C000220558

Blackstone's Police Manual

Crime

Blackstone's Police Manual

Volume 1

Crime

2008

Paul Connor

LLB

OXFORD

UNIVERSITY PRESS

OXFORD
UNIVERSITY PRESS

Great Clarendon Street, Oxford OX2 6DP

Oxford University Press is a department of the University of Oxford.
It furthers the University's objective of excellence in research, scholarship,
and education by publishing worldwide in

Oxford New York

Auckland Bangkok Buenos Aires Cape Town Chennai
Dar es Salaam Delhi Hong Kong Istanbul Karachi Kolkata
Kuala Lumpur Madrid Melbourne Mexico City Mumbai Nairobi
São Paulo Shanghai Taipei Tokyo Toronto

With offices in

Argentina Austria Brazil Chile Czech Republic France Greece
Guatemala Hungary Italy Japan Poland Portugal Singapore
South Korea Switzerland Thailand Turkey Ukraine Vietnam

Published in the United States
by Oxford University Press Inc., New York

First published 1998
Tenth edition, 2007

British Library Cataloguing in Publication Data

Data available

Library of Congress Cataloging in Publication Data

Data available

Typeset by Laserwords Private Limited, Chennai, India
Printed and bound in Great Britain by
William Clowes Ltd, Beccles, Suffolk

ISBN 978-0-19-922927-7

10 9 8 7 6 5 4 3 2 1

Foreword for 2008
Blackstone's Police Manuals

The role of a police officer has become more technical and more demanding over the last decades. To be properly qualified as a frontline officer, particularly a frontline supervisor and manager, there is a huge quantity of law, legal precedent and its interpretation that is required. Unlike a barrister, solicitor or judge, who have the books to hand or a website one click away with their mouse, a police officer frequently has to make crucial legal decisions with partial knowledge of all the facts, the pressure of time and events and the presence of a none-too-cooperative citizen. It is a testimony to the training that officers receive that they get the decisions right most of the time.

However, the training is crucially dependent on the quality of the training materials. These manuals are the product of a partnership between the National Policing Improvement Agency and Blackstone's. The NPIA has a key role in promoting learning and the development of leadership in policing. It is building on more than two decades of national expertise in supporting learning for police officers, and now has responsibility for improving every aspect of learning in the policing from recruit training to the most senior ranks. Alongside Blackstone's we are committed to ensuring that the public is served by qualified, well trained and well led officers and police staff. These manuals are a key part of that mission.

Peter Neyroud QPM
Chief Constable and Chief Executive of the
National Policing Improvement Agency

Preface

Many readers of the Blackstone's Police Manuals are studying for promotion examinations, either to the rank of sergeant or inspector. They may have been informed that the Manuals are overcomplicated and contain unnecessary detail; this is anything but the case. The Manuals aim to bridge the gap between the practical and theoretical worlds of policing, of the law in practice and the letter of the law. Whilst it is conceded that the law is sometimes complicated, this fact alone is not reason enough to prevent its reproduction or discussion. The law is sometimes complex because, of course, it deals with complex situations. How these Manuals differ to the standard approach taken to such issues is to provide the reader with numerous examples and pragmatic explanations, particularly in the 'Keynote' sections, of the law in action. This enables practically-minded individuals to make the connection between the law on the streets and the law as it is applied and interpreted by the courts.

All the Manuals include explanatory keynotes and case law examples, providing clear and incisive analysis of important areas. As well as covering basic law and procedure they take full account of the PACE Codes of Practice and Human Rights implications. They can also be used as a training resource for police probationers, special constables and PCSOs, or as an invaluable reference tool for police staff of all ranks and positions.

Oxford University Press are always happy to receive any useful written feedback from any reader on the content and style of the Manual, especially from those involved in or with the criminal justice system. Please email this address with any comments or queries: police.uk@oup.com.

The law is stated as at 1 June 2007.

Acknowledgements

Blackstone's Police Manuals have become a firmly established 'household name' in the context of police law, particularly to candidates studying for the sergeants' or inspectors' OSPRE Part I examinations.

The production of the Manuals could not be accomplished without the professional participation of a great many people in a variety of capacities.

Many thanks to the production, editorial amd marketing team at Oxford University Press, particularly Peter Daniell, Lindsey Davis and Stuart Johnson.

Thanks must also go to the team of legal checkers and the staff of the National Policing Improvement Agency for their work in reviewing the 2008 editions.

Many thanks to Fraser Sampson who remains the significant contributor to this work.

And last but by no means least I thank my wife, whose continued whole-hearted support and understanding for me and my work has been, and continues to be, the primary reason you are reading these words.

Paul Connor

Contents

Contents

Table of Cases

This table is a compilation of cases referred to in the *Crime* volume of Blackstone's Police Manuals. Case law, containing the decisions of the courts, is one of the primary sources of law in England and Wales.

Cases are referred to by the names of parties. A full citation includes the abbreviation of the law report (of which there are many different series), the volume number and page numbers as follows:

Atkins *v* DPP [2000] 1 WLR 1427
[Names of parties, year case reported, volume no., publication name (Weekly Law Reports), page no.]

In criminal actions the single letter *R* (meaning Rex or Regina) comes first, indicating the state's role as prosecutor, followed by the name of the accused person (the defendant).

In some family cases the report may be headed '*In re Brown*' or, in more modern cases, *Re Brown*, meaning 'in the matter of'. *Ex parte Brown* may also be used, meaning '*Brown*' is the name of the applicant for whom the case is heard. Where a single letter is used for one of the parties, eg T *v* DPP, this means that one of the parties to the case cannot be named for legal reasons.

Cases in the table of cases below are listed alphabetically with references to the relevant paragraph number in this Manual.

Tables of Primary Legislation

These tables are a compilation of all references to Statutes (also known as Acts of Parliament) found in the *Crime* volume of Blackstone's Police Manuals.

Statutes are usually referred to by their short title and date, eg Abortion Act 1967 and in many cases this Manual may refer to just one Part, section (s.) or Schedule (sch.) of an Act. This Manual states the current law as at 1 June 2007 (unless stated otherwise).

The Statutes below are listed alphabetically with references to the relevant paragraph number in this Manual.

UK Statutes

Tables of Secondary Legislation

Secondary, subordinate or delegated legislation is legislation made by a body other than Parliament with powers conferred by Parliament through a specific Act. Secondary legislation is published in the Statutory Instruments (SI) series, and SIs are cited in the following ways:

The Misuse of Drugs Regulations 2001, SI 2001/2066
[Title, year, number]

SIs deal with the detail of how legislation is to work in practice and they can be speedily amended or revoked as necessary. They may also be used to bring legislation into force. This Manual states the current law as at 1 June 2007 (unless stated otherwise).

The tables also contain Codes of Practice, which are not legislation but should be regarded as legally binding on the relevant parties unless exceptional circumstances prevail.

The legislation below is listed alphabetically with references to the relevant paragraph number in this Manual.

For further information on sources of law, please see Chapter 1 Sources of Law in the *Evidence and Procedure* Manual 2008, pages 3–7.

How to use this Manual

Volume numbers for the Manuals

The 2008 Blackstone's Police Manuals each have a volume number as follows:

Volume 1: *Crime*
Volume 2: *Evidence and Procedure*
Volume 3: *Road Policing*
Volume 4: *General Police Duties*

The first digit of each paragraph number in the text of the Manuals denotes the Manual number. For example, paragraph 2.3 is Chapter 3 of the *Evidence and Procedure* Manual and 4.3 is Chapter 3 of the *General Police Duties* Manual.

All index entries and references in the Tables of Legislation and the Table of Cases, etc. refer to paragraph numbers instead of page numbers, making information easier to find.

Length of sentence for an offence

Where a length of sentence for an offence is stated in this Manual, please note that the number of months or years stated is the maximum number and will not be exceeded.

OSPRE® Rules & Syllabus Information

The rules and syllabus for the OSPRE® system are defined within the OSPRE® Rules & Syllabus document published by the National Policing Improvement Agency (NPIA) Examinations and Assessment on behalf of the Police Promotions Examination Board (PPEB). The Rules & Syllabus document is published annually each September, and applies to all OSPRE® assessments scheduled for the calendar year following its publication. For example, the September 2007 Rules & Syllabus document would apply to all OSPRE® Part I and Part II assessments held during 2008.

The document provides details of the law and procedure to be tested within the OSPRE® Part I examinations, information on the Part II assessment centre, and also outlines the rules underpinning the OSPRE® system.

All candidates who are taking an OSPRE® Part I examination or Part II assessment centre are strongly encouraged to familiarise themselves with the Rules & Syllabus document during their preparation. The OSPRE® Part I rules also apply to candidates who take the Part I and then go on to apply for their force's work-based assessment promotion trials.

The document can be downloaded from the Recruitment, Assessment & Selection Section of the NPIA website, which can be found at www.npia.police.uk. Electronic versions are also supplied to all force OSPRE® contacts.

If you have any problems obtaining the Rules & Syllabus document from the above source, please email the OSPRE® Candidate Administration Team at:

exams.ospre@npia.pnn.police.uk

Usually, no further updates to the Rules & Syllabus document will be issued during its year-long lifespan. However, in exceptional circumstances, the NPIA (on behalf of the PPEB) reserves the right to issue an amended syllabus prior to the next scheduled annual publication date.

For example, a major change to a key area of legislation or procedure (e.g. the Codes of Practice) during the lifespan of the current Rules & Syllabus document would render a significant part of the current syllabus content obsolete. In such circumstances, it may be necessary for an update to the syllabus to be issued, which would provide guidance to candidates on any additional material which would be examinable within their Part I.

In such circumstances, an update to the Rules & Syllabus document would be made available through the NPIA website, and would be distributed to all force OSPRE® contacts. The NPIA will ensure that any syllabus update is distributed well in advance of the examination date, to ensure that candidates have sufficient time to familiarise themselves with any additional examinable material. Where possible, any additional study materials would be provided to candidates free of charge.

Please note that syllabus updates will only be made in *exceptional* circumstances, an update will not be made for every change to legislation included within the syllabus. For further guidance on this issue, candidates are advised to regularly check the NPIA website, or consult their force OSPRE® contact, during their preparation period.

1.1 | State of Mind

1.1.1 Introduction

It is traditional when studying or explaining criminal law to strip out the main concepts of *mens rea* (state of mind) and *actus reus* (criminal conduct) at the beginning, followed by a few other key areas such as general defences and incomplete offences (attempts, conspiracies, etc.). This is because these concepts apply across the board and, as such, are fundamental to an understanding of all offences and the idea of criminal liability generally.

In this Manual, the 'state of mind' is considered first, followed by the notion of criminal conduct.

There is a cardinal rule in the criminal law of England and Wales that acts alone cannot amount to a crime unless they are accompanied by a 'guilty mind' or '*mens rea*'.

The idea of 'guilty knowledge' suggested by the original Latin terminology is misleading and there are many different mental states which will fulfil the requirements of many different offences which have nothing to do with 'guilty knowledge' or, sometimes, any other kind of 'knowledge'.

The key to proving *mens rea* in any criminal charge is to show that a defendant had *the required state of mind at the required time*. If you are going to do that, you need to know what the relevant state of mind for the offence is. The coincidence of the state of mind with the criminal act (the *actus reus*) is critical and is dealt with in the next chapter.

1.1.2 Strict Liability

Some criminal offences are said to be offences of 'strict liability'. This expression generally means that there is little to prove beyond the act itself and that the state of mind of the defendant is immaterial. However, in most cases it is more accurate to say that there is no need to prove *mens rea* in relation to one particular aspect of the criminal activity or behaviour. There have been isolated instances in which the courts have held that an offence does not require any *mens rea* to be proved. An example relates to the offence of driving with excess alcohol, contrary to the Road Traffic Act 1988, s. 5 (**see Road Policing, chapter 3.5**), which was stated in *DPP v H* [1997] 1 WLR 1406 not to require proof of any *mens rea*.

Cundy v *Le Cocq* (1884) 13 QBD 207 where the defendant was convicted of selling intoxicating liquor to someone who was drunk (**see General Police Duties, chapter 4.11**). In spite of the fact that the accused showed that he had no idea that the person was drunk, the court held that such knowledge (*mens rea*) was not necessary; if the person supplied with the drink was in fact drunk, that would suffice in proving the offence.

In some other, albeit rare, cases absolute liability is imposed, reducing even further the burden on the prosecution.

Situations where strict or absolute liability is imposed are usually to enforce statutory regulation (e.g. road traffic offences), particularly where there is some social danger or concern presented by the proscribed behaviour. So, where a defendant was charged with possessing a 'prohibited' weapon (**see General Police Duties, chapter 4.7**) the court held that it did not matter whether he *knew* he had the weapon—a CS gas canister—in order to prove 'possession' (*R* v *Bradish* [1990] 1 QB 981).

Some other offences such as public nuisance at common law require only strict liability in relation to some elements of the criminal conduct (**see General Police Duties, chapter 4.5**).

As a general rule, however, there is a presumption that *mens rea* is required for a criminal offence unless parliament clearly indicates otherwise (see *B (A Minor)* v *DPP* [2000] 2 WLR 452). This rule should be borne in mind, not only when approaching the rest of the material in this Manual, but also when considering criminal law in general.

1.1.3 States of Mind

Criminal offences generally can be classified in terms of the level of *mens rea* required. In descending order they are:

1.1.3.1 Offences Requiring a Particular *Mens Rea*

These are often referred to in legal textbooks as crimes of *specific* intent or *ulterior* intent, a distinction which is important when considering defences (**see chapter 1.4**). In policing terms the important thing is to note the specific requirements that must be shown in order to prove that the defendant was guilty of the particular offence, and then to gather any evidence that tends to support or undermine that proposition. In summary, crimes of specific intent are only committed where the defendant is shown to have had a particular intention to bring about a specific consequence at the time of the criminal act. Murder is such a crime, requiring proof of an intention to kill or seriously injure (**see chapter 1.5**). Other examples would be offences such as:

- wounding or inflicting grievous bodily harm *with intent* (Offences Against the Person Act 1861, s. 18 (**see chapter 1.7**));
- blackmail (Theft Act 1968, s. 21 (**see chapter 1.11**));
- contamination of goods (Public Order Act 1986, s. 38(1) (**see chapter 1.13**)).

Ulterior intent means an intention beyond the basic intent of carrying out the core criminal act. For example, where a defendant is charged with burglary (**see chapter 1.11**) under the Theft Act 1968, s. 9(1)(a), you must show the intention, not just to enter a building as a trespasser, but also to *inflict grievous bodily harm, cause damage, or steal*. The italicised intention makes this a crime of ulterior intent.

1.1.3.2 Offences of Basic Intent

Many criminal offences require no further proof of anything other than a basic intention to bring about the given circumstances.

Whereas an offence of burglary under s. 9(1)(a) of the Theft Act 1968 requires proof of the ulterior intent described above, burglary under s. 9(1)(b) simply requires proof that the person entered the building/part of a building as a trespasser and that he/she went on to commit one of the prohibited acts (theft/attempted theft; inflicting/attempting to inflict grievous bodily harm; **see chapter 1.11**). As well as easing the burden of proof on the prosecution in cases of basic intent, the distinction can also be significant when dealing with possible defences (**see chapter 1.4**).

A further important difference in offences of specific or ulterior intent and those requiring only basic intent is that, in the case of the latter type of offence, *recklessness* will often be enough to satisfy the mental element. Recklessness is a particularly important concept in the area of *mens rea* and is dealt with at **para. 1.1.4.2.**

1.1.3.3 Negligence

Although many commentators argue that, by definition, negligence should not appear alongside discussions of *mens rea* as it is not a 'state of mind', it is useful to include it here. Negligence is generally concerned with the defendant's compliance with the standards of reasonableness of ordinary people. Like strict liability, the concept of negligence focuses on the consequences of the defendant's conduct rather than demanding proof of a particular state of mind at the time. Unlike strict liability, negligence still ascribes some notion of 'fault' or 'blame' to the defendant who must be shown to have acted in a way that runs contrary to the expectations of the reasonable person.

The most important criminal offence that can be committed by negligence is manslaughter (manslaughter by gross negligence: **see chapter 1.5**), which is also one of the only offences to include specific reference—at common law—to the word 'negligence'. The requirement to show that an *individual person* was negligent has been one of the main problems in the development of 'corporate manslaughter'. Other offences that can be committed by negligence do not usually contain the word itself but attract that test in relation to the mental element. Good examples are offences involving the standard of driving (**see Road Policing**).

1.1.4 Statutory Expressions

Statutory offences use a number of different terms to describe the respective states of mind which must be proved. The more common expressions are:

- intent
- recklessness
- wilfully
- dishonestly.

These have been developed through our common law system and now have the following meanings.

1.1.4.1 Intent

Like many other concepts of *mens rea* 'intention' is not defined by any statute. If a defendant intends something to happen, he/she wishes to bring about certain consequences. In some offences, say burglary under s. 9(1)(a) of the Theft Act 1968, the defendant's *intention* may be very clear; he/she may enter a house as a trespasser *intending* to steal property inside. As a crime *of ulterior* intent (**see para. 1.1.3.1**), it would need to be proved that the defendant not only entered the house or part of it in such a way, but that at the time he/she also *intended* to steal. Provided there is enough admissible evidence (e.g. the possession of articles for use in the theft, a 'shopping list', an admission by the defendant and an arrangement for the disposal of the property once stolen), this element of the defendant's intention is relatively straightforward.

However, there will often be consequences following from a defendant's actions that he/she did not *intend* to happen. An example might be where, in the above burglary, it was late at night and the householder came across the burglar and suffered a heart attack as a result of the shock. In such an event it would be reasonable to suggest that it was the defendant's behaviour or actions that had brought about the victim's heart attack (**see chapter 1.2**). The defendant, however, may well argue that, although he/she intended to break in and steal, there had never been any *intention* of harming or frightening the occupant. At this point you might well say that the defendant should have thought about that before breaking into someone else's house in the middle of the night. This then brings in the concept of *foresight*, a concept that has caused the courts considerable difficulty over the years—for a number of reasons.

First, there is the Criminal Justice Act 1967 which says (under s. 8) that a court/jury, in determining whether a person has committed an offence:

(a) shall not be bound in law to infer that he intended or foresaw a result of his actions by reason only of its being a natural and probable consequence of those actions; but
(b) shall decide whether he did intend or foresee that result by reference to all the evidence, drawing such inferences from the evidence as appear proper in the circumstances.

Secondly, there is the body of case law which has developed around the area of 'probability', culminating in two cases in the House of Lords (*R v Moloney* [1985] AC 905 and *R v Hancock* [1986] AC 455). Following those cases it is now settled that foresight of the probability of a consequence *does not amount to an intention to bring that consequence about, but may be evidence of it.*

In other words, you cannot claim that a defendant *intended* a consequence of his/her behaviour simply because it was virtually certain to occur. What you can do is to put evidence of the defendant's foresight of that probability before a court who may infer an intention from it. In proving such a point the argument would go like this:

- at the time of the criminal act there was a *probability* of a consequence;
- the greater the probability, the more likely it is that the defendant *foresaw* that consequence;
- if the defendant foresaw that consequence, the more likely it is that the defendant *intended* it to happen.

Whether or not a defendant intended a particular consequence will be a question of fact left to the jury (or magistrate(s) where appropriate). Most of the problematic cases in this area have arisen in relation to murder (**see chapter 1.5**). In such circumstances, where death or serious bodily harm was a *virtual certainty* from the defendant's actions and he/she had appreciated that to be the case, the jury *may* infer that the defendant intended to bring about such consequences (*R v Nedrick* [1986] 1 WLR 1025). Therefore, where the defendant threw a three-month-old baby down onto a hard surface in a fit of rage, the jury *might* have inferred both that death/serious bodily harm was a virtual certainty from the defendant's actions and that he must have appreciated that to be the case; they should therefore have been directed by the trial judge accordingly (*R v Woollin* [1999] 1 AC 82).

Finally, the relevant intent may have been formed, not of the defendant's own volition, but influenced in some way by other external factors. An example is where the defendant's thinking is affected by duress (as to which **see para. 1.4.6**).

1.1.4.2 Recklessness

The concept itself goes beyond a statutory expression and has probably become more important in proving criminal offences than the concept of 'intent' above as proof of recklessness is often enough to fulfil the requirement of *mens rea* (although not in offences requiring 'dishonesty'—**see chapter 1.11**).

The good news is that, following decades of complex differences between objective and subjective recklessness (the former applying only to a very limited number of offences), the law was eventually clarified.

An advantage of recklessness over intention is that the former is easier to prove by the attendant circumstances; a disadvantage is the different elements attributed to the word 'reckless' by different courts considering different offences—there are different sorts of recklessness.

....

EXAMPLE

Consider a schoolgirl who throws a stone into a neighbour's garden, breaking the glass of a greenhouse window. She tells you that she was only 'having a laugh' and did not stop to think of what damage might be caused by the stone. Does the fact that she gave no thought to the consequences of her actions make her 'reckless' or blameless? Had she stopped to think about the possible consequences, would she have seen the risk? Does that matter?

If some reasonable person walking past at the time had seen her about to throw the stone, would that person have realised the possible risk? What if the person walking past had been another schoolgirl of the same age and understanding as the one who threw the stone? Are these questions relevant in determining recklessness?

....

Taking the last question first, yes—all of the above deliberations can be relevant, both to the type of recklessness involved and the liability of the defendant.

In addition, there are not only different types of recklessness, but they are *applied* in different ways to different offences.

Take the example of assault occasioning actual bodily harm (**see chapter 1.7**). In such an offence recklessness can suffice in proving the mental element (*R v Venna* [1976] QB 421). But recklessness as to what? The defendant may have been reckless as to the assault itself and/or to the *harm* that was actually caused *by* the assault. The courts have held that assault occasioning actual bodily harm only requires proof of recklessness *as to the assault* and there is no need to show that the defendant was reckless as to the extent of the harm caused by his/her assault (see *R v Savage* [1992] 1 AC 699).

In offences of criminal damage (**see chapter 1.13**), the situation is slightly different. It is in this context that the concept of 'objective' recklessness caused the most problems for the courts. In such cases, so-called Caldwell recklessness (from the House of Lords decision in *Metropolitan Police Commissioner v Caldwell* [1982] AC 341) applied. This gave rise to difficulties of proof where the defendant failed to consider an *obvious* risk and then went on to damage property. In those cases a defendant was not allowed to claim to have had no *mens rea* simply because he/she had not thought the matter through and if the prosecution show that the relevant risk (in our schoolgirl example above, the risk to property) would have been apparent to a reasonable person, it was not necessary to show that the defendant realised that risk. Of course if a defendant *did* in fact see the risk then clearly this strengthens the prosecution's case in any event. But this notion of obvious risk presented some real problems in practice. For instance, where the defendant, because of his/her mental condition or personal attributes, would not have been able to appreciate the risk *even if he/she had stopped to consider the consequences*. This meant that a defendant could be held criminally liable for the consequences of his/her actions even where he/she could not have foreseen those consequences and the strict application of the rule resulted in some 'harsh' decisions (*Elliot v C* [1983] 1 WLR 939; *R v R* (*Stephen Malcolm*) (1984) 79 Cr App R 334). The abolition of the old *doli incapax* rule (**see chapter 1.4**) meant that, where objective recklessness was the appropriate test—e.g. manslaughter and criminal damage—children who were incapable of appreciating the risks arising from their actions could still be found guilty. Similarly, adults whose mental characteristics prevent them from appreciating the risks created by their behaviour were not able to raise those characteristics as a defence to charges requiring objective recklessness.

Although this type of recklessness was generally confined to offences under the Criminal Damage Act 1971 (as to which, **see chapter 1.13**), it still caused concern among practitioners and academics alike. It is not surprising perhaps that it was a criminal damage case involving children who did not think that their actions would lead to the ultimately disastrous consequences that changed the law. In *R v G & R* [2003] 3 WLR 1060—the House of Lords decided that the former *Caldwell* decision should be departed from. Their Lordships held that a person acts recklessly for the purposes of criminal damage on the following basis: a person will be 'reckless' as to circumstances when s/he is aware of a risk that existed or would exist. A person will be 'reckless' as to a result or consequence when he/she is aware of a risk that it would occur and it is, in the circumstances known to him/her, unreasonable to take the risk.

The House of Lords has concluded (*R v Reid* [1992] 1 WLR 793) that the word reckless may not necessarily be expected to have the same meaning in all statutory provisions. To the practitioner this view causes many problems; to the student of criminal law it is perhaps hardly more helpful than Lewis Carroll's Humpty Dumpty whose words meant whatever he wanted them to mean.

It can be seen therefore that, in offences that can be committed 'recklessly' the test will generally be *subjective*. The requirements of subjective recklessness can be found in the case of *R v Cunningham* [1957] 2 QB 396 and are satisfied in situations where the defendant foresees the consequences of his/her actions as being probable or even possible. In cases requiring subjective recklessness, the fact that the consequences *ought to have been foreseen* by the defendant will not be enough. The most important group of offences where this will be the case is those requiring 'malice' under the Offences Against the Person Act 1861 (**see chapters 1.7 and 1.8**). In such cases the term 'malice' is misleading. What the prosecution will need to show is that the defendant either intended to do harm to the victim or that he/she *foresaw that harm* (though not the extent of that harm) *may be caused but nevertheless went on to take that risk* (*R v Savage* [1992] 1 AC 699).

A good operational example of these issues in action can be seen in *D v DPP* [2005] Crim LR 962. In that case a police officer attending a domestic incident arrested a man in order to prevent a breach of the peace. During a subsequent struggle the defendant bit the officer on the hand. The magistrates' court convicted the defendant of assaulting the officer in the execution of his duty (**see para. 1.7.3.3**) on the basis that the biting of the officer had been 'reckless'. The defendant appealed, arguing that a bite could not be reckless; either it was deliberate or it was accidental. The Divisional Court dismissed the appeal and held that the test of recklessness in this case involved the defendant having foreseen the risk that the victim would be subjected to unlawful force and having gone on to take the risk. While the case endorses the view that there can be a reckless 'battery' (**see para. 1.7.2.2**) the facts of it are not so convincing as, say, an occasion where the defendant causes injury by thrashing his arms around to avoid being handcuffed or by attempting to throw away some property during an arrest.

1.1.4.3 Wilfully

This term implies that a defendant must be shown to have desired the consequences of his/her actions or at least to have foreseen them (subjective recklessness). The term 'wilfully' however is *not* restricted to such occasions and has been taken to include *objective (Caldwell)* recklessness (*R v Sheppard* [1981] AC 394; *R v Newington* (1990) 91 Cr App R 247).

'Wilful' can also mean simply that an action was voluntary, that is, it describes the criminal conduct (*actus reus*) rather than the state of mind (*mens rea*).

1.1.4.4 Dishonestly

The concept of 'dishonesty' is of great importance to a number of mainstream offences, including theft and deception. In proving many of the offences under the Theft Acts 1968 and 1978 you will need to show that the defendant acted dishonestly. This expression is defined for certain purposes within the 1968 Act itself. However, it has also been extended by common law decisions of the courts and it is critical, in dealing with offences requiring proof of dishonesty, that you identify the nature of the state of mind required and the ways in which it can be proved/disproved. For a full discussion of this concept, **see chapter 1.11**.

1.1.5 Transferred Malice

The state of mind required for one offence can, on occasions, be 'transferred' from the original target or victim to another. Known generally as the doctrine of 'transferred malice' because it originates from a case involving malicious wounding (**see chapter 1.7**), the doctrine only operates if the crime remains the same. In other words, a defendant cannot be convicted if he acted with the *mens rea* for one offence but commits the *actus reus* of another offence. For example, in the original case (*R v Latimer* (1886) 17 QBD 359) the defendant lashed out with his belt at one person but missed, striking a third party instead. As it was proved that the defendant had the required *mens rea* when he swung the belt, the court held that the same *mens rea* could support a charge of wounding against any other victim injured by the same act. If the *nature of the offence* changes, then the doctrine will not operate. Therefore if a defendant is shown to have thrown a rock at a crowd of people intending to injure one of them, the *mens rea* required for that offence cannot be 'transferred' to an offence of criminal damage if the rock misses them and breaks a window instead. The House of Lords has acknowledged that this doctrine is somewhat arbitrary and is an exception to the general principles of law (*Attorney-General's Reference (No. 3 of 1994)* [1998] AC 245).

The issue of transferred *mens rea* (which is really what this doctrine amounts to) can be important in relation to the liability of accessories (as to which, **see chapter 1.2**). If the principal's intentions are to be extended to an accessory, it must be shown that those intentions were either contemplated and accepted by that person at the time of the offence, or that they were 'transferred' by this doctrine.

1.1.5 Transferred Malice

1.2 | Criminal Conduct

1.2.1 Introduction

Having considered the concepts that arise out of the relevant state of mind that must exist before a defendant can be found guilty of a criminal offence, the next key element is that of the criminal conduct. Although this may sound an easy concept at first, and many statutory offences spell out exactly the sort of behaviour that will attract liability, there are some important general rules that need to be considered.

For a person to be found guilty of a criminal offence you must show that they:

- acted in a particular way
- failed to act in a particular way (omissions) or
- brought about a state of affairs.

Known as the *actus reus*, this essential characteristic of any offence is the behavioural element.

1.2.2 *Actus Reus*

Mens rea is what a defendant must have had; *actus reus* is what a defendant must have done—or failed to do.

When proving the required *actus reus* you must show:

- that the defendant's conduct was voluntary and
- that it occurred while the defendant still had the requisite *mens rea*.

1.2.2.1 Voluntary Act

Other than in the few specific instances where an 'omission' will suffice (**see para. 1.2.3**), you must generally show that a defendant acted 'voluntarily', that is, by the operation of his/her own free will.

If a person is shoved into a shop window, he/she cannot be said to have damaged it for the purposes of criminal liability, even though he/she was the immediate physical cause of the damage. Similarly, if a person was standing in front of a window waiting to break it and someone came up and pushed that person into the window, the presence of the requisite *mens rea* (**see chapter 1.1**) would still not be enough to attract criminal liability for the resultant damage. In each case, the person being pushed could not be said to be acting of his/her own volition in breaking the window and therefore could not perform the required *actus reus*.

This aspect of voluntariness becomes important, not just when considering offences committed under physical compulsion, but also where the defendant has lost control of his/her own physical actions. Reflexive actions are generally not classed as being willed or voluntary, hence the (limited) availability of the 'defence' of automatism (**see chapter 1.4**).

Likewise, the *unexpected* onset of a sudden physical impairment (such as severe cramp when driving; actions when sleepwalking) can also render any linked actions 'involuntary'. If the onset of the impairment could reasonably have been foreseen or anticipated (e.g. where someone is prone to blackouts) the defendant's actions may be said to have been willed in the respect that he/she could have prevented the loss of control or at least avoided the situation (e.g. driving) which allowed the consequences to come about.

1.2.2.2 Coincidence with *Mens Rea*

Generally it must be shown that the defendant had the requisite *mens rea* at the time of carrying out the *actus reus*. However, there is no need for that 'state of mind' to remain unchanged throughout the entire commission of the offence. If a person (X) poisons another (Y) intending to kill Y at the time, it will not alter X's criminal liability if X changes his mind immediately after giving the poison or even if X does everything he can to halt its effects (see *R v Jakeman* (1983) 76 Cr App R 223). Similarly, if a person 'appropriates' another's property while having the required *mens rea*, giving it back later will not prevent them from committing theft (*R v McHugh* (1993) 97 Cr App R 335 (**see chapter 1.11**)).

Conversely, if the *actus reus* is a continuing act, as 'appropriation' is (**see chapter 1.11**), it may begin without any particular *mens rea* at the start but the required 'state of mind' may come later while the *actus reus* is still continuing. If this happens, whereby the *mens rea* 'catches up' with the *actus reus*, the offence is complete.

This principle can be seen in the offence of rape. The sexual intercourse may be consensual at the time it starts but, if that consent is later withdrawn, any continued intercourse will amount to an offence (*Kaitamaki v The Queen* [1985] AC 147).

A further illustration can be found in a case where a motorist was being directed to pull his car over to the kerb by a police officer. In doing so, the motorist inadvertently drove onto the officer's foot. Having no *mens rea* at the time of driving onto the officer's foot, the defendant was not at that point guilty of battery. However, once the situation was pointed out to him, the fact that he left the car where it was (the *actus reus*) was then joined by the appropriate *mens rea* and he was convicted of assault (*Fagan v Metropolitan Police Commissioner* [1969] 1 QB 439).

1.2.3 Omissions

Criminal conduct is most often associated with *actions*: damaging or stealing property, injuring or deceiving others. In some cases more than one action is required to give rise to criminal liability (e.g. harassment: **see General Police Duties, chapter 4.5**). But occasionally liability is brought about by a failure to act.

Most of the occasions where failure or omission will attract liability are where a *duty to act* has been created. Such a duty can arise from a number of circumstances the main ones being:

D The creation of a Dangerous situation by the defendant. See, for example, *R v Miller* [1983] 2 AC 161 where the defendant, having accidentally started a fire in a house, moved to another room taking no action to counteract the danger he had created.

U Under statute, contract or a person's public 'office'. Examples would be where a police officer failed to intervene to prevent an assault (*R v Dytham* [1979] QB 722) or where a crossing keeper omitted to close the gates at a level crossing and a person was subsequently killed by a train (*R v Pittwood* (1902) 19 TLR 37).

T Where the defendant has Taken it upon himself/herself to carry out a duty and then fails to do so. Such a duty was taken up by the defendant in *R v Stone* [1977] QB 354 when she accepted a duty to care for her partner's mentally-ill sister who subsequently died.

Y In circumstances where the defendant is in a parental relationship with a child or a Young person.

Whether or not there is a sufficient proximity between the defendant and the victim brought about by a duty to act will be a question of law (see generally *R v Singh* [1999] Crim LR 582 and *R v Khan* [1998] Crim LR 830). A graphic and topical example of where such a duty can be created by the defendant is in the case of a lorry driver smuggling illegal immigrants in the back of his vehicle (*R v Wacker* (2003) 2 WLR 374). For offences of people smuggling and immigration generally, **see chapter 1.15**.

In such situations there may be a *duty* to act. Having established such a duty, you must also show that the defendant has *voluntarily* omitted to act as required or that he/she has not done enough to discharge that duty. If a defendant is unable to act (e.g. because someone else has stopped them) or is incapable of doing more because of their own personal limitations, the *actus reus* will *not* have been made out (see *R v Reid* [1992] 1 WLR 793).

Some statutory offences are specifically worded to remove any doubt as to whether they can be committed by omission as well as by a positive act (e.g. torture under the Criminal Justice Act 1988, s. 134, **see chapter 1.8**). Other offences have been held by the courts to be capable of commission by both positive acts and by omission (e.g. false accounting under the Theft Act 1968, s. 17, **see chapter 1.12**).

The distinction between acts and omissions was considered by the High Court in a case concerning withholding medical treatment from chronically ill patients (*NHS Trust A v M* [2001] 2 WLR 942). For a discussion of this case, **see General Police Duties, chapter 4.3.**

An interesting and highly practical issue arose in this area in a case where the defendants' dogs barking in the night were claimed to have caused a neighbour harassment under the Protection from Harassment Act 1997 (as to which **see General Police Duties, chapter 4.5**). The defendants argued that their failure to stop the dogs barking could not amount to a 'course of conduct' for the purposes of that Act. The prosecution argued that the defendants incited the dogs to bark and this was more than a mere failure to act. Although the Divisional Court was not prepared to state that inciting dogs in this way could never amount to a course of conduct, the issue of whether failing to stop the dogs' behaviour could support a charge of harassment was not resolved—*R v Tafurelli* (2004) unreported.

1.2.4 Causal Link or Chain of Causation

Once the *actus reus* has been proved, you must then show a *causal link* between it and the relevant consequences. That is, you must prove that the consequences would not have happened 'but for' the defendant's act or omission.

In a case of simple criminal damage (**see chapter 1.13**) it may be relatively straightforward to prove this causal link: a defendant throws a brick at a window; the window would not have broken 'but for' the defendant's conduct. Where the link becomes more difficult to prove is when the defendant's behaviour triggers other events or aggravates existing circumstances. For example, in *R v McKechnie* [1992] Crim LR 194 the defendant attacked the victim, who was already suffering from a serious ulcer, causing him brain damage. The brain damage prevented doctors from operating on the ulcer which eventually ruptured, killing the victim. The Court of Appeal, upholding the conviction for manslaughter, held that the defendant's criminal conduct had made a significant contribution to the victim's death even though the untreated ulcer was the actual cause of death. In some cases a significant delay can occur between the acts which put in train the criminal consequences. An example is where a defendant transported an accomplice to a place near to the victim's house some 13 hours before the accomplice shot and killed the victim. Despite the delay and despite the fact the accomplice had not fully made up his mind about the proposed shooting at the time he was dropped off by the defendant, there was no intervening event (**see para. 1.2.5**) that diverted or hindered the planned murder—*R* v *Bryce* [2004] 2 Cr App R 35.

In a case which had similar facts to our 'simple damage' example above, the defendant entered the house after throwing the brick through the window. Although the defendant did not attack the occupant, an 87-year-old who died of a heart attack some hours later, the Court of Appeal accepted that there could have been a causal link between the defendant's behaviour and the death of the victim. If so, a charge of manslaughter would be appropriate (*R* v *Watson* [1989] 1 WLR 684).

1.2.5 **Intervening Act**

The causal link can be broken by a new intervening act provided that the 'new' act is 'free, deliberate and informed' (*R* v *Latif* [1996] 1 WLR 104).

If a drug dealer supplies drugs to another person who then kills himself/herself by overdose, the dealer cannot, without more, be said to have *caused* the death. Death would have been brought about by the deliberate exercise of free will by the user (see *R* v *Armstrong* [1989] Crim LR 149). Although the Court of Appeal has accepted that, under certain circumstances, where a person buys a controlled drug from another and immediately injects it, resulting in his/her death, the supplier *can* attract liability for bringing about the person's death (*R* v *Kennedy* [2005] EWCA Crim 685), this was an odd and much criticised decision. The general view is that the supplier is unlikely to be held liable for *causing* death in such a case unless he/she actually takes a more active part in the administering of the drug (see *R* v *Dias* [2002] Cr App R 5).

If the medical treatment which a victim is given results in their ultimate death, the treatment itself will not normally be regarded as a 'new' intervening act (*R* v *Smith* [1959] 2 QB 35). However, in *R* v *Jordan* (1956) 40 Cr App R 152, where the defendant had stabbed the deceased, it was held that death could not be attributed to the defendant. In this case the actual cause of death had been the administration of a drug (terramycin) after the deceased had shown he was intolerant to it (treatment described as 'palpably wrong' by the court) and when his original wound had nearly healed. *R* v *Jordan* has been described as a very particular case, depending on its exact facts. The basic rule is that an intervening act will not generally break the causal link/chain of causation.

There is also a rule which says defendants must 'take their victims as they find them'. This means that if the victim has a particular characteristic—such as a very thin skull or a very nervous disposition—which makes the consequences of an act against them much more acute, that is the defendant's bad luck. Such characteristics (e.g., where an assault victim died after refusing a blood transfusion on religious grounds (*R* v *Blaue* [1975] 1 WLR 1411)) will not break the causal link.

Actions by the victim will sometimes be significant in the chain of causation such as where a victim of a sexual assault was injured when jumping from her assailant's car (*R* v *Roberts* (1972) 56 Cr App R 95). Where such actions take place, the victim's behaviour will not necessarily be regarded as introducing a new intervening acts. If the victim's actions are those which might reasonably be anticipated from any victim in such a situation, there will be no new and intervening act and the defendant will be responsible for the consequences flowing from them. If, however, the victim's actions are done entirely of his/her own volition (as in *Armstrong* above) or where those actions are, in the words of Stuart-Smith LJ 'daft' (see *R* v *Williams* [1992] 1 WLR 380), they *will* amount to a new intervening act and the defendant cannot be held responsible for them.

1.2.6 Principals and Accessories

Once you have established the criminal conduct and the required state of mind, you must identify what degree of involvement the defendant had.

There are two ways of attracting criminal liability for an offence: either as a *principal* or an *accessory*.

A principal offender is one whose conduct has met all the requirements of the particular offence. An accessory is someone who helped in or brought about the commission of the offence. If an accessory 'aids, abets, counsels or procures' the commission of an offence, he/she will be treated by a court in the same way as a principal offender for an indictable offence (Accessories and Abettors Act 1861, s. 8) or for a summary offence (Magistrates' Courts Act 1980, s. 44). The expression 'aid, abet, counsel and procure' is generally used in its entirety when charging a defendant, without separating out the particular element that applies. Generally speaking, the expressions mean as follows:

* aiding = giving help, support or assistance
* abetting = inciting, instigating or encouraging.

Each of these would usually involve the presence of the secondary party at the scene (unless, for example, part of some pre-arranged plan):

* counselling = advising or instructing
* procuring = bringing about.

These activities would generally be expected to take place before the commission of the offence. These are purely guides by which to separate the elements of this concept and will not necessarily apply in all cases. However, if you are trying to show that a defendant *procured* an offence you must show a causal link between his/her conduct and the offence (*Attorney-General's Reference (No. 1 of 1975)* [1975] QB 773). 'Counselling' an offence requires no causal link (*R* v *Calhaem* [1985] QB 808). As long as the principal offender is aware of the 'counsellor's' advice or encouragement, the latter will be guilty as an accessory, even if the principal would have committed the offence anyway (*Attorney-General* v *Able* [1984] QB 795).

1.2.6.1 State of Mind for Accessories

Although the concept of 'state of mind' was addressed in the previous chapter, it is necessary to consider the particular requirements in relation to accessories here.

Generally, the state of mind (*mens rea*) which is needed to convict an accessory is: 'proof of intention to aid as well as of knowledge of the circumstances' (*National Coal Board* v *Gamble* [1959] 1 QB 11 at p. 20). The *minimum* state of mind required of an accessory to an offence is set out in *Johnson* v *Youden* [1950] 1 KB 544. In that case the court held that, before anyone can be convicted of aiding and abetting an offence, he/she must at least know the essential matters that constitute that offence. Therefore the accessory to an offence of drink/driving (**see Road Policing, chapter 3.5**) must at least have been aware that the 'principal' (the driver) had been drinking (see *Smith* v *Mellors and Soar* (1987) 84 Cr App R 279).

There must also be a further mental element, namely an intention to aid the principal. Whether there was such an intention to aid the principal is a question of fact to be decided in the particular circumstances of each case. An example of such a case can be seen in *Gillick* v *West Norfolk & Wisbech Area Health Authority* [1986] AC 112. The case concerned the question as to whether a doctor who prescribed a contraceptive pill for a girl under the age of 16 could be charged with being an accessory to an offence by the girl's partner of having unlawful sexual intercourse (as to which, **see chapter 1.9**).

You can see from this requirement that the wider notions of recklessness and negligence (**see chapter 1.1**) are not enough to convict an accessory.

Occasionally statutes will make specific provision for the state of mind and/or the conduct of accessories and principals. An example can be found in s. 7 of the Protection from Harassment Act 1997 (**see General Police Duties, chapter 4.5**).

1.2.6.2 Joint Enterprise

If an accessory is present at the scene of a crime when it is committed, his/her presence may amount to *encouragement* which would support a charge of aiding or abetting. However, mere presence at the scene of a crime will not usually be enough evidence of guilt (see *R* v *Coney* (1882) 8 QBD 534).

Enormous problems have been encountered where one person involved in a joint venture goes beyond that which was agreed or contemplated by the other(s).

....

EXAMPLE

A person (the 'accessory'), accompanies a friend (the 'principal'), to a public house where the principal intends to attack a third party. When the two arrive at the public house, the principal produces a knife and stabs the third person. Is the accessory liable for the wounding of the victim? The answer will depend on a number of things. The main features that will determine the accessory's liability will be:

- the nature and extent of the offence that was agreed upon and contemplated by the two of them when they set out on their joint enterprise;
- whether the accessory *knew* that the principal had a knife;
- whether the principal used *a different weapon* than the one that the accessory knew about;
- whether the principal *used the knife in a different way* from that agreed upon.

If the accessory knew that the principal intended to attack the victim, but knew nothing about a knife or any intention to stab the victim, the accessory may be liable for the resultant injuries caused by the principal if the joint venture envisaged a physical attack on the third person and the stabbing was simply an 'unusual consequence' arising from the execution of that enterprise (see *R* v *Anderson* [1966] 2 QB 110). If, however, the principal used a different weapon from the one that the accessory knew about or he used it in a wholly different way (e.g. using rope to strangle a victim when the agreed plan was to tie the person up with it), the accessory would not generally be liable for the consequences of the principal's actions (see *R* v *English* [1999] 1 AC 1).

....

What would be the liability of the accessory if, in the above example, the victim had subsequently died from his injuries? This situation has caused further problems for the courts and there are many authorities setting out the liability of accessories in such cases. The overall conclusion appears to be that, if at the time they set out on their joint enterprise, the accessory realised:

• that the principal *might* kill someone and
• that, when killing, the principal might have the *intention* to kill or
• an intention to cause *grievous bodily harm*

then the accessory *may* be liable for murder (*R* v *Powell* [1999] 1 AC 1), subject to the other considerations in *English*. These evidential issues are fairly complex and will usually be a matter for the Crown Prosecution Service. The Court of Appeal confirmed the law in relation to joint enterprise in *Attorney-General's Reference (No. 3 of 2004)* [2005] EWCA Crim 1882. It was alleged that the defendant had recruited two co-defendants to scare someone with a loaded firearm, but one of the co-defendants subsequently went on to shoot the victim dead. The issue turned on whether the first defendant could be convicted of manslaughter on the facts. The primary question raised by the Attorney-General was whether a secondary party to a joint enterprise was guilty of manslaughter if he had contemplated an unlawful act to frighten the victim and the principal carried out that act with the necessary intention for murder.

The court held that the test was whether the secondary party had foreseen the possibility that the primary party would do what he had done. In this case the act done by the primary party (shooting the victim) was of a fundamentally different character from any act contemplated by the person who had recruited him—he had not foreseen the possibility of *any* harm to the victim, let alone any intentional harm. These principles were in accordance with *Powell* which was to be regarded as representing the law. For the *mens rea* of murder generally, **see chapter 1.5**.

In proving joint enterprise in assaults, the intentions of the defendants will be highly relevant, but so too will any foresight of probable or likely consequences. It will not only be necessary to gather any evidence of what harm a defendant or his/her colleagues *intended* to do; it will also be critical to obtain any evidence showing that a defendant envisaged a degree of harm being caused by the others, even though he/she did not wish to bring harm about themselves. The Court of Appeal has held that the issue in joint enterprise generally is not a 'state of mind' or intention, but an objective act which it was contemplated by a defendant would or might be done (*R* v *Day* [2001] Crim LR 984). There are areas of concern in this approach (see the comments in the *Criminal Law Review* accompanying the case report) but, so far as investigations are concerned, the need to establish any available evidence of foresight or contemplation of the consequences is probably the most important point.

The evidential and practical issues become further complicated where the accessory or secondary party is not present during the substantive offence. In such circumstances involved in the example above, the position can be summarised as follows:

Where the principal (P) relies on acts of the accessory (D) which assist him/her in the preliminary stages of a crime later committed in D's absence, it is necessary to prove *intentional assistance by D* in acts which D knew were steps taken by P towards the commission of the crime. Therefore the prosecution must prove:

- an act done by D;
- which *in fact* assisted the later commission of the offence;
- that D did the act deliberately realising that it was capable of assisting the offence;
- that D, at the time of doing the act, contemplated the commission of the offence by P, (e.g. he/she foresaw it as a real or substantial risk or real possibility); and
- that when doing the act D intended to assist P.

(see *R* v *Bryce* [2004] 2 Cr App R 35).

Another practical consideration arises, not from the absence of the accessory, but the failure to trace the *principal*.

If the principal cannot be traced or identified, the accessory may still be liable (see *Hui Chi-ming* v *The Queen* [1992] 1 AC 34). Similarly, an accessory may be convicted of procuring an offence even though the principal is acquitted or has a valid defence for his/her actions. The reasoning for this would seem to be that the principal often supplies the *actus reus* for the accessory's offence. If the accessory also has the required *mens rea*, the offence will be complete and should not be affected by the fact that there is some circumstance or characteristic preventing the principal from being prosecuted.

Additionally, if the accessory had some responsibility and the actual ability to control the actions of the principal, his/her failure to do so may attract liability (e.g. a driving instructor who fails to prevent a learner driver from driving without due care and attention (*Rubie* v *Faulkner* [1940] 1KB 571)).

It is possible for an accomplice to change his/her mind before the criminal act is carried out. However, the exact requirements of making an effective 'withdrawal' before any liability is incurred is unclear. Evidence such as how far the proposed plan had already proceeded before the withdrawal and the amount and nature of any help of encouragement already given by the accessory will be very relevant. Simply fleeing at the last moment because someone was approaching would generally not be enough. In the absence of some overwhelming supervening event, an accessory can only avoid liability for assistance rendered to the principal offender towards the commission of the crime by acting in a way that amounts to the *countermanding* of any earlier assistance such as a withdrawal from the common purpose. Repentance alone unsupported by any action taken to demonstrate withdrawal will not be enough (see e.g. *R* v *Becerra* (1975) 62 Cr App R 212 and *R* v *Mitchell* (1999) 163 JP 75).

For the rules regulating the evidence of accessories and co-accused, **see Evidence and Procedure**.

Particular care needs to be taken when charging defendants with joint enterprise in outbreaks of public disorder (see *R* v *Flounders and Alton* [2002] EWCA Crim 1325).

A person whom the law is intended to protect from certain types of offence cannot be an accessory to such offences committed against them. For example, a girl under 16 years of age is protected (by the Sexual Offences Act 2003 (**see chapter 1.9**)) from people having sexual intercourse with her. If a 15-year-old girl allows someone to have sexual intercourse with her she cannot be charged as an accessory to the offence (*R* v *Tyrrell* [1894] 1 QB 710).

1.2.7 Corporate Liability

Companies which are 'legally incorporated' have a legal personality of their own, that is they can own property, employ people and bring law suits: they can therefore commit offences. There are many difficulties associated with proving and punishing criminal conduct by companies. However, companies have been prosecuted for offences of strict liability (**see para. 1.1.2** and *Alphacell Ltd* v *Woodward* [1972] AC 824); offences requiring *mens rea* (*Tesco Supermarkets Ltd* v *Nattrass* [1972] AC 153); and offences of being an 'accessory' (*R* v *Robert Millar (Contractors) Ltd* [1970] 2 QB 54—aiding and abetting the causing of death by reckless (now dangerous) driving). There are occasions where the courts will accept that the knowledge of certain employees will be extended to the company (see e.g. *Tesco Stores Ltd* v *Brent London Borough Council* [1993] 1 WLR 1037).

Clearly there are some offences that would be conceptually impossible for a legal corporation to commit (e.g. some sexual offences) but, given that companies can be guilty as accessories (see *Robert Millar* above), they may well be capable of aiding and abetting such offences even though they could not commit the offence as a principal.

A company (OLL Ltd) has also been convicted, along with its Managing Director, of manslaughter (following the school canoeing tragedy at Lyme Bay in 1994) (*R* v *Kite* [1996] 2 Cr App R (s) 295). For manslaughter generally, **see chapter 1.5.**

1.2.8 Vicarious Liability

The general principle in criminal law is that liability is *personal*. There are, however, rare occasions where liability can be transmitted *vicariously* to another.

The most frequent occasions are cases where a statutory duty is breached by an employee in the course of his/her employment (see e.g. *National Rivers Authority* v *Alfred McAlpine Homes (East) Ltd* [1994] 4 All ER 286), or where a duty is placed upon a particular individual such as a licensee who delegates some of his/her functions to another (**see General Police Duties, chapter 4.11**). The purpose behind this concept is generally to prevent individuals or organisations from evading liability by getting others to carry out unlawful activities on their behalf. A common law exception to the rule that liability at criminal law is personal can be found in the offence of public nuisance (as to which, **see General Police Duties, chapter 4.5**).

1.3 | Incomplete Offences and Police Investigations

1.3.1 Introduction

There are circumstances where defendants are interrupted or frustrated in their efforts to commit an offence. Such circumstances might come about as a result of police intervention (e.g. where intelligence suggests that a serious offence is to take place on a given date) or as a result of things not going as the defendants had hoped (e.g. the property which they intended to steal not being where they thought it was). In these and other cases several general offences, often called inchoate or incomplete offences, may be used to ensure that the defendant's conduct does not go unpunished.

1.3.2 Incitement

OFFENCE: **Incitement—*Common Law***
- • Triable as per offence incited • Unlimited maximum penalty on indictment
- • Penalty per offence incited on summary conviction (Magistrates' Courts Act 1980, s.45 and Sch. 1, para. 35)

It is an offence unlawfully to incite another to commit an offence.

KEYNOTE

Incitement involves encouraging or pressurising someone to commit an offence. The other person need not actually commit the substantive offence or even form the intention to do so—though if they do go on to commit the offence, the inciter will become a secondary party (see chapter 1.2).

There are also some specific statutory incitements such as inciting someone to commit an offence under the Misuse of Drugs Act 1971 (see chapter 1.6).

Encouraging motorists to break the speed limit by advertising a radar detector has been held to be 'incitement' (*Invicta Plastics Ltd* v *Clare* [1976] RTR 251).

Incitement to murder is punishable under the Offences Against the Person Act 1861, s. 4.

As with accessories (see chapter 1.2), a defendant cannot incite another to commit an offence which exists for the defendant's own protection (e.g. a girl under 16 inciting a man to have unlawful sexual intercourse with her (*R* v *Tyrrell* [1894] 1 QB 710)) (Sexual Offences Act 2003—see chapter 1.9).

It is a necessary element of incitement that the person incited be capable of committing the primary offence themselves (*R* v *Whitehouse* [1977] QB 868 and *R* v *Pickford* [1994] 3 WLR 1022). This principle was confirmed in a sexual offence case involving a boy under the age of 14 who could not have committed

---

the primary offence because of an irrebuttable presumption of law that existed at the time (namely that a boy under the age of 14 was incapable of sexual intercourse)—*R* v *C* [2005] EWCA Crim 2827.

A defendant cannot incite another to commit conspiracy (Criminal Law Act 1977, s. 5(7)).

A defendant cannot incite another to aid, abet, counsel or procure an offence which is not ultimately committed (*R* v *Bodin and Bodin* [1979] Crim LR 176).

1.3.3 Conspiracy

Conspiracies can be divided into statutory and common law conspiracies.

1.3.3.1 Statutory Conspiracy

OFFENCE: **Statutory Conspiracy—*Criminal Law Act 1977, s. 1***
- Triable on indictment • Where conspiracy is to commit murder, an offence punishable by life imprisonment or any indictable offence punishable with imprisonment where no maximum term is specified—life imprisonment • In other cases, sentence is the same as for completed offence

The Criminal Law Act 1977, s. 1 states:

(1) Subject to the following provisions of this Part of this Act, if a person agrees with any other person or persons that a course of conduct will be pursued which, if the agreement is carried out in accordance with their intentions, either—
   (a) will necessarily amount to or involve the commission of any offence or offences by one or more of the parties to the agreement; or
   (b) would do so but for the existence of facts which render the commission of the offence or any of the offences impossible,
   he is guilty of conspiracy to commit the offence or offences in question.

KEYNOTE

A charge of conspiracy can be brought in respect of an agreement to commit indictable or summary offences. Conspiracy is triable only on indictment even if it relates to a summary offence (in which case the consent of the Director of Public Prosecutions will be required). Offences of conspiracy are committed at the time of the agreement, therefore it is immaterial whether or not the substantive offence is ever carried out.

Agreeing with Another

For there to be a conspiracy there must be an agreement. Therefore there must be at least two people involved. Each conspirator must be aware of the overall common purpose to which they all attach themselves. If one conspirator enters into *separate* agreements with different people, each agreement is a separate conspiracy (*R* v *Griffiths* [1966] 1 QB 589).

A person can be convicted of conspiracy even if the other conspirators are unknown (as to the affect of the acquittal of one party to a conspiracy on the other parties, see the Criminal Law Act 1977, s. 5(8)).

A defendant cannot be convicted of a statutory conspiracy if the only other party to the agreement is:

- his/her spouse (or civil partner)
- a person under 10 years of age
- the intended victim (Criminal Law Act 1977, s. 2(2))

A husband and wife can both be convicted of a statutory conspiracy if they conspire with a third party (not falling into the above categories) (*R v Chrastny* [1991] 1 WLR 1381). A person is not guilty of statutory conspiracy if the only other person with whom he agrees is his civil partner. A civil partnership is a same sex partnership registered under the Civil Partnership Act 2004. The 'end product' of the agreement must be the commission of an offence by *one or more of the parties to the agreement*. Once agreed upon, any failure to bring about the end result or an abandoning of the agreement altogether will not prevent the statutory conspiracy being committed. For the situation where the only other conspirator is an undercover officer, **see para. 1.3.6.1**.

Note that if an agreement to commit a *summary offence which is not punishable by imprisonment* is done in contemplation or furtherance of a trade dispute, it must be disregarded (Trade Union and Labour Relations (Consolidation) Act 1992, s. 242).

1.3.3.2 Common Law Conspiracies

OFFENCE: **Conspiracy to Defraud—*Common Law***

- Triable on indictment • Ten years' imprisonment and/or a fine

Conspiracy to defraud involves:

> ... an agreement by two or more [persons] by dishonesty to deprive a person of something which is his or to which he is or would or might be entitled [or] an agreement by two or more by dishonesty to injure some proprietary right [of the victim]...

(*Scott* v *Metropolitan Police Commissioner* [1975] AC 819).

(See also *Blackstone's Criminal Practice*, 2008, section A6.25.)

KEYNOTE

This offence has been endorsed by senior judges as representing an effective—if not *the* most effective—means of dealing with multiple defendants engaged in a fraudulent course of conduct.

The common law offence of conspiracy to defraud can be divided into two main types. The first is contained in the *dictum* of Viscount Dilhorne in *Scott* above, the second involves a dishonest agreement to *deceive* another into acting in a way that is contrary to his/her duty (see *Wai Yu-Tsang* v *The Queen* [1992] 1 AC 269).

Although the requirement for an agreement between at least two people is the same, this offence is broader than statutory conspiracy. There is no requirement to prove that the end result would amount to the commission of *an offence*, simply that it would result in depriving a person of something under the specified conditions or in injuring his/her proprietary right.

You must show *intent* (**see chapter 1.1**) to defraud a victim (*R* v *Hollinshead* [1985] AC 975).

You must also show that a defendant was dishonest as set out in *R* v *Ghosh* [1982] QB 1053 (**see chapter 1.11**).

Clearly there will be circumstances where the defendant's behaviour will amount to both a statutory conspiracy and a conspiracy to defraud. The Criminal Justice Act 1987, s. 12 makes provision for such circumstances and allows the prosecution to choose which charge to prefer.

Examples of common law conspiracies to defraud include:

- Buffet car staff selling their own home-made sandwiches on British Rail trains thereby depriving the company of the opportunity to sell their own products (*R* v *Cooke* [1986] AC 909).
- Directors agreeing to conceal details of a bank's trading losses from its shareholders (*Wai Yu-tsang* above).
- Making unauthorised copies of commercial films for sale (*Scott* above).

A further example can be found in *R* v *Hussain* [2005] EWCA Crim 1866 where the defendant pleaded guilty to conspiracy to defraud after a widespread abuse of the postal voting system. In that case the defendant, an official Labour party candidate, collected uncompleted postal votes from households and completed them in his own favour.

1.3.4 Attempts

The Criminal Attempts Act 1981, s. 1 states:

(1) If, with intent to commit an offence to which this section applies, a person does an act which is more that merely preparatory to the commission of the offence, he is guilty of attempting to commit the offence.

. . .

(2) A person may be guilty of attempting to commit an offence to which this section applies even though the facts are such that the commission of the offence is impossible.

(3) In any case where—

    (a) apart from this subsection a person's intention would not be regarded as having amounted to an intent to commit an offence; but

    (b) if the facts of the case had been as he believed them to be, his intention would be so regarded, then, for the purposes of subsection (1) above, he shall be regarded as having had an intent to commit that offence.

(4) This section applies to any offence which, if it were completed, would be triable in England and Wales as an indictable offence, other than—

    (a) conspiracy (at common law or under section 1 of the Criminal Law Act 1977 or any other enactment);

    (b) aiding, abetting, counselling, procuring or suborning the commission of an offence;

    (c) offences under section 4(1) (assisting offenders) or 5(1) (accepting or agreeing to accept consideration for not disclosing information about a relevant offence) of the Criminal Law Act 1967.

KEYNOTE

Most attempts at committing criminal offences will be governed by s. 1. Although some statutory exceptions apply, the sentence generally for such attempts will be:

- for murder—life imprisonment
- for indictable offences—the same maximum penalty as the substantive offence
- for either way offences—the same maximum penalty as the substantive offence *when tried summarily.*

If the attempted offence is triable summarily only, it cannot be an offence under s. 1. However, if the only reason the substantive offence is triable summarily is because of a statutory limit imposed in some cases (e.g. criminal damage to property of a low value) the offence can be attempted (see chapter 1.13). Some summary offences include an element of attempt (e.g. drink drive offences—see Road Policing, chapter 3.5).

If the offence attempted is triable only on indictment, the attempt will be triable only on indictment. Similarly, if the offence attempted is an 'either way' offence, so to will the attempt be triable either way (s. 4(1)).

Many other statutory offences contain references to 'attempts', including:

- Theft Act 1968, s. 9 (burglary)
- Firearms Act 1968, s. 17 (using firearm to resist arrest)
- Official Secrets Act 1920, s. 7 (encouraging others to commit offences).

Section 3 of the Criminal Attempts Act 1981 deals with such statutory provisions and they will generally be governed by the same principles as those set out here.

More than Merely Preparatory

A defendant's actions must be shown to have gone beyond mere preparation towards the commission of the substantive offence. Whether the defendant did or not go beyond that point will be a question of fact for the jury/magistrate(s). There is no specific formula used by the courts in interpreting this requirement. An example of where the defendant was held to have done no more than merely preparatory acts was *R v Bowles* [2004] EWCA Crim 1608. In that case the defendant had been convicted of several offences involving dishonesty against an elderly neighbour. The neighbour's long-standing will left her estate to charity but, following his arrest, police officers searched the defendant's premises and found a new will, fully complete except for the signature. The defendant and his wife were named as the main beneficiaries and were to inherit the neighbour's house. Although the defendant's son was said to have been heard making reference to the fact that he was going to inherit the house, the 'new' will had been drafted over six months earlier and there was no evidence of any steps to have it executed, nor was there any evidence of it being used. On this basis the Court of Appeal held that the making of the will was no more than merely preparatory and the defendant's conviction for attempting to make a false instrument (as to which **see para. 1.12.11.4**) was quashed. Courts have accepted an approach of questioning whether the defendant had 'embarked on the crime proper' (*R v Gullefer* [1990] 1 WLR 1063) but there is no requirement for him/her to have passed a point of no return leading to the commission of the substantive offence. However, to prove an 'attempt' you must show an *intention* (**see chapter 1.1**) on the part of the defendant to commit the substantive offence.

This requirement means that a higher level or degree of *mens rea* may be required to prove an attempt than for the substantive offence. For instance, nothing less than an *intent* to kill can support a charge of attempted murder (*R v Whybrow* (1951) 35 Cr App R 141), while in proving the substantive offence, an intention to cause grievous bodily harm will suffice (**see chapter 1.7**). A defendant's intention may be *conditional*, that is, he/she may only intend to steal from a house if something worth stealing is later found inside. The conditional nature of this intention will not generally prevent the charge of attempt being brought and the defendant's intentions will, in accordance with s. 1(3) above, be judged *on the facts as he/she believed them to be*. However, careful drafting of the charge may be required in cases where there is doubt as to the precise extent of the defendant's knowledge at the time he/she was caught (see *R v Husseyn* (1977) 67 Cr App R 131n).

Although 'intent to commit' the offence is required under s. 1(1), there are occasions where a state of mind that falls short of such a precise intention may suffice. For instance, in cases of attempted rape (**see chapter 1.9**) the courts have accepted that recklessness as to whether the victim is consenting was (under the earlier sexual offences legislation) sufficient *mens rea* for attempted rape because it is sufficient for the substantive offence (*R v Khan* [1990] 1 WLR 813).

In proving an 'attempt' it is enough to show that a defendant was in one of the states of mind required for the substantive offence and that he/she did his/her best, so far as he/she was able, to do what was necessary for the commission of the full offence (*Attorney-General's Reference (No. 3 of 1992)* [1994] 1 WLR 409).

1.3.4.1 Interfering with Vehicles

OFFENCE: **Interfering with Vehicles—*Criminal Attempts Act 1981, s. 9***

> • Triable summarily • Three months' imprisonment and/or a fine

The Criminal Attempts Act 1981, s. 9 states:

(1) A person is guilty of the offence of vehicle interference if he interferes with a motor vehicle or trailer or with anything carried in or on a motor vehicle or trailer with the intention that an offence specified in subsection (2) below shall be committed by himself or some other person.

(2) The offences mentioned in subsection (1) above are—

    (a) theft of the motor vehicle or trailer or part of it;

    (b) theft of anything carried in or on the motor vehicle or trailer; and

    (c) an offence under section 12(1) of the Theft Act 1968 (taking and driving away without consent);

    and, if it is shown that a person accused of an offence under this section intended that one of those offences should be committed, it is immaterial that it cannot be shown which it was.

(3)–(4) . . .

(5) In this section 'motor vehicle' and 'trailer' have the meanings assigned to them by section 185(1) of the Road Traffic Act 1988.

KEYNOTE

'Interference' is not defined and there are no conclusive cases on the subject at the time of writing. This offence is one of specific intent (**see chapter 1.1**) and you must prove that the defendant interfered with the vehicle, etc. with one of the intentions listed—(note, however, that it is not necessary to show which *particular* intention).

For the definitions of motor vehicle and trailer, see Road Policing, chapter 3.1.

Where a person suspected of committing this offence has any articles with them, the further offence of going equipped (s. 25 of the Theft Act 1968) should be considered (**see chapter 1.11**). The above offence is a specified offence for the purposes of the Vehicles (Crime) Act 2001, s. 3(4)(b) (as to which, **see Road Policing**).

See also the offence of tampering **Road Policing, chapter 3.8**.

1.3.5 Impossibility

Practical difficulties have arisen where, despite the best (or worst) efforts of the defendant, his/her ultimate intention has been impossible (such as trying to extract cocaine from a powder which is, unknown to the defendant, only talc). Impossibility is now far clearer following the Criminal Attempts Act 1981 and its interpretation through the courts. It differs however in some incomplete offences.

....

EXAMPLE

Taking an example of someone who tries to handle goods which are not in fact stolen, the following rules would apply:

- A defendant could *not* be guilty of inciting another, nor of common law conspiracy to defraud in these circumstances. The *physical* impossibility of what they sought to do would preclude such a charge.
- A defendant *could* be guilty of a statutory conspiracy with another to handle 'stolen' goods and also of attempting to handle 'stolen' goods under these circumstances. The physical impossibility would not prelude such charges as a result of the Criminal Attempts Act 1981 and the House of Lords' decision in *R* v *Shivpuri* [1987] AC 1. The only form of impossibility which would preclude liability under the Criminal Attempts Act 1981 or for a statutory conspiracy would be the *legal* impossibility.

....

1.3.6 Inter-relationship and Police Operations

A good rule of thumb is that *most* incomplete offences cannot be mixed, and that most cannot be attempted. For instance, you *cannot* conspire to aid and abet, neither can you attempt to conspire. There are, as ever, limited exceptions to this rule. So, for instance, you *can* attempt to incite another to commit an offence.

Where the issues of involvement in an incomplete offence *are* of practical relevance to police officers is in the area of covert operations. Is it a conspiracy if one of the conspirators is an undercover police officer? Can a person commit an offence of incitement if the person they try to incite is a police informer? These questions, along with the regulatory framework governing the whole area of covert police operations, are discussed below.

1.3.6.1 Entrapment, Incitement and Undercover Operations

One of the arguments that is often raised by defendants who are caught by undercover officers is that they were induced or pressurised into committing the offence by the officers and that, as a result, either they should not be prosecuted or the evidence of the officer(s) should be excluded.

In *R* v *Loosely; Attorney-General's Reference (No. 3) of 2000* [2001] 1 WLR 2060, the House of Lords took the chance to set out in detail the legal position in relation to these issues. Their Lordships held that it is both unfair and an abuse of process if a person is incited or pressurised by an undercover officer into committing a crime which the person would otherwise not have committed. If, however, the police officer(s) did no more than present a person with an 'unexceptional opportunity' to commit a criminal offence and the person took that opportunity, this would not amount to such an abuse of process.

The cases arose out of prosecutions of two different matters, both involving the supply of Class A drugs to undercover police officers. From a long judgment it is possible to draw out the following 'checklist' of issues when dealing with cases where evidence of undercover officers and test purchases is involved:

1.3.6.2 Entrapment

This area of policing, along with the relevant decisions in our domestic courts, has been considered at length by the European Court of Human Rights in *Edwards* v *United Kingdom* (2005) 40 EHRR 24. In that case the Court re-stated the rights of defendants who are to be prosecuted on the basis of evidence obtained by undercover officers and, once again, highlighted the tensions between protecting the sensitive sources of that evidence while affording the defendant a fair trial.

- As a starting point—it is not acceptable for the 'State' (police officers or other agents) to lure its citizens into committing acts that are against the law and then to prosecute those citizens for doing so—this amounts to entrapment, a misuse of power and abuse of the courts' process.
- If police officers acted only as 'detectives' and 'passive observers' of criminal activity that was to take place anyway, there would be no real problem in drawing the line between what is allowable and what is not.
- However, some offences need a degree of active involvement by the police if those offences are to be successfully prosecuted. In such cases the police officers themselves become the reporters and witnesses of the offence as well as the investigators.
- The yardstick for judging the activities of the police in this regard is to ask whether the officers' conduct preceding the offence was no more than might have been expected from others in the circumstances. That is, did they do no more than give the defendant the 'unexceptional opportunity' to commit a crime as described above? If the answer is 'yes', the consequences below are not relevant. If the answer is 'no', there are several potential consequences for any subsequent trial (and possibly police conduct proceedings—as to which, **see General Police Duties**).

Or, to put it another way (as the Court of Appeal did), the trial judge's task in such cases is to distinguish between legitimate crime detection and illegitimate crime creation (*R* v *Byrne* [2003] EWCA Crim 1073).

- The greater the inducement or persistence by the officers—the more readily the courts will conclude that they have overstepped the line.
- The greater the degree of intrusiveness into the 'target's' life—the closer the courts will scrutinise the 'proportionality' of the operation.
- The courts will also look at the defendant's personal circumstances including his/her vulnerability and experience. What might be insignificant in terms of an inducement to one person may not be seen as so insignificant in relation to another.

The consequences are as follows:

- Courts have a general discretion to exclude evidence on grounds of unfairness under the Police and Criminal Evidence Act 1984, s. 78 (**see Evidence and Procedure, chapter 2.9**).
- Courts also have a common law power to stay (discontinue) proceedings and order the release of a defendant where it becomes apparent that there has been a serious abuse of power by the State (*R* v *Horseferry Road Magistrates' Court, ex parte Bennett* [1994] 1 AC 42).
- Courts also have a general duty to consider the fairness of any defendant's trial under Article 6 of the European Convention on Human Rights (**see General Police Duties, chapter 4.3**). However, it should be noted that violations of Article 8 (right to privacy)

will not by themselves usually give rise to exclusion of any evidence obtained as a result (*PG* v *United Kingdom* [2002] Crim LR 308).

The use of informants in this area is particularly hazardous and will invite suggestions that the police did more than present the defendant with an unexceptional opportunity to commit their crimes. The accurate keeping and maintenance of records as required by the Regulation of Investigatory Powers Act 2000 here is critical (**see General Police Duties, chapter 4.12**). Where participating informants are involved, the same legal principles apply but the issues become far more complicated and policy regarding 'participating informant' status will be crucial. This is an area in which the expertise of the Crown Prosecution Service will be needed from a very early stage.

1.3.6.3 Incitement

The other side of the coin is where, rather than approaching others, an undercover police officer is approached to take part in a proposed offence. There are several types of situation where this can arise—bringing with them the issues discussed in the earlier part of this chapter.

In relation to incitement, there is no need for the person 'incited' to have any intention of going on to commit the offence (**see para. 1.3.2**). The Divisional Court has held that there is no requirement for 'parity of *mens rea*' between the inciter and the incited (*DPP* v *Armstrong* [2000] Crim LR 379). In that case the defendant had approached an undercover police officer asking him to supply child pornography. At his trial, the defendant argued that, as the officer in reality had no intention of supplying the pornography, there was no offence of incitement. On appeal by the prosecutor, the Divisional Court held that incitement, like conspiracies (**see para. 1.3.3**) and attempts (**see para. 1.3.4**) were auxiliary offences where criminal liability was attributed to the defendant where the full offence had not been committed. Consequently the intent of the person incited was irrelevant. The Court also held that the issue of impossibility (**see para. 1.3.5**) did not arise in circumstances such as Armstrong's because it had been 'possible' for the officer to supply the material.

A further situation involving police operations is where a defendant enters into an agreement with another person to commit an offence but that other person is in fact a police officer. Under normal circumstances, forming an agreement with another person to carry out an offence is a conspiracy (**see para. 1.3.3.1**). If, however, one of only two conspirators is an undercover officer who has no intention of going through with the agreement, there is a strong argument that there can be no 'true' conspiracy as the only other person had no intention of going through with the plan (see the comments of Lord Griffiths in *Yip Chiu-Cheung* v *The Queen* [1995] 1 AC 111). This situation is different from that of incitement because, in conspiracies, the intention of at least two parties *is* the basis of the whole offence. In cases where the only other 'conspirator' is a police officer, incitement may be a more appropriate charge but the advice of the CPS would clearly be needed.

Making *an offer* which amounts *in itself* to a criminal offence (e.g. an offer to supply a controlled drug, **see chapter 1.6**) to an undercover officer may still amount to the offence and a defendant cannot claim that the offer was not 'real' because of the identity of the recipient (see *R* v *Kray*, unreported, 10 November 1998).

This area of law has received a great deal of attention recently, primarily as a result of 'sting' operations carried out by public authorities and, more recently, by investigative journalists. So far as the police are concerned, one of the greatest dangers in cases such as these is the possibility that the evidence obtained may be excluded because the officers concerned are deemed to have acted as *agents provocateur* and to have violated the defendant's rights under the European Convention on Human Rights (see *Teixeira de Castro v Portugal* (1998) 28 EHRR 101). Generally, the involvement of the officers will be judged in the light of the seriousness of the case (see, for example, *Nottingham City Council v Mohammed Amin* [2000] 1 WLR 1071, where it was held that police officers posing as members of the public to flag down unlicensed mini-cab drivers was not unfair to the defendants). However, this entire area of the law has also been revised—and restricted—by the Regulation of Investigatory Powers Act 2000 (as to which **see General Police Duties, chapter 4.12**).

1.4 | General Defences

1.4.1 Introduction

'General defences' in criminal law are concerned with cases where the prosecution are unable to prove all elements beyond reasonable doubt because of some specific characteristics of the defendant or circumstances of a particular offence. This failure may come about at trial but will often be apparent at the evidence gathering stage of a proposed prosecution. There are two main reasons why police officers need to be aware of any defences that a person may have in answer to a criminal charge:

- because they have a duty to investigate crime *impartially and fairly*—if there is evidence that supports a person's defence, the police officer should be collecting it in the same way as evidence of the offence itself—it is not their job just to collect the evidence that proves someone *did* do something wrong;
- because the police will need to be able to deal with any likely defences when they interview the accused person.

Some offences have particular defences attached to them (e.g. criminal damage), others exist only in relation to murder. These defences are discussed in the relevant chapters. This chapter is concerned with 'general defences', that is, those circumstances which may negate a conviction or even the bringing of a charge for a number of different offences.

When considering defences, either statutory or at common law, it is necessary to examine the impact of the Human Rights Act 1998 and any relevant provisions made under the European Convention on Human Rights. In particular the right to life (Article 2), the rights to liberty and security of person (Article 5) and the right to the peaceful enjoyment of property and possessions (Protocol 1, Article 1) may be relevant in assessing the lawfulness or otherwise of a person's conduct.

In addition, it has been argued that some statutory defences infringe the presumption of innocence (imposed at both common law and under Article 6). This argument was considered by the House of Lords in the context of the statutory defences under the Misuse of Drugs Act 1971 (**see chapter 1.6**) in *R* v *Lambert* [2002] 2 AC 545. In *Lambert* it was argued that the statutory defence effectively shifted the legal burden of proof from the prosecution to the defendant, making it incompatible with the Convention. Among other things, their Lordships decided that the statutory defence did not shift the *legal* burden of proof at all, by interpreting the statutory defence as imposing no more than an *evidential* burden onto the defendant. Such an approach *was* compatible with the Convention and the Human Rights Act 1998. In *Lambert* their Lordships also considered the effects of some other statutory defences and held that there was no general incompatibility between them and the presumption of innocence. The same—very technical—arguments came before the House of Lords again, this time in the context of s. 5(2) of the Road Traffic Act 1998 (statutory defence to driving while over the prescribed limit; **see Road Policing, para. 3.5.3.1**) and

s. 11(2) of the Terrorism Act 2000 (statutory defence with regard to belonging to proscribed organisation; **see General Police Duties, para. 4.6.14.3**) in *Attorney-General's Reference (No. 4 of 2002) Sheldrake* v *DPP* [2004] UKHL 43. In the case of the Road Traffic Act provision it was held that, although the section did in fact infringe the presumption of innocence under Article 6, the burden placed on the defendant was reasonable because it was in pursuance of a legitimate aim. Insofar as the terrorism matter was concerned, it was held that s. 11(2) imposed a *legal* burden on the defendant and one which was neither proportionate nor reasonable. However, when applying the relevant subsection, the courts should 'read down' the wording in a way that imposed an *evidential* burden on the defendant. For a further discussion of these issues, **see Evidence and Procedure, chapter 2.7**.

1.4.2 Automatism

Strictly speaking, automatism is not a 'defence'; it is an absence of a fundamental requirement for any criminal offence, namely the 'criminal conduct' (*actus reus*). In **chapter 1.2** we considered the need for criminal conduct to be *voluntary* and *willed*. It therefore follows that, if a defendant has total loss of control over his/her actions, he/she cannot be held liable for those actions and provided the loss of control is *total*, there may be grounds to claim a defence of automatism. The most well known example of this defence is the road traffic one where a swarm of bees flies into a car. The reflex action by the driver may result in an accident but if the driver's actions were involuntary, and not sufficient to support a criminal charge, the defence of automatism would be available. Other examples might include a person inadvertently dropping and damaging property when suddenly seized by cramp or discharging a firearm as a result of an irresistible bout of sneezing.

If the loss of control is brought about by voluntary intoxication or by insanity, the defence becomes narrower and more complicated (see below).

1.4.3 Intoxication: Voluntary or Involuntary

There is no general defence of intoxication. If there were, a high proportion of criminal behaviour would clearly go unpunished. There are several summary offences which involve drunkenness, **see General Police Duties, chapters 4.6 and 4.11**: there are also some statutory offences where specific provision is made for drunkenness (e.g. the Public Order Act 1986, **see General Police Duties, chapter 4.6**). Additionally, if a defendant is *involuntarily* intoxicated (say, through having his/her drink 'spiked'), he/she may lack the relevant *mens rea* or state of mind for an offence.

If a defendant simply misjudges the amount or strength of intoxicants which he/she takes, this will not be regarded as involuntary and the restrictions discussed below will apply (*R* v *Allen* [1988] Crim LR 698). Similarly, if the defendant can be shown to have formed the required *mens rea* (**see chapter 1.1**) the limited defence of intoxication—whether involuntary or otherwise—will not be available (*R* v *Kingston* [1995] 2 AC 355).

The source of the intoxication can be drink or drugs. In the latter case, however, the courts will consider the known effects of the drug in deciding whether or not the defendant had formed the required degree of *mens rea*; the characteristics of the drugs will also be relevant in determining whether the defendant behaved recklessly in taking them.

1.4.3.1   Specific and Basic Intent

The division of crimes into specific and basic intent (**see chapter 1.1**) is relevant when considering a defendant's intoxication.

If a defendant was intoxicated voluntarily at the time of the alleged offence, he/she can only rely on that fact *if the offence is one of specific intent*. The courts have accepted that, when so intoxicated, a defendant may be incapable of forming the specific intent required (such as an intention to steal or to wound in the case of burglary, **see chapter 1.11**).

Conversely, the courts have also accepted that a defendant is still capable of forming basic intent even when completely inebriated (see *DPP* v *Majewski* [1977] AC 443).

The defence of voluntary intoxication applies to offences where a specific intent is required (e.g. murder or s. 18 wounding or criminal attempts); it is also suggested (see *Blackstone's Criminal Practice*, 2008, section A3.10) that the defence would logically extend to other offences requiring particular states of mind such as 'dishonesty'.

Where the defendant forms a 'mistaken belief' based on the fact that he/she is intoxicated and not thinking straight, that belief may sometimes be raised as a defence. In cases of criminal damage where a defendant has mistakenly believed that the property being damaged is his/her her own property, and that mistaken belief has arisen from the defendant's intoxicated state, the courts have accepted the defence under s. 5 of the Criminal Damage Act 1971 (*Jaggard* v *Dickinson* [1981] QB 527) (**see chapter 1.13**). However, this appears to be confined to the wording of that particular statute and the courts have refused to accept similar defences of mistaken, drunken belief (see *R* v *O'Grady* [1987] QB 995 where the defendant mistakenly believed he was being attacked and so 'defended' himself) or where the defendant mistakenly believed that the victim of a rape was consenting to sexual intercourse. More recently, the Court of Appeal has confirmed that the decision in *O'Grady* (a defendant on a charge of murder cannot rely on a mistake induced by their own voluntary intoxication in claiming self-defence) also applies to manslaughter—*R* v *Hatton* (2006) 1 Cr App R 16.

One further qualification is that if a defendant becomes intoxicated in order to gain false courage to go and commit a crime, he/she will not be able to claim a defence of intoxication *even if the crime is one of specific intent*. This is because he/she has already formed the intent required and the intoxication is merely a means of plucking up courage to carry it out (*Attorney-General for Northern Ireland* v *Gallagher* [1963] AC 349).

1.4.4   Insanity

There is a presumption in law that all people are sane. That presumption is clearly rebuttable (**see Evidence and Procedure, chapter 2.7**) and evidence of a defendant's insanity may be put before a court. Where a person wishes to raise insanity as a defence, the burden of proof (albeit on a balance of probabilities) rests with the defendant.

If a defendant claims to have been 'insane' at the time of the offence (to attract an acquittal in a summary trial or an order of the court when tried on indictment), that claim will be judged against the M'Naghten rules. The rules (*M'Naghten's Case* (1843) 10 Cl & F 200) state:

> ... to establish a defence on the ground of insanity, it must be clearly proved that, at the time of the committing of the act, the party accused was labouring under such a defect of reason, from disease of the mind, as not to know the nature and quality of the act he was doing; or, if he did know it, that he did not know he was doing what was wrong.

The question of whether the defendant's attributes or condition amount to a 'disease of the mind' is a question of law and not a question of medical opinion (*R* v *Sullivan* [1984] AC 156). (Contrast the 'special defence' to murder in **chapter 1.5**.)

An epileptic fit and a hypoglycaemic episode in a diabetic have both been deemed to be similar to insanity in respect of a defence to a criminal charge and therefore the M'Naghten rules above should be applied (*Sullivan* and *R* v *Quick* [1973] QB 910).

A special verdict of 'not guilty by reason of insanity' is provided by the Trial of Lunatics Act 1883.

1.4.5 Inadvertence and Mistake

In addition to mistaken belief brought about by intoxication (**see para. 1.4.3.1**), there are also occasions where a defendant makes a mistake about some circumstance or consequence. Claims that a defendant 'made a mistake' or did something 'inadvertently' will only be an effective defence if they negate the *mens rea* for that offence. Therefore, if someone picks up another person's shopping at a supermarket till or wanders out of a shop with something they have yet to pay for, their mistake or inadvertence, in each case, might negative any *mens rea* of 'dishonesty' (**see chapter 1.11**). As the requirement for the *mens rea* in such a case is *subjective* then the defendant's mistake or inadvertence will be judged subjectively. The same will generally be true for offences requiring subjective recklessness. It does not matter whether the mistake was 'reasonable' (*DPP* v *Morgan* [1976] AC 182). The appropriate test is whether the defendant's mistaken belief was an honest and genuine one. If the alleged offence is one which will be judged *objectively* (**see chapter 1.1**) then inadvertence will not be a defence and any 'mistake' will have to involve the defendant ruling out any risk of the prohibited consequence. (See *Chief Constable of Avon and Somerset* v *Shimmen* (1986) 84 Cr App R 7 where a martial arts 'expert' mistakenly believed he could aim a kick at a window without breaking it. As he had not 'ruled out any risk' of the window breaking—which it did—his mistake was not accepted as a defence.) There are occasions where a genuine mistake on the part of the defendant may amount to a defence (**see chapter 1.9**). However, as a general rule, a defendant cannot rely on a mistake induced by their own voluntary intoxication—a rule that applies equally to cases of manslaughter and murder (as to which **see chapter 1.5**)—*R* v *O'Grady* [1987] QB 995 and *R* v *Hatton* [2005] EWCA Crim 2951.

In *R* v *Lee* [2000] Crim LR 991, a case arising from an assault on two arresting police officers, the Court of Appeal reviewed the law in this area, reaffirming the following points:

- A genuine or honest mistake could provide a defence to many criminal offences requiring a particular state of mind, including assault with intent to resist arrest (*R* v *Brightling* [1991] Crim LR 364).
- A defence of mistake had to involve a mistake of fact, not a mistake of law (see below).
- People under arrest are not entitled to form their own view as to the lawfulness of that arrest. They have a duty to comply with the police and hear the details of the charge against them (*R* v *Bentley* (1850) 4 Cox CC 406).
- Belief in one's own innocence, however genuine or honestly held, cannot afford a defence to a charge of assault with intent to resist arrest under s. 38 of the Offences Against the Person Act 1861 (as to which, **see chapter 1.7**).

A defendant attempted to argue that his honest and reasonable mistake as to the *facts* of his arrest (as opposed to the law) after he was lawfully arrested for a public order offence was different from the decision in *Lee*. The Divisional Court did not agree with him (see *Hewitt* v *DPP* [2002] EWHC 2801).

In relation to offences involving negligence, inadvertence would clearly not amount to a defence and any 'mistake' would generally need to be shown to be a reasonable one.

Generally, it is no defence to claim a mistake as to the law because all people are presumed to know the law once it is made. With statutory instruments a defendant can show that the instrument in question was not in force at the time of the offence or that the behaviour that it sought to control was beyond the powers (*ultra vires*) of that instrument (see *Boddington* v *British Transport Police* [1998] 2 WLR 639 where the defendant sought to challenge the bye-laws preventing smoking on trains formerly owned by British Rail but now operated by private companies).

There is one particular example, however, where a mistaken belief in the legal position is specifically provided for in a criminal offence. This is where a person appropriates property in the belief that he/she has a legal right to deprive another person of it under s. 2 of the Theft Act 1968 (**see chapter 1.11**).

1.4.6 Duress

Where a person is threatened with death or serious physical injury unless they carry out a criminal act, they may have a defence of *duress* (see *R* v *Graham* [1982] 1 WLR 294). The threat of serious physical injury does not appear to include serious *psychological* injury (see *R* v *Baker* [1997] Crim LR 497), which seems slightly at odds with the situation regarding injury generally (see *R* v *Ireland* [1998] AC 147 and **chapter 1.7**). Where relevant intent is an essential ingredient of the offence, the defendant might claim that he/she only formed that intent as a result of duress (e.g. an intent to supply controlled drugs—**see para. 1.6.5.2**). However, unless it is shown that the intent had—or could have—been formed *only* by reason of that duress (e.g. the duress was the only thing causing the defendant to form that intent), the defence will fail (see *R* v *Fisher* [2004] EWCA Crim 1190.

It would seem that the threat need not be made solely to the person who goes on to commit the relevant offence and there are authorities to suggest that threats of death/serious harm to loved ones may allow a defence of duress (see *Blackstone's Criminal Practice*, 2008, section A3.22).

The defence is not available in respect of an offence of murder (*R* v *Howe* [1987] AC 417) or attempted murder (*R* v *Gotts* [1992] 2 AC 412), as a principal or secondary offender. It is, however, available in other offences even in offences of strict liability (*Eden DC* v *Braid* [1998] COD 259—taxi driver threatened and forced to carry excessive number of people in breach of his licensing conditions).

There are several key elements to this defence:

- the threat must have driven the defendant to commit the offence;
- the defendant must have acted as a sober and reasonable person sharing his/her characteristics would have done;
- the threatened injury must be anticipated at or near the time of the offence (i.e. not sometime in the distant future).

If a defendant knowingly exposes himself/herself to a risk of such a threat of death or serious physical injury, he/she cannot then claim duress as a defence. For instance, if a person joins a violent gang or an active terrorist organisation, he/she cannot then claim duress as a defence to any crimes he/she may go on to commit under threat of death or serious injury from another member or rival of that organisation (see *R v Sharp* [1987] QB 853). However, if the purpose of the organisation or gang is not predominantly violent or dangerous (e.g. a gang of shoplifters) then the defence of duress *may* be available in relation to offences committed while under threat of death or serious physical injury from other gang members (*R v Shepherd* (1987) 86 Cr App R 47).

The House of Lords summarised the defence of duress in *R v Hasan* [2005] UKHL 22. This case provides a good practical example of how this defence may or may not apply and the importance of evidence gathering by the police. In that case the defendant had been convicted of aggravated burglary and raised the defence of duress. He claimed that a drug dealer known for his use of violence had threatened to injure him and his family if he did not carry out the burglary. The prosecution argued that he should have foreseen the risk of being compelled to commit criminal offences by his association with violent criminals and further, that remarks made 'off the record' in a later interview showed that any threats had not been made until after the burglary. The House of Lords held that the defence of duress is excluded when, as a result of the defendant's voluntary association with others engaged in criminal activity, he or she foresaw or ought reasonably to have foreseen the risk of being subjected to any compulsion by threats of violence. However, the law of duress does not require there to have been foresight of coercion to commit crimes *of the kind with which the defendant is charged*. The test should be an objective one of what the defendant in all the circumstances and knowing what he or she did, ought reasonably to have foreseen. The general policy behind the law here was to discourage association with known criminals, and the courts should be slow to excuse the criminal conduct of those who did so.

The defence and the relevant cases were considered in *R v Quayle* [2005] 1 WLR 3642 by the Court of Appeal where a number of defendants had been variously convicted of cultivating, possessing, producing and importing cannabis (**see chapter 1.6**).

The Attorney-General made a reference in respect of a defence of 'medical necessity'. The question referred by the Attorney-General involved a number of strands but in essence concerned whether or not the defence of necessity was available in respect of drugs offences such as possession of cannabis with intent to supply (**see para. 1.6.5.6**) where the defendant intended to supply the drug for the purpose of alleviating pain from a pre-existing illness (such as multiple sclerosis). It was also argued that the common law defence of necessity should be expanded to prevent or remove any inconsistency with statutory legislation such as the European Convention on Human Rights. Dismissing the appeals, the court held that necessary 'medical use' claimed on an individual basis was in conflict with the purpose and effect of the legislative scheme (in particular the Misuse of Drugs Act 1971 Act and the relevant Regulations). No such use was permitted under the legislation, even on doctor's prescription, except in the context of ongoing trials for medical research purposes. The legislative scheme did not permit unqualified individuals to prescribe cannabis to themselves as patients or to assume the role of a doctor by obtaining, prescribing and supplying it to other 'patients'. Neither can a defendant rely on the same defence by presenting it as a 'human rights' issue (*R v Altham* [2006] EWCA Crim 7).

For the defence of necessity of circumstances to be potentially available, there have to be 'extraneous circumstances capable of objective scrutiny by judge and jury' (per *Hassan* above) and the legal defences of duress by threats and 'necessity' (duress of circumstances—**see para. 1.4.7**) should be confined to cases where there was an imminent danger of physical injury and pain.

1.4.6.1 Marital Coercion

Closely linked to the defence of duress is the defence of 'marital coercion' whereby a *wife* charged with any offence other than treason or murder, may raise the defence that she committed the offence in the presence and under the coercion of her husband (see the Criminal Justice Act 1925, s. 47 and *R* v *Shortland* [1996] 1 Cr App R 116).

1.4.7 Duress of Circumstances

As well as cases where a person receives a direct threat in order to make them commit an offence, there may be times when circumstances leave the defendant no real alternative. If a doctor is suddenly called upon to use his/her car to get someone to hospital for emergency treatment then those circumstances may provide a defence for driving while disqualified (see e.g. *R* v *Martin* [1989] 1 All ER 652). Similarly, threats of immediate violence may allow a defence of duress of circumstances for someone who drives dangerously in order to escape the threat (*R* v *Willer* (1986) 83 Cr App R 225). In such cases the court will consider the reasonableness of the defendant's behaviour in light of the prevailing circumstances. If the defendant commits a very serious offence in order to avoid very minor or trivial consequences then this defence is unlikely to be available.

Although it was said for a long time that there was no defence of 'necessity' in the law of England and Wales, there is now authority for this defence, albeit in very narrow circumstances (*R* v *A (Children) (Conjoined Twins: Surgical Separation)* [2001] 2 WLR 480).

This type of duress should be distinguished from that at **para. 1.4.6**. There the duress comes from a threat made to the defendant compelling him/her to commit an offence: a gun to the head type of situation where one person says to another '*Do this or else. . .*'. With duress of circumstances, there is no such threat being made. Rather there is a threatening situation or set of circumstances from which the defendant wishes to escape and, in so doing, feels impelled to commit an offence as the lesser of two present evils. Here the threat is 'situational' and the defendant feels '*If I don't do this, then I will suffer death or serious physical injury. . .*'. A good example is in *R* v *Willer* (1986) 83 Cr App R 225 where the defendant, while in his car, feared he would be attacked by a gang of youths and drove across a shopping precinct in order to avoid the assault. In answer to a charge of what was then 'reckless' (now 'dangerous', **see Road Policing, chapter 3.2**) driving, the defendant raised the defence of duress of circumstances.

This growing defence was examined by the Court of Appeal in a case where someone jumped onto the bonnet of the car that the appellant was driving. The appellant drove for some distance with the man on the bonnet of the car, braking after a short time to go over a speed ramp. The man fell from the bonnet and the appellant drove on, running the man over and causing him grievous bodily harm (as to which, **see chapter 1.7**). In determining whether or not the defence of 'duress of circumstances' was available, the court held that the jury must ask two questions in relation to the appellant:

- Was he (or might he have been) impelled to act as he did because, as a result of what he reasonably believed, he had good cause to fear he would suffer death or serious injury if he did not do so?
- If so, would a sober person of reasonable firmness and sharing the same characteristics, have responded to the situation in the way that he did?

If each question were answered with a 'yes', the defence would be made out (*R v Cairns* [1999] 2 Cr App R 137).

The important aspect to this defence then is that it will only avail the defendant as long as he/she is acting under compulsion of the prevailing circumstances when committing the offence. It appears that the defendant need only hold an *honest* belief that those circumstances exist without necessarily having *reasonable grounds* for that belief (see *DPP v Rogers* [1998] Crim LR 202) and there is no need for the threat to be 'real'. There is certainly no need for the threat (perceived threat) to amount to a criminal offence and the Court of Appeal has accepted the possibility of a 'duress of circumstances' defence being applicable where a defendant acts in fear of the consequences of declaring war on Iraq (see *R v Jones (Margaret)* [2004] EWCA Crim 1981). However, the defendant's actions in order to avoid that perceived threatening situation must be reasonable and in proportion to the threat presented. Therefore defendant(s) in situation(s) like *Willer* and *Cairns* would not be able to claim duress of circumstances if they drove at their victims repeatedly until all had been injured to a point whereby they no longer posed a threat.

An attempt to extend the defence was made in *R v Altham* [2006] EWCA Crim 7, where the defendant had been charged with possessing a controlled drug (cannabis). The defendant appealed against his conviction and argued that he needed to smoke the drug to ease the pain he suffered as a consequence of injuries he had received in a car accident. It was argued that the defence of duress of circumstances should be open to the defendant on the basis that he was suffering serious physical harm. This was countered by the prosecution who argued that pain can never amount to serious physical harm. The appeal was dismissed and the court stated that the defence could not be available in this type of circumstance because it would allow unlawful activity to be undertaken and it would be in direct conflict with the purpose and effect of the intention of the Misuse of Drugs Act 1971.

It seems that, apart from the offence of murder or attempted murder (or treason), the defence is available against any other charge (including hijacking, *R v Abdul-Hussain* [1999] Crim LR 570). The Court of Appeal has said that there is an urgent need for legislation in this area (*Abdul-Hussain* above).

For the development of this defence in the area of dangerous and careless driving, **see Road Policing, chapter 3.2**.

1.4.8 Defence of Self, Others or Property

There are circumstances where the use of force against person or property will be permissible. This aspect of criminal law has attracted a great deal of interest as a result of several widely-reported court cases. As a result, there have been calls for a change in the legislation in order to provide greater perceived protection for those who cause injury in defending their lives or property. Whatever future changes this may bring, it is almost certain that the effect of Human Rights Act 1998 will be to impose even stricter conditions on those occasions whereby a person might lawfully injure—or kill—a person in the defence of another (see below). There are also those cases where a person is specifically empowered to use force, such as when executing a warrant (**see General Police Duties, chapter 4.4**). But there are times when the use of force generally will be justified by the circumstances, i.e.:

- preventing crime
- defending yourself or another
- protecting property.

In practical terms, the decision to claim self-defence can also carry some risks for a defendant. If a defendant claims, for example, that the victim struck the first blow, allowing him to defend himself, that allegation may amount to an attack on the character of the victim and give rise to the provisions for 'bad character' evidence (see **Evidence & Procedure, chapter 2.7**) (*R v Blackford* [2005] EWCA Crim 1645).

1.4.8.1 Preventing Crime

The Criminal Law Act 1967, s. 3(1) states:

> A person may use such force as is reasonable in the circumstances in the prevention of crime, or in effecting or assisting in the lawful arrest of offenders or suspected offenders or of persons unlawfully at large.

Since the Privy Council decision in *Beckford* v *The Queen* [1988] AC 130 and the case of *R v Clegg* [1995] 1 AC 482, the requirement is *such force as is reasonable in the circumstances*.

Where such a defence is raised in relation to the taking of someone's life, the provisions of Article 2 of the European Convention on Human Rights will now be applicable. The requirements of Article 2 are more stringent than the test under s. 3. Under Article 2 the test will be whether the force used was no more than *absolutely necessary* and lethal force will be 'absolutely necessary' only if it is strictly proportionate to the legitimate purpose being pursued. In order to meet those criteria, regard will be had to:

- the nature of the aim being pursued
- the inherent dangers to life and limb from the situation
- the degree of risk to life presented by the amount of force employed.

The only circumstances under which lethal force might be permissible here are where the defendant was acting *to defend another person from unlawful violence* (Article 2(2)), not in the general prevention of crime. The other circumstances where such force may be used are in effecting the lawful arrest, or preventing the escape of another and in lawfully acting to quell a riot or insurrection.

1.4.8.2 Defence of Self or Another

It is uncertain whether 'self-defence' is limited to the defence of oneself and 'friends and family', or whether it extends to acts done in defence of any other person. The distinction is of little importance given the general defence in relation to the prevention of crime under the Criminal Law Act 1967.

A defendant must believe that the degree of force used is reasonable in the circumstances *as he/she honestly believes them to be* (*Beckford*). Therefore if a defendant believes he/she is being attacked or is facing a lethal threat, he/she may use a degree of force which would be reasonable if that were actually the case.

However, a defendant cannot rely on a mistake induced by their own voluntary intoxication when trying to establish 'self-defence' (*R v O'Grady* [1987] QB 995).

Note that there is no requirement to let the believed attacker 'strike the first blow' (*Beckford*) or for the person defending themselves to retreat (see *R v Bird* [1985] 1 WLR 816). A 'pre-emptive' strike may be justified by the circumstances.

Whether or not a defendant did act in self-defence is a question of fact which should be left to a jury—even if the defendant has not raised the issue (*DPP (Jamaica)* v *Bailey* [1995] 1 Cr App R 257).

In deciding whether or not the force used by a defendant was reasonable in the circumstances, the court will have regard to the 'anguish' of the moment and the defendant will not be expected to have *'weighed to a nicety the exact measure of his [/her] necessary defensive actions'* (per Lord Morris in *Palmer* v *The Queen* [1971] AC 814). However, in applying the test under *Palmer*, courts may take into account matters such as the relative height, build and strength of the defendant and the person against whom the force was used and the injuries caused; the court can also take into account the gender of the parties (see e.g. *R (On the Application of Buckley)* v *DPP* [2004] EWHC 2533 where even an open-handed push was held to have been unreasonable force in all the circumstances). Therefore it is important to record as much of this detail as possible.

If the degree of force used by the defendant is found to have been excessive in a trial for murder, there is no room for an argument of self-defence to *reduce* the defendant's liability to manslaughter; the defence is either accepted completely (in which case the defendant is 'not guilty') or it is not (in which case he/she is convicted) (*R* v *Clegg* [1995] 1 AC 482).

If the defendant mistakenly believes that he/she is being attacked, that belief does not have to be 'reasonable' (*R* v *Williams* (*Gladstone*) [1987] 3 All ER 411). In such cases the defendant's actions will be judged against the circumstances as he/she believed them to be at the time. Therefore, where a defendant mistakenly believed he was being attacked by strangers and 'defended' himself against them, his actions were to be judged as though that were actually the case—even though the strangers were in fact police officers and court officials and the defendant's mistake was not an entirely reasonable one (*Blackburn* v *Bowering* [1994] 1 WLR 1324).

If any lethal force is used, the test under Article 2 of the European Convention on Human Rights will apply (see above).

The situation with regard to protection of property is considered below. For a discussion of trespassory entry of buildings **see para. 1.11.4**.

1.4.8.3 Defence of Property

There is a distinction between the actions that the law will allow in defending yourself or someone else and that which it will allow when defending property. Again it is unclear how far a person may act in defence of his/her own or another's property. For the statutory defences to destroying or damaging another's property in defence of one's own, **see chapter 1.13**. In such situations where the Criminal Damage Act 1971 is involved there are some further considerations arising out of the statutory defence (see *DPP* v *Bayer* [2004] 1 Cr App R 38). Given the general requirements of reasonableness set out above, it would be difficult—though not impossible—to argue that deliberately killing another was a reasonable and necessary response to a threat to one's property alone. However, Article 2(2) of the European Convention on Human Rights does not permit the taking of life in order to protect property.

1.4.9 Police Officers

When using force against others, police officers will be criminally liable for any assaults they commit, in the same way as any other person—and the penalties if found guilty can generally be expected to be more severe. Assaults in such circumstances can be seen by the courts as a breach of public trust and, as such, any harm done is not only done to the victim, but to society's confidence in its public services. This approach can be seen in a case involving assaults by prison officers on a prisoner in their charge (*R* v *Fryer* [2002] 2 Cr App R(S) 122). In *Fryer* the Court of Appeal also took account of the relevant ranks and seniority of the officers when passing sentence.

However, just as the same offences and sentences will apply, similarly, the same general *defences* will potentially be available to the officer. One specific issue that can often arise where force is used by a police officer is the technique employed by the officer in applying force or striking someone. This may consist of a particular technique that the officer has been trained to use—either with some form of weapon such as a baton, or without, such as a hand or knee strike. The issue of whether a particular technique is a 'proper' or 'recognised' one is not the same as the question of the *lawfulness* of any force used on that occasion. Clearly the controlled use of a technique in which an officer has been trained may help a court in determining the issue of the lawfulness or otherwise of the use of force. So too will any training that the officer has (or has not) received in relation to the use of force and personal protection. However, there are times when using an 'authorised technique' will nevertheless be unlawful; conversely there will be circumstances in which the use of an improvised strike or use of an object may be lawful. All will turn on the circumstances of the case.

1.4.10 Infancy

Children under the age of 10 are irrebuttably presumed to be incapable of criminal responsibility (*doli incapax*) by virtue of s. 50 of the Children and Young Persons Act 1933. A similar rebuttable presumption formerly existed for children aged 10, 11, 12 or 13, but this was abolished by virtue of s. 34 of the Crime and Disorder Act 1998.

The current situation is that only children under the age of 10 are specifically exempted from the criminal law on account of their age.

<table>
<tr><td>

1.5

</td><td>

Homicide

</td></tr>
</table>

1.5.1 Introduction

Homicide covers not only the offences of murder and manslaughter, but also other occasions where a person causes, or is involved in, the death of another. The common law which has grown up around the subject of homicide is important, not only because of the gravity of the offences themselves, but also because the cases have defined a number of key issues in criminal law which are applicable to many other offences.

In all cases of homicide the general criminal conduct (*actus reus*) is the same—the killing of another person—but there are often complex arguments over *causation*. For further discussion of both these points, **see chapter 1.2**.

Although offences of homicide are still relatively rare in day-to-day policing, many assaults can turn into homicides simply by the consequent and causally-connected death of the victim. For this reason, it is necessary that police officers have at least a general understanding of the key concepts.

As a result of several high profile cases involving homicide, a number of technical changes have been made to the availability of alternative verdicts by the Domestic Violence, Crime and Victims Act 2004 (see s. 6). These are more matters for the courts and legal representatives than for police officers and investigators.

1.5.2 Murder

OFFENCE: **Murder—*Common Law***
- Life imprisonment (mandatory)

Murder is committed when a person unlawfully kills another human being under the Queen's Peace, with malice aforethought (see *Blackstone's Criminal Practice*, 2008, section B1).

KEYNOTE

A conviction for murder carries a mandatory sentence of life imprisonment (in the case of a defendant who is under 18, 'detention at Her Majesty's pleasure': Powers of Criminal Courts (Sentencing) Act 2000, s. 90).

'Unlawful killing' means actively causing the death of another without justification and includes occasions where someone fails to act after creating a situation of danger (**see chapter 1.2**).

'Another human being' includes a baby who has been born alive and has an existence independent of its mother. If a person injures a baby while it is in its mother's womb and it subsequently dies from those injuries *after being born*, it may be appropriate to bring a charge of murder.

If the defendant intended only to cause serious injury to the mother, that intention cannot support a charge of *murder* in respect of the baby if it goes on to die after being born alive. It may, however, support

---

a charge of *manslaughter*. This departure from the earlier law is clear from the House of Lords' ruling in *Attorney-General's Reference (No. 3 of 1994)* [1998] AC 245, a ruling that overturned the Court of Appeal's previous decision in the same case. The House of Lords ruled that the doctrine of 'transferred malice' (see chapter 1.1) does not fully apply in cases of unborn children (*in utero*). Any liability of the defendant for the subsequent death of a child that he/she injured before it was born alive will depend on the defendant's intentions at the time of causing the injury. Clearly an intention to kill the mother could be sufficient in bringing a charge of murder following the subsequent and connected death of the child.

'Under the Queen's Peace' appears to exclude deaths caused during the legitimate prosecution of warfare (see the War Crimes Act 1991). Under the provisions of the Offences Against the Person Act 1861 any British citizen who commits a murder anywhere in the world may be tried in England or Wales.

It should be noted that the only state of mind or *mens rea* (see chapter 1.1) that will support a charge of attempted murder is an *intention to kill*. Nothing less will suffice.

Where a charge of murder is brought there may be specific restrictions on the applicability of a defence that might otherwise be available. For example, a claim of self-defence based on a mistake arising out of voluntary drunkenness will not be allowed in a prosecution for murder (or manslaughter)—see para. 1.4.3.

1.5.2.1 Malice Aforethought

After the cases of *R* v *Moloney* [1985] AC 905 and *R* v *Hancock* [1986] AC 455, the *mens rea* required for murder is an intention:

- to kill, or
- to cause grievous bodily harm.

Murder is therefore a crime of 'specific intent' (see chapter 1.1).

The term 'malice aforethought' is often associated with some form of premeditation; this is not required.

1.5.2.2 Year and a Day

A rule which no longer applies is the 'year and a day' requirement. Since the Law Reform (Year and a Day Rule) Act 1996 there is no longer a need to show that a victim died within a year and a day of the defendant's actions (s. 1).

If a victim of an alleged murder dies *more than three years after receiving their injury* then the consent of the Attorney-General (or Solicitor-General) is needed before bringing a prosecution (s. 2(2)(b)). That consent is also needed if the defendant has already been convicted of an offence committed under the circumstances connected with the death (s. 2(2)(a)).

1.5.3 Special Defences

As a conviction for murder leaves a judge no discretion in sentencing a defendant, a number of 'special defences' have developed around the offence. These 'defences' are now provided by the Homicide Act 1957 and, rather than securing an acquittal, allow for a conviction of voluntary manslaughter instead of murder. As such these defences fall outside the more common defences that are generally available in respect of criminal offences (as to which, see chapter 1.4).

These 'special defences' are:

- diminished responsibility
- provocation
- suicide pact.

1.5.3.1 Diminished Responsibility

The Homicide Act 1957, s. 2 states:

(1) Where a person kills or is party to the killing of another, he shall not be convicted of murder if he was suffering from such abnormality of mind (whether arising from a condition of arrested or retarded development of mind or any inherent causes or induced by disease or injury) as substantially impaired his mental responsibility for his acts or omissions in doing or being a party to the killing.

(2) On a charge of murder, it shall be for the defence to prove that the person charged is by virtue of this section not liable to be convicted of murder.

(3) A person who but for this section would be liable, whether as principal or as accessory, to be convicted of murder shall be liable instead to be convicted of manslaughter.

(4) The fact that one party to a killing is by virtue of this section not liable to be convicted of murder shall not affect the question whether the killing amounted to murder in the case of any other party to it.

KEYNOTE

'Abnormality of mind' has been held to be 'a state of mind so different from that of ordinary human beings that the reasonable man would term it abornmal' (*R* v *Byrne* [1960] 2 QB 396). This includes the mental inability to exert control over one's behaviour and to form rational judgement.

'Impairment of mental responsibility'—this impairment must be 'substantial'. Whether or not that is the case will be a question of fact for the jury to decide. Minor lapses of lucidity will not be enough. There may be any number of causes of the 'abnormality' of the mind. Examples accepted by the courts to date have included pre-menstrual symptoms (*R* v *Reynolds* [1988] Crim LR 679) and 'battered wives' syndrome' (*R* v *Hobson* [1998] 1 Cr App R 31). A further example arose in the case of *R* v *Dietschmann* [2003] 1 AC 1209 where the House of Lords accepted that a mental abnormality caused by a grief reaction to the recent death of an aunt with whom the defendant had had a physical relationship could suffice. In that case their Lordships went on to hold that there is no requirement to show that the 'abnormality of mind' was the *sole* cause of the defendant's acts in committing the killing.

The burden of proving these features lies with the defence and the standard required is one of a balance of probabilities (see **Evidence and Procedure, chapter 2.7**). While this issue of 'reverse onus of proof' has created some inconsistent decisions across different statutory provisions—and in particular its relationship with the European Convention on Human Rights—in *R* v *Lambert* [2001] 2 WLR 211, the Court of Appeal held that this burden of proof did not breach an individual's right to a presumption of innocence or the right to a fair trial under the Convention.

1.5.3.2 Provocation

The Homicide Act 1957, s. 3 states:

Where on a charge of murder there is evidence on which a jury can find that the person charged was provoked (whether by things done or by things said or by both together) to lose his self-control, the question whether the provocation was enough to make a reasonable man do as he did shall be left to be determined by the jury; and in determining that question the jury shall take into account everything both done and said according to the effect which, in their opinion, it would have on a reasonable man.

KEYNOTE

The question of provocation here is not a general consideration of the ordinary English meaning of the word, but a highly technical pleading that has developed through the common law. The real relevance of this area to police officers will be in the gathering and recording of any evidence that might support or undermine the claim that the defendant was 'provoked'.

The main questions to be considered are:

- Was the defendant actually provoked?
- Might a reasonable person have acted as the defendant did under the same circumstances?

Whether the defendant *was* in fact provoked will be a matter for the jury.

It is clear that words (*DPP* v *Camplin* [1978] AC 705) or even sounds (*R* v *Doughty* [1986] 83 Cr App R 319 (baby crying)) have amounted to 'provocation'. It is also clear that the words or acts need not be directed towards the defendant, nor need they originate from the ultimate victim. Therefore a defendant may be sufficiently provoked by things which X says to Y that he/she kills Z and the 'defence' of provocation could be available. In addition to the 'battered wives' syndrome' mentioned above, where the provocation has been endured by the defendant over a prolonged period (such as the abused wife in *R* v *Ahluwalia* [1992] 4 All ER 889), he/she may be able to show an eventual and sudden lack of self-control brought about by that prolonged behaviour or by a particular event which proved to be 'the last straw' (*R* v *Humphreys* [1995] 4 All ER 1008). If a defendant simply panics or acts out of fear, as opposed to losing control, the defence will not be made out. Unlike the general defence of 'duress' (**see chapter 1.4**), there is no defence of 'provocation by circumstances'; the provocation must come from something done by or to a third person (*R* v *Acott* [1997] 1 WLR 306).

If there is no loss of control by the defendant, then the provocation defence will not be available. See, for example, *R* v *Cocker* [1989] Crim LR 740 where the defendant had endured pleas from his chronically-ill wife to kill her. He had not lost control at the time of the killing—quite the reverse—and the judge had no alternative but to pass a life sentence. Several relatively recent cases (*R* v *James* [2006] EWCA Crim 14 and *Attorney General for Jersey* v *Holley* [2005] UKPC 23) have led the courts to support the approach to the standard of self-control as laid down in the case of *Luc Thiet Thuan* v *The Queen* [1997] AC 131. Here, the defendant's characteristics could affect the gravity of the provocation to be taken into account (a subjective inquiry for the jury) but the standard of self-control to be expected of the particular individual should be the same as the 'reasonable man' (a second and objective inquiry for the jury).

1.5.3.3 Suicide Pact

The Homicide Act 1957, s. 4 states:

(1) It shall be manslaughter, and shall not be murder, for a person acting in pursuance of a suicide pact between him and another to kill the other or be a party to the other being killed by a third person.

KEYNOTE

The *defendant* must show that:

- a suicide pact had been made, and
- he/she had the intention of dying at the time the killing took place.

'Suicide pact' is defined by the Homicide Act 1957, s. 4(3) as:

a common agreement between two or more persons having for its object the death of all of them, whether or not each is to take his own life, but nothing done by a person who enters into a suicide pact shall be treated as done by him in pursuance of the pact unless it is done while he has the settled intention of dying in pursuance of the pact.

(See also para. 1.5.6.2 for the offence of assisting a suicide.)

1.5.4 Manslaughter

Traditionally this subject is divided into two classifications—voluntary and involuntary manslaughter.

The three sets of circumstances where 'special defences' may reduce a murder charge to one of manslaughter make up one type or classification of the offence (so-called *voluntary* manslaughter). They have been covered in **paras 1.5.3.1 to 1.5.3.3 above**. In that sense, voluntary manslaughter is more a finding by a court than an offence with which someone can be charged. The second classification (*involuntary* manslaughter) occurs where the defendant causes the death of another but is not shown to have had the required *mens rea* for murder.

As with murder (**see para. 1.5.2**) a defendant on a charge of manslaughter cannot rely on a mistake induced by their own voluntary intoxication in claiming self defence—*R* v *Hatton* (2006) 1 Cr App R 16 (**see para. 1.4.3**).

OFFENCE: **Manslaughter—*Common Law***
- Triable on indictment • Life imprisonment

KEYNOTE
Manslaughter, like murder is the unlawful killing of another human being. What it does not require is the intention to kill or to cause grievous bodily harm.

The second classification of manslaughter, that is, those cases which do not involve the 'special defences' under the Homicide Act 1957 (**see para. 1.5.3**) can be separated into occasions where a defendant:

- kills another by an *unlawful act* which was *likely to cause bodily harm*, or
- kills another by *gross negligence*.

1.5.4.1 Manslaughter by Unlawful Act

In order to prove manslaughter by an unlawful act (constructive manslaughter), you must prove:

- An unlawful act by the defendant, that is, an act which is *unlawful in itself*, irrespective of the fact that it ultimately results in someone's death. The act must be inherently unlawful. An act that only becomes unlawful by virtue of the way in which it is carried out will not be enough. A good example is 'driving'. Driving is clearly not an inherently unlawful act but becomes so if done inconsiderately on a road or public place (**see Road Policing, chapter 3.2**). Therefore if someone drives inconsiderately and thereby causes the death of another, the act of driving—albeit carried out in a way that attracts criminal liability—is *not* an 'unlawful act' for the purposes of constructive manslaughter (see *Andrews* v *DPP* [1937] AC 576). This is one reason why there are statutory offences addressing most instances of death that are caused by poor standards of driving. The act need not be directed or aimed at anyone and can include acts committed against or towards property (*R* v *Goodfellow* (1986) 83 Cr App R 23).

Generally, if the actions of the victim break the chain of causation between the defendant's unlawful act and the cause of death, the defendant will not be responsible for the death of that victim (**see chapter 1.2**).

This is why drug dealers who supply controlled drugs cannot generally be held liable for the ultimate deaths of their 'victims' (See *R* v *Dalby* [1982] 1 WLR 621 and *R* v *Armstrong* [1989] Crim LR 149). Although the Court of Appeal accepted that, where a person buys a controlled drug from another and immediately injects it, resulting in his/her death, the supplier might attract liability for bringing about the person's death (*R* v *Kennedy* [2005] EWCA Crim 685), by far the greater weight of authorities suggest that the supplier is unlikely to be convicted of manslaughter in such a case unless they have done something more (e.g. helping apply a tourniquet)—see generally *R* v *Dias* [2002] 2 Cr App R 5.

An *omission* to do something will not suffice (**see chapter 1.2**). Any unlawful killing caused by an omission would either come under the circumstances outlined in **chapter 1.2** or under those required to prove gross negligence (**see para. 1.5.4.2**).

- That the act involved a risk of somebody being harmed. That risk will be judged *objectively*, that is; would the risk be apparent to a reasonable and sober person watching the act? (See *R* v *Church* [1966] 1 QB 59.) Such acts might include dropping a paving stone off a bridge into the path of a train (*DPP* v *Newbury* [1977] AC 500), setting fire to your house (*Goodfellow* above) or firing a gun at police officers and then holding someone else in front of you when the officers return fire (*R* v *Pagett* (1983) 76 Cr App R 279). 'Harm' must be physical; the risk of emotional or psychological harm does not appear to be enough (see *R* v *Dawson* (1985) 81 Cr App R 150). In *R* v *C* [2006] EWCA Crim 17 the deceased—aged 15—had been out walking with friends and had met the defendants who had been drinking alcohol all afternoon. The defendants were verbally abusive and threatening to the deceased and her group. One defendant punched one of the deceased's group and another attacked the deceased herself, pulling her hair back and punching her in the face. Two boys intervened and stopped the attack, at which point the deceased ran off but collapsed and died later that night. The medical evidence showed that, unknown to her doctors or her family, the deceased had a severely diseased heart, and that she might not have died had she not been running.

On appeal it was held that the manslaughter charge (of which the first defendant was convicted) should have been withdrawn from the jury. Although the attack was unpleasant and accompanied by bullying, any injuries caused had been slight. None of the defendants had intended to cause really serious harm to any of the victims and they did not intend that the deceased should die. The Court of Appeal reiterated the general principle that a person who inflicts a slight injury that unforeseeably leads to the death of the victim nevertheless commits manslaughter (per *R* v *Church* [1966] 1 QB 59). However, to hold the defendants liable for the deceased's death in the circumstances of this case would have involved an 'unwarranted extension of the law'. The court observed that the law of unlawful act manslaughter required the commission of an unlawful act which was recognised, by a sober and reasonable person, as being dangerous and likely to subject the victim to the risk of some physical harm which in turn caused their death. In the instant case the only act committed against the deceased that was 'dangerous' was the assault and the physical harm resulting from it did not cause her death.

- That the defendant had the required *mens rea* for the relevant 'unlawful act' (e.g. for an assault or criminal damage) which led to the death of a victim. If he/she did not have that *mens rea*, the offence of manslaughter will not be made out. See, for example, *R v Lamb* [1967] 2 QB 981 where the defendant pretended to fire a revolver at his friend. Although the defendant believed that the weapon would not fire, the chamber containing a bullet moved round to the firing pin and the defendant's friend was killed. As Lamb did not have the *mens rea* required for an assault (**see chapter 1.7**) his conviction for manslaughter was quashed.

There is no logical reason why, if a defendant uses a motor vehicle as a means to commit an 'unlawful act' (e.g. an assault) that he/she cannot be charged with manslaughter as long as the 'act' goes beyond poor driving. There are, however, reasons of policy (see *R v Lawrence* [1982] AC 510) why, in all but the most deliberate of cases, the offence under the Road Traffic Act 1988, as amended, should be used (**see Road Policing, chapter 3.2**).

1.5.4.2 Manslaughter by Gross Negligence

Manslaughter is the only criminal offence at common law capable of being committed by negligence. The degree of that negligence has been the source of considerable debate over the years and particular problems have arisen in trying to distinguish the level of negligence required for manslaughter and that required to prove 'recklessness' (as to which, **see chapter 1.1**).

A charge of manslaughter may be brought where a person, by an instance of *gross negligence*, has brought about the death of another. The ingredients of this offence were reviewed and re-stated by the Court of Appeal and essentially consist of death resulting from a negligent breach of a duty of care owed by the defendant to the victim in circumstances so reprehensible as to amount to gross negligence (*R v Misra and Srivastava* [2004] EWCA Crim 2375). The most difficult task in defining the degree of negligence that will qualify as 'gross' falls to the trial judge when he/she addresses the jury. Whether a defendant's conduct will amount to gross negligence is a question of fact for the jury to decide in the light of all the evidence (*R v Bateman* (1925) 19 Cr App R 8).

Although the lack of clarity around this offence has resulted in its being challenged under the European Convention on Human Rights, the Court of Appeal has held that its ingredients are sufficiently certain for those purposes (*R v Misra and Srivastava*). What is clear from the decided cases is that civil liability, although a starting point for establishing the breach of a duty of care, is not enough to amount to 'gross negligence', neither is objective 'recklessness' (**see chapter 1.1**) (*R v Adomako* [1995] 1 AC 171).

The test in *Adomako* as summarised by Lord Mackay seems to provide the leading authority on the area. Lord Mackay put the test for the jury as being:...'whether, having regard to the risk of death involved, the conduct of the defendant was so bad in all the circumstances as to amount in their judgment to a criminal act or omission'.

For the practical difficulties and the inconsistencies in the case law on this area generally, see *Blackstone's Criminal Practice*, 2008, section B1.55.

1.5.4.3 Corporate Manslaughter

The requirement that there be at least some evidence of the state of mind of defendant even in cases involving gross negligence has always presented problems where the defendant is a limited company. As an entirely separate legal 'person', a limited company can clearly be capable of committing criminal offences and it is not unusual for companies to be prosecuted for criminal offences, particularly those involving strict liability (as to which, **see chapter 1.1**). Where the offence in question requires proof of a state of mind by the defendant, however, corporate liability becomes a little more problematic. Companies can still commit such offences, which include manslaughter, a fact made very clear by the prosecution of P&O ferries after the sinking of the *Herald of Free Enterprise* in 1987. However, the problem of identifying a 'directing mind' of an officer of the company has prevented the successful prosecution of corporate liability cases on a number of occasions (including in the P&O case). A case that attracted a great deal of attention in this area followed the Southall rail crash. In *Attorney-General's Reference (No. 2 of 1999)* [2000] 3 WLR 195, the Court of Appeal confirmed that a defendant might be convicted of gross negligence manslaughter without the need to prove his/her particular state of mind at the time provided it is shown:

- that the defendant owed the deceased a duty of care
- that the defendant breached that duty of care, and
- that the breach was so grossly negligent that the defendant could be deemed to have had such a disregard for the life of the deceased as to deserve criminal punishment

(per *R* v *Adomako* [1995] 1 AC 171).

However, the state of mind of the defendant might still be relevant as the jury need to take *all* the circumstances into account when considering the breach of duty of care above. As a result, a 'corporate defendant' could only be convicted of manslaughter by gross negligence through the mind and will of its directors and senior managers.

Where this area is of direct relevance to police officers is in the early investigation of fatal incidents where the appropriate health and safety standards appear to have been breached. While the investigation of such incidents is primarily the responsibility of the Health and Safety Executive, there will be occasions where it is proper for the police to conduct a manslaughter investigation and to treat the scene as a crime scene (see also *R* v *DPP, ex parte Jones (Timothy)* [2000] Crim LR 858).

1.5.5 Causing or Allowing the Death of a Child or Vulnerable Adult

In addition to the categories of manslaughter discussed above, there is a specific offence to cater for circumstances where a relevant person causes or allows the death of a child or vulnerable adult. This offence came about as a result of the practical difficulties that arise where a child or other vulnerable person dies as a result of the unlawful act of one of several people but it cannot be shown which of them actually caused the death or allowed it to occur.

OFFENCE: **Causing or Allowing the Death of a Child or Vulnerable Adult—*Domestic Violence, Crime and Victims Act 2004, s. 5***
- Triable on indictment • 14 years' imprisonment

The Domestic Violence, Crime and Victims Act 2004, s. 5 states:

(1) A person ('D') is guilty of an offence if—
    (a) a child or vulnerable adult ('V') dies as a result of the unlawful act of a person who—
        (i) was a member of the same household as V, and
        (ii) had frequent contact with him,
    (b) D was such a person at the time of that act,

(c) at that time there was a significant risk of serious physical harm being caused to V by the unlawful act of such a person, and

(d) either D was the person whose act caused V's death or—

   (i) D was, or ought to have been, aware of the risk mentioned in paragraph (c),

   (ii) D failed to take such steps as he could reasonably have been expected to take to protect V from the risk, and

   (iii) the act occurred in circumstances of the kind that D foresaw or ought to have foreseen.

KEYNOTE

This offence has a number of key components that must be proved before it is made out.

First you must show that the victim was a child or vulnerable adult. 'Child' means a person under the age of 16 and 'vulnerable adult' means a person aged 16 or over whose ability to protect themselves from violence, abuse or neglect is significantly impaired through physical or mental disability or illness, through old age or otherwise (s. 5(6)).

It will then be necessary to prove that the victim died *as a result of the unlawful act* of a person who fits a number of criteria. For these purposes 'act' includes 'omissions' and an act or omission will generally only be 'unlawful' if it would have amounted to an offence (see s. 5(5) and (6)). The first criterion that must be shown to apply to the defendant is that, *at the time of the act* they were a member of the same household as the victim *and* had frequent contact with him or her. For these purposes a person will be a member of a particular household if they visit it so often and for such periods of time that it is reasonable to regard them as a member of it—even if they do not actually live there (s. 5(4)(a)). Where, as often happens, the victim lived in different households at different times, the 'same household' criterion will mean the household in which the victim was living at the time of the act that caused their death (s. 5(4)(b)).

Finally it must be shown that, at the time, there was a significant risk of serious physical harm being caused to the victim by the unlawful act of a person meeting these criteria. 'Serious harm' means grievous bodily harm for the purposes of the Offences against the Person Act 1861 (**see para. 1.7.6.2**).

Once these elements have been established, the offence is completed in one of two ways: directly (i.e. by the defendant's act causing the victim's death) or indirectly and the prosecution does not have to prove which alternative applies (see s. 5(2)). However, in cases where indirect causation is suspected, three further things must be shown, namely that:

(1) the defendant was (or ought to have been) aware of the risk of grievous bodily harm;

(2) the defendant failed to take such steps as he or she could reasonably have been expected to take to protect the victim from the risk; *and*

(3) the act occurred in the kind of circumstances that the defendant foresaw (or ought to have foreseen).

Unless the defendant is the mother or father of the victim (a) they cannot be charged with an offence under this section if they were under 16 at the time of the act and (b) restrictions will be made on what steps would have been reasonable for a defendant to have taken while under that age (see s. 5(3)).

1.5.6 Aiding Suicide and Assisted Dying

Although suicide involves taking your own life, there are two particular areas that are relevant to policing. These are considered below.

1.5.6.1 Assisted Dying

The laws relating to homicide set out in previous paragraphs have meant that the deliberate taking of another's life will, without a specific recognised defence, be a criminal offence.

Although there are several generic defences (**see chapter 1.4**) as well as the specific defences to murder (**see para. 1.5.3**), there is no defence of 'mercy killing' or formal recognition of euthanasia under our current legal system. In addition, there is a specific offence of helping another to take their own life (**see para. 1.5.6.2**).

1.5.6.2 Aiding Suicide

OFFENCE: **Aiding Another to Commit Suicide—*Suicide Act 1961, s. 2***

- Triable on indictment • Fourteen years' imprisonment

The Suicide Act 1961, s. 2 states:

> (1) A person who aids, abets, counsels or procures the suicide of another, or an attempt by another to commit suicide, shall be liable...

KEYNOTE

This offence is an alternative verdict on a charge of murder/manslaughter (Suicide Act 1961, s. 2(2)). The House of Lords has held that the Suicide Act 1961 is not incompatible with the European Convention on Human Rights; at the same time, it upheld a decision of the Director of Public Prosecutions refusing to undertake not to prosecute in a case where a sufferer of motor neurone disease wanted her husband to help her die. In the case, which attracted a huge amount of publicity, their Lordships held that the DPP had no power to give an undertaking not to prosecute in advance of an offence actually being committed and that, even if he/she *did* have that power, using it in such a way would be an abuse of process because the circumstances of the offence could not possibly be known in advance (*R (On the Application of Pretty)* v *DPP* [2002] 1 AC 800). The late Mrs Pretty also failed in her attempt to have the ruling overturned at the European Court of Human Rights. Although the news media insisted on referring to these trials as 'right to die' hearings it is important to distinguish issues concerning the 'right' of an individual to die under certain circumstances (**see General Police Duties, chapter 4.3**) and the issues arising out of 'assisted suicide' which were decided in Mrs Pretty's case. s. 1 of the 1961 Act. For guidance on the scope of aiding, abetting, counselling and procuring, **see chapter 1.2**. This offence has the unusual feature of creating criminal liability for aiding and abetting *an attempt*. In addition, while it is impossible to aid and abet suicide where the other person in fact had no intention of committing suicide, the *possibility* of their suicide will be enough to support the above offence (see *R* v *S* (2005) unreported).

1.5.7 Solicitation of Murder

OFFENCE: **Encouraging Another to Murder—*Offences Against the Person Act 1861, s. 4***

- Triable on indictment • Life imprisonment

The Offences Against the Person Act 1861, s. 4 states:

> Whosoever shall solicit, encourage, persuade or endeavour to persuade, or shall propose to any person, to murder any other person, whether he be a subject of Her Majesty or not...shall be guilty of a misdemeanour...

KEYNOTE

This relatively rare offence has received greater attention lately as in the contexts of contract killings and terrorism. An example of the latter can be seen in the case of *R* v *El-Faisal* [2004] EWCA Crim 343 where

---

the defendant, a minister of Islam, was convicted of this offence after creating audio tapes containing public speeches given by him encouraging the killing of non-believers.

The proposed victim may be outside the United Kingdom.

It does not matter whether or not the person is in fact encouraged to commit murder. This offence may be appropriate in cases where a person is trying to arrange a 'contract killing' (see *R* v *Adamthwaite* (1994) 15 Cr App R (S) 241 where the person 'encouraged' was an undercover police officer). For this reason this offence may be preferred in cases where the defendant has 'conspired' with *one* other person and that person is an undercover police officer (see chapter 1.3).

For the offence of making threats to kill, see para. 1.7.5.

1.5.8 Domestic Homicide Reviews

In addition to the individual concerns arising in any homicide, there can be wider policing concerns where the death occurred in particular circumstances. One such area is that of domestic homicides. As a result there are further legal powers and procedures available in such circumstances. In summary, the Secretary of State may direct that a domestic homicide review be held:

- where the death of a person aged 16 or over has, or appears to have, resulted from violence, abuse or neglect by:
  — a person to whom they were related or with whom they were (or had been) in an intimate personal relationship; or
  — a member of the same household;
- with a view to identifying the lessons to be learnt from the death (see the Domestic Violence, Crime and Victims Act 2004, s. 9).

Among the bodies and organisations that can be directed to take part in such a review are chief officers of police for police areas in England and Wales and local authorities.

1.6 | Misuse of Drugs

1.6.1   Introduction

The misuse of controlled drugs has become such a pervasive feature of Western society that it now affects almost every aspect of community life. As such, this subject is one of the most written about, argued about and legislated about in our criminal law. The impact of the misuse of drugs on crime and community safety has become so significant that it is also one of the most frequently encountered areas of criminal law for police officers.

The majority of the law in this area is statutory and is supported by a considerable body of case law.

1.6.2   Classification

Drugs which are subject to the provisions of the Misuse of Drugs Act 1971 are listed in Parts I to II to Schedule 2 of the Act.

The divisions are made largely on the basis of each substance's potential effects on both the person taking it and society in general.

Classification is important in determining the sentencing powers of the courts.

- **Class A**—This class includes the most notorious and dangerous drugs such as heroin and morphine, opiates, cocaine, some amphetamines and LSD; it also includes fungus (of any kind) which contains psilocin ('magic mushrooms'). It also includes the drug 'crystal meth' (methylamphetamine).
- **Class B**—This class includes codeine and some amphetamines.
- **Class C**—This class includes some commonly-abused prescription drugs. It includes cannabis resin and ketamine.

There has been much publicity and attention devoted the reclassification of cannabis (which took place in 2004) from a Class B drug to a Class C drug. The fact remains that cannabis is still illegal and possession, production and supply of the drug remain offences; only the penalty for such offences has changed.

If the charge alleges possession of one particular drug then that drug must be identified.

While crystal meth is a Class A drug, the leaves produced by the khat plant (sometimes chewed for a mild stimulant effect) are not controlled drugs for the purposes of the 1971 Act even though the substance produced is banned in some other jurisdictions in Europe and the United States of America.

Note that, although a substance may appear in sch. 2 to the Act, there may be restrictions on the occasions where possession is treated as an offence (**see para. 1.6.5.5**).

The main practical effect of the classification of controlled drugs is the mode of trial which may affect the available powers and sentence. Difficulties in identifying a plant, pill or powder precisely mean that officers will frequently have to rely on criminal intelligence and/or their 'reasonable suspicions' when dealing with suspected drugs offences.

It is not necessary, when prosecuting an offence, to distinguish between the various chemical forms in which a drug exists (i.e. as a salt, ester or other form) (*R* v *Greensmith* [1983] 1 WLR 1124).

A defendant's admission may, in some cases, be relied upon to prove his/her knowledge as to what a particular substance is (see *R* v *Chatwood* [1980] 1 WLR 874).

1.6.2.1 Cannabis

The Misuse of Drugs Act 1971, s. 37 states:

> 'cannabis' (except in the expression 'cannabis resin') means any plant of the genus *Cannabis* or any part of any such plant (by whatever name designated) except that it does not include cannabis resin or any of the following products after separation from the rest of the plant, namely—
> (a) mature stalk of any such plant,
> (b) fibre produced from mature stalk of any such plant, and
> (c) seed of any such plant,
>
> 'cannabis resin' means the separated resin, whether crude or purified, obtained from any plant of the genus *Cannabis*;

KEYNOTE

There can scarcely have been anyone in England and Wales who failed to notice all the media coverage over the change of class for cannabis from B to C. At the time of writing there is now a debate as to whether the drug should be reclassified as class B once again. Whatever its classification, as cannabis and cannabis resin are both in the same class for the purposes of the 1971 Act there would be no duplicity if a person is charged with possessing either one or the other in the same charge (*R* v *Best* [1980] 70 Cr App R 21).

1.6.2.2 Drug Testing

Section 63B of the Police and Criminal Evidence Act 1984 enables the police to require urine or non-intimate samples to be taken from adults in police detention under certain circumstances. The purpose of such tests is to ascertain whether the person has any specified Class A drug in their body. The power to require such a sample can be activated in a number of ways (**see Evidence and Procedure, chapter 2.11**).

The Powers of Criminal Courts (Sentencing) Act 2000 makes further provision for the courts to impose drug treatment and testing orders. For a full discussion of these powers, **see Evidence and Procedure, chapter 2.11**.

1.6.3 Possession

Possession appears to be a straightforward concept. However, as with many other such 'straightforward' concepts, the courts have wrangled over its meaning for so long that it is not so straightforward after all.

1.6.3.1 Physical Control

A good starting point in understanding 'possession' is to realise that it is a neutral concept, not implying any kind of blame or fault. This is the key feature to understand first before going on to consider specific offences under *any* legislation. In order to be in possession of *anything*, the common law requires physical control of the object plus knowledge of its presence. This requirement is particularly problematic where containers of some sort (whether they be boxes, handbags, cigarette packets or whatever) are involved or where the person claims not to have realised what it was that he/she 'possessed'. In such cases, the common law makes the same requirements; you need to show that the person had physical control of the container together with a knowledge that it contained *something*. Once you have established possession, you then need to show that the substance/object/material possessed was in fact proscribed by the relevant statute.

In *R v Forsyth* [2001] EWCA Crim 2926, the defendant argued that there was a distinction between a person carrying something *in* a container and a person carrying *something inside something else* in a container! In that particular case, the defendant was found in possession of a box which contained a safe; inside the safe was a significant quantity of a controlled drug. The defendant argued that this type of possession should be differentiated from the situation where someone simply had possession of a box with drugs in it. The Court of Appeal ruled that there was no difference and the issues of proof were the same.

1.6.3.2 Knowledge of Possession

In relation to controlled drugs, the issue becomes complicated further by the specific defences provided by the 1971 Act. The very reason those defences (**see para. 1.6.5**) have been drafted in this way is to reflect the common law concept of possession and to provide some protection from its effects where drugs are concerned (see *R v Bett* [1999] 1 WLR 2109).

So, if a person has a container with him/her and that container is found to have controlled drugs in it, he/she is in possession of those drugs *provided he/she knew that there was something in the container*. That does not mean that, at this point, the person necessarily commits an offence (and he/she may still have a statutory defence); it means that he/she was in 'possession' of the drugs. This merely satisfies one element of a number of possible offences; just as if you were trying to prove that a person was 'driving' a vehicle. (Driving is also a neutral concept and only satisfies one element within a number of possible offences.)

The Misuse of Drugs Act 1971 creates offences under certain circumstances where a person has been shown to have been in 'possession' of a controlled drug. However, the Act also provides a defence which unfortunately includes a mental element on the part of the defendant. It is true that this situation in relation to possession is impracticable—like many others in our system—and it is not even consistently applied (e.g. in cases of strict liability such as some firearms offences involving 'possession' (see *R v Bradish* [1990] 1 QB 981 and **General Police Duties, chapter 4.7**)). Nevertheless, until the concept of 'possession' at common law is changed to include an element of blame or fault, these rules will continue to apply and presumably statutes will continue to contain defences which, like s. 28 of the 1971 Act, are aimed at correcting any unjust results.

Nevertheless it is clear from the House of Lords' decisions in *Warner v Metropolitan Police Commissioner* [1969] 2 AC 256 and *R v Boyesen* [1982] AC 768, and also the Court of Appeal judgment in *R v McNamara* (1988) 87 Cr App R 246 that the basic elements required are that a person 'knows' that he/she is in possession of something which is, in fact, a prohibited or controlled object or substance.

Some of the further practical difficulties that can arise from this view of 'possession' were highlighted in *Adams* v *DPP* [2002] EWHC 438 (Admin). In that case a small quantity of controlled drugs was found in the defendant's home during the execution of a search warrant. There was no proof that the drugs were owned by the defendant, nor that she was specifically aware of their presence but the defendant *did* know that her home was used by various people who were highly likely to bring controlled drugs into it. She was convicted of possession. In hearing her appeal against conviction by way of case stated, the Administrative Court held that, where knowledge of possession of drugs was limited to the fact that a visitor had brought drugs into the defendant's home intending to take them, that was not sufficient evidence from which it was appropriate to infer that she had control over the drugs.

The Court also held that giving consent (explicitly or impliedly) for the use of a controlled drug did not of itself constitute possession. Similarly, an inference that the defendant knew whose drugs had been found in her home did not amount to evidence of control over the drug itself—even though she may well have been able to exercise control over what actually took place in her home.

The Court went on to point out that the social concern arising from people permitting the use of drugs on their premises would be addressed by the amended offence under s. 8 of the Misuse of Drugs Act 1971 (**see para. 1.6.5.9**).

1.6.3.3 Points to Prove

To prove possession of a controlled drug then, you must show that a defendant both:

- *had* a controlled drug in his/her possession; and
- *knew* that he/she had something in his/her possession which was in fact a controlled drug.

....

EXAMPLE

Consider the following circumstances: After a stop and search, a defendant is found with a knife in his pocket. The knife has traces of brown powder on the blade. Later examination shows the powder to be heroin.

In order to prove 'possession' of the heroin you must show:

- that the defendant actually had the knife
- that the knife had a substance which was a controlled drug on it and that
- the defendant knew *of the existence of the substance* (i.e. the powder).

....

1.6.3.4 Quality

You would not have to show that he/she knew what the powder was. That is, you do not need to show that the defendant knew the *quality* of what he/she possessed.

If the defendant admits to knowing that the powder was there but thought it was sand, he/she is in possession of it (see *R* v *Marriott* [1971] 1 WLR 187).

Therefore if a defendant had a packet of cigarettes with him/her and admitted to knowing that he/she had them, he/she would be in possession of a controlled drug if one cigarette was shown to have contained cannabis. The fact that the defendant thought they contained tobacco would be irrelevant (*Searle* v *Randolph* [1972] Crim LR 779) (although clearly they may be able to raise the defence under s. 28: see below).

1.6.3.5 Quantity

The *quantity* of a controlled drug, however, may be so small that the defendant could not possibly have known about it; therefore it could not be 'possessed'.

Each case will have to be decided on its merits but the House of Lords have suggested that if something is 'visible, tangible and measurable', that may be sufficient (*Boyesen*). If the amount recovered is too small to support a charge of possession, it might be used to prove earlier possession of the drug (see *R* v *Graham* [1970] 1 WLR 113n and *Hambleton* v *Callinan* [1968] 2 QB 427 (traces of a controlled drug in a urine sample held to be possible evidence of earlier possession of that drug)).

Quantity is not only relevant to the fact of possession; it is also relevant to the intention of the person in whose possession the drug is found. Larger quantities (particularly if they are also divided into smaller amounts) may be indicative of an intention to supply and may be assumed to be proof of that intention in some circumstances (**see para. 1.6.5.6**).

1.6.3.6 Regulated Possession and Supply of Controlled Drugs

The statutory framework governing controlled drugs does not simply ban substances and their possession outright. People working at various levels within the system need to be able to access, analyse and prescribe substances that are controlled by the 1971 Act. To that end, the framework takes account of the differing legitimate activities that may be relevant to individual people or particular circumstances. The majority of the exceptions and conditions imposed on this lawful possession and use can be found in the Misuse of Drugs Regulations 2001 (SI 2001/3998) as amended.

The importance of the 2001 Regulations lies in the fact that they exempt certain drugs and certain people (pharmacists, medical staff and laboratory workers etc)—including police officers—from the main offences of possession, supply and importation.

Among the key regulations are:

- Regulation 4—which sets out those controlled drugs which will be exempted from the main offences of importation/exportation when they are contained in medicinal products.
- Regulation 5—allowing people holding a licence issued by the Secretary of State to produce, supply, offer to supply or have in their possession a controlled drug—*provided* that their activities (e.g. of supplying etc.) are carried out in accordance with their licence and any conditions attached to it. If the licence holder goes outside the terms of his/her licence (say by offering to supply a drug that is not covered by it) or fails to comply with any conditions attached to the licence (e.g. by keeping the drugs in a different place from that specified), he/she commits the relevant offence(s) in the ordinary way.
- Regulation 6—this allows anyone who is *lawfully* in possession of a controlled drug to give the drug back to the person from whom he/she obtained it and would cover registered heroin addicts properly returning methadone to a chemist. Regulation 6 also allows others to possess and supply certain controlled drugs under strict conditions.

Regulation 6 allows police constables to have any controlled drug in their possession, or to supply such a drug to anyone who is lawfully allowed to have it (reg. 6(5)–(7)). These exemptions only apply where the constable is *acting in the course of his/her duty as such*.

Other people who are given the same protection are HM Customs & Excise officers, postal workers and people engaged in conveying the drug to someone who may lawfully possess it. This last category would include civilian support staff, exhibits officers and others who, although not police constables, are nevertheless properly engaged in conveying controlled drugs to others.

The remainder of the regulations are generally concerned with exemptions for doctors, dentists, vets and others who may need to store or supply controlled drugs; the 2001 Regulations also impose requirements on some such people in relation to record keeping and the provision of information when requested.

The Regulations make provision for medical practitioners and some nurses (extended formulary nurse prescribers) to prescribe controlled drugs under certain circumstances. Where controlled drugs are supplied lawfully by healthcare providers, other regulations (e.g. the Misuse of Drugs (Supply to Addicts) Regulations 1997 (SI 1997/1001)) may also be relevant and should be consulted.

The 2001 Regulations provide that records of activity, authority and prescription may be preserved in computerised form in accordance with specified best practice guidance. The Secretary of State or an authorised person can request that a computerised register form be produced by sending a copy of it to the appropriate person.

1.6.4 Defences

In addition to the generic defences available in criminal law (as to which **see chapter 1.4**), offences under the Misuse of Drugs Act 1971 may attract specific defences set out in the legislation. So far as the generic defences are concerned, there have been several (unsuccessful) attempts to claim defences such as 'medical necessity' in respect of possession, supply and production of controlled drugs (**see para. 1.4.6**). In addition, the Court of Appeal would not allow a defendant to rely on effectively the same defence by presenting it as a human rights issue (*R v Altham* [2006] EWCA Crim 7). In that case the defendant argued that, criminalising his use of cannabis to treat his severe medical symptoms was subjecting him to inhuman or degrading treatment, in contravention of Article 3 of the European Convention on Human Rights. The court held that the prohibition in Article 3 was against subjection to torture or to inhuman or degrading treatment or punishment. The state had not done anything to the defendant to exacerbate his condition or to cause him inhuman or degrading treatment, and its obligation under Article 3 did not extend to permitting him (even though he suffered from chronic pain) to smoke cannabis as a form of pain relief.

Before considering the various offences under the Misuse of Drugs Act 1971 it is useful to address the specific statutory defences provided by ss. 5 and 28 of the Act.

1.6.4.1 Section 5 Defence to Unlawful Possession

Section 5 provides a defence to an offence of unlawful *possession*:

(4) In any proceedings for an offence under subsection (2) above in which it is proved that the accused had a controlled drug in his possession, it shall be a defence for him to prove—
(a) that, knowing or suspecting it to be a controlled drug, he took possession of it for the purpose of preventing another from committing or continuing to commit an offence in connection with that drug and that as soon as possible after taking possession of it he took all such steps as were reasonably open to him to destroy the drug or to deliver it into the custody of a person lawfully entitled to take custody of it; or

(b) that, knowing or suspecting it to be a controlled drug, he took possession of it for the purpose of delivering it into the custody of a person lawfully entitled to take custody of it and that as soon as possible after taking possession of it he took all such steps as were reasonably open to him to deliver it into the custody of such a person.

KEYNOTE

This defence envisages two distinct situations. The purpose in taking possession of the controlled drug under s. 5(4)(a) must be to:

- prevent *another*
- from committing (in the future) or
- continuing to commit

an offence in connection with *that* drug.

The first situation might arise where a parent, guardian or carer finds a child in possession of something which appears to be a controlled drug. Provided that that person takes all reasonable steps to destroy the drug or to take it to someone lawfully entitled to possess it (like a general practitioner or police officer), *as soon as possible after taking possession of it,* he/she commits no offence *of unlawful possession.*

The finer technical issues of this defence were examined in *R v Murphy* [2003] 1 WLR 422. In that case the defendant found some cannabis in his father's car which was outside a prison at the time. The defendant took the drug and buried it in the hope that it would be destroyed by the forces of nature over time. The Administrative Court held that the trial judge had been right not to leave the s. 5(4)(a) defence to the jury. The defendant had to show that he had taken all steps that were reasonably open to him to destroy the drug directly and relying on the forces of nature did not provide this defence on that occasion.

The second situation (under s. 5(4)(b)) may arise where a person finds what he/she believes to be a controlled drug and he/she takes possession of it *solely for the purpose of delivering it to a person lawfully entitled to take custody of it.* The defendant must prove that this was his/her intention at the time of taking possession (*R v Dempsey and Dempsey* [1986] 82 Cr App R 291).

In either case above, s. 5(4) will not provide a defence to any other offence connected with the controlled drug (e.g. supplying or offering to supply).

1.6.4.2 General Defence under Section 28

However, there is a more general defence provided by s. 28 of the Act. Section 28 applies to offences of:

- unlawful production (s. 4(2))
- unlawful supply (s. 4(3))
- unlawful possession (s. 5(2))
- possession with intent to supply (s. 5(3))
- unlawful cultivation of cannabis (s. 6(2))
- offences connected with opium (s. 9).

The defences under s. 28 are *not* available in cases of conspiracy as they are not offences under the 1971 Act (*R v McGowan* [1990] Crim LR 399). In *R v Lambert* [2001] 3 WLR 206 the House of Lords considered the requirements of the defences under ss. 5(4) and 28 in relation to their effect on the presumption of innocence (imposed at both common law and under Article 6). It was argued that the statutory defence shifted the legal burden of proof from the prosecution onto the defendant and, therefore, was incompatible with the Convention. Their Lordships held that the defences could legitimately be read by the courts in a way that moved the *evidential* burden only onto the defendant. Such an approach, they held, was compatible with the Convention and the Human Rights Act 1998.

Section 28 states:

(2) Subject to subsection (3) below, in any proceedings for an offence to which this section applies it shall be a defence for the accused to prove that he neither knew of nor suspected nor had reason to suspect the existence of some fact alleged by the prosecution which it is necessary for the prosecution to prove if he is to be convicted of the offence charged.

(3) Where in any proceedings for an offence to which this section applies it is necessary, if the accused is to be convicted of the offence charged, for the prosecution to prove that some substance or product involved in the alleged offence was the controlled drug which the prosecution alleges it to have been, and it is proved that the substance or product in question was that controlled drug, the accused—

(a) shall not be acquitted of the offence charged by reason only of proving that he neither knew nor suspected nor had reason to suspect that the substance or product in question was the particular controlled drug alleged; but

(b) shall be acquitted thereof—

(i) if he proves that he neither believed nor suspected nor had reason to suspect that the substance or product in question was a controlled drug; or

(ii) if he proves that he believed the substance or product in question to be a controlled drug, or a controlled drug of a description, such that, if it had in fact been that controlled drug, or a controlled drug of that description, he would not at the material time have been committing any offence to which this section applies.

KEYNOTE

This defence envisages three distinct situations:

- a lack of knowledge by the defendant of some fact which is alleged by the prosecution;
- a general lack of knowledge by the defendant about the drug in question;
- a conditional belief held by the defendant about the drug in question.

These situations are discussed below.

1.6.4.3 Lack of Knowledge of Some Alleged Fact

Section 28(2) allows a defence where the defendant did not *know, suspect* or *have reason to suspect* the existence of some fact which is essential to proving the case.

....

EXAMPLE

Consider the following example. A youth is stopped in the street by a stranger who asks him to drop off an envelope at a nearby address in exchange for £1. As the youth approaches the address he is arrested for possessing a controlled drug (which had been inside the envelope), with intent to supply.

Section 28(2) would allow the youth to discharge the evidential burden by showing that he neither knew, nor suspected that the envelope contained a controlled drug, and that he neither knew nor suspected that he was supplying it to another. Both of these elements would be facts which the prosecution would have to allege in order to prove the offence.

If the youth knew the person to be a local drug dealer, or the reward for his errand was disproportionately large—say £100—then he may not be able to discharge this, albeit evidential, burden.

It has been held that the test for 'reason to suspect' is an *objective* one (*R* v *Young* [1984] 1 WLR 654). Consequently, where a 'reason to suspect' was not apparent to a defendant because he/she was too intoxicated to see it, the defence will not apply.

1.6.4.4 General Lack of Knowledge about Drug in Question

The wording of s. 28(3)(a) prevents defendants from claiming a 'defence' when what they thought was one type of controlled drug was in fact another, different controlled drug.

Section 28(3)(b) however, has two strands, one concerned with the defendant's general lack of knowledge about the drug in question and the other (see below) concerning the defendant's conditional belief.

Section 28(3)(b)(i) will allow a defendant to prove that he/she did not believe or suspect the substance in question to be a controlled drug and that he/she had no reason so to suspect.

This clearly overlaps with s. 28(2) and the youth in the above example would also be able to claim this lack of knowledge. If he believed the envelope to contain amphetamine when it turned out to contain heroin, however, this lack of knowledge would not be permitted as a defence under s. 28(3).

1.6.4.5 Conditional Belief about Drug in Question

In contrast to s. 28(3)(a), the second strand of s. 28(3)(b)(ii) allows a defendant to discharge the evidential burden by showing that he/she *did* believe the drug in question to be a particular controlled drug. It is then open to them to claim that, had the drug in question actually been the drug which he/she believed it to be, then he/she would not have committed any of the offences in **para. 1.6.4** above.

EXAMPLE

A registered heroin addict may have been prescribed methadone. If she collects her prescription from a chemist but is mistakenly given pethidine instead, she may be able to discharge the evidential burden by showing that she *believed* the drug in question to be methadone *and* that, if it had been, she would not have committed an offence by possessing it.

1.6.5 Offences Involving the Misuse of Controlled Drugs

Clearly there are occasions when the production, supply and possession of controlled drugs will be lawful and most of these occasions are addressed in either the Misuse of Drugs Regulations 2001 (SI 2001/3998) or in s. 28 of the Misuse of Drugs Act 1971 (**see para. 1.6.4**).

In the offences which follow, the aspects which generally make the behaviour 'unlawful' are either the lack of authority under the relevant regulations, or the absence of the circumstances outlined in the defences under s. 28.

1.6.5.1 Production

OFFENCE: **Producing Controlled Drug—*Misuse of Drugs Act 1971, s. 4(2)***

      • Triable either way • Class A (life imprisonment and/or fine on indictment; six months' imprisonment and/or prescribed sum summarily) • Class B (14 years' imprisonment and/or fine on indictment; six months' imprisonment and/or prescribed sum summarily) • Class C (five years' imprisonment and/or fine on indictment; three months' imprisonment and/or fine summarily)

The Misuse of Drugs Act 1971, s. 4 states:

(2) Subject to section 28 of this Act, it is an offence for a person—
    (a) to produce a controlled drug in contravention of subsection (1) [of section 4]...; or
    (b) to be concerned in the production of such a drug in contravention of that subsection by another.

KEYNOTE

'Produce' means producing by manufacture, cultivation or any other method and 'production' has a corresponding meaning (Misuse of Drugs Act 1971, s. 37).

    Converting one form of a Class A drug into another has been held to be 'producing' (*R* v *Russell* (1992) 94 Cr App R 351) as has harvesting, cutting and stripping a cannabis plant (*R* v *Harris* [1996] 1 Cr App R 369).

1.6.5.2 Supply

OFFENCE: **Supplying Controlled Drug—*Misuse of Drugs Act 1971, s. 4(3)***

      • Triable either way • Class A (life imprisonment and/or fine on indictment; six months' imprisonment and/or prescribed sum summarily) • Class B (14 years' imprisonment and/or fine on indictment; six months' imprisonment and/or prescribed sum summarily) • Class C (five years' imprisonment and/or fine on indictment; three months' imprisonment and/or fine summarily)

The Misuse of Drugs Act 1971, s. 4 states:

(2) Subject to section 28 of this Act, it is an offence for a person—
    (a) to supply or offer to supply a controlled drug to another in contravention of subsection (1) above; or
    (b) to be concerned in the supplying of such a drug to another in contravention of that subsection; or
    (c) to be concerned in the making to another in contravention of that subsection of an offer to supply such a drug.

KEYNOTE

The word supply 'connotes more than the mere transfer of physical control of [something] from one person to another' (per Lord Keith in *Holmes* v *Chief Constable of Merseyside Police* [1976] Crim LR 125). The offence of supplying requires a further element, namely that the person receiving the item (the controlled drug) is thereby enabled to apply it to his/her own purposes. Whether or not a person has 'supplied' a controlled drug to another is a question of fact.

'Supplying' includes distributing (s. 37(1)).

    This offence most frequently occurs where one person hands over a controlled drug to another, in which case there is little argument about the meaning of supply.

1.6.5.3 Specific Situations

There is a whole spectrum along which the supply of controlled drugs can take place. Ranging from handing someone their own cannabis after holding it for a while to taking orders for class A drugs from school children, the different prevailing circumstances of the 'supply' must be taken into account. Section 4A of the Misuse of Drugs Act 1971 recognises this and requires courts to treat certain conditions as 'aggravating' factors when considering the seriousness of the offence under s. 4(3) if committed by a person aged 18 or over.

The conditions are either:

1. that the offence was committed on or in the vicinity of school premises at a relevant time. 'Vicinity' is not defined and will be left to each court relying on its local knowledge. Other buildings and premises (e.g. cafes and shopping centres) can fall within this description and courts may decide that a route used to get to or from a school or a place where school children gather (even if trespassing) may be in the 'vicinity'. School premises are land used for the purposes of a school but *excluding* any land occupied solely as a dwelling *by a person employed at the school* (s. 4A(8)). A 'relevant time' is any time when the school premises are in use by people under the age of 18 (and one hour before the start/after the end of any such time) (s. 4A(5)); or
2. that in connection with the commission of the offence the offender used a 'courier' who, at the time the offence was committed, was under the age of 18. A person uses a courier if he/she causes or permits another person (the courier):
   (a) to deliver a controlled drug to a third person, or
   (b) to deliver a 'drug related consideration' (basically any money, goods etc. obtained or intended to be used in connection with the supply of a controlled drug) to him/herself or a third person. (s. 4A(6) and (7)).

Other specific situations involving the supply of controlled drugs (which may or may not also be accompanied by the aggravating factors of s. 4A) are considered below.

The concept of supplying another with a drug generally conjures up something along the lines of a straightforward sale or exchange. It has been held that, where a person holds on to a controlled drug belonging to another for a short while and then hands it back, there is no 'supply' (although there may be unlawful possession) (*R v Dempsey and Dempsey* (1986) 82 Cr App R 291, see below). If the person looking after the drugs for another is in some way benefiting from that activity, then the return of those drugs to the depositor *will* amount to 'supplying', and the offences of supplying or possession with intent to supply will be applicable (*R v Maginnis* [1987] AC 303, see below). *Dempsey* involved a registered drug addict who was in lawful possession of a controlled drug and who asked his partner to hold on to some of that drug while he went to administer the remainder of it to himself in a gents' toilet. Both the addict and his partner were arrested, the addict being subsequently charged with 'supplying' his partner with the drug. The Court of Appeal held that, if the partner had simply been given the drug for safekeeping until the addict's return, there would be no 'supplying'. If however, she had been given the drug for her own use, then there clearly *would* be a 'supplying' of that drug and the offence under s. 4(3)(a) would be complete.

Leaving Drugs with Another

Other situations where the *initial* possession of the controlled drug is itself unlawful have also raised difficult questions. If a drug trafficker leaves drugs with a third person temporarily, what criminal liability is incurred by the third person when he/she returns the drugs to the trafficker? Will returning the drug to its owner under these circumstances, which are different from those in *Dempsey* (above) amount to 'supplying'? This situation was faced by the House of Lords in *R v Maginnis* [1987] AC 303. In that case their Lordships decided that Maginnis would have been 'supplying' the controlled drug had he returned it to the drug trafficker who had left a package of cannabis resin in Maginnis' car. Therefore he was in possession with intent to supply and so committed an offence under s. 5(3) (**see para. 1.6.5.6**). Once again however, the court expressed the view that if the person left with temporary possession of the controlled drug was not benefiting from so possessing it, there would be no 'supplying'. That being the case, it is at least arguable that the third person is *aiding and abetting* the trafficker to possess with intent to supply (as to which, **see chapter 1.2**).

This issue has been further complicated by a decision involving a person who claimed that he had been coerced into holding controlled drugs for unnamed dealers. When found in possession of the drugs, the defendant claimed the defence of duress (as to which, **see chapter 1.4**) and said that he had only been an 'involuntary custodian' of them, intending to return them at a later date. The Court of Appeal decided that it was irrelevant whether a person was a voluntary or involuntary custodian of the drugs and that an intention to return them to their depositor amounted to an 'intention to supply' (*R v Panton* (2001) *The Times*, 27 March).

If a police informer provides a controlled drug to another in order that the other be arrested, there will still be a 'supplying' of the drug (*R v X* [1994] Crim LR 827).

Injecting Others

Injecting another with his/her own controlled drug has been held not to amount to 'supplying' in a case where the defendant assisted pushing down the plunger of a syringe that the other person was already using. Parker CJ's comments in that case suggest that simply injecting another person with their own drug would not amount to 'supplying' (*R v Harris* [1968] 1 WLR 769). It may, however, amount to an offence of 'poisoning' under s. 23 of the Offences Against the Person Act 1861 (**see chapter 1.8**). The key problem with charging the supplier of drugs for self-injection by someone who then dies as a result lies in the issues of causation. While there are some authorities that say a supplier of a drug for self-injection which leads to the death of the recipient *can potentially* amount to unlawful act manslaughter (**see chapter 1.5**) great difficulties have arisen and the general view is that the supplier is unlikely to be held liable for *causing* death in such a case (see *R v Dias* [2002] 2 Cr App R 5). Where the defendant carries out the injection as opposed to merely the supply of the drug, liability for causing the death of another in this way can be made out however—even if the drug injected is not a controlled drug (see *R v Andrews* [2003] Crim LR 477—injection of insulin with consent; see also *R v Rogers* [2003] 1 WLR 1374—applying and holding a tourniquet to the arm of a drug abuser while injecting heroin can amount to the *actus reus* for manslaughter).

Dividing up controlled drugs which have been jointly purchased will amount to 'supplying' (*R v Buckley* (1979) 69 Cr App R 371).

The Court of Appeal has held that there is no statutory defence of 'religious use' to the above offence and that, even where it was accepted that the supply was for religious purposes, bringing a prosecution for the offence did not amount to an infringement the defendant's rights under Articles 8 and 9 of the European Convention on Human Rights (*R v Taylor* [2002] 1 Cr App R 314).

The offence of offering to supply a controlled drug is complete when the offer is made. It is irrelevant whether or not the defendant actually has the means to meet the offer or even intends to carry it out (see *R* v *Goodard* [1992] Crim LR 588). If the offer is made by conduct alone (i.e. without any words), it may be difficult to prove this offence. If words are used, the defence under s. 28 (**see para. 1.6.4**) does not appear to apply (see *R* v *Mitchell* [1992] Crim LR 723). If the offer is made to an undercover police officer, the offence is still committed and the defendant cannot claim that such an offer was not a 'real' offer (*R* v *Kray*, 10 November 1998, unreported).

In each case it will be a question of fact for the magistrate(s)/jury to decide whether or not the conduct amounted to a supply or offer to supply.

1.6.5.4   Points to Prove

In order to prove the offence of being concerned in the supply/offer to supply a controlled drug, you must show:

- the actual supply of, or making of an offer to supply, a controlled drug
- the participation of the defendant in that enterprise, and
- knowledge by the defendant that the enterprise involved the supply of, or making of an offer to supply, a controlled drug

(per the Court of Appeal in R v Hughes (1985) 81 Cr App R 344).

If the object of a conspiracy (**see chapter 1.3**) is to supply a controlled drug to a co-conspirator, any subsequent charge must make that clear; stating that the defendants conspired to supply the drug to 'another' implies that the supply was to be made to someone *other than any of the conspirators* (*R* v *Jackson* [2000] 1 Cr App R 97n).

1.6.5.5   Possession

OFFENCE: **Possession of Controlled Drug—*Misuse of Drugs Act 1971, s. 5(2)***
- Triable either way • Class A (seven years' imprisonment and/or fine on indictment; six months' imprisonment and/or prescribed sum summarily) • Class B (five years' imprisonment and/or fine on indictment; three months' imprisonment and/or fine summarily) • Class C (two years' imprisonment and/or fine on indictment; three months' imprisonment and/or fine summarily) • If possession of cannabis or cannabis resin

The Misuse of Drugs Act 1971, s. 5 states:

(2) Subject to section 28 of this Act and to subsection (4) below, it is an offence for a person to have a controlled drug in his possession in contravention of subsection (1) . . .

KEYNOTE

See para. 1.6.3 above for meaning of 'possession'.

In 2004, the Home Secretary consulted the Advisory Council on the Misuse of Drugss (ACMD) for advice on changing the classification of cannabis. The Advisory Council was clear that cannabis is a harmful drug and should remain illegal; however the toxicity and harmfulness of cannabis is not comparable either with Class A drugs, such as crack, heroin or ecstasy, or with substances such as amphetamines, which are Class B (under the Misuse of Drugs Act 1971). The Council therefore recommended that cannabis and all cannabis preparations, including cannabis resin, should be reclassified to Class C. The Government accepted the recommendation and cannabis was re-classified as a Class C drug. The fact that cannabis has been re-classified does not mean that possession is no longer a crime, as the then Home Secretary stated, 'all controlled drugs are harmful, all will remain illegal'.

Where the controlled drug involved is a fungus containing psilocin (a class A drug) or an ester of psilocin (commonly known as magic mushrooms) possession will not be unlawful in certain circumstances. In summary, those circumstances are generally where the fungus is growing *uncultivated* and it:

- is picked by a person already in *lawful possession* of it (for example the landowner on whose land the mushrooms are growing) for the purpose of delivering it (as soon as is reasonably practicable) into the custody of a person lawfully entitled to take custody of it and it remains in that person's possession for (and in accordance with) that purpose; or
- it is picked by anyone either for the purpose of delivering it (as soon as reasonably practicable) into the custody of a person lawfully entitled to take custody of it or destroying it (as soon as is reasonably practicable) and it is held for that purpose.

Note that there is no defence of medical necessity to the offence of possession of a controlled drug and the courts will not condone any form of self-prescription where controlled drugs are involved (**see para. 1.4.6**).

1.6.5.6   Possession with Intent to Supply

OFFENCE: **Possession with Intent to Supply—*Misuse of Drugs Act 1971, s. 5(3)***
- Triable either way • Class A (life imprisonment and/or fine on indictment; six months' imprisonment and/or prescribed sum summarily) • Class B (14 years' imprisonment and/or fine on indictment; six months' imprisonment and/or prescribed sum summarily) • Class C (14 years' imprisonment and/or fine on indictment; three months' imprisonment and/or fine summarily)

The Misuse of Drugs Act 1971, s. 5 states:

(3) Subject to section 28 of this Act, it is an offence for a person to have a controlled drug in his possession, whether lawfully or not, with intent to supply it to another in contravention of section 4(1) of this Act.

KEYNOTE

This is a crime of *specific* intent (**see chapter 1.1**).

It is important to note that the lawfulness or otherwise of the *possession* is irrelevant; what matters here is the lawfulness of the intended supply. If a vet or a police officer or some other person is in lawful possession of a controlled drug but they intend to supply it unlawfully to another, this offence will be made out.

You must show that the intention was that *the person in possession of the controlled drug* (rather than some third party) would supply it at some point in the future (*R* v *Greenfield* [1984] 78 Cr App R 179).

If more than one person has possession of the relevant controlled drug, you must show an individual intention to supply it by each person charged; it is not enough to show a joint venture whereby one or more parties simply knew of another's intent (*R* v *Downes* [1984] Crim LR 552). Given the decision of the Court of Appeal in *Kray* (**see para. 1.6.5.3**), possession with intent to supply a controlled drug to a person who is in fact an undercover police officer would appear to amount to an offence under this section.

All that is necessary in proving the offence under s. 5(3) is to show that the defendant had a controlled drug in his/her possession and intended to supply that substance to another. If the substance in the defendant's possession is a Class A drug and he/she intended to supply it to another person, the fact that he/she thought the drug was some other type of drug does not matter (*R* v *Leeson* [2000] 1 Cr App R 233).

While the possession by a defendant of drugs paraphernalia (e.g. clingfilm, paper, scales, contact details, etc.) will be relevant evidence to show that he/she was an active dealer in drugs generally, it does not prove the intention to supply and the trial judge will give a jury very careful directions as to the probative value of such items found in the defendant's possession (see *R* v *Haye* [2003] Crim LR 287).

Where a Rastafarian was prosecuted for possessing cannabis with intent to supply others as part of their religious worship, he claimed that his rights under Articles 8 and 9 of the European Convention (as to which, **see General Police Duties, chapter 4.3**) had been unnecessarily and disproportionately interfered with. The Court of Appeal, while reducing the sentence, held that such a prosecution had been properly brought (*R* v *Taylor* [2002] Crim LR 314).

In proving an intention to supply you may be able to adduce evidence of the defendant's unexplained wealth (*R* v *Smith* (*Ivor*) [1995] Crim LR 940) or the presence of large sums of money with the drugs seized (see *R* v *Wright* [1994] Crim LR 55).

For the meaning of 'supply', **see para. 1.6.5.2**. Note that the Drugs Act 2005 introduces a statutory presumption that, where a person has a certain quantity of drugs in their possession, their intention was to supply others. At the time of writing this provision has not been brought into force.

1.6.5.7 Cultivation of Cannabis

OFFENCE: **Cultivation of Cannabis—*Misuse of Drugs Act 1971, s. 6***

- Triable either way • 14 years' imprisonment and/or a fine
on indictment • Six months' imprisonment and/or prescribed sum summarily

The Misuse of Drugs Act 1971, s. 6 states:

(1) Subject to any regulations under section 7 of this Act for the time being in force, it shall not be lawful for a person to cultivate any plant of the genus *Cannabis*.
(2) Subject to section 28 of this Act, it is an offence to cultivate any such plant in contravention of subsection (1) above.

KEYNOTE

'Cultivate' is not defined but it appears that you would have to show some element of attention (such as watering or feeding) to the plant by the defendant in order to prove this offence. This offence does not permit police officers to tend plants which have been seized as evidence in order to preserve them as exhibits for court!

In proving the offence, you need only show that the plant is of the genus *Cannabis* and that the defendant cultivated it; you need not show that the defendant knew it to be a cannabis plant (*R* v *Champ* [1981] 73 Cr App R 367).

A person may be licensed to cultivate cannabis plants by the Secretary of State (under reg. 12 of the Misuse of Drugs Regulations 2001).

1.6.5.8 Supply of Articles

OFFENCE: **Supplying Articles for Administering or Preparing Controlled Drugs—*Misuse of Drugs Act 1971, s. 9A***

- Triable summarily • Six months' imprisonment and/or fine

The Misuse of Drugs Act 1971, s. 9A states:

(1) A person who supplies or offers to supply any article which may be used or adapted to be used (whether by itself or in combination with another article or other articles) in the administration by any person of a controlled drug to himself or another, believing that the article (or the article as adapted) is to be so used in circumstances where the administration is unlawful, is guilty of an offence.

(2) . . .

(3) A person who supplies or offers to supply any article which may be used to prepare a controlled drug for administration by any person to himself or another believing that the article is to be so used in circumstances where the administration is unlawful is guilty of an offence.

KEYNOTE

This offence is designed to address the provision of drug 'kits'.

'Supply' for these purposes is likely to be interpreted in the same way as for the earlier sections in the 1971 Act.

Hypodermic syringes, or parts of them, are not covered by this offence (s. 9A(2)).

The administration for which the articles are intended must be 'unlawful'. Section 9A states:

(4) For the purposes of this section, any administration of a controlled drug is unlawful except—
  (a) the administration by any person of a controlled drug to another in circumstances where the administration of the drug is not unlawful under section 4(1) of this Act, or
  (b) the administration by any person of a controlled drug to himself in circumstances where having the controlled drug in his possession is not unlawful under section 5(1) of this Act.

(5) In this section, references to administration by any person of a controlled drug to himself include a reference to his administering it to himself with the assistance of another.

1.6.5.9 Occupiers, etc.

OFFENCE: **Occupier or Manager of Premises Permitting Drug Misuse—**
Misuse of Drugs Act 1971, s. 8

• Triable either way • Class A or B (14 years' imprisonment and/or fine on indictment; six months' imprisonment and/or prescribed sum summarily) • Class C (14 years' imprisonment and/or a fine on indictment; three months' imprisonment and/or fine summarily)

The Misuse of Drugs Act 1971, s. 8 states:

A person commits an offence if, being the occupier or concerned in the management of any premises, he knowingly permits or suffers any of the following activities to take place on those premises, that is to say—

(a) producing or attempting to produce a controlled drug in contravention of section 4(1) of this Act;

(b) supplying or attempting to supply a controlled drug to another in contravention of section 4(1) of this Act, or offering to supply a controlled drug to another in contravention of section 4(1);

(c) preparing opium for smoking;

(d) smoking cannabis, cannabis resin or prepared opium.

KEYNOTE

The courts have adopted a 'common sense' approach to the interpretation of whether someone is an 'occupier' or not (see *R* v *Tao* [1977] QB 141). You will not need to prove that a defendant falls within some narrow legal meaning of an occupier. What is important in proving this offence is showing that the defendant had enough control over the premises to prevent the sort of activity listed above (see *R* v *Coid* [1998] Crim LR 199).

If a person cannot be shown to be an occupier in this sense, it may be that he/she can be shown to be involved in the planning, organising and actual use of the premises by taking part in more than just menial tasks. If so, this level of involvement may amount to 'management' of the premises (see *R* v *Josephs* (1977) 65 Cr App R 253).

'Premises' is not defined and has not been clarified at common law but the meaning has been given a wide definition elsewhere (such as in the Police and Criminal Evidence Act 1984; see **General Police Duties, chapter 4.4**).

The permitting or suffering of these activities requires a degree of *mens rea* (**see chapter 1.1**)—*Sweet* v *Parsley* [1970] AC 132—even if that degree is little more than wilful blindness (see *R* v *Thomas* (1976) 63 Cr App R 65). For the purposes of s. 8(b)—and therefore presumably s. 8(a)—it is not necessary to show that the defendant knew exactly which drugs were being produced, supplied etc.; only that they were 'controlled drugs' (*R* v *Bett* [1999] 1 All ER 600).

However, the precise activities that are described under s. 8 will need to be proved. So, for instance, if the offence charged is one of knowingly permitting the smoking of cannabis (under subs. (d)), it must be shown that this actually took place; it is not enough that the owner/occupier had given permission for this to happen (see *R* v *Auguste* (2003) *The Times,* 15 December).

An occupier who permits the growing of cannabis plants also commits this offence (*Taylor* v *Chief Constable of Kent* [1981] 1 WLR 606).

An occupier will not commit the above offence *in relation to the smoking of cannabis or cannabis resin* if the premises are covered by a research licence from the Secretary of State (see reg. 13 of the Misuse of Drugs Regulations 2001).

1.6.5.10 Closure Notices

Section 1 of the Anti-social Behaviour Act 2003 states:

(1) This section applies to premises if a police officer not below the rank of superintendent (the authorising officer) has reasonable grounds for believing—
   (a) that at any time during the relevant period the premises have been used in connection with the unlawful use, production or supply of a Class A controlled drug, and
   (b) that the use of the premises is associated with the occurrence of disorder or serious nuisance to members of the public.

KEYNOTE

This provision is primarily designed to allow the police to close so-called 'crack houses'. If the above conditions are met the authorising officer may authorise the issuing of a closure notice.

The 'relevant period' referred to means the period of three months ending with the day on which the authorising officer considers whether to authorise the issue of a closure notice in respect of the premises (s. 1(10)).

'Premises' are defined as including any land or other place (whether enclosed or not) and any outbuildings which are or are used as part of the premises (s. 11).

The authorising officer may authorise the issue of a closure notice in respect of premises to which this section applies if s/he is satisfied:

(a) that the local authority for the area in which the premises are situated has been consulted;

(b) that reasonable steps have been taken to establish the identity of any person who lives on the premises or who has control of or responsibility for or an interest in the premises.

An authorisation may be given orally or in writing, but if it is given orally the authorising officer must confirm it in writing as soon as is practicable (s. 1(3)).

Note that it is immaterial whether any person has been convicted of an offence relating to the use, production or supply of a controlled drug (though clearly it will help in showing relevant grounds to support a closure notice and a closure order (see below) if someone has been convicted in connection with the use of the premises). The Secretary of State may make regulations specifying premises or descriptions of premises to which this power does not apply (s. 1(9)).

There is also a general power for local authorities to make a closure order in relation to noise and nuisance being caused in connection with the use of premises under s. 40 of the Act.

1.6.5.11 The Notice

The notice, which must be served by a police officer, must also:

- give notice that an application will be made under s. 2 for the closure of the premises
- state that access to the premises by any person (other than a person who habitually resides in the premises or the owner of the premises) is prohibited
- specify the date and time when and the place at which the application will be heard
- explain the effects of a closure order
- state that failure to comply with the notice amounts to an offence
- give information about the names of and means of contacting people and organisations in the area that provide advice about housing and legal matters.

Service of the notice will be effected by fixing a copy of the notice to:

- at least one prominent place on the premises
- each normal means of access to the premises
- any outbuildings which appear to the constable to be used with or as part of the premises; and

by giving a copy of the notice to at least one person who appears to the constable to have control of or responsibility for the premises and also to any person who lives on the premises or who has control of or responsibility for or an interest in the premises. (see s. 1(6)).

For the purpose of effecting service of the notice a constable may enter any premises to which the section applies, using reasonable force if necessary (s. 1(7A)).

1.6.5.12 The Closure Order

If a closure notice has been issued under s. 1 a police officer must apply to a magistrates' court for the making of a closure order and that application must be heard by the court not later than 48 hours after the notice has been served (s. 2).

However, the court may adjourn the hearing on the application for a period of not more than 14 days to enable the occupier or another person with control of, responsibility for or an interest in the premises to show why an order should not be made (s. 2(6)).

The magistrates' court cannot use a power under other enactments relating to adjournments to adjourn any hearing of that application for more than 14 days (see *Commissioner of Police for the Metropolis* v *Hooper* [2005] EWHC 199 (Admin)).

The magistrates' court may make a closure order only if it is satisfied that:

- the premises in respect of which the closure notice was issued have been used in connection with the unlawful use, production or supply of a Class A controlled drug
- the use of the premises is associated with the occurrence of disorder or serious nuisance to members of the public, and
- the making of the order is necessary to prevent the occurrence of such disorder or serious nuisance for the period specified in the order.

(s. 2 (3)).

A closure order is an order that all or any part of the premises are closed to all people for such period (not exceeding three months) as the court decides (s. 2(4)). The police can apply for an order to be extended at any time before it expires but that application must be authorised by an officer not below the rank of superintendent after consultation with the local authority (see s. 5). An order cannot be extended beyond a total of six months (s. 5(5)). Further specific provisions are made by the Act in relation to the discharge of closure notices and the bringing of appeals.

1.6.5.13 Enforcement

A police officer or an authorised person may enter the premises in respect of which the order is made and/or do anything reasonably necessary to secure the premises against entry by any person and may use reasonable force to do so (see s. 3).

A police officer or authorised person may also enter the premises at any time while the order is in force for the purpose of carrying out essential maintenance of or repairs to the premises (s. 3(5)).

A police officer or authorised person seeking to enter the premises for these purposes must, if required to do so by or on behalf of the owner, occupier or other person in charge of the premises, produce evidence of his/her identity and authority before entering the premises (s. 3(4)).

1.6.5.14 Obstructing or Breaching Closure Order

OFFENCE: **Obstruction and Breaching Closure Order—*Anti-social Behaviour Act 2003, s. 4***

- Triable summarily • Six months' imprisonment and/or fine

The Anti-social Behaviour Act 2003, s. 4 states:

(1) A person commits an offence if he remains on or enters premises in contravention of a closure notice.
(2) A person commits an offence if—
    (a) he obstructs a constable or an authorised person acting under section 1(6) or 3(2),
    (b) he remains on premises in respect of which a closure order has been made, or
    (b) he enters the premises.

> **KEYNOTE**
>
> A person does not commit an offence under subs. (1) or subs. (2)(b) or (c) if he/she has a reasonable excuse for entering or being on the premises (as the case may be) (s. 4(4)).
>
> Any person who occupies or owns any part of a building or structure in which closed premises are situated and in respect of which the closure order does not have effect may apply to the court for an order allowing access to any part of the premises.
>
> For the general offence of obstructing police see **General Police Duties**.

1.6.5.15 Importation of Controlled Drugs

It is an offence under the Misuse of Drugs Act 1971, s. 3 to import or export a controlled drug unless authorised by the regulations made under the Act. The relevant offences and their respective penalties are contained in the Customs and Excise Management Act 1979. Schedule 1 to the 1979 Act provides for the following penalties for the improper importation or exportation of controlled drugs:

- **Class A**—life imprisonment
- **Class B**—14 years' imprisonment
- **Class C**—14 years' imprisonment.

1.6.5.16 Assisting or Inducing Offence Outside United Kingdom

OFFENCE: **Assisting or Inducing Misuse of Drugs Offence Outside UK—*Misuse of Drugs Act 1971, s. 20***
- Triable either way • 14 years' imprisonment and/or a fine on indictment
- Six months' imprisonment and/or fine summarily

The Misuse of Drugs Act 1971, s. 20 states:

> A person commits an offence if in the United Kingdom he assists in or induces the commission in any place outside the United Kingdom of an offence punishable under the provisions of a corresponding law in force in that place.

> **KEYNOTE**
>
> In order to prove this offence, you must show that the offence outside the United Kingdom actually took place. The circumstances where this offence is likely to be committed will clearly overlap with the offences of importation/exportation (see para. 1.6.5.15).
>
> 'Assisting' has been held to include taking containers to another country in the knowledge that they would later be filled with a controlled drug and sent on to a third country (*R* v *Evans* (1977) 64 Cr App R 237). For an offence to amount to one under 'corresponding law' for these purposes, a certificate relating to the domestic law concerned with the misuse of drugs must be obtained from the government of the relevant country (s. 36).

1.6.5.17 Incitement

OFFENCE: **Incitement—*Misuse of Drugs Act 1971, s. 19***
- Triable and punishable as for substantive offence incited

The Misuse of Drugs Act 1971, s. 19 states:

It is an offence for a person to incite another to commit such an offence.

KEYNOTE

Although the offence of incitement exists for most other offences generally (see chapter 1.3), the Act makes a specific offence of inciting another to commit an offence under its provisions. On the arguments in *DPP* v *Armstrong* [2000] Crim LR 379 (see chapter 1.3), it would seem that a person inciting an undercover police officer may commit an offence under s. 19 even though there was no possibility of the officer actually being induced to commit the offence.

1.6.6 Enforcement

In addition to the general policing powers available for serious offences (**see General Police Duties, chapter 4.4**), the 1971 Act provides a number of specific enforcement powers.

1.6.6.1 Powers of Entry, Search and Seizure

The Misuse of Drugs Act 1971, s. 23 states:

(1) A constable or other person authorised in that behalf by a general or special order of the Secretary of State (or in Northern Ireland either of the Secretary of State or the Ministry of Home Affairs for Northern Ireland) shall, for the purposes of the execution of this Act, have power to enter the premises of a person carrrying on business as a producer or supplier of any controlled drugs and to demand the production of, and to inspect, any books or documents relating to dealings in any such drugs and to inspect any stocks of any such drugs.

(2) If a constable has reasonable grounds to suspect that any person is in possession of a controlled drug in contravention of this Act or of any regulations made thereunder, the constable may—

    (a) search that person, and detain him for the purpose of searching him;

    (b) search any vehicle or vessel in which the constable suspects that the drug may be found, and for that purpose require the person in control of the vehicle or vessel to stop it;

    (c) seize and detain, for the purposes of proceedings under this Act, anything found in the course of the search which appears to the constable to be evidence of an offence under this Act.

        In this subsection 'vessel' includes a hovercraft within the meaning of the Hovercraft Act 1968; and nothing in this subsection shall prejudice any power of search or any power to seize or detain property which exercisable by a constable apart from this subsection.

(3) If a justice of the peace (or in Scotland a justice of the peace, a magistrate or a sheriff) is satisfied by information on oath that there is reasonable ground for suspecting—

    (a) that any controlled drugs are, in contravention of this Act or of any regulations made thereunder, in the possession of a person on any premises; or

    (b) that a document directly or indirectly relating to, or connected with, a transaction or dealing which was, or an intended transaction or dealing which would if carried out be, an offence under this Act, or in the case of a transaction or dealing carried out or intended to be carried out in a place outside the United Kingdom, an offence against the provisions of a corresponding law in force in that place, is in the possession of a person on any premises, he may grant a warrant authorising any constable acting for the police area in which the premises are situated at any time or times within one month from the date of the warrant, to enter, if need be by force, the premises named in the warrant, and to search the premises and any persons found therein and, if there is reasonable ground for suspecting that an offence under this Act has been committed in relation to any controlled drugs found on the premises or in the possession of any such persons, or that a document so found is such a document as is mentioned in paragraph (b) above, to seize and detain those drugs or that document, as the case may be.

KEYNOTE

This is a very wide statutory provision granting authority for a broad range of enforcement measures in connection with controlled drugs.

Particular care will need to be taken when drafting the application for a warrant under s. 23. Where police officers are on premises under the authority of such a warrant it will be important to have established the precise *extent* of the warrant. If such a warrant authorises the search of *premises only*, that in itself will not give the officers authority to search *people* found on those premises unless the officer can point to some other power authorising the search (*see e.g. Chief Constable of Thames Valley Police* v *Hepburn* (2002) *The Times*, 19 December).

However, where the warrant authorises the search of premises *and* people, the Divisional Court has held that it is reasonable to restrict the movement of people within the premises to allow the search to be conducted properly (see *DPP* v *Meaden* (2004) *The Times*, 2 January).

For the procedure involved in applying for, and executing warrants, **see General Police Duties,** chapter 4.4.

The Police and Criminal Evidence Act 1984, code A (**see General Police Duties**), applies to the exercise of any power to search people for controlled drugs specifically included in a warrant issued under s. 23.

The Serious Organised Crime and Police Act 2005 has not changed the duration of a warrant issued under s. 23 of the Misuse of Drugs Act 1971. A warrant issued under s. 23 of the Act lasts for a period of one month from the date of issue.

1.6.6.2 **Obstruction**

OFFENCE: **Obstruction—*Misuse of Drugs Act 1971, s. 23(4)***
- Triable either way • Two years' imprisonment and/or a fine on indictment • Six months' imprisonment and/or fine summarily

The Misuse of Drugs Act 1971, s. 23 states:

(4) A person commits an offence if he—
   (a) intentionally obstructs a person in the exercise of his powers under this section; or
   (b) conceals from a person acting in the exercise of his powers under subsection (1) above any such books, documents, stocks or drugs as are mentioned in that subsection; or
   (c) without reasonable excuse (proof of which shall lie on him) fails to produce any such books or documents as are so mentioned where their production is demanded by a person in the exercise of his powers under that subsection.

KEYNOTE

The offence of obstructing a person in the exercise of his/her powers is only committed if the obstruction was intentional (*R* v *Forde* (1985) 81 Cr App R 19). For the offence of obstructing a police officer generally, see chapter 1.7.

1.6.6.3   Travel Restriction Orders

The Criminal Justice and Police Act 2001 makes provision for courts to impose travel restrictions on offenders convicted of drug trafficking offences. Travel restriction orders prohibit the offender from leaving the United Kingdom at any time during the period beginning from his/her release from custody (other than on bail or temporary release for a fixed period) and up to the end of the order. The minimum period for such an order is two years (s. 33(3)).

Where a court

- has convicted a person of a drug trafficking offence
- and it has determined that a sentence of four years or more is appropriate

it is under a *duty* to consider whether or not a travel restriction order would be appropriate (s. 33). If the court decides not to impose an order, it must give its reasons for not doing so.

An offender may also be required to surrender his/her UK passport as part of the order.

The offences which are covered by travel restriction orders include the production and supply of controlled drugs (**see paras 1.6.5.1** and **1.6.5.2**), the importation/exportation offences described at **para. 1.6.5.15** along with attempting, or inciting—either at common law (**see chapter 1.3**) or under the Misuse of Drugs Act 1971, s. 19 (**see para. 1.6.5.17**).

The Secretary of State may add to this list (see s. 34(2)).

An offender may apply to the court that made a restriction order to have it revoked or suspended (s. 35) and the court must consider the strict criteria set out in s. 35 when considering any such suspension or revocation. If an order is suspended, the offender has a legal obligation to be back in the United Kingdom when the period of suspension ends (s. 35(5)(a)).

The general importance of all this to police officers is the offence below.

OFFENCE: **Contravening a Travel Restriction Order—*Criminal Justice and Police Act 2001, s. 36***
- Triable either way • Five years' imprisonment and/or a fine on indictment
- Six months' imprisonment and/or fine summarily

The Criminal Justice and Police Act 2001, s. 36 states:

(1) A person who leaves the United Kingdom at a time when he is prohibited from leaving it by a travel restriction order is guilty of an offence . . .
(2) A person who is not in the United Kingdom at the end of a period during which a prohibition imposed on him by a travel restriction order has been suspended shall be guilty of an offence . . .

KEYNOTE

These offences make no specific requirement for a particular state of mind. The first offence simply requires proof of two things—that there was an order in existence in respect of the offender and that he/she left the United Kingdom during the time it was in force. Strangely there is no requirement that the person leave the United Kingdom *voluntarily* in order to be guilty (although they would have a pretty good argument if they were taken out of the jurisdiction against their will or without their knowledge).

However, travel restriction orders do not prevent the proper exercise of any prescribed power to remove a person from the United Kingdom (see s. 37—the relevant powers are set out in the Travel Restriction Order (Prescribed Removal Powers) Order 2002 (SI 2002/313)). For instance, if the Secretary of State deports someone who is under a travel restriction order, that person would not commit the above offence.

The second offence requires proof that there was a suspended order in existence in respect of the offender and that, at the end of the suspension period, the offender was not in the United Kingdom. Given that this offence simply envisages a set of circumstances (that the defendant is not in the United Kingdom when the suspension order ends) it is interesting—though of no great practical relevance—to consider whether this offence could ever be 'attempted'.

Failing to deliver up a UK passport when required by an order will be a summary offence carrying six months' imprisonment and/or a fine (s. 36(3)).

1.6.7 Intoxicating Substances

OFFENCE: **Supply of Intoxicating Substance—***Intoxicating Substances (Supply) Act 1985, s. 1*

- Triable summarily • Six months' imprisonment and/or a fine

The Intoxicating Substances (Supply) Act 1985, s. 1 states:

(1) It is an offence for a person to supply or offer to supply a substance other than a controlled drug—

    (a) to a person under the age of 18 whom he knows, or has reasonable cause to believe, to be under that age; or

    (b) to a person—

        (i) who is acting on behalf of a person under that age; and

        (ii) whom he knows, or has reasonable cause to believe, to be so acting,

        if he knows or has reasonable cause to believe that the substance is, or its fumes are, likely to be inhaled by the person under the age of 18 for the purpose of causing intoxication.

KEYNOTE

This offence is aimed at curbing 'glue sniffing'. Retailers who sell solvents to people apparently under 18, or to people apparently acting on the behalf of someone under 18, would commit this offence.

The requirement as to the personal knowledge of the age and intentions of the person supplied makes this a difficult offence to prove.

It is a defence for a person charged with this offence to show that at the time he/she made the supply or offer he/she was both:

- under the age of 18 and
- acting otherwise than in the course or furtherance of a business (s. 1(2)).

For the law relating to the supply of alcohol to people under 18, see **General Police Duties**, chapter 4.11.

OFFENCE: **Supply of Butane Lighter Refill to Person under 18—*Cigarette Lighter Refill (Safety) Regulations 1999, reg. 2***

    • Triable summarily • Six months' imprisonment and/or a fine

The Cigarette Lighter Refill (Safety) Regulations 1999 (SI 1999/1844), reg. 2 states:

> No person shall supply any cigarette lighter refill canister containing butane or a substance with butane as a constituent part to any person under the age of eighteen years.

KEYNOTE

For this offence there is no requirement that the person believed or even suspected the person to be under 18. The 1999 Regulations are made under the Consumer Protection Act 1987, s. 11.

For the meaning of 'supply', see para. 1.6.5.2.

1.7.1 Introduction

Non-fatal offences against others cover a wide range of behaviour from a raised fist to a calculated wounding. The importance of this subject lies not only in the number of occasions when officers will need to refer to it, but also because it deals with violence and the fear of violent crime—areas in which victims are particularly traumatised. As courts are being urged to focus on the effects of a defendant's conduct upon their victim, the scope for bringing a charge of assault is widening.

1.7.2 Key Issues

While there are several distinct categories of offence that can be committed against other people, there are some features that are important for both understanding the law and the practical application of it. These key issues are set out below.

1.7.2.1 Assault and Battery

Assault and battery are, strictly speaking, two separate things. What people generally think of as being an 'assault' (e.g. a punch on the nose) is a 'battery', that is, the infliction of unlawful force on someone else. While it would cover a punch on the nose, an 'assault' in its proper legal sense has a much wider meaning and includes any act whereby the defendant 'intentionally—or recklessly—causes another person to apprehend immediate and unlawful personal violence' (*Fagan* v *Metropolitan Police Commissioner* [1969] 1 QB 439).

1.7.2.2 Assault or Battery?

Although these terms—assault and battery—have distinct legal meanings they are often referred to as simply 'assaults' or 'common assault'. It is, however, important to separate the two expressions when charging or laying an information against a defendant as to include both may be bad for duplicity (*DPP* v *Taylor* [1992] QB 645).

The term battery, or the application of 'force', creates a misleading impression as a very small degree of physical contact will be enough. That force can be applied directly or indirectly. For example, where a defendant punched a woman causing her to drop and injure a child she was holding, he was convicted of assaulting that child (*Haystead* v *Chief Constable of Derbyshire* [2000] 3 All ER 890). The *actus reus* needed to prove an assault is an act which caused the victim to apprehend the immediate infliction of unlawful force, although 'apprehension' does not mean 'fear' and there is no need to show that the victim was actually in fear. The force or violence apprehended by the victim does not have to be a 'certainty'. Causing a fear of some possible violence can be enough (see *R* v *Ireland* [1998]

AC 147) provided that the violence feared is about to happen in the immediate future (see *R* v *Constanza* [1997] 2 Cr App R 492).

There is some academic debate as to whether battery and assault are still common law offences or whether they are now statutory offences. What is clear is that the Criminal Justice Act 1988, s. 39 stipulates that they must be tried summarily and sets out the maximum penalty that may be imposed (**see para. 1.7.3**).

While some offences can be committed by an act or an *omission* (e.g. manslaughter (**see chapter 1.5**)) for a charge of assault to succeed there must be an *act* (*Fagan*).

It also is important to remember that the state of mind of the *victim* in an assault is relevant to the *actus reus*. The victim must apprehend the immediate use of unlawful force. For these reasons, if a defendant threatened someone with an imitation pistol, he/she could still be charged with assault provided the victim *believed* that the pistol was real—the defendant had caused an apprehension of possible immediate force being used (*Logdon* v *DPP* [1976] Crim LR 121).

Words can amount to an assault provided they are accompanied by the required *mens rea*. This was made clear by the decision in *R* v *Ireland* [1998] AC 147 where it was held that telephone calls to a victim, followed by silences, could amount to an assault. In *Ireland*, the House of Lords accepted that '*a thing said is also a thing done*' and rejected the view that words can never amount to an assault. *Ireland* involved the making of threatening telephone calls which led the victims to fear that unlawful force would be used against them. The House of Lords accepted that, in such cases, even *silence* could fulfil the requirements for the *actus reus* of assault if it brought about the desired consequences (e.g. fear of the immediate use of unlawful force).

Where the words threatening immediate unlawful force come in the form of letters, the Court of Appeal has held that an assault may have been committed (see *Constanza* above).

1.7.2.3 Conditional Threats

As well as constituting an assault, words can also *negate* an assault if they make a conditional threat, e.g., where you attend an incident and one person says to another '*If these officers weren't here I'd chin you!*' (*Tuberville* v *Savage* (1669) 1 Mod R3—a very ancient and therefore long-standing authority). In this type of case the defendant is making a *hypothetical* threat and is really saying 'if it weren't for the existence of certain circumstances, I would assault you'. This should be contrasted with occasions where the defendant makes an immediate threat conditional upon some real circumstance, e.g. '*If you don't cross the road, I'll break your neck*'. Such threats have been held, in a civil case, to amount to an assault (*Read* v *Coker* (1853) 13 CB 850).

1.7.2.4 What is 'Immediate'?

Although the force threatened must be immediate, that immediacy is—like most legal interpretation—somewhat elastic. Courts have accepted that, where a person makes a threat from outside a victim's house to the victim who is inside, an assault is still committed even though there will be some time lapse before the defendant can carry out the threat.

In *Ireland* the House of Lords suggested that a threat to cause violence 'in a minute or two' might be enough to qualify as an assault. The victim must be shown to have feared the use of *force*; it will not be enough to show that a person threatened by words—or silence—feared more calls or letters. The fear of force is the key to assault.

1.7.2.5   **Intentionally or Recklessly**

The *mens rea* needed to prove common assault is either:

- an intention to cause apprehension of immediate unlawful violence, or
- subjective recklessness (i.e. foresight) as to that consequence (**see chapter 1.1**).

When considering the *mens rea of* any assault, it is important to separate the assault or battery (**see para. 1.7.2.2**) from *any further consequences caused by* that assault or battery. The *mens rea* needed for the assault/battery is set out above. If a defendant's behaviour causes another to fear immediate and unlawful personal violence, he/she commits an 'assault' provided it can be shown that, at the time, the defendant *intended* to cause that fear or was *subjectively reckless* as to whether such a fear would result from his/her actions.

So what happens where the defendant's actions cause more than just fear; they cause more serious injury? Unfortunately that appears to depend on the extent of the injury and the wording of the offence charged. Among the more serious offences under the Offences Against the Person Act 1861 (**see para. 1.7.6**) are causing 'actual bodily harm' (s. 47) and 'wounding' or inflicting/causing 'grievous bodily harm' (ss. 18 and 20). The *mens rea* required for an offence under s. 47, causing actual bodily harm, is the same as that required for the basic offence of assault (*R v Savage* [1992] 1 AC 699). This is because s. 47 makes no specific requirement for any greater degree of *mens rea* by the defendant and, in effect, the offence of causing actual bodily harm becomes simply an assault or battery with a more serious outcome. From the defendant's point of view this is really pot luck because there is no requirement for him/her to have intended or even foreseen the actual bodily harm. In the case of woundings and grievous bodily harm, the situation is different because ss. 18 and 20 use the word 'maliciously' (**see para. 1.7.6.2**). This element introduces the element of intention or subjective recklessness *in relation to the injuries suffered by the victim* (*Savage* above), thereby adding a further requirement to the *mens rea*.

....

EXAMPLE

Take the example of two people in a pub. They are arguing. One person, the defendant, threatens to throw a pint of beer over the other, the victim. At this point the defendant has caused the victim to fear that immediate unlawful personal violence will be used against him—an 'assault'. In order to prove an offence of assault under the Criminal Justice Act 1988, you must show that, at the time of the threat, the defendant either intended to cause the fear of violence or was subjectively reckless in that regard. If such an intention or recklessness cannot be shown, there is no offence of assault.

After the threat, a third person pushes past the defendant, accidentally knocking him into the victim and spilling the beer over him. At this point there has been no 'assault' by the defendant because there has been no *actus reus* by him, irrespective of his intentions.

The defendant continues to argue and then raises his glass and throws the contents over the victim. Clearly there has now been a voluntary application of unlawful force—a 'battery'—which the defendant intended to apply and he commits an offence under the Criminal Justice Act 1988. In the act of throwing the beer, however, the defendant's hand slips and he in fact hits the victim in the face with his beer glass causing a broken tooth. At this point the defendant's actions have gone beyond those intended by him and his victim has suffered injuries which the defendant had neither intended nor considered. Nevertheless, at the time of the assault (and battery) the defendant had the required *mens rea* for the assault/battery and therefore is liable for any actual bodily harm suffered by the victim as a result. Therefore the defendant commits the offence of assault occasioning actual bodily harm under s. 47 of the Offences Against the Person Act 1861, even though he neither intended nor considered the injuries to his victim.

Having a small amount of beer left in the glass, the defendant flicks the 'dregs' from the glass at the victim. The defendant loses his grip on the glass and it flies from his hand, hitting the victim in the eye and breaking on impact. The victim suffers a deep wound to the eye. Although the defendant is still liable for any actual bodily harm, he can only be liable for the more serious offences of wounding and causing/inflicting *grievous* bodily harm if it can be shown that he acted 'maliciously'. Malice for these purposes means that he must have intended to cause the harm or realised that there was a risk of at least some harm being suffered by the victim. If he did realise that the victim was at risk of being harmed by his actions, the defendant may be liable for an offence under s. 20 of the Offences Against the Person Act 1861 (**see para. 1.7.6.2**). If it can be shown that he intended to bring about *serious* harm, the defendant may be liable for the offence under s. 18 of the 1861 Act (**see para. 1.7.6.3**).

If the victim goes on to die from the injury, the defendant would be guilty of murder, or manslaughter by unlawful or dangerous act, depending on the level of *mens rea* (**see chapters 1.1 and 1.5**).

Given the requirements for *mens rea*, together with the respective penalties, it is not surprising that charges of 'actual bodily harm' might be preferred over charges of malicious wounding or inflicting grievous bodily harm.

A further example of the issues arising in the context of an arrest can be seen in *D* v *DPP* [2005] Crim LR 962 (**see para. 1.1.4.2**).

....

1.7.2.6 Consent

A key element in proving an assault is the *unlawfulness* of the force used or threatened. Although the courts have accepted consent as a feature which negatives any offence, they have been reluctant to accept this feature in a number of notable cases.

Consent to Sado-masochistic Injuries

These cases have developed as a question of public policy and were summarised in the House of Lords in the so-called 'spanner trial' (*R* v *Brown* [1994] 1 AC 212).

That case involved members of a sado-masochist group who inflicted varying degrees of injuries on one another for their own gratification. Charged with many offences against the person, the group claimed that they had consented to the injuries and therefore no assault or battery had taken place. Their Lordships followed an earlier policy that *all assaults which result in more than transient harm will be unlawful unless there is good reason for allowing the plea of 'consent'*. Good reason will be determined in the light of a number of considerations:

- the practical consequences of the behaviour
- the dangerousness of the behaviour
- the vulnerability of the 'consenting' person.

Further difficulties in clarifying what will amount to 'true' or effective consent were added by the decision of the Court of Appeal in *R* v *Wilson* [1997] QB 47. In that case the court accepted that a husband might lawfully brand his initials on his wife's buttocks with a hot knife provided she consented (as she appeared to have done). The reasoning behind the judgment seems to be based on the fact that the branding was similar to a form of tattooing (see below), but also on the policy grounds that consensual activity between husband and wife is not a matter for criminal investigation. This causes several problems, not least of which is the fact that sado-masochistic 'branding' was denounced by the House of Lords in *Brown* above. Therefore, if a situation arose where a husband and wife took part in mutual branding in the privacy of their home, their criminal liability would arguably depend on whether they caused the harm for purposes of sado-masochistic pleasure or out of some affectionate wish to be permanently adorned with the mark of their loved one. It is also unclear how far the policy aspect of the decision in *Wilson* would extend and whether or not it would encompass unmarried or homosexual couples.

Sado-masochistic injury may justifiably be made the subject of criminal law on grounds of the 'protection of health'. It was for this reason that the European Court of Human Rights held that there had been no violation of the defendants' right to private life (under Article 8) in the *Brown* case above. Although the defendants asserted that the interference by the criminal law in their consensual sexual practices amounted to an unnecessary restriction of their individual rights under Article 8, the Court held that this was a justifiable intrusion on the grounds set out above (*Laskey, Jaggard and Brown* v *United Kingdom* (1997) 24 EHRR 39).

Legitimate Consent to Risk of Injury

Clearly there are times when a person may consent to even serious harm such as during properly-conducted sporting events (see *Attorney-General's Reference (No. 6 of 1980)* [1981] QB 715), tattooing and medical operations. Where the activity falls outside those parameters, such as an off-the-ball incident in a football match (*R* v *Lloyd* (1989) 11 Cr App R (S) 36) or an unauthorised prize fight, the plea of consent will not apply. However, the Court of Appeal has stated that the criminal prosecution of those who inflict injury on another in the course of a sporting event is reserved for those situations where the conduct was sufficiently grave to be properly categorised as criminal—*R* v *Barnes* [2004] EWCA Crim 3246. In that case the defendant appealed against his conviction for inflicting grievous bodily harm (**see para. 1.7.6**) after he caused a serious leg injury by way of a tackle during a football match. The tackle took place after the victim had kicked the ball into the goal but, while accepting that the tackle was hard, the defendant maintained that it had been a fair challenge and that the injury caused was accidental. The Court held that where injuries were sustained in the course of contact sports, public policy limited the availability of the defence of consent to situations where there had been implicit consent to what had occurred. Whether conduct reached the required threshold to be treated as 'criminal' would depend on all the circumstances. The fact that the actions of the defendant had been within the rules and practice of the game would be a firm indication that what had occurred was not criminal, although in highly competitive sports even conduct *outside the rules* could be expected to occur in the heat of the moment, and such conduct still might not reach the threshold level required for it to be criminal. The Court held that the threshold level was an objective one to be determined by the type of sport, the level at which it was played, the nature of the 'act', the degree of force used, the extent of the risk of injury and the state of mind of the defendant.

Other more straightforward policy considerations would include the implied consent by people getting on to crowded tube trains or moving around at a packed concert venue. In these cases it will be a matter of fact to decide whether the behaviour complained of went beyond what was acceptable in those particular circumstances.

Where a dentist who had been suspended by the General Dental Council continued to operate on patients, her failure to inform those patients of her suspension did not affect their true 'consent' and the dentist's actions were not an 'assault' (*R* v *Richardson* [1999] QB 444). The situation would be very different if the dentist had no formal qualifications at all, or if her actions went beyond the proper professional activities of a dentist (e.g. an indecent touching of patients).

One area where the issue of legitimate consent has raised considerable debate is that of infection with a sexually transmitted disease. Here there are two aspects to the 'consent'—one is consent to the sexual activity itself, the other is consent to the risk of contracting the disease (such as HIV). It is clear from the authorities that consent to the former does not necessarily provide consent to the latter (**see para. 1.7.6.2**).

1.7.2.7 Lawful Chastisement

For many years the common and statute law allowed for those acting in *loco parentis* of a child to be able to use reasonable force in controlling the behaviour of that child. What was 'reasonable' varied widely and became increasingly difficult to define let alone justify given the breadth and depth of social attitudes and conventions within England and Wales.

In a case involving an allegation of assault by a stepfather on his stepson, the European Court of Human Rights held that the United Kingdom was in breach of its obligation to protect individuals from inhuman or degrading punishment (under Article 3 of the European Convention on Human Rights—**see General Police Duties, chapter 4.3**) because the law in this area was not clear enough (*A* v *United Kingdom* (1999) 27 EHRR 611). Additionally, Protocol 1, Article 2 (the right to education) of the Convention requires a state to have regard to the religious and philosophical convictions of parents in its schools. This requirement was at the centre of a successful challenge against corporal punishment in a state school (*Campbell* v *United Kingdom* (1982) 4 EHRR 293). The School Standards and Framework Act 1998 outlaws corporal punishment in all British schools, although staff may use reasonable force in restraining violent or disruptive pupils (Education Act 1996, s. 550A). The Divisional Court has held that this legislation removes entirely the defence of reasonable chastisement from any teacher when they are acting as such (*Williamson* v *Secretary of State for Education and Employment* [2001] EWHC Admin 960, later affirmed by the House of Lords [2005] UKHL 15). The legislation gave effect to a clear parliamentary intention to abolish corporal punishment in all schools including independent schools and did not infringe the human rights of any of the claimants.

So far as the general issue of lawful chastisement by parents and carers is concerned, the Children Act 2004 provides that battery of a person under 18 years of age cannot be justified on the ground that it constituted reasonable punishment in relation to an offence under s. 47 of the Offences against the Person Act 1861 (assault occasioning actual bodily harm) or an offence under s. 18 or 20 (wounding or causing grievous bodily harm)—as to which **see para. 1.7.6** (s. 58).

In addition, the 2004 Act goes on to provide that battery of a person under 18 years of age causing actual bodily harm to the person cannot be justified in any *civil* proceedings on the ground that it constituted reasonable punishment (s. 58(3)).

1.7.3 Offences

Having considered the key common elements in this area, the specific offences are set out below.

1.7.3.1 Common Assault and Battery

OFFENCE: **Common Assault/Battery—*Criminal Justice Act 1988, s. 39***
  • Triable summarily • Six months' imprisonment

OFFENCE: **Racially or Religiously Aggravated—*Crime and Disorder Act 1998, s. 29(1)(c)***

- Triable either way • Two years' imprisonment and/or a fine on indictment
- Six months' imprisonment and/or a fine summarily

KEYNOTE

Common assault was deemed by the legislators to be one of those offences where it was necessary to increase the maximum penalty available to the courts if it was committed under racially or religiously aggravated circumstances (see the Crime and Disorder Act 1998, s. 29(1)(c)). A further effect of the racially or religiously aggravated offence is that it can be tried on indictment without having to be included alongside another indictable offence as is the case with common assaults generally (see the Criminal Justice Act 1988, s. 40).

The Divisional Court has held that the words 'white man's arse licker' and 'brown Englishman' when used to accompany an assault on an Asian victim did not necessarily make the assault 'racially aggravated' and that the prosecution had not done enough to show that the assailants' behaviour fell under the definition set out in s. 28 of the 1998 Act (*DPP* v *Pal* [2000] Crim LR 756).

For a full explanation of the meaning of 'racially or religiously aggravated', **see General Police Duties, chapter 4.5.**

Under the racially—and now religiously—aggravated public order offences the courts have held that police officers are entitled to the same protection under the legislation as anyone else (see *R* v *Jacobs* [2001] 2 Cr App R (S) 38) and the same principle ought to apply to physical assault.

If an assault upon a police officer is 'racially or religiously aggravated' per the requirements of s. 28 of the Crime and Disorder Act 1998, it may be preferable to consider this offence rather than one of the offences under the Police Act 1996 (as to which, **see para. 1.7.3.3**).

CPS Charging Standards state that a charge under s. 39 of the Act will be appropriate where injuries amount to no more than the following:

- grazes
- scratches
- abrasions
- minor bruising
- swelling
- reddening of the skin
- superficial cuts
- a 'black eye'

The injury sustained by the victim should always be considered first, and in most cases the degree of injury will determine whether the appropriate charge is an assault under s. 39 of the Act or a more serious assault under s. 47 of the Offences Against the Person Act 1861. There will be borderline cases, such as where an undisplaced broken nose has resulted. Generally, where injuries amount to no more than those described above, common assault will be the appropriate charge.

1.7.3.2 Assault with Intent to Resist Arrest

OFFENCE: **Assault with Intent to Resist Arrest—*Offences Against the Person Act 1861, s. 38***

- Triable either way • Two years' imprisonment

The Offences Against the Person Act 1861, s. 38 states:

> Whosoever ... shall assault any person with intent to resist or prevent the lawful apprehension or detainer of himself or of any other person for any offence, shall be guilty of a misdemeanour ...

KEYNOTE

This is a crime of *specific intent* (see chapter 1.1). It must be shown that the defendant intended to resist or prevent a lawful arrest. It must also be shown that the defendant knew the arrest was lawful. Provided they were acting within their powers, this offence can apply to arrests made, not only by police officers, but also by store detectives, Benefits Agency staff and custody assistants. There are other specific offences created for the protection of court security officers and prisoner custody officers (not police officers) under the Criminal Justice Act 1991, ss. 78 and 90. If the person assaulted was assisting a police officer in the execution of his/her duty, the offence below may also apply.

Once the lawfulness of the arrest is established, the state of mind necessary for the above offence is an intention to resist/prevent that arrest, accompanied by knowledge that the person assaulted was trying to make or help in the arrest. It is irrelevant whether or not the person being arrested had actually committed an offence. These principles were set out recently by the Court of Appeal in a case where the defendant mistakenly believed that the arresting officers had no lawful power to do so. The Court held that such a mistaken belief does not provide a defendant with the defence of 'mistake' (see chapter 1.4). Similarly, a belief in one's own innocence, however genuine or honestly held, cannot afford a defence to a charge under s. 38 (*R* v *Lee* [2000] Crim LR 991).

1.7.3.3 Assaults on Police

There is an offence which deals specifically with assaults on police officers.

OFFENCE: **Assault Police—*Police Act 1996, s. 89***
- Triable summarily • Six months' imprisonment and/or a fine

The Police Act 1996, s. 89 states:

> (1) Any person who assaults a constable in the execution of his duty, or a person assisting a constable in the execution of his duty, shall be guilty of an offence...

KEYNOTE

It is critical to this offence that the officer was acting in the execution of his/her duty when assaulted. Given the almost infinite variety of situations that police officers may find themselves in, it is difficult to define the precise boundaries of the execution of their duty. There have been many instances of officers being assaulted after entering premises as technical 'trespassers' or not following statutory or common law requirements when stopping and questioning people. If it is not proved that the constable was in the execution of his/her duty then part of the *actus reus* will be missing. However, a court may infer from all the circumstances that an officer was in fact acting in the execution of his/her duty (*Plowden* v *DPP* [1991] Crim LR 850).

Where the assault is made in reaction to some form of physical act by the officer, it must be shown that the officer's act was not in itself unlawful. Two cases serve as good examples here. In the first, police officers attended a house to investigate a domestic incident. The defendant's female partner and her children told the officers they believed that if the defendant remained at the premises she might be subjected to violence by him. The officers tried to speak with the defendant but he ignored them. Despite warnings from the officers, the defendant refused to leave the premises and he was arrested to prevent a breach of the peace. During a subsequent struggle with the defendant one of the officers was injured. The defendant argued that the officers were wrong to believe that there was a risk of imminent or immediate violence and there was insufficient evidence for that belief. Dismissing the appeal, the Divisional Court held that the officers had to assess whether, by leaving the defendant in the house that night, there was a risk that his partner would be subjected to violence by him. In doing so there were matters that the officers had to consider such as the fact that the defendant had been drinking and it was reasonable for the officers to take into account the partner's fear of violence by him and the statements of her children. The officers were entitled to take into account the fact that the defendant had failed to respond to their requests to address the situation and had attempted to intimidate them. Therefore it had been reasonable in the circumstances of the case for the police to believe that a breach of the peace would be committed in the imminent future if the defendant remained at the premises and consequently his arrest had been lawful (*Wragg* v *DPP* [2005] EWHC 1389).

In the second case, the defendant was convicted of assaulting a police officer in the execution of his duty after the police had gone to her home address to arrest her son. The defendant followed her son into the police vehicle and refused to get out. She was given a warning and was verbally abusive, and only got out of the car when a second one arrived. She started to walk towards her house at which point a police officer took hold of her arms. The defendant bit the police officer on the arm and was prosecuted on the basis that the police officer had arrested her for a breach of the peace and that the assault had occurred in the execution of that duty. Allowing her appeal, the Divisional Court held that the defendant had exhibited nothing more than an aggressive manner and that, while her conduct may have given rise to an imminent threat of violence, there was no evidence to suggest that it involved any violence justifying the conclusion that she had actually committed a breach of the peace in the presence of the police officer. In the circumstances, her arrest had been unlawful and the conviction for assaulting a police officer in the execution of his duty could not stand (*R (On the Application of Hawkes)* v *DPP* [2005] EWHC 3046).

Although the common law complaint of breach of the peace still exists where appropriate (**see General Police Duties, chapter 4.6**) the question of the lawfulness of any arrest will become even more important to this offence in light of the re-wording of s. 24 of the Police and Criminal Evidence Act 1984. Other than the powers of arrest and detention (**see General Police Duties, chapter 4.4**), police officers have no general power to take hold of people in order to question them or keep them at a particular place while background enquiries are made about them. Therefore, if an officer does hold someone by the arm in order to question them without arresting them, there may well be a 'battery' by that officer (*Collins* v *Wilcock* [1984] 1 WLR 1172). The courts have accepted, however, that there may be occasions where a police officer is justified in taking hold of a person to attract their attention or to calm them down (*Mepstead* v *DPP* (1996) 160 JP 475).

However, where a prisoner is arrested and brought before a custody officer, that officer is entitled to assume that the arrest has been lawful. Therefore, if the prisoner goes on to assault the custody officer, that assault will nevertheless be an offence under s. 89(1) even if the original arrest turns out to have been unlawful (*DPP* v *L* [1999] Crim LR 752).

There is no need to show that the defendant knew—or suspected—that the person was in fact a police officer or that he/she was acting in the lawful execution of his/her duty (*Blackburn* v *Bowering* [1994] 1 WLR 1324). However, if the defendant claims to have been acting in self-defence under the mistaken and honestly held belief that he/she was being attacked, there may not be sufficient *mens rea* for a charge of assault (for defences of mistake generally, **see chapter 1.4**).

These offences are simply a form of common assault upon someone carrying out a lawful function. There is a further offence which deals with behaviour not amounting to an actual assault.

1.7.3.4 **Obstructing a Police Officer**

OFFENCE: **Obstruct Police—*Police Act 1996, s. 89***

> • Triable summarily • One month's imprisonment and/or a fine

The Police Act 1996, s. 89 states:

> (2) Any person who resists or wilfully obstructs a constable in the execution of his duty, or a person assisting a constable in the execution of his duty, shall be guilty of an offence...

KEYNOTE

Resistance suggests some form of physical opposition; obstruction does not and may take many forms. For instance, warning other drivers of a speed check operation (*Betts* v *Stevens* [1910] 1KB 1), providing misleading information (*Ledger* v *DPP* [1991] Crim LR 439), or deliberately drinking alcohol before providing breath specimen (*Ingleton* v *Dibble* [1972] 1 QB 480). Obstruction has been interpreted as making it more difficult for a constable to carry out his/her duty (*Hinchcliffe* v *Sheldon* [1955] 1 WLR 1207). Refusing to answer an officer's questions is not obstruction (*Rice* v *Connolly* [1966] 2 QB 414)—unless perhaps the defendant was under some duty to provide information. Any obstruction must be *wilful*, that is the defendant must intend to do it (see chapter 1.1). The obstruction will not be 'wilful' if the defendant was simply trying to help the police, even if that help turned out to be more of a hindrance (*Willmot* v *Atack* [1977] QB 498).

Obstruction can be caused by omission but only where the defendant was already under some duty towards the police or the officer. There is also a common law offence of refusing to go to the aid of a constable when asked to do so in order to prevent or diminish a breach of the peace (*R* v *Waugh* (1986) *The Times*, 1 October).

Tipping off people who were about to commit crime has been held to amount to obstruction (*Green* v *Moore* [1982] QB 1044), and some extreme forms of obstruction may amount to more serious offences such as perverting the course of justice or concealing offences (see chapter 1.14). There are also specific statutory offences of 'tipping off' in relation to money laundering and drug trafficking offences.

1.7.3.5 **Assault/Obstructing Designated or Accredited Persons**

OFFENCE: **Assaulting Designated or Accredited Person—*Police Reform Act 2002, s. 46(1)***

> • Triable summarily • Six months' imprisonment and/or a fine

The Police Reform Act 2002, s. 46 states:

> (1) Any person who assaults—
>   (a) a designated person in the execution of his duty,
>   (b) an accredited person in the execution of his duty, or
>   (c) a person assisting a designated or accredited person in the execution of his duty, is guilty of an offence...

KEYNOTE

This, and the following offence, relates to individuals who are designated or accredited under the provisions of the Police Reform Act 2002.

As with the corresponding offence against police officers (as to which, see para. 1.7.3.3) issues relating to the person's 'execution of duty' are paramount and particular care will need to be taken to prove that the relevant person had complied with all the applicable requirements as to wearing of uniform, badges and the production of their designation/accreditation (see General Police Duties, chapter 4.2). If a person is acting outside his/her powers as specifically designated or accredited, he/she will not have the protection of this offence. Also in common with the police offences, this offence (and the offence of obstruction below) applies to an assault on/wilful obstruction of someone who is helping the relevant officer.

Any acts causing more than minor or superficial injury may be dealt with under the general offences for assaults and woundings in this chapter. The fact that a victim was acting in the capacity of a designated/ accredited person (or assisting them) at the time would still be relevant when considering sentence.

There is a special offence regarding assaults etc. on members of international joint investigation teams working in a force area (see the Police Reform Act 2002, s. 104).

OFFENCE: **Obstructing Designated or Accredited Person—*Police Reform Act 2002, s. 46(2)***

- Triable summarily • One month's imprisonment and/or a fine

The Police Reform Act 2002, s. 46 states:

(2) Any person who resists or wilfully obstructs—
    (a) a designated person in the execution of his duty,
    (b) an accredited person in the execution of his duty, or
    (c) a person assisting a designated or accredited person in the execution of his duty, is guilty of an offence . . .

KEYNOTE

As with the previous offence, the important issue here will be proof that the relevant person was in fact acting in the execution of their duty. For a discussion of the ingredients needed in proving this offence in the context of the corresponding offence against police officers, see para. 1.7.3.3.

Again, if a person is acting outside his/her powers as specifically designated or accredited, he/she will not have the protection of this offence.

1.7.4 Assaults on Providers of Emergency Services

In light of the increase of assaults on emergency workers, the Emergency Workers (Obstruction) Act 2006 was passed. The Act is designed to offer protection to persons outside the police (to members of the Fire Brigade and staff of the NHS, for example) who face an increasing and unacceptable amount of violence simply by carrying out their functions.

1.7.4.1 Obstructing or Hindering Emergency Workers

OFFENCE: **Obstructing or Hindering Certain Emergency Workers Responding to Emergency Circumstances—*Emergency Workers (Obstruction) Act 2006, s. 1***

- Triable summarily • Fine

The Emergency Workers (Obstruction) Act 2006, s. 1 states:

(1) A person who without reasonable excuse obstructs or hinders another while that other person is, in a capacity mentioned in subsection (2) below, responding to emergency circumstances, commits an offence.

(2) The capacity referred to in subsection (1) above is—
    (a) that of a person employed by a fire and rescue authority in England and Wales;
    (b) in relation to England and Wales, that of a person (other than a person falling within paragraph (a)) whose duties as an employee or as a servant of the Crown involve—
        (i) extinguishing fires; or
        (ii) protecting life and property in the event of a fire;
    (c) that of a person employed by a relevant NHS body in the provision of ambulance services (including air ambulance services), or of a person providing such services pursuant to arrangements made by, or at the request of, a relevant NHS body;
    (d) that of a person providing services for the transport of organs, blood, equipment or personnel pursuant to arrangements made by, or at the request of, a relevant NHS body;
    (e) that of a member of Her Majesty's Coastguard;
    (f) that of a member of the crew of a vessel operated by—
        (i) the Royal National Lifeboat Institution, or
        (ii) any other person or organisation operating a vessel for the purpose of providing a rescue service,
    or a person who musters the crew of such a vessel or attends to its launch or recovery.

KEYNOTE

It should be noted that these offences not only cover a wide variety of occupations within the emergency services but also cover those individuals as they respond to 'emergency circumstances' by:

- going anywhere for the purpose of dealing with emergency circumstances occurring there; or
- dealing with emergency circumstances or preparing to do so.

(s. 1(3)(a) and (b) of the Act)

    Section 1(4) of the Act defines an 'emergency' circumstance as a present or imminent circumstance likely to cause:

  (i) serious injury to or the serious injury (including mental illness) of a person;

  (ii) serious harm to the environment (including the life and health of plants and animals);

(iii) serious harm to any building or other property; or

(iv) a worsening of any such injury, illness or harm;

or which is likely to cause the death of a person.

    'Relevant NHS body' means (in relation to England and Wales) an NHS foundation trust, NHS trust, Special Health Authority, Primary Care Trust or Local Health Board. In relation to Northern Ireland the same phrase means a Health and Social Services trust or a Health and Social Services Board.

1.7.4.2   Obstructing or Hindering Persons Assisting Emergency Workers

OFFENCE: **Obstructing or Hindering Persons Assisting Emergency Workers— *Emergency Workers (Obstruction) Act 2006, s. 2***

- Triable summarily • Fine

The Emergency Workers (Obstruction) Act 2006, s. 2 states:

(1) A person who without reasonable excuse obstructs or hinders another in the circumstances described in subsection (2) below commits an offence.

(2) Those circumstances are where the person being obstructed or hindered is assisting another while that person is, in a capacity mentioned in section 1(2) of this Act, responding to emergency circumstances.

KEYNOTE

Section 3(1) states that a person may be convicted of an offence under ss. 1 and 2 of the Act notwithstanding that the act is effected by means other than physical means or is effected by action directed only at any vehicle, vessel, apparatus, equipment or other thing or any animal used or to be used by a person referred to in that section.

For the purposes of ss. 1 and 2 of the Act, circumstances to which a person is responding are to be taken to be emergency circumstances if the person believes and has reasonable grounds for believing they are or may be emergency circumstances (s. 3(2)).

1.7.5 Threats to Kill

OFFENCE: **Making a Threat to Kill**—*Offences Against the Person Act 1861, s. 16*
- Triable either way • Ten years' imprisonment on indictment
- Six months' imprisonment and/or a fine summarily

The Offences Against the Person Act 1861, s. 16 (amended by Criminal Law Act 1977; s. 65, sch. 12) states:

A person who without lawful excuse makes to another a threat, intending that that other would fear it would be carried out, to kill that other or a third person shall be guilty of an offence . . .

KEYNOTE

The proviso that the threat must be made 'without lawful excuse' means that a person acting in self-defence or in the course of his/her duty in protecting life (e.g. an armed police officer) would not commit this offence (provided that his/her behaviour was 'lawful'; see chapter 1.4).

You must show that the threat was made (or implied (*R* v *Solanke* [1969] 3 All ER 1383)) with the intention that the person receiving it would fear that it would be carried out. It is the intention of the person who makes the threat which is important in this offence. It does not matter whether the person to whom the threat is made *does* fear that the threat would be carried out, or that the person whose life is threatened so fears (unless that person is the same person to whom the threat is made). The threat may be to kill another person at some time in the future or it may be an immediate threat, but the threatened action must be directly linked with the defendant. Simply passing on a threat on behalf of a third person would probably be insufficient for this offence.

1.7.6 Offences Involving Significant or Lasting Injury

If an assailant causes any significant or lasting injury then one of the following offences may apply.

These offences—and the injuries they cause—can be committed in many different ways, with or without weapons or implements. In relation to injuries brought about by driving motor vehicles, although there is a specific offence of dangerous driving (**see Road Policing, para. 3.2.3**) the Court of Appeal has held that there is nothing wrong in principle in charging a driver with causing grievous bodily harm (**see para. 1.7.6.2**) as well as dangerous driving in appropriate circumstances (*R* v *Bain* (2005) EWCA Crim 07). It follows that bringing about other forms of significant or lasting injury with a motor vehicle could be dealt with under the offences in this part of the chapter. However, in *Bain* it was held that where a driver was charged with both offences (causing grievous bodily harm and dangerous driving), a court could not impose consecutive terms of imprisonment for both offences arising out of the same incident.

1.7.6.1 Assault Occasioning Actual Bodily Harm

OFFENCE: **Assault Occasioning Actual Bodily Harm—*Offences Against the Person Act 1861, s. 47***

- Triable either way • Five years' imprisonment on indictment • Six months' imprisonment and/or a fine summarily

OFFENCE: **Racially or Religiously Aggravated—*Crime and Disorder Act 1998, s. 29(1)(b)***

- Triable either way • Seven years' imprisonment and/or a fine on indictment
- Six months' imprisonment and/or a fine summarily

The Offences Against the Person Act 1861, s. 47 states:

> Whosoever shall be convicted ... of any assault occasioning actual bodily harm shall be liable ... to be kept in penal servitude ...

KEYNOTE

It must be shown that 'actual bodily harm' was a consequence, directly or indirectly, of the defendant's actions. Such harm can include shock (*R* v *Miller* [1954] 2 QB 282) and mental 'injury' (*R* v *Chan-Fook* [1994] 1 WLR 689).

So what is 'actual bodily harm'? In *DPP* v *Smith* [1961] AC 290, it was noted that the expression needed 'no explanation' and, in *Chan-Fook*, the court advised that the phrase consisted of 'three words of the English language which require no elaboration and in the ordinary course should not receive any. While the phrase 'bodily harm' has its ordinary meaning, it has been said to include any hurt calculated to interfere with the health or comfort of the victim: such hurt need not be permanent, but must be more than transient and trifling (*R* v *Donovan* [1934] 25 Cr App Rep 1, CCA).

The Administrative Court has accepted that a momentary loss of consciousness caused by a kick but without any physical injury can be 'actual harm' because it involved an injurious impairment of the victim's sensory abilities which did not fall within the 'trifling' category described in *Donovan* above (see *T* v *DPP* [2003] Crim LR 622).

For a discussion of the relevant *mens rea* for this offence, see para. 1.7.2.5. The state of mind required is the same as that for an assault or battery.

In an interesting decision the Divisional Court accepted that the cutting of a person's hair against their will could amount to actual bodily harm (*DPP* v *Smith (Ross Michael)* [2006] EWHC 94). In *Smith* the defendant cut off his ex-partner's ponytail, deliberately and without her permission. The court held that, even though medically and scientifically speaking, the hair above the surface of the scalp is no more than dead tissue, it remains part of the body and is attached to it. While it is so attached, it falls within the meaning of 'bodily' in the phrase 'actual bodily harm' as it is concerned with the body of the individual victim. Therefore the same would be true of fingernails.

Futher examples of what will amount to 'actual bodily harm' can be found in the CPS Charging Standards and include:

- Loss or breaking of teeth

- Temporary loss of sensory functions, which may include loss of consciousness (*T* v *Director of Public Prosecutions* [2003] EWHC 266 (Admin))
- Extensive or multiple bruising
- Displaced broken nose
- Minor fractures
- Minor but not merely superficial, cuts of a sort probably requiring medical treatment (e.g. stitches)
- Psychiatric injury that is more than merely emotions such as fear, distress or panic.

Where psychiatric injury is relied upon as the basis for an allegation of assault occasioning actual bodily harm, and the matter is not admitted by the defence, then expert evidence must be called by the prosecution (*R* v *Chan-Fook* [1994] 1 WLR 689).

As with common assault, this offence was deemed by the legislators to be one where it was necessary to increase the maximum penalty available to the courts if it was committed under racially aggravated circumstances (see Crime and Disorder Act 1998, s. 29(1)(b)).

1.7.6.2 Wounding or Inflicting Grievous Bodily Harm

OFFENCE: **Wounding or Inflicting Grievous Bodily Harm—*Offences Against the Person Act 1861, s. 20***
- Triable either way • Five years' imprisonment on indictment
- Six months' imprisonment and/or a fine summarily

OFFENCE: **Racially or Religiously Aggravated—*Crime and Disorder Act 1998, s. 29(1)(a)***
- Triable either way • Seven years' imprisonment and/or a fine on indictment
- Six months' imprisonment and/or a fine summarily

The Offences Against the Person Act 1861, s. 20 states:

> Whosoever shall unlawfully and maliciously wound or inflict any grievous bodily harm upon any other person, either with or without any weapon or instrument, shall be guilty of a misdemeanour ...

KEYNOTE

Wounding means the breaking of the continuity of the whole of the outer skin, or the inner skin within the cheek or lip. A cut which goes right through all the layers of a person's skin, whether caused externally (e.g. a knife wound) or internally (e.g. a punch causing a tooth to puncture the cheek), will amount to a wound. It does not include the rupturing of internal blood vessels.

The definition of wounding may encompass injuries that are relatively minor in nature, for example a small cut or laceration. An assault resulting in such minor injuries should more appropriately be charged contrary to s. 47 of the Act. An assault contrary to s. 20 should be reserved for the type of wounds considered to be serious (thus equating the offence with the infliction of grievous, or serious, bodily harm).

The word 'inflict' has caused problems in the past. However, the House of Lords in *R* v *Ireland* [1998] AC 147 has made it clear that no 'assault' (see para. 1.7.2.2) is needed for this offence and that harm could be 'inflicted' indirectly (in this case by menacing telephone calls inflicting psychiatric harm). Therefore there is now little if any difference between inflicting harm and 'causing' harm (see para. 1.7.6.3). It should be enough to show that the defendant's behaviour brought about the resulting harm to the victim.

There have also been many judicial attempts at defining grievous bodily harm. In *R* v *Saunders* [1985] Crim LR 230 it was held that the expression meant 'serious or really serious harm'. This harm will now include psychiatric harm (*Ireland*). Examples of what will amount to 'grievous bodily harm' can be found in the CPS Charging Standards and include:

- injury resulting in some permanent disability or visible disfigurement
- broken or displaced limbs or bones
- injuries requiring blood transfusion or lengthy treatment.

Following the well-publicised case of Mohammed Dica in 2003, there was an acceptance that the deliberate infection of another with the HIV virus could amount to grievous bodily harm—although there were still significant difficulties with regard to 'consent' if the infection had taken place as a result of consensual sexual activity. This issue was explored further by the Court of Appeal in *R* v *Konzani* [2005] EWCA Crim 706. In that case the defendant appealed against convictions for inflicting grievous bodily harm on three women contrary to s. 20 above. The defendant had unprotected consensual sexual intercourse with the women, but without having disclosed that he was HIV positive. The women subsequently contracted the HIV virus. In hearing the appeals, the Court held that there was a critical distinction between taking a risk as to the various potentially adverse (and possibly problematic) consequences of unprotected consensual intercourse, and the giving of informed consent *to the risk of infection with a fatal disease*. Before consent to the risk of contracting HIV could provide a defence, that consent had to be an *informed* consent in this latter sense (see *R* v *Dica* [2004] EWCA Crim 1103). Therefore, simply having an honestly held belief that the other person was consenting would only help if that consent would itself have provided a defence to the passing of the infection.

This approach was confirmed in *R* v *B* (2006) (unreported) where the Court of Appeal stated that, while a defendant's condition (being HIV positive) was immaterial in relation to the consent issue in an offence of rape, the defendant would have no defence to the harm created by the sexual activity merely by virtue of that consent, as the consent related to the sexual activity and not to the disease.

'Maliciously'—although the word maliciously suggests some form of evil premeditation, 'malice' here amounts to subjective recklessness (**see chapter 1.1**). It means that the defendant must realise that there is a risk of some harm being caused to the victim. The defendant does not need to foresee the degree of harm which is eventually caused, only that his/her behaviour may bring about some harm to the victim.

1.7.6.3 Wounding or Causing Grievous Bodily Harm with Intent

OFFENCE: **Wounding or Causing Grievous Bodily Harm with Intent—*Offences Against the Person Act 1861, s. 18***

- Triable on indictment only • Life imprisonment

The Offences Against the Person Act 1861, s. 18 states:

> Whosoever shall unlawfully and maliciously by any means whatsoever wound or cause any grievous bodily harm to any person with intent to do some grievous bodily harm to any person, or with intent to resist or prevent the lawful apprehension or detainer of any person, shall be guilty of felony ...

KEYNOTE

This is a crime of *specific intent* (**see chapter 1.1**). Although there are similarities with the offence under s. 20 (see above), you must show the appropriate *intent* (e.g. to do grievous bodily harm to *anyone* or to resist/prevent the lawful apprehension/detention of *anyone*); recklessness and foresight are not sufficient. Factors that may indicate such a specific intent include:

- a repeated or planned attack

- deliberate selection of a weapon or adaptation of an article to cause injury, such as breaking a glass before an attack
- making prior threats
- using an offensive weapon against, or kicking a victim's head.

Where the intent was to cause grievous bodily harm, the issue of 'malice' will not arise. However, where the intent was to resist or prevent the lawful arrest of someone, the element of maliciousness as set out above (see para. 1.7.6.2) will need to be proved. The word 'cause', together with the expression 'by any means whatsoever', seems to give this offence a wider meaning than s. 20. However, the increasingly broad interpretation of the s. 20 offence means that there is little difference in the *actus reus* needed for either offence.

The provisions of ss. 28 and 29 of the Crime and Disorder Act 1998 in relation to racially or religiously aggravated assaults do not apply to this offence as it was felt by the legislators that there was nothing to be gained by creating a special offence, given that the maximum sentence available is already life imprisonment. However, the courts must still take notice of any element of racial or religious aggravation when determining sentence (s. 153 of the Powers of Criminal Courts (Sentencing) Act 2000).

Miscellaneous Offences Against the Person

1.8.1 Introduction

In addition to the relatively common offences examined in the previous chapter, there are further offences against the person that, while not as prevalent, are nevertheless important.

1.8.2 Torture

OFFENCE: **Torture—*Criminal Justice Act 1988, s. 134***
- Triable on indictment • Life imprisonment

The Criminal Justice Act 1988, s. 134 states:

(1) A public official or person acting in an official capacity, whatever his nationality, commits the offence of torture if in the United Kingdom or elsewhere he intentionally inflicts severe pain or suffering on another in the performance or purported performance of his official duties.

(2) A person not falling within subsection (1) above commits the offence of torture, whatever his nationality, if—

(a) in the United Kingdom or elsewhere he intentionally inflicts severe pain or suffering on another at the instigation or with the consent or acquiescence—
  (i) of a public official; or
  (ii) of a person acting in an official capacity; and
(b) the official or other person is performing or purporting to perform his official duties when he instigates the commission of the offence or consents to or acquiesces in it.

(3) It is immaterial whether the pain or suffering is physical or mental or whether is caused by an act or an omission.

KEYNOTE

The consent of the Attorney-General (or Solicitor-General) is needed before bringing a prosecution under s. 134. This offence, although it sounds quite extreme, could be committed by a police officer in the course of his/her duties, and may have significant implications for Custody Officers.

Although the offence has a statutory defence of 'lawful authority, justification or excuse' (see below), Article 3 of the European Convention on Human Rights contains an absolute prohibition on torture. Irrespective of the prevailing circumstances, there can be no derogation from an individual's absolute right under Article 3 to freedom from torture, inhuman or degrading treatment or punishment.

These three features have been identified as having the following broad characteristics:

- Torture—deliberate treatment leading to serious or cruel suffering.
- Inhuman treatment—treatment resulting in intense suffering, both physical and mental.

- Degrading treatment—treatment giving rise to fear and anguish in the victim, causing feelings of inferiority and humiliation.

(See *Ireland* v *United Kingdom* (1974–1980) 2 EHRR 25.)

It has been held by the European Commission of Human Rights that causing mental anguish without any physical assault could be a violation of Article 3 (*see Denmark* v *Greece* (1969) 12 YB Eur Conv HR special Vol.).

Article 3 does not only prohibit the deliberate application of pain and suffering, but also a range of other behaviour. Oppressive interrogation techniques such as sleep deprivation, exposure to continuous loud noise and forcing suspects to adopt uncomfortable postures for prolonged lengths of time have been held to fall within the second and third categories of inhuman and degrading treatment (*Ireland* v *United Kingdom*).

In each case, it must be shown that the prohibited behaviour went beyond the 'minimum level of severity'. In determining whether the behaviour did go beyond that level, and under which particular category that behaviour falls, the courts will take into account factors such as the age, sex, state of health and general life experience of the victim. 'Severe pain or suffering' can be mental as well as physical and can be caused by omission.

1.8.2.1 Defence

The Criminal Justice Act 1988, s. 134 states:

(4) It shall be a defence for a person charged with an offence under this section in respect of any conduct of his to prove that he had lawful authority, justification or excuse for that conduct.

1.8.3 Poisoning

OFFENCE: **Poisoning—*Offences Against the Person Act 1861, s. 23***
- Triable on indictment • Ten years' imprisonment

The Offences Against the Person Act 1861, s. 23 states:

Whosoever shall unlawfully and maliciously administer to or cause to be administered to or taken by any other person any poison or other destructive or noxious thing, so as thereby to endanger the life of such person, or so as thereby to inflict upon such person any grievous bodily harm, shall be guilty of [an offence]...

KEYNOTE

Other than the requirement for 'malice', this offence is mainly concerned with the consequences caused to the victim and not the defendant's intentions.

'Causing to be administered' would cover indirect poisoning or even inducing someone to poison themselves. 'Administering' is a very broad term which has been held to include the spraying of gas into another's face (*R* v *Gillard* (1988) 87 Cr App R 189). As such this would appear to include the use of CS spray by police officers but the 'administering' would also have to be shown to be both unlawful and malicious.

Whether a substance is poisonous, destructive or noxious will depend on both its quality and quantity. Some substances may become poisonous or noxious only in large amounts whereas others may be so *per se*.

This offence would certainly cover the administering of a controlled drug to another or inducing another to take a controlled drug.

There is a requirement to prove a consequence with this offence, namely the endangering of a person's life or the infliction of grievous bodily harm.

1.8.3.1 Poisoning with Intent

OFFENCE: **Poisoning with Intent—*Offences Against the Person Act 1861, s. 24***
• Triable on indictment • Five years' imprisonment

The Offences Against the Person Act 1861, s. 24 states:

Whosoever shall unlawfully and maliciously administer to or cause to be administered to or taken by any other person any poison or other destructive or noxious thing, with intent to injure, aggrieve, or annoy any such person, shall be guilty of a misdemeanour...

KEYNOTE

Unlike the previous offence under s. 23, there is no requirement as to the actual consequences of a defendant's actions under s. 24 and this offence is concerned with the defendant's intentions.

This is an offence of *specific intent* which means that recklessness will not suffice and that self-induced intoxication may provide a defence (see chapters 1.1 and 1.4).

There is a further, more extreme offence of using noxious substances to cause harm or intimidation under the Anti-terrorism, Crime and Security Act 2001, s. 113. This offence, which carries 14 years' imprisonment on indictment, occurs where a person takes any action which:

• involves the use of a noxious substance or other noxious thing;
• has or is likely to have an effect set out below; and
• is designed to influence the government or to intimidate the public or a section of the public.

The effects are:

• causing serious violence against a person, or serious damage to property, anywhere in the world;
• endangering human life or creating a serious risk to the health or safety of the public or a section of the public; or
• inducing in members of the public the fear that the action is likely to endanger their lives or create a serious risk to their health or safety.

Clearly the recent concerns over terrorist activity have greatly increased the relevance of this piece of legislation to policing.

1.8.4 False Imprisonment

OFFENCE: **False Imprisonment—*Common Law***
• Triable on indictment • Unlimited maximum penalty

It is an offence at common law falsely to imprison another person.

KEYNOTE

This offence is the first in an ascending order of aggravated offences against the person and is more usually dealt with under civil law or as kidnapping/abduction (see below).

These offences, although relatively uncommon, have become particularly relevant with the introduction of a specific offence of committing a criminal offence with intent to commit a relevant sexual offence (as to which see chapter 1.9).

The elements required for this offence are the unlawful and intentional/reckless restraint of a person's freedom of movement (*R* v *Rahman* (1985) 81 Cr App R 349). Locking someone in a vehicle or keeping them in a particular place for however short a time may amount to false imprisonment if done unlawfully. An unlawful arrest may amount to such an offence (see General Police Duties, chapter 4.4) and it is not uncommon for such an allegation to be levelled at police officers against whom a public complaint has been made.

The state of mind required to prove this offence is 'subjective' recklessness (*R* v *James* (1997) *The Times*, 2 October). (For a discussion of this concept, see chapter 1.1.)

1.8.5 Kidnapping

OFFENCE: **Kidnapping—*Common Law***

- Triable on indictment • Unlimited maximum penalty

It is an offence at common law to take or carry away another person without the consent of that person and without lawful excuse.

KEYNOTE

Kidnapping is the second of the aggravated offences described above. The required elements of this offence are the unlawful taking or carrying away of one person by another by force or fraud (*R* v *D* [1984] AC 778). These requirements go beyond those of mere restraint needed for false imprisonment. Parents may be acting without lawful excuse, for instance, if they are acting in breach of a court order in respect of their children (see chapter 1.10).

The taking or carrying away of the victim must be without the consent of the victim. If the victim consents to an initial taking but later withdraws that consent, the offence would be complete. If the consent is obtained by fraud, the defendant cannot rely on that consent and the offence—or attempted offence—will be made out (see *R* v *Cort* [2003] 3 WLR 1300). If the victim is a child, the consent will probably be that of the parents but the more appropriate charge in such a case may be one under the Child Abduction Act 1984 (see chapter 1.10).

The state of mind required for this offence appears to be the same as that for false imprisonment, indeed the only thing separating the two offences seems to be *actus reus* (*R* v *Hutchins* [1988] Crim LR 379). For *actus reus* generally, see chapter 1.2.

1.8.6 Hostage Taking

OFFENCE: **Hostage Taking—*Taking of Hostages Act 1982, s. 1***

- Triable on indictment • Life imprisonment

The Taking of Hostages Act 1982, s. 1 states:

(1) A person, whatever his nationality, who, in the United Kingdom or elsewhere—
   (a) detains any other person ('the hostage'), and
   (b) in order to compel a State, international governmental organisation, or person to do or abstain from doing any act, threatens to kill, injure or continue to detain the hostage, commits an offence.

KEYNOTE

The consent of the Attorney-General (or Solicitor-General) is needed before bringing a prosecution for this, the third aggravated offence. To be guilty, a defendant must detain a person *and* threaten to kill, injure or continue to detain them with the intentions outlined under s. 1(1)(b). It is therefore an offence of 'ulterior' or 'specific' intent (see chapter 1.1).

1.8.7 False Imprisonment, Kidnapping and Hostage Taking Compared

To summarise:

- Detaining someone without any lawful authority can amount to false imprisonment. The detention or restraint may be committed recklessly.
- Taking or carrying someone away without any lawful authority or without the person's consent can amount to kidnapping. Again this may be done 'recklessly'.
- Detaining a person (with or without authority) in order to compel a State, governmental organisation or person to do/not to do something will be hostage taking if it is accompanied by the relevant threats. This offence cannot be committed by recklessness and requires proof of the requisite intent.

In any of these cases the overall motive of the defendant or the wider consequences of the offence may bring it within the category of 'terrorism' (as to which, **see General Police Duties, chapter 4.6**). These areas of law have become more relevant to police officers, not only as a result of the increased threat of terrorist activity, but also in the totally separate area of 'forced marriage'.

1.9 | Sexual Offences

1.9.1 Introduction

Sexual offences represent a particularly important area of criminal law for two main reasons: the sensitivity required in their investigation and prosecution and their potential effect on the victim. Such offences can cause significant emotional harm to the victim, harm which may take far longer to 'heal' than many physical injuries. For that reason, together with the growth in the range of legal provisions that have been created to tackle the behaviour of sex offenders, sexual offences have been addressed in this separate chapter.

It is important to note that there is overlap between many of the offences, for example a mentally disordered person could be raped under s. 1 (because of his/her lack of ability to give true consent) or subjected to sexual activity contrary to s. 30 (due to an inability to refuse). In all circumstances it is essential that the most appropriate option is chosen.

1.9.1.1 Human Rights Considerations

A factor affecting this area of criminal law is the relevance of the European Convention on Human Rights. It is clear that sexual activities are aspects of a person's 'private life' as protected by Article 8 of the Convention (see *Dudgeon* v *United Kingdom* (1981) 4 EHRR 149 and *ADT* v *United Kingdom* [2000] Crim LR 1009). This concept applies to homosexual and heterosexual relationships (*X* v *United Kingdom* (1997) 24 EHRR 143).

Any attempt by the criminal law to place restrictions on the consensual sexual activities of individuals has to be considered very carefully in light of the Human Rights Act 1998.

The Sexual Offences Act 2003 and its compatibility with the ECHR were considered in *R* v *G & Secretary of State for the Home Department* [2006] EWCA Crim 821. The Court of Appeal held that the imposition of strict liability in relation to the offence under s. 5 of the Act (rape of a child under 13) did not infringe ECHR, Article 6.2 (presumption of innocence).

1.9.1.2 Anonymity

Under the Sexual Offences (Amendment) Act 1992, victims of most sexual offences (including rape, incest, and indecency with children) are entitled to anonymity throughout their lifetime. This means that there are restrictions on the way in which trials and cases may be reported and the courts have powers to enforce these provisions. Further protection preventing victims from cross-examination by their alleged attackers is provided by the Youth Justice and Criminal Evidence Act 1999. The 1999 Act also imposes restrictions on the introduction of evidence in most of the sexual offences covered in this chapter.

1.9.2   **The Sexual Offences Act 2003**

The Sexual Offences Act creates a whole series of sexual offences and sets out the elements that will be needed in proving the relevant offences and also introduces some further practical measures such as the presumptions about consent that will be made by a court under certain circumstances. Some of these are considered later in this chapter. The Act is very clear in its drafting and brings some much needed clarity to this area of criminal law, borrowing its style from other legislation. In many of the mainstream offences it creates, the Act uses the approach of describing actions of a hypothetical offender 'A' towards the victim 'B'. This approach has generally worked well in discrimination legislation.

The Act has some recurring themes and terms; in order to understand—and prove—many of the offences set out in the Act, it is necessary to understand some of the themes and terms first.

1.9.2.1   **The Definition of 'Sexual'**

This is an important concept in the statutory framework. Some activities carried out in order to gain sexual gratification are difficult to classify—and certainly to prove—as 'sexual' in the ordinary meaning of the word. Fetishes in particular—for things such as feet and shoes—have caused difficulties in this regard.

What a Reasonable Person would Consider

Therefore the Act abandons the notion of indecency, preferring the definition 'sexual' and setting out what activity will be sexual for the purposes of the relevant offences.

Section 78 provides that penetration, touching or any other activity will be sexual if a reasonable person would consider that:

(a) whatever its circumstances or any person's purpose in relation to it, it is sexual by its very nature or,

(b) because of its nature it *may* be sexual and because of its circumstances or the purpose of any person in relation to it, it is sexual.

Therefore, activity under (a) covers things that a reasonable person would always consider to be sexual (for example, masturbation), while activity under (b) covers things that may or may not be considered sexual by a reasonable person depending on the circumstances or the intentions of the person carrying it out (or both). For instance, a doctor inserting a finger into a vagina might be sexual under certain circumstances, but if done for a purely medical purpose in a hospital, it would not be.

If the activity would not appear to a reasonable person to be sexual, then it will not meet either criteria and, irrespective of any sexual gratification the person might derive from it, the activity will not be 'sexual'. Therefore weird or exotic fetishes that no ordinary person would regard as being sexual or potentially sexual will not be covered. This pretty well follows the common law developments in this area (see for example *R* v *Court* [1989] AC 28 and *R* v *Tabassum* [2000] Crim LR 686).

1.9.2.2   **The Definition of 'Touching'**

This activity is relevant to a number of specific offences. Section 79(8) states that touching includes touching:

• with any part of the body

- with anything else
- through anything

and in particular, touching amounting to penetration.

'Touching' for the purposes of an offence under s. 3 (**see para. 1.9.4.2**) includes the touching of a victim's clothing. This is clear from the Court of Appeal's decision in *R* v *H* (2005) *The Times*, 8 February. There it was held that it was not Parliament's intention to preclude the touching of a victim's clothing from amounting to a sexual 'assault'. Where touching was not automatically by its nature 'sexual' the test under s. 78(b) applies (**see para. 1.9.2.1**). In a case where that section applies it will be appropriate for a trial judge to ask the jury to determine whether touching was 'sexual' by answering two questions. First, would the jury, as 12 reasonable people, consider that the touching could be sexual and, if so, whether in all the circumstances of the case, they would consider that the purpose of the touching *had in fact been* sexual.

1.9.3 Rape

OFFENCE: **Rape—*Sexual Offences Act 2003, s.1***
- Triable on indictment • Life imprisonment

The Sexual Offences Act 2003, s. 1 states:

(1) A person (A) commits an offence if—
  (a) he intentionally penetrates the vagina, anus or mouth of another person (B) with his penis,
  (b) B does not consent to the penetration, and
  (c) A does not reasonably believe that B consents

KEYNOTE

Rape is an offence that can *only* be committed via the use of the penis. It can be committed if the defendant penetrates the vagina, anus or mouth of the victim with the penis.

Consent is a key aspect of rape. In proving rape you must show that the victim did not in fact consent at the time and that the defendant did not reasonably believe that s/he consented. The wording is supported by the further provision that whether or not the defendant's belief is reasonable will be determined having regard to all the circumstances (s. 1(2)). Both this, and the aspects of the criminal conduct required to prove rape are considered in greater detail below.

Sections 75 and 76 apply to this offence (**see paras 1.9.3.3 and 1.9.3.4**).

If the victim is a child under 13, you simply have to prove intentional penetration and the child's age. No issue of 'consent' arises and a specific offence under s. 5 is committed.

Section 103(2)(b) of the Criminal Justice Act 2003 provides that a defendant's propensity to commit offences of the kind with which he/she is charged may (without prejudice to any other way of doing so) be established by evidence that he/she has been convicted of an offence of 'the same category'. An offence under s. 1, if committed in relation to a person under the age of 16, or under s. 5 (including aiding, abetting, counselling, procuring, inciting or attempting the commission of such an offence) falls within the relevant sexual offences category (see the Criminal Justice Act 2003 (Categories of Offences) Order 2004 (SI 3346/2004)). Many of the other offences that follow in this chapter, along with their predecessors under earlier legislation, are also covered and will fall within the relevant sexual offences category. For a further discussion of this highly controversial legislation **see Evidence and Procedure**.

1.9.3.1 Criminal Conduct

To prove rape you must show that the defendant penetrated the vagina, mouth or anus of the victim. It should be noted that penetration is a continuing act from entry to withdrawal (s. 79(2)). The 'continuing' nature of this act is of practical importance when considering the issue of consent and the statutory presumptions (see below). While it is not necessary to prove ejaculation, clearly the presence of semen or sperm is important in proving the elements of a sexual offence, as is other scientific evidence recovered from the victim, the offender and the scene etc. References to a part of the body (for example, penis, vagina) will include references to a body part which has been surgically constructed, particularly if it is through gender reassignment (s. 79(3)).

1.9.3.2 Consent

The issue of consent is a question of fact and is critical to proving the offence of rape. It is also potentially the most difficult aspect of the offence to prove and that is why the legislation has included some specific sections raising presumptions and conclusions in certain circumstances. Whereas an act of intercourse or physical intimacy may be proved or corroborated by forensic evidence, the true wishes of the victim at the time of the offence are much more difficult to prove beyond a reasonable doubt. Any consent given must be 'true' consent, not simply a *submission* induced by fear or fraud. Some people however are not capable of giving the required consent—these are generally addressed in the following chapter.

The starting point in examining consent is s. 74 which states that a person consents if he or she agrees by choice and has the freedom and capacity to make that choice. Therefore, if the person does not have any real choice in the matter, or their choice is not a genuine exercise of their free will, then they have not 'consented'.

In *R* v *B* (2006) (unreported) the Court of Appeal stated that whether an individual had a sexual disease or condition, such as being HIV positive, was not an issue as far as consent was concerned. The case related to a man who was alleged to have raped a woman after they had met outside a nightclub in the early hours of the morning. When arrested, the man informed the custody officer that he was HIV positive, a fact he had not disclosed to the victim prior to sexual intercourse. At the original trial, the judge directed that this non-disclosure was relevant to the issue of consent. On appeal the court stated that this was not the case and that the consent issue for a jury to consider was whether or not the victim consented to sexual intercourse, not whether she consented to sexual intercourse with a person suffering from a sexually transmitted disease.

The next key considerations in relation to consent are the important provisions set out at ss. 75 and 76. These are presumptions about consent and can be divided into *evidential* presumptions and *conclusive* presumptions. They are of considerable practical significance in evidence gathering and interviewing suspects.

1.9.3.3 Section 75—Evidential Presumptions and Consent

The Sexual Offences Act 2003, s. 75 states:

(1) If in proceedings for an offence to which this section applies it is proved—
    (a) that the defendant did the relevant act,
    (b) that any of the circumstances specified in subsection (2) existed, and
    (c) that the defendant knew that those circumstances existed,
    the complainant is to be taken not to have consented to the relevant act unless sufficient evidence is adduced to raise an issue as to whether he consented, and the defendant is to be taken

not to have reasonably believed that the complainant consented unless sufficient evidence is adduced to raise an issue as to whether he reasonably believed it.

KEYNOTE

This means that, if the prosecution can show that the defendant carried out the relevant act in relation to certain specified sexual offences (for example, penetration in rape) and that any of the circumstances below existed and the defendant knew they existed, it will be presumed that the victim did not consent. Then the defendant will have to satisfy the court, by reference to evidence, that this presumption should not be made.

The circumstances are that:

(a) *any person* was, at the time of the relevant act (or immediately before it began), using violence against *the complainant* or causing *the complainant* to fear that immediate violence would be used against him/her;

(b) *any person* was, at the time of the relevant act or immediately before it began, causing *the complainant* to fear that violence was being used, or that immediate violence would be used, against *another person*;

(c) *the complainant* was, and the defendant was not, unlawfully detained at the time of the relevant act;

(d) *the complainant* was asleep or otherwise unconscious at the time of the relevant act;

(e) because of *the complainant's* physical disability, *the complainant* would not have been able at the time of the relevant act to communicate to the defendant whether the complainant consented;

(f) *any person* had administered to or caused to be taken by the complainant, without the complainant's consent, a substance which, having regard to when it was administered or taken, was capable of causing or enabling the complainant to be stupefied or overpowered at the time of the relevant act.

It can be seen that these conditions cover a range of circumstances, including the use or threat of violence by any person (not just the defendant) against the victim of the sexual offence and circumstances where the victim was asleep or had been drugged.

The 'relevant act' for each offence covered by s. 75 will generally be obvious but is set out specifically at s. 77. The use of the term 'sufficient evidence' is a new feature in criminal legislation and comes about as a result of the Human Rights Act 1998 and Article 6(2) of the European Convention on Human Rights. Provisions where the burden to adduce 'sufficient evidence' is on the defendant, as in s. 75(1), may not breach Art. 6 provided the public interest is sufficient to warrant it (for example, *R v Lambert* [2001] 3 WLR 206; *Attorney-General's Reference (No. 4 of 2002)* [2003] HRLR 15). In the case of rape there are strong public interest and policy considerations to support this presumption.

1.9.3.4 Conclusive Presumptions about Consent

Section 76 of the Sexual Offences Act 2003 states that, if it is proved in some sexual offences (listed in s. 77) that the defendant did the relevant act and that he/she:

(a) intentionally deceived the complainant as to the nature or purpose of the relevant act or

(b) intentionally induced the complainant to consent to the relevant act by impersonating a person known personally to the complainant,

there will be a *conclusive* presumption both that the victim did not consent and also that the defendant did not believe she or he consented.

These provisions deal with the problems where the defendant either misrepresents the nature or purpose of what he or she is doing (for example, pretending that inserting a finger into the victim's vagina is for medical reasons) or impersonates the victim's partner. Section 76 requires that a misunderstanding was created by the defendant and that it was done deliberately. Once it is proved, beyond a reasonable doubt, that these circumstances existed then it is conclusive and the defendant cannot argue against them.

As with s. 75, the 'relevant act' for each offence covered by s. 76 will generally be obvious but is set out specifically at s. 77.

Even if freely given, consent may still be withdrawn at any time. Once the 'passive' party to sexual penetration withdraws consent, any continued activity (for example, penetration in rape—*R* v *Cooper* [1994] Crim LR 531) can amount to a sexual offence provided all the other ingredients are present.

1.9.4 Sexual Assault

There are several specific, accurate and easy to prove offences: these are discussed below.

1.9.4.1 Assault by Penetration

OFFENCE: **Assault by Penetration—*Sexual Offences Act 2003, s. 2***
- Triable on indictment • Life imprisonment

The Sexual Offences Act 2003, s. 2 states:

(1) A person (A) commits an offence if—
   (a) he intentionally penetrates the vagina or anus of another person (B) with a part of his body or anything else,
   (b) the penetration is sexual,
   (c) B does not consent to the penetration, and
   (d) A does not reasonably believe that B consents.

KEYNOTE

As with all the offences in the Sexual Offences Act 2003 except rape, this offence can be committed by a male or a female against a male or female.

While the offence of rape considered in **para. 1.9.3** above involves penetration by the penis, this offence involves penetration by any part of the body or anything else whatsoever. It is therefore a very broad offence covering insertion into the vagina or anus (though not the mouth) of *anything*, provided that the penetration is 'sexual' (**see para. 1.9.2.1**). Penetration must be intentional, made without the consent of the victim and you must show that the defendant did not reasonably believe that the victim did consent. Whether a belief is reasonable is to be determined having regard to all the circumstances, including any steps the defendant has taken to ascertain whether the victim consents (s. 2(2)).

The introduction of the series of sexual offences under the 2003 Act has raised some questions as to the extent to which they mirror or replace similar offences under the former regime. The Court of Appeal has held that, so far as the above offence is concerned, its introduction attracting a potential sentence of life imprisonment means that it must be dealt with at a higher level than the previous generic offence of indecent assault. The ingredient of penetration has always been regarded by the law as being particularly serious and the starting point in s. 2 offences for sentencing ought to be in the region of four years (*Attorney-General's Reference (No. 104 of 2004)* [2004] EWCA Crim 2672).

Sections 75 and 76 apply to this offence (**see paras 1.9.3.3 and 1.9.3.4**).

If the victim is a child under 13, you simply have to prove intentional, sexual penetration and the child's age. No issue of 'consent' arises and a specific offence under s. 6 is committed.

An offence under s. 2 if committed in relation to a person under the age of 16 or under s. 6 (including aiding, abetting, counselling, procuring, inciting or attempting the commission of such an offence) falls within the relevant sexual offences category for the purposes of s. 103(2)(b) of the Criminal Justice Act 2003 (a defendant's propensity to commit offences of the kind with which he/she is charged—**see para. 1.9.3**).

1.9.4.2 Sexual Assault by Touching

OFFENCE: **Sexual Touching—*Sexual Offences Act 2003, s. 3***

> • Triable either way • If victim is child under 13—fourteen years' imprisonment; otherwise ten years' imprisonment on indictment • Six months' imprisonment summarily

The Sexual Offences Act 2003, s. 3 states:

(1) A person (A) commits an offence if—
    (a) he intentionally touches another person (B),
    (b) the touching is sexual,
    (c) B does not consent to the touching, and
    (d) A does not reasonably believe that B consents.

KEYNOTE

The part of the body touched does not have to be a sexual organ or orifice. Touching for the purposes of the above offence includes touching a person's clothing. Therefore, where a man approached a woman and asked '*Do you fancy a shag?*', grabbing at a pocket on her tracksuit bottoms as she tried to walk away, he was properly convicted of the s. 3 offence (*R* v *H* (2005) *The Times*, 8 February).

As with the offence under s. 2, you need to prove that the conduct was intentional (rather than accidental), that it was sexual (**see para. 1.9.2.1**) that the victim did not consent and that the defendant did not reasonably believe that the victim consented.

Whether a belief is reasonable is to be determined having regard to all the circumstances, including any steps the defendant has taken to ascertain whether the victim consents (s. 3(2)).

Sections 75 and 76 apply to this offence (**see paras 1.9.3.3 and 1.9.3.4**).

If the victim is a child under 13, you simply have to prove intentional, sexual touching and the child's age. No issue of 'consent' arises and a specific offence under s. 7 is committed.

An offence under s. 3 if committed in relation to a person under the age of 16 or under s. 7 (including aiding, abetting, counselling, procuring, inciting or attempting the commission of such an offence) falls within the relevant sexual offences category—**see para. 1.9.3**.

1.9.4.3 Causing Sexual Activity without Consent

OFFENCE: **Causing a Person to Engage in Sexual Activity without Consent—*Sexual Offences Act 2003, s. 4***

> • If involves penetration: of the victim's anus or vagina, of victim's mouth with penis, of any other person's anus or vagina with a part of victim's body or by victim, or of any person's mouth by victim's penis—triable on indictment; life imprisonment
> • Otherwise triable either way; ten years' imprisonment on indictment; six months' imprisonment summarily

The Sexual Offences Act 2003, s. 4 states:

(1) A person (A) commits an offence if—
    (a) he intentionally causes another person (B) to engage in an activity,
    (b) the activity is sexual,
    (c) B does not consent to engaging in the activity, and
    (d) A does not reasonably believe that B consents.

KEYNOTE

The offence can involve a number of permutations—for example a woman making a man penetrate her, a man forcing someone else to masturbate him or a woman making another woman masturbate a third person. Apart from the defendant and the victim, there may be others involved who also consent. Clearly they may be liable for aiding and abetting under the right circumstances. If the permutations involve penetration, the chances are it will carry life imprisonment. You need to prove that the conduct was intentional, that the 'activity' engaged in was sexual (see para. 1.9.2.1), that the *victim* (rather than any other participant) did not consent and that the defendant did not reasonably believe that the victim consented.

Whether a belief is reasonable is to be determined having regard to all the circumstances, including any steps the defendant has taken to ascertain whether the victim consents (s. 4(2)).

Sections 75 and 76 apply to this offence (see paras 1.9.3.3 and 1.9.3.4).

There is a specific offence of causing or *inciting* a child under 13 to engage in sexual activity (s. 8). It is important to remember that an individual can commit an offence of incitement even if the activity he/she is encouraging, etc. does not take place. In *R v Walker* (2006) (unreported), the Court of Appeal held that s. 8 of the Act created two offences: (i) intentionally causing, and (ii) intentionally inciting a child under 13 to engage in sexual activity. The offence was centred on the concept of incitement and the acts had to be intentional or deliberate, but it was not a necessary ingredient for incitement of sexual activity that the defendant had intended the sexual activity to take place.

An offence under s. 4 if committed in relation to a person under the age of 16 or under s. 8 (including aiding, abetting, counselling, procuring, inciting or attempting the commission of such an offence) falls within the relevant sexual offences category for the purposes of s. 103(2)(b) of the Criminal Justice Act 2003 (a defendant's propensity to commit offences of the kind with which he/she is charged—see para. 1.9.3).

1.9.5 Child Sex Offences

In addition to the generic sexual offences above (such as rape) where the victim is a child, the Sexual Offences Act 2003 creates several specific offences relating to sexual activity involving or directed towards children. These are set out below. In considering each offence it is important to remember the relevant ages, both of offenders and victims. In addition, the Act makes special exceptions to some offences of aiding, abetting or counselling some offences involving children. In summary a person will not be guilty of aiding, abetting or counselling the specified offence against a child if he/she acts for the purpose of:

- protecting the child from sexually transmitted infection,
- protecting the physical safety of the child,
- preventing the child from becoming pregnant, or
- promoting the child's emotional well-being by the giving of advice,

and not for the purpose of obtaining sexual gratification or for the purpose of causing or encouraging the activity constituting the offence or the child's participation in it (s. 73).

The full list of offences is set out in s. 73(2); basically it covers specific offences against children under 13 and offences involving sexual activity with a child under 16.

1.9.5.1 Sexual Activity with a Child

OFFENCE: **Sexual Activity with a Child—*Sexual Offences Act 2003, s. 9***

- If involves penetration: of victim's anus or vagina by a part of defendant's body or anything else, of victim's mouth with defendant's penis, of defendant's anus or vagina by a part of victim's body or of defendant's mouth by victim's penis—triable on indictment; 14 years' imprisonment • Otherwise triable either way; 14 years' imprisonment on indictment; six months' imprisonment summarily

The Sexual Offences Act 2003, s. 9 states:

(1) A person aged 18 or over (A) commits an offence if—
    (a) he intentionally touches another person (B),
    (b) the touching is sexual, and
    (c) either—
       (i) B is under 16 and A does not reasonably believe that B is 16 or over, or
      (ii) B is under 13.

KEYNOTE

The person committing this offence must be at least 18. If the defendant is under 18, he or she commits a specific offence, punishable by 5 years' imprisonment (if tried on indictment) under s. 13. Similarly, if the person committing the offence is in a position of trust in relation to the victim, he or she commits a specific offence under s. 16.

You must show that the defendant intentionally touched the victim sexually (see para. 1.9.2.1) and either that the victim was under 13 (in which case the offence is complete) or that the victim was under 16 and that the defendant did not reasonably believe he or she was 16 or over. In either case consent is irrelevant.

There is a further specific offence (s. 10) of a person aged 18 or over intentionally causing or inciting (see chapter 1.3) another to engage in the type of sexual activity set out above. The sexual activity caused or envisaged may be with the defendant or with a third person. In the case of incitement there is no need for the sexual activity itself to take place. If the person committing the offence is in a position of trust in relation to the victim, he or she commits a specific offence under s. 17 (see para. 1.9.5.5).

An offence under s. 9 or 10 (including aiding, abetting, counselling, procuring, inciting or attempting the commission of such an offence) falls within the relevant sexual offences category for the purposes of s. 103(2)(b) of the Criminal Justice Act 2003 (a defendant's propensity to commit offences of the kind with which he/she is charged—see para. 1.9.3).

1.9.5.2 Sexual Activity in Presence of a Child

OFFENCE: **Engaging in Sexual Activity in the Presence of a Child—*Sexual Offences Act 2003, s. 11***

- Triable either way • Ten years' imprisonment on indictment • Six months' imprisonment summarily

The Sexual Offences Act 2003, s. 11 states:

(1) A person aged 18 or over (A) commits an offence if—
    (a) he intentionally engages in an activity,
    (b) the activity is sexual,

(c) for the purpose of obtaining sexual gratification, he engages in it—

    (i) when another person (B) is present or is in a place from which A can be observed, and

    (ii) knowing or believing that B is aware, or intending that B should be aware, that he is engaging in it, and

(d) either—

    (i) B is under 16 and A does not reasonably believe that B is 16 or over, or

    (ii) B is under 13.

KEYNOTE

The person committing this offence must be at least 18. If the defendant is under 18, he or she commits a specific offence, punishable by 5 years' imprisonment (if tried on indictment) under s. 13. Similarly, if the person committing the offence is in a position of trust in relation to the victim, he or she commits a specific offence under s. 18.

The activity in which the offender is engaged must be 'sexual' (**see para. 1.9.2.1**) and intentional and must be in order to obtain sexual gratification (for the defendant). The display of sexual images or sexual activity might, in certain circumstances, be appropriate, for example, for medical or educational reasons, hence the requirement that the offence depended on the corrupt purpose of 'sexual gratification'. However, the offence under s. 12 of the Act does not require that such gratification has to be taken immediately; i.e. the section does not require that the offence can only be committed if the purposed sexual gratification and the viewed sexual act, or display of images, were simultaneous, contemporaneous or synchronised. For example, the defendant may cause a child to watch a sexual act to put the child in a frame of mind for future sexual abuse, as well as where the defendant does so to obtain enjoyment from seeing the child watch the sexual act (*R* v *Abdullahi* [2006] EWCA Crim 2060). The approach to 'sexual gratification' taken in *Abdullahi* appears equally applicable to other offences where this phrase appears (the offence under s. 11 of the Act, for example).

You must show that a person under 16 is present or is in a place from which the defendant can be observed *and* that the defendant knew, believed or intended that the child was aware that s/he was engaging in that activity. Therefore, it is not necessary to show that the child was in fact aware of the activity in every case (although that would clearly help in terms of proving the defendant's state of mind). Because of the wording in s. 79(7), 'observation' includes direct observation or by looking at any image.

In relation to the child you must show also that either the child was under 13 (in which case the offence is complete) or that s/he was under 16 and that the defendant did not reasonably believe him/her to be 16 or over.

This offence is aimed at, for example, people masturbating in front of children or performing sexual acts with others where they know they can be seen (or they want to be seen) by children directly or via a camera/video phone etc.

For the specific offence of causing a child to watch a sexual act or an image of such an act, see below.

1.9.5.3 Causing a Child to Watch a Sex Act

OFFENCE: **Causing a Child to Watch a Sexual Act—*Sexual Offences Act 2003, s. 12***

    • Triable either way • Ten years' imprisonment on indictment • Six months' imprisonment summarily

The Sexual Offences Act 2003, s. 12 states:

(1) A person aged 18 or over (A) commits an offence if—

(a) for the purpose of obtaining sexual gratification, he intentionally causes another person (B) to watch a third person engaging in an activity, or to look at an image of any person engaging in an activity,

  (b) the activity is sexual, and
  (c) either—
      (i) B is under 16 and A does not reasonably believe that B is 16 or over, or
      (ii) B is under 13.

KEYNOTE

The person committing this offence must be at least 18. If the defendant is under 18, he or she commits a specific offence, punishable by 5 years' imprisonment (if tried on indictment) under s. 13. Similarly, if the person committing the offence is in a position of trust in relation to the victim, he or she commits a specific offence under s. 19.

While the related offence under s. 11 is concerned with the engaging in sexual activity which the person knows, believes or intends to be observed by a child, the above offence is concerned with intentionally causing a child to watch a third person engaging in such activity *or* to look at an image of a person *engaging in such activity*. 'Image' includes a moving or still image and includes an image produced by any means and, where the context permits, a three-dimensional image (s. 79(4)); it also includes images of an imaginary person (s. 79(5)).

As with the s. 11 offence, you must show that the defendant acted for the purposes of obtaining sexual gratification. For issues in relation to the term 'sexual gratification' see the explanation given in **para. 1.9.5.3**. Similarly, you must also show that either the child was under 13 (in which case the offence is complete) or that s/he was under 16 and that the defendant did not reasonably believe him/her to be 16 or over.

1.9.5.4 Arranging Intended Child Sex Offences

OFFENCE: **Arranging or Facilitating Commission of Child Sex Offences—**
Sexual Offences Act 2003, s. 14

  • Triable either way • 14 years' imprisonment on indictment • Six months' imprisonment summarily

The Sexual Offences Act 2003, s. 14 states:

  (1) A person commits an offence if—
      (a) he intentionally arranges or facilitates something that he intends to do, intends another person to do, or believes that another person will do, in any part of the world, and
      (b) doing it will involve the commission of an offence under any of sections 9 to 13.

KEYNOTE

This offence addresses the activities of those who arrange or facilitate child sex offences. The relevant offences are those set out in ss. 9–13 of the Act set out in the earlier paragraphs of this chapter.

The offence applies to activities by which the defendant intends to commit one of those relevant child sex offences him/herself, or by which the defendant intends or believes another person will do so, in either case in any part of the world. The offence is complete whether or not the sexual activity actually takes place. Examples of the offence would include a defendant approaching a third person to procure a child to take part in sexual activity with him or where the defendant makes travel arrangements for another in the belief that the other person will commit a relevant child sex offence.

This part of the Act specifically excludes the actions of those who are protecting the child in question. The exception will apply to a person acting for the child's protection who arranges or facilitates something that s/he believes another person will do, but that s/he does not intend to do or intend another person to do. Acting for the child's protection must fall within one of the following:

- protecting the child from sexually transmitted infection,
- protecting the physical safety of the child,
- preventing the child from becoming pregnant, or
- promoting the child's emotional well-being by the giving of advice,

and not for obtaining sexual gratification or for causing or encouraging the activity constituting the relevant child sex offence or the child's participation in it. This statutory exception (contained in s. 14(2) and (3)) covers activities such as health workers supplying condoms to people under 16 who are intent on having sex in any event and need protection from infection; it also potentially extends to covert investigative operations.

If carrying out the above offence will involve the commission of an offence under s. 9 or 10 (arranging or facilitating the commission of a child sex offence—**see para. 1.9.5.1**) it will fall within the relevant sexual offences category for the purposes of s. 103(2)(b) of the Criminal Justice Act 2003 (a defendant's propensity to commit offences of the kind with which he/she is charged—**see para. 1.9.3**). So too will aiding, abetting, counselling, procuring, inciting or attempting the commission of such an offence.

OFFENCE: **Meeting a Child Following Sexual Grooming**—*Sexual Offences Act 2003, s. 15*

- Triable either way • Ten years' imprisonment on indictment • Six months' imprisonment summarily

The Sexual Offences Act 2003, s. 15 states:

(1) A person aged 18 or over (A) commits an offence if—
   (a) having met or communicated with another person (B) on at least two earlier occasions, he—
      (i) intentionally meets B, or
      (ii) travels with the intention of meeting B in any part of the world,
   (b) at the time, he intends to do anything to or in respect of B, during or after the meeting and in any part of the world, which if done will involve the commission by A of a relevant offence,
   (c) B is under 16, and
   (d) A does not reasonably believe that B is 16 or over.

KEYNOTE

This offence is designed to deal with the increase in child grooming as a result of developments in communications technology (such as the Internet). The initial behaviour by the defendant involves either a communication with the victim (who must be under 16) on at least two previous occasions *or* a meeting with the victim on at least two previous occasions. The communications or meetings can (and often will) be innocuous, such as family occasions or during the course of youth activities, sports fixtures and so on. The communications can include text messaging or interactions on Internet 'chat rooms'. The meetings or communications can have taken place in any part of the world (s. 15(2)).

Once these earlier meetings or communications have taken place, the offence itself is triggered by either:

- an intentional meeting with the victim, or
- the defendant travelling with the intention of meeting the victim.

At the time of either of the above, the defendant must intend to do anything to or in respect of the victim, during or even after the meeting, that would amount to a relevant offence. A relevant offence here is generally any offence under Part I of the Act (all the offences covered in this chapter). Note that the intended offence does not have to take place.

You must show that the victim was under 16 and that the defendant did not reasonably believe that s/he was 16 or over.

1.9.5.5 Abuse of Position of Trust

OFFENCE: **Abuse of Position of Trust—*Sexual Offences Act 2003, ss. 16–19***

It is a function of Local Safeguarding Children Boards (LSCBs) to develop policies and procedures for safeguarding and promoting the welfare of children, including policies and procedures in relation to the investigation of allegations concerning persons who work with children, including teachers and educational support staff.

'Position of Trust'

The Sexual Offences Act 2003, s. 21 states:

(1) For the purposes of sections 16 to 19, a person (A) is in a position of trust in relation to another person (B) if—
  (a) any of the following subsections applies, or
  (b) any condition specified in an order made by the Secretary of State is met.
(2) This subsection applies if A looks after persons under 18 who are detained in an institution by virtue of a court order or under an enactment, and B is so detained in that institution.
(3) This subsection applies if A looks after persons under 18 who are resident in a home or other place in which—
  (a) accommodation and maintenance are provided by an authority under section 23(2) of the Children Act 1989 (c. 41) . . . , or
  (b) accommodation is provided by a voluntary organisation under section 59(1) of that Act . . . ,
  and B is resident, and is so provided with accommodation and maintenance or accommodation, in that place.
(4) This subsection applies if A looks after persons under 18 who are accommodated and cared for in one of the following institutions—
  (a) a hospital,
  (b) an independent clinic,
  (c) a care home, residential care home or private hospital,
  (d) a community home, voluntary home or children's home,
  (e) a home provided under section 82(5) of the Children Act 1989, or
  (f) a residential family centre,
  and B is accommodated and cared for in that institution.
(5) This subsection applies if A looks after persons under 18 who are receiving education at an educational institution and B is receiving, and A is not receiving, education at that institution.
(6) . . .
(7) This subsection applies if A is engaged in the provision of services under, or pursuant, to anything done under—
  (a) sections 8 to 10 of the Employment and Training Act 1973 (c. 50), or
  (b) section 114 of the Learning and Skills Act 2000 (c. 21),
  and, in that capacity, looks after B on an individual basis.
(8) This subsection applies if A regularly has unsupervised contact with B (whether face to face or by any other means)—
  (a) in the exercise of functions of a local authority under section 20 or 21 of the Children Act 1989 (c. 41),
  (b) . . .

(9) This subsection applies if A, as a person who is to report to the court under section 7 of the Children Act 1989 ... on matters relating to the welfare of B, regularly has unsupervised contact with B (whether face to face or by any other means).

(10) This subsection applies if A is a personal adviser appointed for B under—

(a) section 23B(2) of, or paragraph 19C of Schedule 2 to, the Children Act 1989,

(b) ...

and, in that capacity, looks after B on an individual basis.

(11) This subsection applies if—

(a) B is subject to a care order, a supervision order or an education supervision order, and

(b) in the exercise of functions conferred by virtue of the order on an authorised person or the authority designated by the order, A looks after B on an individual basis.

(12) This subsection applies if A—

(a) is an officer of the Service or Welsh family proceedings officer (within the meaning given by section 35 of the Children Act 2004) appointed for B under section 41(1) of the Children Act 1989,

(b) is appointed a children's guardian of B under rule 6 or rule 18 of the Adoption Rules 1984 (S.I. 1984/265), or

(c) is appointed to be the guardian ad litem of B under rule 9.5 of the Family Proceedings Rules 1991 (S.I. 1991/1247) ...

and, in that capacity, regularly has unsupervised contact with B (whether face to face or by any other means).

(13) This subsection applies if—

(a) B is subject to requirements imposed by or under an enactment on his release from detention for a criminal offence, or is subject to requirements imposed by a court order made in criminal proceedings, and

(b) A looks after B on an individual basis in pursuance of the requirements.

KEYNOTE

Although fairly long winded, the key to this list lies in establishing whether the defendant looked after people under 18 in the contexts described or his/her relationship with the victim fell into one of the other categories at subss. (7)–(13). Further clarification for the interpretation of these definitions is set out in s. 22.

The importance of the categories in subss. (2)–(5) is that the evidential presumptions described below will apply.

A position of trust may also exist under conditions specified by statutory instrument made by the Home Secretary (s. 21(1)(b)).

In summary, positions of trust include the wide range of settings in which a child is being lawfully detained or accommodated, including situations such as foster care, residential care and education. Those who look after children on an individual basis such as Connexions Personal Advisors and people with unsupervised contact appointed under the relevant parts of the Children Act 1989 will be covered.

Note that there is a separate category of sexual offences involving people with mental disorders and, in particular, care workers who are looking after them (see para. 1.9.6).

There are specific procedures in place for dealing with allegations of abuse made against teachers and educational support staff. These are overseen by the relevant Local Safeguarding Children Boards.

Essentially the above provisions make it a specific offence for a person aged 18 or over in a position of trust to engage in sexual activity which is prohibited by the general child sex offences considered earlier in this chapter (ss. 9–12—see paras 1.9.5.1 to 1.9.5.3) in relation to a child, namely:

• sexual activity with a child;

• causing or inciting a child to engage in sexual activity;

- sexual activity in the presence of a child;
- causing a child to watch a sexual act.

There are however some key differences. For instance, in such cases involving an abuse of a position of trust, the 'child' victim can be 16 or 17 years old. Another difference is that the maximum sentence is generally lower in the corresponding offences by a person in a position of trust. In addition, except in cases where the victim is under 13, it must be shown that the defendant did not reasonably believe that the victim was 18 or over. Once it is proved that the victim was under 18 an evidential burden passes to the defendant. This means that, unless the defendant can point to some evidence to raise an arguable case to the contrary, it will be presumed that he or she did not reasonably believe that the victim was 18 or over.

There are further provisions relating to presumptions of knowledge by the defendant. Generally, if the position of trust held by the defendant falls within the first four categories set out in subss. (2)–(5) (basically where the defendant looks after children at an institution and the victim is at that institution), there will be a further evidential burden on the defendant. In such cases, it will be presumed that a defendant knew (or could reasonably have been expected to know) of the circumstances that gave rise to the position of trust. In other words, where the defendant works in an institution where the victim is, it will be presumed that the defendant knew (or could reasonably have been expected to know) that there was a position of trust between him/her and the victim unless he/she can point to some evidence to the contrary.

There is an exception to the offences under ss. 16–19 where a lawful sexual relationship existed between the defendant and the victim before the position of trust arose (s. 24) and where the defendant and the victim were lawfully married to each other at the time (s. 23). An offence under s. 16 or 17 (abuse of position of trust: sexual activity with a child or causing etc. a child to engage in sexual activity) if committed in relation to a person under the age of 16 will fall within the relevant sexual offences category for the purposes of s. 103(2)(b) of the Criminal Justice Act 2003 (a defendant's propensity to commit offences of the kind with which he/she is charged—see para. 1.9.3). This will also apply—where relevant—to aiding, abetting, counselling, procuring, inciting or attempting the commission of such an offence. The omissions from the above statutory extract relate to Northern Ireland: for the full wording of the requirements and presumptions reference should be made to the statutory text.

1.9.5.6   Sex Offences with Family Members

OFFENCE: **Sexual Activity with Child Family Member—*Sexual Offences Act* 2003, ss. 25 *and* 26**

- Where defendant is 18 or over at the time of the offence and if involves penetration: of victim's anus or vagina by a part of defendant's body or anything else, of victim's mouth with defendant's penis, of defendant's anus or vagina by a part of victim's body or of defendant's mouth by victim's penis—triable on indictment: 14 years' imprisonment • Otherwise triable either way; 14 years' imprisonment on indictment; six months' imprisonment and/or fine summarily • Or, where defendant is under 18 at the time of the offence; five years' imprisonment on indictment; six months' imprisonment and/or fine summarily

The Sexual Offences Act 2003. s. 25 states:

(1) A person (A) commits an offence if—
  (a) he intentionally touches another person (B),
  (b) the touching is sexual,
  (c) the relation of A to B is within section 27,
  (d) A knows or could reasonably be expected to know that his relation to B is of a description falling within that section, and

(e) either—
    (i) B is under 18 and A does not reasonably believe that B is 18 or over, or
    (ii) B is under 13.

KEYNOTE

Where the defendant intentionally incites another person (the victim) to touch him/her or to allow him/herself to be touched by the defendant, there is a specific—and to all practical purposes identically worded—offence under s. 26.

For the relevant definitions of touching and sexual see the earlier paragraphs in this chapter.

There are two further elements that must be proved in relation to these offences. The first is the existence of the relevant family relationship between the defendant and the victim, the second is the age of the victim.

Note that, where the relevant family relationship is proved, it will be presumed that the defendant knew or could reasonably have been expected to know that he or she was related to the victim in that way. Similarly where it is proved that the victim was under 18, there will be a presumption that the defendant did not reasonably believe that the victim was 18 or over. In respect of both the relationship and the age of the defendant under these circumstances, the defendant will have an evidential burden to discharge in that regard (see s. 25(2) and (3)).

The relevant family relationships are set out in s. 27. These cover all the close family relationships that you would expect, along with adoptive relationships. In summary the relationships are where:

- the defendant or the victim is the other's parent, grandparent, brother, sister, half-brother, half-sister, aunt or uncle or
- the defendant is or has been the victim's foster parent.

Additional categories are where the defendant and victim live or have lived in the same household, or the defendant is or has been regularly involved in caring for, training, supervising or being in sole charge of the victim and:

- one of them is or has been the other's step-parent,
- they are cousins,
- one of them is or has been the other's stepbrother or stepsister, or
- they have the same parent or foster parent.

For a full definition of the various familial relationships and their application to the specific offences, reference should be made to the statutory text.

There are exceptions for situations where the defendant and the victim are lawfully married at the time or where (under certain circumstances) the sexual relationship pre-dates the family one—for example, where two divorcees each have a child of 17 who are engaged in a sexual relationship before their respective parents marry and move all four of them into the same household.

An offence under s. 25 or 26 if committed in relation to a person under the age of 16 (including aiding, abetting, counselling, procuring, inciting or attempting the commission of such an offence) will fall within the relevant sexual offences category for the purposes of s. 103(2)(b) of the Criminal Justice Act 2003 (a defendant's propensity to commit offences of the kind with which he/she is charged—**see para. 1.9.3**).

1.9.5.7   **Other Offences with Family Members**

The Sexual Offences Act goes on to clarify and extend a number of other sexual offences involving adult family members (see ss. 64–65). These replace the former offences of incest and generally create either way offences punishable by up to two years' imprisonment. They can be committed by both parties where one relative (who is 16 or over) intentionally penetrates the vagina or anus of another relative (aged 18 or over) with anything, or penetrates their mouth with his penis and in each case the relative knows (or could reasonably be expected to know) that s/he is related to the other in the way described. The relatives are parent, grandparent, child, grandchild, brother, sister, half-brother, half-sister, aunt, uncle, nephew or niece (this does not include adopted children).

1.9.5.8   Indecent Photographs

OFFENCE: **Indecent Photographs—*Protection of Children Act 1978, s. 1***
- Triable either way • Ten years' imprisonment on indictment • Six months' imprisonment and/or a fine summarily

The Protection of Children Act 1978, ss. 1, 1A and 1B state:

1 Indecent photographs of children

(1) Subject to sections 1A and 1B, it is an offence for a person—
   (a) to take, or permit to be taken or to make, any indecent photograph or pseudo-photograph of a child. . . ; or
   (b) to distribute or show such indecent photographs or pseudo-photographs; or
   (c) to have in his possession such indecent photographs or pseudo-photographs, with a view to their being distributed or shown by himself or others; or
   (d) to publish or cause to be published any advertisement likely to be understood as conveying that the advertiser distributes or shows such indecent photographs or pseudo-photographs, or intends to do so.
(2) For purposes of this Act, a person is to be regarded as distributing an indecent photograph or pseudo-photograph if he parts with possession of it to, or exposes or offers it for acquisition by, another person.
(3) . . .
(4) Where a person is charged with an offence under subsection (1)(b) or (c), it shall be a defence for him to prove—
   (a) that he had a legitimate reason for distributing or showing the photographs or pseudo-photographs or (as the case may be) having them in his possession; or
   (b) that he had not himself seen the photographs or pseudo-photographs and did not know, nor had any cause to suspect, them to be indecent.
(5) References in the Children and Young Persons Act 1933 (except in sections 15 and 99) to the offences mentioned in Schedule 1 to that Act shall include an offence under subsection (1)(a) above.

1A Marriage and other relationships

(1) This section applies where, in proceedings for an offence under section 1(1)(a) of taking or making an indecent photograph of a child, or for an offence under section 1(1)(b) or (c) relating to an indecent photograph of a child, the defendant proves that the photograph was of the child aged 16 or over, and that at the time of the offence charged the child and he—
   (a) were married, or
   (b) lived together as partners in an enduring family relationship.
(2) Subsections (5) and (6) also apply where, in proceedings for an offence under section 1(1)(b) or (c) relating to an indecent photograph of a child, the defendant proves that the photograph was of the child aged 16 or over, and that at the time when he obtained it the child and he—
   (a) were married, or
   (b) lived together as partners in an enduring family relationship
(3) This section applies whether the photograph showed the child alone or with the defendant, but not if it showed any other person.
(4) In the case of an offence under section 1(1)(a), if sufficient evidence is adduced to raise an issue as to whether the child consented to the photograph being taken or made, or as to whether

the defendant reasonably believed that the child so consented, the defendant is not guilty of the offence unless it is proved that the child did not so consent and that the defendant did not reasonably believe that the child so consented.

(5) In the case of an offence under section 1(1)(b), the defendant is not guilty of the offence unless it is proved that the showing or distributing was to a person other than the child.

1B Exception for criminal proceedings, investigations etc.

(1) In proceedings for an offence under section 1(1)(a) of making an indecent photograph or pseudo-photograph of a child, the defendant is not guilty of the offence if he proves that—
  (a) it was necessary for him to make the photograph or pseudo-photograph for the purposes of the prevention, detection or investigation of crime, or for the purposes of criminal proceedings, in any part of the world,
  (b) at the time of the offence charged he was a member of the Security Service, and it was necessary for him to make the photograph or pseudo-photograph for the exercise of any of the functions of the Service, or
  (c) at the time of the offence charged he was a member of GCHQ, and it was necessary for him to make the photograph or pseudo-photograph for the exercise of any of the functions of GCHQ.

OFFENCE: **Indecent Photographs—*Criminal Justice Act 1988, s. 160***
  • Triable either way • Five years' imprisonment on indictment • Six months' imprisonment and/or a fine

The Criminal Justice Act 1988, ss. 160 and 160A state:

160 Possession of indecent photograph of child

(1) Subject to subsecton (1A) it is an offence for a person to have any indecent photograph or pseudo-photograph of a child in his possession.
(2) Where a person is charged with an offence under subsection (1) above, it shall be a defence for him to prove—
  (a) that he had a legitimate reason for having the photograph or pseudo-photograph in his possession; or
  (b) that he had not himself seen the photograph or pseudo-photograph and did not know, nor had any cause to suspect, it to be indecent; or
  (c) that the photograph or pseudo-photograph was sent to him without any prior request made by him or on his behalf and that he did not keep it for an unreasonable time.

160A Marriage and other relationships

(1) This section applies where, in proceedings for an offence under section 160 relating to an indecent photograph of a child, the defendant proves that the photograph was of the child aged 16 or over, and that at the time of the offence charged the child and he—
  (a) were married, or
  (b) lived together as partners in an enduring family relationship.
(2) This section also applies where, in proceedings for an offence under section 160 relating to an indecent photograph of a child, the defendant proves that the photograph was of the child aged 16 or over, and that at the time when he obtained it the child and he—
  (a) were married, or
  (b) lived together as partners in an enduring family relationship.
(3) This section applies whether the photograph showed the child alone or with the defendant, but not if it showed any other person.
(4) If sufficient evidence is adduced to raise an issue as to whether the child consented to the photograph being in the defendant's possession, or as to whether the defendant reasonably believed that the child so consented, the defendant is not guilty of the offence unless it is proved that the child did not so consent and that the defendant did not reasonably believe that the child so consented.

KEYNOTE

Once the defendant realises, *or should realise*, that material is indecent, any distribution, showing or retention of the material with a view to its being distributed will result in a *prima facie* offence being made out under the 1978 Act if the person depicted turns out to be a child (*R* v *Land* [1999] QB 65). This is because s. 160(4) provides no defence of mistake as to a child's age.

A person will be a 'child' for the purposes of both Acts above if it appears from the evidence as a whole that he/she was, at the material time, under the age of 18 (Protection of Children Act 1978, s. 2(3) and Criminal Justice Act 1988, s. 160(4)).

However, if the impression conveyed by a pseudo-photograph is that the person shown is a child or where the predominant impression is that the person is a child, that pseudo-photograph will be treated for these purposes as a photograph of a child, notwithstanding that some of the physical characteristics shown are those of an adult (s. 7(8) of the 1978 Act).

'Pseudo-photographs' include computer images and the above offences will cover the situation where part of the photograph is made up of an adult form. Downloading images from the Internet will amount to 'making' a photograph for the purposes of s. 1(1)(a) of the 1978 Act (*R* v *Bowden* [2000] 2 WLR 1083). 'Making' pseudo-photographs includes voluntarily browsing through indecent images of children on and from the Internet (*R* v *Smith and Jayson* [2002] EWCA Crim 683). In *Smith and Jayson* the Court of Appeal held that a person receiving an unsolicited e-mail attachment containing an indecent image of a child would not commit an offence under s. 1(1) by opening it if he/she was unaware that it contained or was likely to contain an indecent image. This was because s. 1(1)(a) does not create an absolute offence (see also *Atkins* v *DPP* [2000] 1 WLR 1427). This may create a potential 'loophole' for paedophiles using the Internet, but all the relevant circumstances of their viewing will need to be considered. In proving the 1978 Act offence you have to show that the act of 'making' the image was deliberate and intentional with the knowledge that it was, or was likely to be, an indecent photograph or pseudo-photograph of a child. Any title that accompanied the e-mail, along with the level of IT literacy of the defendant and any subsequent e-mail correspondence that he/she had with the sender after opening the attachment, will be directly relevant to the issue of the defendant's state of mind (*mens rea*) in this offence.

In *Smith and Jayson* the Court of Appeal went on to say that, once an image is downloaded, the length of time it remains on the screen is irrelevant.

In *R* v *Porter* [2006] EWCA Crim 560, the court considered the issues surrounding retrieval. The defendant had been charged with offences under s. 160 of the Act following the seizure of his computer. On the hard drive of the computer there were images of child pornography. However, these files had been deleted and the recycle bin emptied so that the deleted images could only be retrieved using specialist software which the defendant did not have. Although originally convicted, the defendant's conviction was quashed. The Court stated that if a person cannot gain access to retrieve deleted images on a computer then he was no longer in custody or control of those images. It could not be said that an image that a person cannot retrieve from a computer hard drive is in that person's possession simply because it is on the hard drive. Whether the defendant is in custody or control of the image is a question for the jury, but if at the material time the image is beyond the defendant's control then he cannot be in possession of it.

The statutory defence under s. 160(2)(b) of the 1988 Act above is broader than it seems at first. Although the wording requires that the defendant (1) has not seen the material and (2) did not know or have *any* cause to suspect it was indecent, the defendant will be acquitted of the offence under s. 160 if he/she proves that (1) he/she had not seen the material and (2) did not know (and had no cause to suspect) that it was *an indecent photograph of a child*. This was confirmed by the Court of Appeal in *R* v *Collier* [2004] EWCA Crim 1411 and arose from an argument where the material relating to children had been among other adult material that the defendant *did* know was indecent—he just did not know that it was an indecent photograph *of a child*. While this is a very technical distinction, it is very relevant when evidence gathering and interviewing suspects for the s. 160 offence.

Evidence indicating an interest in paedophile material generally can also be relevant to show that it was more likely than not that a file containing an indecent image of a child *had* been created deliberately. Such evidence has been held by the Court of Appeal to be relevant for this purpose, along with evidence showing how a computer had been used to access paedophile news groups, chatlines and websites (*R v Mould* [2001] 2 Crim App R(S) 8). A further decision on the making of a 'pseudo-photograph' has held that an image consisting of two parts of two different photographs taped together (the naked body of a woman taped to the head of a child) would not suffice (*Goodland* v *DPP* [2000] 1 WLR 1427). In that case the Divisional Court accepted that such an image, *if photocopied*, could fall within the meaning of a 'pseudo-photograph'. The Court of Appeal has confirmed that the offence under s. 1(1)(a) is justified by the requirement to protect children from being exploited and does not contravene Article 8 or Article 10 of the European Convention on Human Rights (*R v Smethurst* [2001] Crim LR 657). The finer IT issues that are typically involved in these cases were further considered in *R v Dooley* [2005] EWCA Crim 3093. In that case the defendant appealed against convictions on six counts of possession of indecent photographs of a child with a view to their being distributed (contrary to s. 1(1)(c) of the 1978 Act, above). The defendant belonged to an internet-based file sharing network that allowed users to share files stored in a folder named 'my shared folder' on their computer. The defendant's computer was found to have six indecent images of children stored in the shared folder but many thousands of other such images were stored elsewhere on the computer. The defendant maintained that he had intended to remove the pictures from the shared folder. The appeal turned on the judge's preliminary ruling on the meaning of 'with a view to' under s. 1(1)(c). The Court of Appeal agreed with the judge's ruling that there was a distinction between 'with the intention of' and 'with a view to'—where a defendant had knowledge that images were likely to be accessed by other people, any images would be downloaded 'with a view to distribute'. If one of the reasons the defendant left the pictures in the shared folder was so others could have access to them, he would be in possession of the images 'with a view to their being distributed'. However, as the court accepted that the defendant did *not* leave the pictures in the shared folder for that reason, his conviction could not stand.

A legitimate purpose for possessing such material might be where someone has the material as an exhibits officer or as a training aid for police officers or social workers.

The consent of the Director of Public Prosecutions is needed before prosecuting an offence under the Protection of Children Act 1978.

Distributing will include lending or offering to another. Clearly cases falling within the above legislation will vary significantly and there needs to be some distinction between the seriousness of different types of material. The Court of Appeal has set out five broad levels of seriousness and these are of use, not only in helping police officers and investigators understand how the offences will be dealt with by the criminal courts, but also in explaining this to victims and witnesses. The levels are:

(1) images depicting erotic posing with no sexual activity;
(2) sexual activity between children, or solo masturbation by a child;
(3) non-penetrative sexual activity between adults and children;
(4) penetrative sexual activity between children and adults, and;
(5) sadism or bestiality.

(*R v Oliver* [2003] 1 Cr App R 28).

The Court of Appeal also recognised that much of this material involves abuse of the child featuring in it and held that, so far as an offender's involvement was concerned, the seriousness of an offence increased with his/her proximity to, and responsibility for, the original abuse. In considering all these factors, courts will distinguish between pseudo-photographs which had involved no abuse or exploitation of children, and photographic images that involved real children. The Court of Appeal indicated that the imprisonment would normally follow where the material had been shown or distributed to others or where the offender had been in possession of a large amount of level 2 material or a small amount of material of level 3 or above.

Note that although the offences include video recordings, possession of exposed but undeveloped film (i.e. film in the form in which it is taken out of a camera) does not appear to be covered. The offence at s. 1(1)(b) and (c) of the 1978 Act can only be proven if the defendant showed/distributed the photograph etc. or intended to show or distribute the photograph etc. *to someone else.* This is clear from the decisions in *R* v *Fellows* [1997] 1 Cr App R 244 and *R* v *T* [1999] 163 JP 349. If no such intention can be proved, or if the defendant only had the photographs etc. for his/her own use, the appropriate charge would be under the 1988 Act.

Sections 1 and 2 of the Criminal Evidence (Amendment) Act 1997 apply to an offence under s. 1 of the Protection of Children Act 1978 (and to conspiracies, attempts or incitements in the circumstances set out in the 1997 Act) **(see Evidence and Procedure, chapter 2.12).**

1.9.5.9 Defences to Indecent Photographs of Marriage and Other Relationships

There is a specific defence to offences under s. 1(1) (a), (b) and (c) of the Protection of Children Act 1978 (making, distributing or possessing with a view to distributing). This defence arises where the defendant can prove that the photograph was of a child aged 16 or over, the photograph only showed the defendant and the child, and that, at the time of the offence, they were married or lived together as partners in an enduring family relationship (s. 1A). This is a very narrow defence, restricted to photographs (as opposed to pseudo-photographs, which are not covered) in the restricted circumstances set out. If the defendant cannot show these elements, the defence will not apply. If the defendant *can* show these elements, then the following further conditions of the defence will apply:

- In the case of an offence under s. 1(1)(a) (taking or permitting to be taken etc.), the defendant will have an evidential burden of showing that the child consented or that the defendant reasonably believed that the child consented to the making of the photograph (s. 1A(4)).
- In the case of an offence under s. 1(1)(b) (distributing or showing), you must prove that the distributing or showing was to a person other than the child in the photograph (s. 1A(5)).
- In the case of an offence under s. 1(1)(c) (possession with a view to distribution or showing etc.), the defendant will have an evidential burden of demonstrating that the image was to be shown/distributed to no person other than the child and that the child consented to the defendant's possession of the photograph (s. 1A(6)).

Similar provisions are made in relation to the offence under s. 160 of the Criminal Justice Act 1988 (possession)—see s. 160A.

1.9.5.10 Exception in Indecent Photographs for Criminal Proceedings and Investigations

There is a limited defence in relation to the making of an indecent photograph or pseudo-photograph under s. 1(1)(a) of the Protection of Children Act 1978 where the defendant proves that:

- it was *necessary* for him/her to make the photograph or pseudo-photograph for the purposes of the prevention, detection or investigation of crime or for criminal proceedings in any part of the world, or

- at the time, s/he was a member of the Security Service or GCHQ (Government Communications Headquarters) and it was *necessary* for the exercise of any of the functions of the Service/GCHQ. (s. 1B).

In order to assist police officers and prosecutors the Association of Chief Police Officers (ACPO) and the Crown Prosecution Service (CPS) have published a Memorandum of Understanding. This Memorandum sets out the factors that will be taken into account in deciding whether the intention of someone accused of an offence under s. 1(1)(a) attracted criminal liability when 'making' a photograph etc. As the Memorandum points out:

> This reverse burden is intended to allow those people who need to be able to identify and act to deal with such images to do so. It also presents a significant obstacle to would-be abusers and those who exploit the potential of technology to gain access to paedophilic material for unprofessional (or personal) reasons.

The purpose of the Memorandum is therefore twofold: to reassure those whose duties properly involve the prevention, detection or investigation of this type of crime and also as a warning to others who might claim this defence having taken it upon themselves to investigate such offences. In summary the following criteria will be considered:

- How soon after its discovery the image was reported and to whom.
- The circumstances in which it was discovered.
- The way in which the image was stored and dealt with, and whether it was copied.
- Whether the person's actions were reasonable, proportionate and necessary.

1.9.5.11 Child Prostitution, Pornography and Payment for Sex

OFFENCE: **Paying for Sexual Services of a Child—*Sexual Offences Act 2003, s. 47***
- If victim is child under 13; triable on indictment; life imprisonment • Where victim is under 16 at the time of the offence and if involves penetration of victim's anus or vagina by a part of defendant's body or anything else, of victim's mouth with defendant's penis, of defendant's anus or vagina by a part of victim's body or by victim with anything else—triable on indictment; 14 years' imprisonment
- Otherwise triable either way; seven years' imprisonment on indictment; six months' imprisonment and/or fine summarily

The Sexual Offences Act 2003, s. 47 states:

(1) A person (A) commits an offence if—
  (a) he intentionally obtains for himself the sexual services of another person (B),
  (b) before obtaining those services, he has made or promised payment for those services to B or a third person, or knows that another person has made or promised such a payment.

KEYNOTE

In proving this offence you must show that the defendant intentionally obtained the sexual services of a child for him/herself; you must also show that, before doing so, he/she made or promised payment either to the child or another person, or that he/she knew that someone else had made or promised such payment.

If the child is under 13, the offence is complete at this point. If the child is under 18, you must prove that the defendant did not reasonably believe that the child was 18 or over (s. 47(1)(c)).

Payment means any financial advantage, including the discharge of an obligation to pay or the provision of goods or services (including sexual services) gratuitously or at a discount (s. 47(2)). This is a very wide definition and would include situations where the child victim or some other person is given drugs or other goods/services at a cheaper rate in exchange for sexual services from the child.

OFFENCE: **Causing, Inciting, Controlling, Arranging or Facilitating Child Prostitution or Pornography—*Sexual Offences Act 2003, ss. 48–50***
  • Triable either way • 14 years' imprisonment on indictment • Six months' imprisonment and/or fine summarily

The Sexual Offences Act 2003, s. 48 states:

(1) A person (A) commits an offence if—
  (a) he intentionally causes or incites another person (B) to become a prostitute, or to be involved in pornography, in any part of the world...

The Sexual Offences Act 2003, s. 49 states:

(1) A person (A) commits an offence if—
  (a) he intentionally controls any of the activities of another person (B) relating to B's prostitution or involvement in pornography in any part of the world...

The Sexual Offences Act 2003, s. 50 states:

(1) A person (A) commits an offence if—
  (a) he intentionally arranges or facilitates the prostitution or involvement in pornography in any part of the world of another person (B)...

KEYNOTE

These offences are aimed at those who seek to recruit children for prostitution or to take part in pornography, or otherwise control these activities and arrangements anywhere in the world.

If the child is under 13, the offences are complete once the relevant conduct of the defendant has been proved and any belief s/he may have had as to the child's age is irrelevant to guilt. If the child is under 18, you must prove that the defendant did not reasonably believe that the child was 18 or over (see subs. (1)(b) of each).

A person is involved in pornography if an indecent image of that person is recorded and pornography and similar expressions are to be interpreted accordingly (s. 51(1)). This will cover every type of recording of images including camera phones, video footage and computer scanned images.

Prostitute means a person (A) who, *on at least one occasion and whether or not compelled to do so*, offers or provides sexual services to another person in return for payment or a promise of payment to A or a third person (s. 51(2)). Therefore the mere offering of the provision of services is covered and there is no need to show that the 'prostitute' (victim) was compelled to act in this way.

Payment means any financial advantage, including the discharge of an obligation to pay or the provision of goods or services (including sexual services) gratuitously or at a discount (s. 51(3)).

Therefore these offences would be committed if the child is recruited on a one-off basis, as well as on those occasions where the child is habitually involved. Note that, unlike the general offence of controlling prostitution (see para. 1.9.10.2) there is no need to show that the causing or inciting was done for gain. The expressions used in the sections are deliberately wide and will, in places, overlap. Controlling the activities of the child would include, for example, setting the relevant price or specifying which room or equipment is to be used. Arranging will include taking an active part in the transport or travel arrangements or organising relevant facilities (such as hotel rooms etc.).

1.9.5.12 Harmful Publications

OFFENCE: **Harmful Publications—*Children and Young Persons (Harmful Publications) Act 1955, s. 2***

- Triable summarily • Four months' imprisonment and/or a fine

The Children and Young Persons (Harmful Publications) Act 1955, s. 2 states:

> (1) A person who prints, publishes, sells or lets on hire a work to which this Act applies, or has any such work in his possession for the purpose of selling it or letting it on hire, shall be guilty of an offence...

KEYNOTE

A prosecution for this offence can only be brought with the consent of the Attorney-General (or Solicitor-General). The sort of 'works' to which the Act applies are set out in s. 1 and include books, magazines or other like works of a kind likely to fall into the hands of children or young persons which consist wholly or mainly of stories told in pictures which portray:

- the commission of crimes, or
- acts of violence or cruelty, or
- incidents of a repulsive or horrible nature,

in such a way that the work as a whole would tend to corrupt a child or young person.

Power of Search

A search warrant may be issued under s. 3 of the 1955 Act.

Defence

The Children and Young Persons (Harmful Publications) Act 1955, s. 2 states:

> (1) ... in any proceedings taken under this subsection against a person in respect of selling or letting on hire a work or of having it in his possession for the purpose of selling it or letting it on hire, it shall be a defence for him to prove that he had not examined the contents of the work and had no reasonable cause to suspect that it was one to which this Act applies.

KEYNOTE

For a possible alternative charge it is worth considering s. 2(1) of the Obscene Publications Act 1959. In such a case a jury only has to be satisfied that there was a likelihood of vulnerable persons seeing the relevant obscene material and there is no need to show that a vulnerable person actually saw the material or would have seen it. This means that the charge may be particularly suitable where obscene material is made generally available on the Internet (see *R* v *Perrin* [2002] EWCA Crim 747). Where video recordings are involved, the provisions of the Video Recordings Act 1984 may also be of use. For further detail on both statutes, *see Blackstone's Criminal Practice*, 2008, Part B.

1.9.5.13 Offences Outside the United Kingdom

Section 72 of the Sexual Offences Act 2003 generally makes it an offence in England and Wales for British citizens or UK residents to commit acts against children under 16 outside the United Kingdom. In addition to being offences in England and Wales, they must also amount to an offence in the other country (although the description and title of the offence need not be the same). The Act goes on to make certain provisions in relation to proving that the offence committed was in fact an offence in the other country.

1.9.6 Sexual Offences Against People with a Mental Disorder

The Sexual Offences Act 2003 is centred largely upon the fact that certain mental disorders deprive the sufferer of the ability to refuse involvement in sexual activity. This is different from, and wider than, a lack of consent at the time and focuses on the victim's inability to refuse.

1.9.6.1 Definition of 'Mental Disorder'

The relevant definition is now that of a 'mental disorder'. The definition used is that of the Mental Health Act 1983 which defines mental disorder as 'mental illness, arrested or incomplete development of mind, psychopathic disorder and any other disorder or disability of mind' (s. 1(2)).

1.9.6.2 Sexual Activity with Mentally Disordered Person

OFFENCE: **Sexual Activity with a Person with a Mental Disorder**—*Sexual Offences Act 2003, s. 30*
 • If involves penetration of victim's anus or vagina, of victim's mouth with defendant's penis, or of defendant's mouth by victim's penis—triable on indictment; life imprisonment • Otherwise triable either way; 14 years' imprisonment on indictment; six months' imprisonment and/or fine summarily

The Sexual Offences Act 2003, s. 30 states:

(1) A person (A) commits an offence if—
    (a) he intentionally touches another person (B),
    (b) the touching is sexual,
    (c) B is unable to refuse because of or for a reason related to a mental disorder, and
    (d) A knows or could reasonably be expected to know that B has a mental disorder and that because of it or for a reason related to it B is likely to be unable to refuse.

KEYNOTE

This is very similar to the general offence of sexual touching under s. 3(as to which see para. 1.9.4.2).
 For a discussion of the requirements to prove 'touching' and 'sexual' see para. 1.9.2.
 In order to prove the above offence you must show, not only that the sexual touching was intentional, but also that the victim was *unable to refuse* and that this inability was because of, or for a reason related to a mental disorder. The Act goes on to provide that a person is unable to refuse if:

• they lack the capacity to choose whether to agree to the touching (whether because they lack sufficient understanding of the nature or reasonably foreseeable consequences of what is being done, or for any other reason), or

• they are unable to communicate such a choice to the defendant. s. 30(2).

 Once you have established these elements, you must also show that the defendant knew or could reasonably have been expected to know both that the victim had a mental disorder *and* that because of it (or for a reason related to it) he or she was likely to be unable to refuse. In *Hulme* v *DPP* [2006] EWHC 1347, the Divisional Court examined a decision reached by a magistrates' court in relation to a complainant who was a cerebral palsy sufferer with a low IQ (aged 27). The magistrates' court had decided that the complainant was unable to refuse to be touched sexually; the Divisional Court agreed and the conviction against the defendant (who was 73) was upheld.

If the defendant obtains the victim's agreement to sexual touching by means of any inducement (offered or given), or a threat or deception for that purpose, the defendant commits a specific (and similarly punishable) offence under s. 34. An example of such an offence would be where the defendant promises to give the victim some reward in exchange for allowing sexual touching or where he or she deceives the victim into believing that the touching is necessary for some other purpose. If the defendant uses an inducement, threat or deception to *cause* the victim to engage in or agree to engage in sexual activity, there is a further specific offence (similarly punishable) under s. 35.

In these specific cases of inducements, threats or deception there is still the need to prove that the defendant knew (or could reasonably have been expected to know) of the victim's mental disorder but *no need to prove that the victim was unable to refuse.*

Causing or inciting a person with a mental disorder impeding choice to engage in sexual activity with another person generally (i.e. without threats, inducements or deception) is a separate offence, punishable in the same way, under s. 31. As that is an 'incomplete' or unfinished offence (as to which **see chapter 1.3**) it is not necessary to prove that the sexual activity took place.

Any of the offences under ss. 30, 31, 34 or 35 if committed in relation to a person under the age of 16 will fall within the relevant sexual offences category for the purposes of s. 103(2)(b) of the Criminal Justice Act 2003 (a defendant's propensity to commit offences of the kind with which he/she is charged—**see para. 1.9.3**). This will also apply—where relevant—to aiding, abetting, counselling, procuring, inciting or attempting the commission of such an offence.

1.9.6.3 Sexual Activity in Presence of Mentally Disordered Person

OFFENCE: **Sexual Activity in Presence of a Person with a Mental Disorder—** *Sexual Offences Act 2003, s. 32*

> • Triable either way • Ten years' imprisonment on indictment • Six months' imprisonment and/or fine summarily

The Sexual Offences Act 2003, s. 32 states:

(1) A person (A) commits an offence if—
  (a) he intentionally engages in an activity,
  (b) the activity is sexual,
  (c) for the purpose of obtaining sexual gratification, he engages in it—
    (i) when another person (B) is present or is in a place from which A can be observed, and
    (ii) knowing or believing that B is aware, or intending that B should be aware, that he is engaging in it,
  (d) B is unable to refuse because of or for a reason related to a mental disorder, and
  (e) A knows or could reasonably be expected to know that B has a mental disorder and that because of it or for a reason related to it B is likely to be unable to refuse.

KEYNOTE

This is very similar to the corresponding offence relating to children under s. 11 (as to which **see para. 1.9.5.2**).

As with the previous offence, you will need to show that the defendant intentionally engaged in sexual activity; you will also have to show that he or she did so:

- when a person (who was unable to refuse because of, or for reason related to, a mental disorder) was present or in a place from which the defendant could be observed, and
- that the defendant knew/believed/intended that the mentally disordered person was aware that he or she was engaging in that activity

for the purposes of sexual gratification.

For the requirements in proving the victim's inability to refuse see the previous offence under s. 30.

Because of the wording of s. 79(7) 'observation' includes direct observation or by looking at any image. For the specific offence of causing a person with a mental disorder impeding choice to watch a sexual act or an image of such an act see below.

If the victim agrees to be present or in the place referred to in s. 32(1)(c)(i) above because of any inducement (offered or given), or a threat or deception practised by the defendant for that purpose, the defendant commits a specific (and similarly punishable) offence under s. 36. An example of such an offence would be where the defendant pays the mentally disordered person to stay in a particular place while the activity occurs. In these specific cases of inducements, threats or deception there is still the need to prove that the defendant knew (or could reasonably have been expected to know) of the victim's mental disorder but *no need to prove that the victim was unable to refuse.*

1.9.6.4 Causing Person with Mental Disorder to Watch Sexual Act

OFFENCE: **Causing a Person with a Mental Disorder to Watch a Sexual Act—**
Sexual Offences Act 2003, s. 33

- Triable either way • Ten years' imprisonment on indictment • Six months' imprisonment summarily

The Sexual Offences Act 2003, s. 33 states:

(1) A person (A) commits an offence if—
    (a) for the purpose of obtaining sexual gratification, he intentionally causes another person (B) to watch a third person engaging in an activity, or to look at an image of any person engaging in an activity,
    (b) the activity is sexual, and
    (c) B is unable to refuse because of or for a reason related to a mental disorder, and
    (d) A knows or could reasonably be expected to know that B has a mental disorder and that because of it or for a reason related to it B is likely to be unable to refuse.

KEYNOTE

For the key elements to prove in relation to this offence see the earlier offences above.

While the related offence under s. 32 is concerned with engaging in sexual activity which the person knows, believes or intends to be observed by a person with a mental disorder impeding their choice, the above offence is concerned with intentionally causing such a person to watch a third person engaging in such activity *or* to look at an image of a person engaging in such activity. 'Image' includes a moving or still image and includes an image produced by any means and, where the context permits, a three-dimensional image (s. 79(4); it also includes images of an imaginary person (s. 79(5)).

If the victim agrees to watch or look because of any inducement (offered or given), or a threat or deception practised by the defendant for that purpose, the defendant commits a specific (and similarly punishable) offence under s. 37. An example of such an offence would be where the defendant (with the appropriate motive) deceives the mentally disordered person into watching a film which is actually a live video feed of sexual activity. In these specific cases of inducements, threats or deception there is still the need to prove that the defendant knew (or could reasonably have been expected to know) of the victim's mental disorder but *no need to prove that the victim was unable to refuse.*

1.9.6.5 Care Workers

There are specific sexual offences that apply to people who are involved in the care of the mentally disordered victim. These offences follow similar wording to those general offences set out above (namely engaging in, causing or inciting sexual activity, sexual activity in the presence of a mentally disordered person etc.). In proving these offences (which appear in ss. 38–41 of the Act) you must show that the person was in a relationship of care as defined at s. 42. These are generally people whose employment has brought them into regular face to face contact with the victim in care homes, voluntary homes or hospitals. The offences are similar to those involving a position of trust (**see para. 1.9.5.5**). In these offences there is no need to prove that the victim was unable to refuse to take part in the activity but you must show that the defendant knew or could reasonably have been expected to know that the victim has a mental disorder. Given that the defendant will be a care worker with direct personal knowledge of the victim's circumstances, there is a presumption against the defendant that he or she had (or could reasonably have been expected to have) such knowledge and the defendant will have to discharge an evidential burden in that regard if he/she is using this issue as part of his/her defence.

An offence under s. 38 (care workers: sexual activity with a person with a mental disorder) or s. 39 (care workers: causing or inciting sexual activity) if committed in relation to a person under the age of 16 (including aiding, abetting, counselling, procuring, inciting or attempting the commission of such an offence) will fall within the relevant sexual offences category for the purposes of s. 103(2)(b) of the Criminal Justice Act 2003 (a defendant's propensity to commit offences of the kind with which he/she is charged—**see para. 1.9.3**).

1.9.6.6 Protection of People Suffering from Mental Disorders

The Mental Health Act 1983 provides for the care and treatment of people suffering from mental disorders and supplies powers for enforcing some of its provisions.

If those powers are executed in good faith, the 1983 Act also provides some protection against criminal and civil liability for the police officers and care workers who use them (see s. 139).

The 1983 Act is supported by a Code of Practice that sets out guidance for the police and other agencies when dealing with people suffering from mental disorders.

1.9.6.7 Mentally Disordered People Found in Public Places

Section 136 of the Mental Health Act 1983 creates a power for police officers to remove such a person under certain conditions.

Section 136 states:

(1) If a constable finds in a place to which the public have access a person who appears to him to be suffering from mental disorder and to be in immediate need of care or control, the constable may, if he thinks it necessary to do so in the interests of that person or for the protection of other persons, remove that person to a place of safety within the meaning of section 135 above.

(2) A person removed to a place of safety under this section may be detained there for a period not exceeding 72 hours for the purpose of enabling him to be examined by a registered medical practitioner and to be interviewed by an approved social worker and of making any necessary arrangements for his treatment or care.

KEYNOTE

Given the number of people who are suffering from some form of mental disorder and who are receiving 'care in the community', this a significant power which is provided for the protection of the person themselves and of others.

The power places a lot of responsibility and latitude on the officer who must decide whether:

- the person is suffering from mental disorder (see below)
- the person is in immediate need of care or control, and
- it is necessary in the person's interest or for someone else's protection that he/she be removed to a place of safety

before the power is applicable. This power appears to be consistent with Article 5 of the European Convention on Human Rights which sets out the limited circumstances where the detention or arrest of an individual will be permitted (see General Police Duties, chapter 4.3).

The definition of 'mental disorder' under s. 1(2) is very wide and means:

- mental illness
- arrested or incomplete development of mind
- psychopathic disorder (a persistent disorder or disability resulting in abnormally aggressive or seriously irresponsible conduct)
- any other disorder or disability of mind.

Under s. 135(6), a 'place of safety' is:

- residential accommodation provided by social services
- a hospital
- a police station
- a mental nursing home, or
- any other suitable place where the occupier is willing to receive the patient temporarily.

Anyone being taken to a place of safety or detained at such a place will be treated as being in legal custody (s. 137(1)). (This expression is only relevant in relation to escaping and assisting in an escape; it is very different from 'in police detention' used under s. 118 of the Police and Criminal Evidence Act 1984. A mentally disordered person removed from a public place is *not* in police detention even if taken to a police station.)

Note that this power is a power of removal from a public place; it is not a power of arrest nor does it provide a power to detain/further detain someone who is already in police detention.

It is an offence to assist someone removed under s. 136 to escape (see s. 128).

Interestingly, in considering the lawfulness of an enforced placement of an old woman in a secure ward under Article 5(1)(e) of the European Convention, the European Court of Human Rights recently decided that the key issue was whether or not the detention was in the person's 'best interests', rather than whether the precise wording of the article had been complied with (see *HM* v *Switzerland* (2002) LTL 26 February). The Court held that, not only was the enforced detention of the woman (who suffered from dementia and was unable to care for herself) against her will lawful, but also that keeping her in a closed ward which she was not allowed to leave did not amount to a deprivation of liberty. Whatever its other implications for mental health law, this approach is at least consistent with the intention and wording of s. 136 which is very much aimed at allowing the State to take immediate, short-term action to protect the best interests of someone who is clearly unable to look after themselves. This element should also be considered alongside the positive obligations of the police and others to protect life (under Article 2 of the European Convention—see General Police Duties, chapter 4.3).

1.9.6.8 Warrant to Search for Patients

Where there is reasonable cause to suspect that a person believed to be suffering from a mental disorder has been, or is being ill-treated or neglected or is unable to care for himself/herself and is living alone, a warrant may be issued by a magistrate (s. 135).

The warrant allows a constable to enter any premises specified and to remove the person to a place of safety. In doing so, the officer must be accompanied by a social worker and a doctor (s. 135(4)).

A warrant may also be issued in respect of a patient ordered to be detained by a court.

1.9.6.9 Power to Retake Escaped Patients

Section 138 provides a power to retake people who have been in legal custody under the 1983 Act.

A person removed to a place of safety under s. 136 or a person removed under a warrant, who subsequently escapes while being taken to or detained in a place of safety, cannot generally be retaken after 72 hours have elapsed. That time period starts either when the person escapes or when his/her liability to be detained began, whichever expires first (s. 138(3)). This means that, if the person escapes *before* reaching the place of safety, the 72 hours begins then; if the person escapes *from* the place of safety, the 72 hours begins at the time he/she arrived there.

There is also a power for a court to issue a warrant for the arrest of a convicted mental patient who is unlawfully at large (Criminal Justice Act 1967, s. 72(3)).

1.9.6.10 Ambit of the Mental Health Act 1983

The ambit of the Mental Health Act 1983 was recently reviewed in *St George's Healthcare NHS Trust v S* [1998] 3 WLR 936, by the Court of Appeal. There it was held that:

- The 1983 Act should not be invoked to overrule the decision of a patient concerning medical treatment simply because that decision appears to be irrational.
- A person detained under the 1983 Act should not be forced to receive medical treatment which is not connected with his/her mental condition unless his/her capacity to give consent is seriously diminished.

1.9.7 Sexual Displays and Voyeurism

While many of the sexual offences dealt with in this chapter concern the sexual activity itself, or the encouragement of it, there are several offences that involve sexual 'displays' of some description and of voyeurism; there is also a specific offence of sexual activity in public lavatories. All of these are addressed below.

1.9.7.1 Indecent Exposure

Although it is often trivialised, the behaviour of those who indecently expose themselves in public is both distressing and often symptomatic of a psychological disorder which can manifest itself in other, far more destructive ways.

OFFENCE: **Outraging Public Decency—*Common Law***
>   • Triable either way • Unlimited powers of sentence on indictment • Six months' imprisonment and/or fine summarily

It is an offence at common law to commit an act of a lewd, obscene or disgusting nature and outrage public decency.

KEYNOTE

This offence is committed by the deliberate commission of an act that is, *per se*, lewd, obscene or disgusting (*R* v *Rowley* [1991] 4 All ER 649). If an act is not lewd, obscene' etc. then the motives or intentions of the defendant cannot make it so. Therefore, where the defendant's acts involved leaving messages that were not in themselves obscene in public toilets, his motives (to induce young boys to engage in gross indecency with him) did not bring his actions under this offence (*Rowley* above). In *Rowley* the court cited a speech by Lord Simon in *Knuller (Publishing, Printing and Promotions) Ltd* v *DPP* [1973] AC 435. Lord Simon had said that 'outraging public decency' goes considerably beyond offending the sensibilities of, or even shocking, reasonable people and that the recognised minimum standards of decency were likely to vary from time to time.

The offence can be committed by exposing the penis or engaging in simulated sexual acts (*R* v *Mayling* [1963] 2 QB 717) but it may also be committed in other ways and is not restricted to offences committed by men.

The act must be committed where it might be seen by the public generally and it must be shown that more than one person could have seen the act take place (*R* v *Walker* [1996] 1 Cr App R 111).

It is not necessary to prove that someone was *in fact* annoyed or insulted (*R* v *May* (1989) 91 Cr App R 157).

OFFENCE: **Exposure—*Sexual Offences Act 2003, s. 66***
>   • Triable either way • Two years' imprisonment on indictment • Six months' imprisonment summarily

The Sexual Offences Act 2003, s. 66 states:

(1) A person commits an offence if—
    (a) he intentionally exposes his genitals, and
    (b) he intends that someone will see them and be caused alarm or distress.

KEYNOTE

This offence requires only the intentional exposure of the genitals with the dual intention of their being seen by someone else and that this other person will be caused alarm or distress.

There is no need to show that the defendant acted for sexual gratification and simply exposing the genitals out of loutish behaviour will suffice if the other ingredients are present.

The offence is not restricted to public places and there is no need to show that anyone saw the genitals or was alarmed or distressed.

1.9.7.2 Voyeurism

OFFENCE: **Voyeurism—*Sexual Offences Act 2003, s. 67***

> • Triable either way • Two years' imprisonment on indictment • Six months' imprisonment summarily

The Sexual Offences Act 2003, s. 67 states:

(1) A person commits an offence if—
   (a) for the purpose of obtaining sexual gratification, he observes another person doing a private act, and
   (b) he knows that the other person does not consent to being observed for his sexual gratification.
(2) A person commits an offence if—
   (a) he operates equipment with the intention of enabling another person to observe, for the purpose of obtaining sexual gratification, a third person (B) doing a private act, and
   (b) he knows that B does not consent to his operating equipment with that intention.
(3) A person commits an offence if—
   (a) he records another person (B) doing a private act,
   (b) he does so with the intention that he or a third person will, for the purpose of obtaining sexual gratification, look at an image of B doing the act, and
   (c) he knows that B does not consent to his recording the act with that intention.

KEYNOTE

Unlike the previous offence of exposure, these offences require proof of the defendant's motive of sexual gratification.

A person is doing a private act if they are in a place which, in the circumstances, would reasonably be expected to provide privacy, and:

- their genitals, buttocks or breasts are exposed or covered only with underwear
- they are using a lavatory, or
- they are doing a sexual act that is not of a kind ordinarily done in public (s. 68).

The three offences described above require proof that the victim does not consent to the observing, recording or operating of the relevant equipment *for the purpose of the defendant or another's sexual gratification* (i.e. they might have consented to being observed, recorded etc. for other reasons). The first offence involves a defendant observing another doing a private act (which will include looking at an image—s. 79(5)) with the relevant motive of gaining sexual gratification. The second offence deals with people operating equipment such as hoteliers or landlords using webcams to enable others to view live footage of their residents or tenants, in each case for the sexual gratification of those others. There is no need to show that the defendant intended to gain sexual gratification themselves.

The third offence deals with the recording of the private act with the intention that the person doing the recording or another will look at the image and thereby obtain sexual gratification. It does not matter that those who eventually look at the recording know that the victim did not consent, though all elements of the offence would be corroborated by the accompanying material (e.g. the descriptions of the pages on an internet website). A practical example of this offence can be seen in *R v Turner* [2006] EWCA Crim 63 where the defendant—the manager of a gym—had recorded images of women showering and using the sun beds. The court regarded this as an abuse of the defendant's position of trust which took him 'over the custodial threshold' and he was sentenced (following an appeal) to nine months' imprisonment.

Finally, there is also a specific offence under s. 67(4) of installing equipment or adapting structures (e.g. drilling peepholes) with the intention of committing the first offence themselves or enabling others to do so. Structures will include tents, vehicles or vessels or other temporary or movable structures.

The restricted wording of subs. (4) appears not to cover the situation where the defendant installs equipment to *record* the private act (under subs. (2)) rather than observing it live.

It can be seen that, these offences do not extend to activities such as, for example, covertly filming up women's skirts as they go about the public act of shopping and travelling to work.

1.9.7.3 Sexual Activity in a Public Lavatory

OFFENCE: **Sexual Activity in a Public Lavatory—*Sexual Offences Act 2003, s. 71***
- Triable summarily • Six months' imprisonment and/or a fine

The Sexual Offences Act 2003, s. 71 states:

(1) A person commits an offence if—
  (a) he is in a lavatory to which the public or a section of the public has or is permitted to have access, whether on payment or otherwise,
  (b) he intentionally engages in an activity, and,
  (c) the activity is sexual.

KEYNOTE

This offence will apply to any lavatory to which the public or a section of it has access. For the purposes of this offence only, an activity is sexual if a reasonable person would, in all the circumstances but regardless of any person's purpose, consider it to be sexual. This is a narrower definition than the more general one of 'sexual' used in other sections of the Act (see s. 78).

1.9.8 Preparatory Offences

In addition to the many substantive offences covered by this chapter, there are specific provisions to prevent the consequences set out in those offences from happening. These 'preparatory' offences should be considered in conjunction with the general principles applying to incomplete offences.

1.9.8.1 Any Offence with Intent to Commit Sexual Offence

OFFENCE: **Committing Criminal Offence with Intent to Commit a Sexual Offence—*Sexual Offences Act 2003, s. 62***
- Where the offence committed is kidnapping or false imprisonment—triable on indictment only; life imprisonment • Otherwise triable either way; ten years' imprisonment on indictment; six months' imprisonment and/or a fine summarily

The Sexual Offences Act 2003, s. 62 states:

(1) A person commits an offence under this section if he commits any offence with the intention of committing a relevant sexual offence.

KEYNOTE

Relevant sexual offence means an offence under part I of the Act (virtually all regularly occurring sexual offences) including aiding, abetting, counselling or procuring such an offence (s. 62(2)). It does not extend to other sexual offences such as those under the Protection of Children Act 1978.

This offence is designed to deal with the commission of any criminal offence where the defendant's intention is to commit a relevant sexual offence. In addition to the more obvious offences of kidnapping and blackmail, this would appear to cover a vast array of possible circumstances where the defendant's ulterior motive in committing the first offence is to carry out the relevant sexual offence. As there is no express requirement for there to be any immediate link in time between the two offences, the wording appears to cover any situation from the theft of drugs or equipment to be used in the course of the sexual offence and going equipped for burglary, to the taking of a vehicle or even dangerous driving with the intention in each case of committing the further relevant sexual offence.

1.9.8.2 Trespass with Intent to Commit Sexual Offence

OFFENCE: **Trespass with Intent to Commit a Relevant Sexual Offence—*Sexual Offences Act 2003, s. 63***

- Triable either way • Ten years' imprisonment on indictment • Six months' imprisonment and/or a fine summarily

The Sexual Offences Act 2003, s. 63 states:

(1) A person commits an offence if—
   (a) he is a trespasser on any premises,
   (b) he intends to commit a relevant sexual offence on the premises, and
   (c) he knows that, or is reckless as to whether, he is a trespasser.

KEYNOTE

A person is a trespasser if they are on the premises without the owner or occupier's consent, whether express or implied. Generally, the defendant ought to know whether he/she is trespassing or not and recklessness will be enough in that regard.

Premises here will include a structure or part of a structure (including a tent, vehicle or vessel or other temporary or movable structure)—s. 63(2)—which is wider than the term 'building' used in the Theft Act offence of burglary.

Relevant sexual offence has the same meaning as in the s. 62 offence (see para. 1.9.8.1).

This offence is one of intention rather than consequence and so there is no need to prove that the substantive sexual offence took place. There is still considerable overlap between the above offence and burglary and, if the person is caught going equipped for burglary and also has the intention of committing a relevant sexual offence at the time, he/she may commit the more general offence under s. 62.

Note that the defendant must intend to commit the relevant offence on the premises.

1.9.8.3 Administering Substance with Intent

OFFENCE: **Administering Substance with Intent—*Sexual Offences Act 2003, s. 61***

- Triable either way • Ten years' imprisonment on indictment • Six months' imprisonment and/or a fine summarily

The Sexual Offences Act 2003, s. 61 states:

(1) A person commits an offence if he intentionally administers a substance to, or causes a substance to be taken by, another person (B)—
   (a) knowing that B does not consent, and
   (b) with the intention of stupefying or overpowering B, so as to enable any person to engage in a sexual activity that involves B.

KEYNOTE

This offence is aimed at the use of the so-called date rape drugs but is far wider than that. For instance it would cover the spiking of a victim's soft drinks with alcohol if done with the relevant intent.

'Administering or causing to be taken' covers a broader range of conduct than the parallel offences of poisoning.

The key elements are the defendant's intentionally administering the substance (*any* substance), in the knowledge that the victim does not consent and with the intention of overpowering or stupefying the victim in order that *any person* can engage in sexual activity involving the victim.

As this is an offence of intent rather than consequence there is no need for the victim to be stupefied or overpowered or for the sexual activity to take place.

So far as proof of the relevant elements is concerned see para. 1.9.3.3.

1.9.9 Control of Sex Offenders

In addition to the creation of specific criminal offences regulating and punishing certain types of sexual or sexually motivated behaviour, Parliament has also provided a framework for the control and monitoring of sex offenders. This framework is covered in the following paragraphs.

1.9.9.1 Statutory Regulation of Sex Offenders

Statutory regulation of the behaviour of sex offenders has increased significantly over recent years.

Part 2 of the Sexual Offences Act 2003 sets out the notification requirements for sex offenders and introduces sexual offences prevention orders, along with other measures for reducing the opportunities for sex offenders to continue to present a threat to victims anywhere in the world.

What follows is a summary of the main practical provisions but reference should be made to the statutory text for complete coverage.

1.9.9.2 Offenders Covered by Notification Requirements

A person is subject to the notification requirements for the period set out in s. 82 (the notification period) if:

- they are convicted of an offence listed in Schedule 3—this covers most of the commonly occurring sex offences set out elsewhere in this chapter (for example, the offences of rape or assualt by penetration);
- they are found not guilty of such an offence by reason of insanity;
- they are found to be under a disability and to have done the act charged against them in respect of such an offence; or

- they are cautioned in respect of such an offence, not only in England and Wales but for an offence in Northern Ireland as well. (s. 80).

In a decision relating to the former legislation, the Court of Appeal has confirmed that conditional discharges count as 'convictions' and therefore a person receiving such a punishment was subject to the notification requirements (*R* v *Longworth* [2004] EWCA Crim 2145). The reasoning behind this decision is likely to be applied to the notification requirements under the Sexual Offences Act 2003 set out below (although the Court of Appeal expressly declined to speculate on this point). The reasoning behind the finding that conditional discharges were 'convictions' in *Longworth* was because s. 14(1) of the Powers of Criminal Courts (Sentencing) Act 2000 provides that a discharge is to be regarded as a conviction 'for the purposes of the proceedings in which the order was made' and the Court of Appeal held that the notification requirements (under the old legislation) fell within the scope of those purposes.

Where the above findings, convictions or cautions are made, the court or the police may issue a certificate that will be evidence of that fact (see s. 92) and the Secretary of State may make regulations setting out the form of certificate to be used.

A person subject to the notification requirements is referred to in the legislation as a 'relevant offender'.

Clearly many sex offenders were already subject to the previous notification requirements under part 1 of the Sex Offenders Act 1997. Some of these people continue to be subject to the notification requirements. For the full details as to these offenders see s. 81.

Some relevant offenders will have attracted that status (and the relevant notification requirements below) by reason of a conviction etc. for one of the sexual offences abolished by the Sexual Offences Act 2003 (buggery or gross indecency between men under ss. 12 or 13 of the Sexual Offences Act 1956). Schedule 4 to the 2003 Act and Home Office Circular 19/2004 deal with the procedure whereby such offenders may apply to the Secretary of State for removal of their notification requirements.

A challenge to the compatibility of the notification requirements with the European Convention on Human Rights was unsuccessful in *Forbes* v *Secretary of State for the Home Department* [2005] EWHC 1597. That case arose from the very specific excise offence of importing obscene material involving children, but courts can be expected to follow the general principles applied in that case.

1.9.9.3 The Notification Period

Section 82 sets out the notification period. This is as follows:

Description of relevant offender	Notification period
A person who, in respect of the offence, is or has been sentenced to imprisonment for a term of 30 months or more	An indefinite period beginning with the relevant date
A person who, in respect of the offence or finding, is or has been admitted to a hospital subject to a restriction order	An indefinite period beginning with that date
A person who, in respect of the offence, is or has been sentenced to imprisonment for a term of more than 6 months but less than 30 months	10 years beginning with that date

Description of relevant offender	Notification period
A person who, in respect of the offence, is or has been sentenced to imprisonment for a term of 6 months or less	7 years beginning with that date
A person who, in respect of the offence or finding, is or has been admitted to a hospital without being subject to a restriction order	7 years beginning with that date
A person within section 80(1)(d) (cautioned)	2 years beginning with that date
A person in whose case an order for conditional discharge is made in respect of the offence	The period of conditional discharge
A person of any other description	5 years beginning with the relevant date

Where a person is under 18 on the relevant date, references to a period of 10 years, 7 years, 5 years or 2 years are substituted by a reference to half that period (s. 82(2)).

Meaning of Cautioned

Cautioned means cautioned by a police officer after the person concerned has admitted the offence, or reprimanded or warned within the meaning given by s. 65 of the Crime and Disorder Act 1998 (see Evidence and Procedure)—s. 133.

The wording of s. 134 means that conviction includes a conditional discharge (though not an absolute discharge). The Act makes specific provisions for offenders who are sentenced for more than one offence and for those who, having been initially found to be under a disability, are later tried for the offence.

1.9.9.4 Initial Notification

A relevant offender must notify the police of certain information within a specified time period from the 'relevant date'. Generally the relevant date will be the date of conviction, finding, caution or, in the case of people covered by the Sex Offenders Act 1997, the appropriate date under that Act.

Relevant offenders must, within the period of three days beginning with the relevant date (or, if later, the commencement of part 2 of the Act), notify to the police the information set out in subs. (5)—(s. 83(1)). There are some exceptions made in relation to offenders covered by the earlier legislation and those who have already complied with s. 83(1) at the date of being dealt with by the court.

The information required under subs. (5) is the relevant offender's:

- date of birth
- national insurance number
- name on the relevant date *and* on the date on which notification is given. If s/he used one or more other names on those dates, each of those names
- home address on the relevant date *and* on the date on which notification is given

and the address of any other premises in the United Kingdom at which, at the time the notification is given, he/she regularly resides or stays.

In calculating the time under s. 83(1) account is not generally taken of time spent in custody by order of a court, detention in a hospital or while out of the United Kingdom (see s. 83(6)).

Home address means the address of the relevant offender's sole or main residence in the United Kingdom, or where he/she has no such residence, the address or location of a place in the United Kingdom where he/she can regularly be found and, if there is more than one such place, such one of those places as the person may select (s. 83(7)). This means that, if the offender is of no fixed abode, they can give details of any shelter or other place where they are regularly to be found.

1.9.9.5 Notification Requirements: Changes

Within the period of three days beginning with:

- his or her using a name which has not been notified to the police under the relevant legislative provisions
- any change of home address
- his or her having resided or stayed, for a 'qualifying period' (seven days *or* two or more periods in any 12 months which together amount to seven days), at any premises in the United Kingdom the address of which has not been notified to the police under the relevant legislative provision, or
- his or her release from custody pursuant to an order of a court or from imprisonment, service detention or detention in a hospital,

a relevant offender must notify to the police that name, the new home address, the address of those premises or (as the case may be) the fact that s/he has been released, and (in addition) the information set out in s. 83(5)–s. 84(1).

Any notification under the above requirement can be given in advance of the change, provided the actual change takes place within a given 'margin' of time either side of the notified date. For that reason the relevant offender must also specify the date when the event is expected to occur (s. 84(2)). As long as the change notified in advance takes place no earlier than two days before the date notified or no more than three days after, the offender does not need to notify the police of the actual date when it took place. However, if the change takes place outside this margin, the offender must notify the change as required by s. 84(1)—e.g. within three days of the actual change. Similarly, if the change takes place three days or more after the date notified in advance, the offender must also tell the police within six days that the change s/he gave advance notice of did not occur as specified (see s. 84(3) and (4)).

As with the initial notification requirements, account is not generally taken of time spent in custody by order of a court, detention in a hospital or while out of the United Kingdom (see s. 84(5)).

1.9.9.6 Notification Requirements: Periodic Notification

A relevant offender must also re-notify the police of the details in s. 83(5) above within one year of either the initial notification or the notification of the changes unless s/he has already notified them within that period (under s. 84) as a result of changing circumstances (s. 85). In summary this means that, if a relevant offender does not change their name or address, or stay away from home for seven days or more, they will have to re-notify the police of the relevant details within a year of their initial notification and every year afterwards. Under s. 85(3), if the offender is detained or is abroad when their periodic notification becomes due, they have until three days after their release/return to the United Kingdom to re-notify.

1.9.9.7 Notification Requirements: Travel Outside the United Kingdom

The Secretary of State has the power to make regulations setting out the notification requirements for relevant offenders who travel outside the United Kingdom (s. 86). The current regulations are the Sexual Offences Act 2003 (Travel Notification Requirements) Regulations 2004 (S1 2004/1220).

1.9.9.8 Method of Notification and Related Matters

A relevant offender complies with the obligations to notify the police set out above by attending at such police station in his local police area as the Secretary of State may by regulations prescribe—see the Sexual Offences Act 2003 (Prescribed Police Stations) Regulations 2005 (SI 2005/210) for a list of specific police stations identified for this purpose—(or, if there is more than one, at any of them), and giving an oral notification to any police officer, or to any person authorised for the purpose by the officer in charge of the station (s. 87(1)). 'Local police area' means:

- the police area in which the offender's home address is situated or,
- if they do not have a home address, the police area in which the home address last notified is situated or,
- if they do not have a home address or in the absence of any such notification, the police area in which the court which last dealt with them for a relevant matter is situated (see s. 88).

If the notification relates to staying away from home for seven days or more, or to an advance change of address, the offender may give the notification at a police station in the police area of the other address (s. 87(2)).

When the offender gives a notification to the police (other than in relation to travel outside the United Kingdom), the police can fingerprint and/or photograph the offender (s. 87(4)) for the purpose of verifying the identity of the relevant offender. 'Photograph' includes any process by means of which an image may be produced and therefore would include new methods such as iris scans (see s. 88(2)).

1.9.9.9 Notification Orders

In addition to the above, a chief officer of police may apply to a magistrates' court for an order against a person who has been convicted, cautioned or had another relevant finding recorded against him or her for a relevant offence outside the United Kingdom (see s. 97). Basically a relevant offence here means an offence abroad which, had it been committed here, would also have been a sch. 3 offence. This provision closed a loophole in the earlier sex offenders registration and monitoring scheme and applies where the relevant offender lives in the chief officer's police area or where the chief officer believes that s/he is intending to come to that police area. This means that a chief officer can apply to a magistrates' court for a notification order against a foreign national who has been convicted abroad and who is intending to come to the chief officer's police area. Notification orders will, broadly speaking, make the offender subject to the notification requirements, however there are specific differences in relation to the calculation of the relevant periods (see s. 97(3) and (4) and s. 98).

1.9.9.10 Interim Notification Orders

In addition, the police may apply for an interim notification order while the application for a full notification order is determined (s. 100). Such an interim order may be necessary because the relevant paperwork is likely to delay the hearing for the main order. Once an interim notification order is granted, the relevant offender becomes subject to the notification requirements above and the notification period starts from the date of service of the order (s. 100(5) and (6)).

An offender has a right of appeal against both interim or full notification orders to the Crown Court (s. 101).

1.9.9.11 Young Offenders: Parental Directions

Section 89 of the Sexual Offences Act 2003 makes provisions for young offenders and allows the courts to direct a person with parental responsibility for the offender to comply with their notification requirements instead—until either the young offender reaches 18 or an earlier date specified by the court. Under a parental direction the parent must ensure that the young offender attends at the police station with him or her, when a notification is being given (s. 89(2)(b)).

A chief officer may (by complaint to any magistrates' court whose commission area includes any part of his or her police area) apply for a parental direction in respect of any relevant offender who is under 18 and who resides in that police area, or who the chief officer believes is in or is intending to come to his or her police area (see s. 89(4) and (5)). A court may alter or discharge a parental direction order on application by the offender, parent or relevant chief officer (s. 90). A variation or alteration might be needed where, for example, the offender's parents divorce or where they cannot exercise enough control over the offender to ensure compliance with the notification requirements. For the general provisions relating to youth offending **see Evidence and Procedure.**

1.9.9.12 Failure to Notify

OFFENCE: **Failing to Comply with Notification Requirements—*Sexual Offences Act 2003, s. 91***

> • Triable either way • Five years' imprisonment on indictment • Six months' and/or fine summarily

The Sexual Offences Act 2003, s. 91 states:

(1) A person commits an offence if he—
   (a) fails, without reasonable excuse, to comply with section 83(1), 84(1), 84(4)(b), 85(1), 87(4) or 89(2)(b) or any requirement imposed by regulations made under section 86(1); or
   (b) notifies to the police, in purported compliance with section 83(1), 84(1) or 85(1) or any requirement imposed by regulations made under section 86(1), any information which he knows to be false.

KEYNOTE

Reasonable excuse will be a question of fact in all the circumstances for the court to decide. In relation to a parental direction, it is more likely that the person will have such an excuse, particularly if they have done all they can to ensure that the young offender comes with them to the police station.

This is a continuing offence, in that the offender continues to commit it for each and every day that s/he fails to give notification as required (s. 91(3)). Although the offender can only be prosecuted once for the same continuing failure, if he/she is convicted for the above offence and then fails again to comply, s/he commits another offence.

1.9.9.13 Supply of Information for Verification

Section 94 provides that a specified person or body may supply information to the Secretary of State (or a person supplying a relevant function to the Secretary of State) for the purposes of the prevention, detection, investigation or prosecution of offences under part 2 of the Act, for use in verifying that information. The information is that which was notified to the police under ss. 83, 84 or 85 (see above) or the equivalent earlier legislation (s. 2(1)–(3) of the Sex Offenders Act 1997). Those people and bodies are:

- a chief officer of police
- the National Policing Improvement Agency (NPIA).
- the Director General of the Serious Organized Crime Agency

Verification and Use

Verifying the information here means checking its accuracy by comparing it with information held by the Secretary of State or bodies responsible for functions such as social security, child support, employment or training, the Passports Agency or the Driver and Vehicle Licensing Agency (DVLA). Checking accuracy includes compiling a report, though this part of the Act does not authorise anything that would amount to a breach of the Data Protection Act 1998. The recipient of the report must be one of the people/bodies set out above and they may use the information only for the purposes of the prevention, detection, investigation or prosecution of an offence under part 2 but can retain it whether or not it is in fact used for that purpose (see s. 95).

1.9.9.14 Orders to Control Sex Offenders

In addition to the notification requirements for relevant offenders (**see para. 1.9.10**), there are other powers available in the appropriate circumstances to restrain or prevent sex offending. The Sexual Offences Act 2003 creates a series of different orders which, although civil in nature, are of significant value to the police in preventing and controlling the activities of sex offenders and people who have presented a risk of sexual harm to children. The first of these orders is the Sexual Offences Prevention Order (SOPO).

1.9.9.15 Sexual Offences Prevention Orders

SOPOs are civil law measures to prevent offending and protect the public. They have replaced the old sex offender orders and restraining orders (although someone who is still subject to those older orders remains under the relevant obligations contained in them).

A court can make a SOPO in a number of circumstances where it is satisfied that it is necessary to do so for the purpose of protecting the public (or any particular member(s) of the public) from serious sexual harm from the defendant. In summary, the SOPO can be made where:

- the court deals with (rather than simply 'convicts') a person for a sch. 3 offence
- the court decides that a defendant is not guilty of an offence listed in sch. 3 or sch. 5 (these include offences of murder and manslaughter, causing the death of a child or vulnerable adult, violence, fear or intimidation as well as sexual offences and firearms

offences; they also include those offences relating to 'dangerous offenders' created by the Criminal Justice Act 2003 by reason of insanity, or that he is under a disability and has done the act charged against him in respect of such an offence, or

- a chief officer applies for one in respect of a 'qualifying offender' (see below) and certain conditions are met. (see s. 104).

1.9.9.16   Police Application for SOPO

As described above, the police can apply for a SOPO in respect of certain people in certain circumstances. Section 104(5) provides that a chief officer may, by complaint to a magistrates' court, apply for an order under this section in respect of a person who resides in his or her police area or who the chief officer believes is in, or is intending to come to, his or her police area if it appears to the chief officer that:

- the person is a qualifying offender (basically this means they have been convicted of, cautioned for or found not guilty by reason of insanity or to have been under a disability, in respect of an offence under sch. 3 or 5 here or by a foreign court for an equivalent offence), *and*
- the person has, since the appropriate date (e.g. date of first conviction or caution) acted in such a way as to give reasonable cause to believe that it is *necessary* (rather than just desirable or a 'good idea') for such an order to be made.

The court will have to decide whether the order is necessary to protect the public or any particular member(s) of the public in the United Kingdom from serious physical or psychological harm, caused by the defendant committing one or more offences listed in sch. 3 (s. 106(3)). In doing so, the court will consider the acts of the defendant since the relevant date. Therefore the availability of good quality intelligence as to the defendant's conduct within the relevant period will be critical.

As this procedure is a civil one, the standard of proof required in proving the elements above is on a balance of probabilities (**see Evidence and Procedure, chapter 2.7**).

1.9.9.17   The Order

Section 107 of the Sexual Offences Act 2003 states:

(1) A sexual offences prevention order—
    (a) prohibits the defendant from doing anything described in the order, and
    (b) has effect for a fixed period (not less than 5 years) specified in the order or until further order.
(2) The only prohibitions that may be included in the order are those necessary for the purpose of protecting the public or any particular members of the public from serious sexual harm from the defendant.

KEYNOTE

A SOPO can cover any activity by the offender at all, whether or not that activity amounts to a criminal offence or a civil wrong, provided it is shown to be necessary for the purposes of protecting the public (or any particular member of the public) from serious sexual harm from the defendant. This phrase is defined under s. 106 and is discussed in the previous paragraph.

> The order will last for at least five years but can be for an indefinite period, provided that period is specified in the order. Further orders can be made after the original expires but there can only be one SOPO in respect of the same offender at any one time (see s. 107(6)).

Effect on Notification Requirements

If an offender is not subject to the notification requirements discussed in previous paragraphs, he/she will become subject to them for the duration of a SOPO (s. 107(4)). In such circumstances the relevant date is the date of service of the order (s. 107(5)).

This means that, in relation to the initial notification requirements under s. 83(1), for example, the relevant offender will have three days *from service of the order* within which to comply with his or her obligations.

Where the offender is already subject to the notification requirements and those requirements will cease during the period of the SOPO, he/she will still have to comply with those notification requirements for the duration of the order (s. 107(3)). Conversely, if the notification requirements last *longer* than any SOPO made since conviction, finding or caution, then the SOPO does not have any effect on them and they continue as originally imposed by the court.

1.9.9.18 Changes to a SOPO

Where a SOPO has been made, an application to vary, renew or discharge the order can be made, either by the defendant or:

- the chief officer of police for the area in which the defendant resides or
- a chief officer of police who believes that the defendant is in, or is intending to come to, his or her police area or,
- where the order was made on an application under s. 104(5), the chief officer of police who made the application. (s. 108).

It may become necessary for a SOPO to be varied or renewed. For instance, the original order may be limited to a certain geographical area and the defendant intends to move, or it is discovered that s/he is travelling more widely and frequently than originally believed. An order may be renewed, or varied so as to impose additional prohibitions on the defendant, only if it is necessary to do so for the purpose of protecting the public or any particular members of the public from serious sexual harm from the defendant (and any renewed or varied order may contain only such prohibitions as are necessary for this purpose)—s. 108(5).

A court must not discharge a SOPO before the end of five years beginning with the day on which it was made, without the consent of the defendant and, if it was made on the application of a chief officer of police, that chief officer. If it was not made on application by a chief officer, then the chief officer for the area where the defendant resides must also consent before such a variation can be made (s. 108(6)).

1.9.9.19 Approach by Court in Similar Processes

In assessing how SOPOs will be received and interpreted by the courts, there are some useful decisions arising out of the earlier legislation. For instance, a good example of some of the practical aspects of applying for an order under the previous system can be found in the case of *Jones (Peter)* v *Greater Manchester Police Authority* [2002] ACD 4. There a man had been convicted of 30 sexual offences against young males and an order was made against him. The order prevented the man from entering public parks, playgrounds or public swimming baths and from enticing, approaching, communicating with or being in the company of anyone under the age of 18; it also prevented him from leaving the country without first notifying the police and getting permission from the court. The order was to last for life. In dismissing the defendant's appeal, the Crown Court nevertheless amended the order to take out the reference to parks and reduced the age of those with whom the defendant could not associate to 16 years. The defendant appealed on the basis that evidence of a consultant psychologist and a probation officer which had been put before the Crown Court was evidence of 'mere propensity' to commit sexual offences and had no place in an enquiry relating to an order against him. He also argued that the admission of such evidence breached Articles 6 and 8 of the European Convention on Human Rights and that the proceedings were criminal in nature. The Divisional Court did not agree with him, re-affirming that proceedings for an order were civil in nature for the purposes of Article 6 (see *B* v *Chief Constable of the Avon and Somerset Constabulary* [2001] 1 WLR 340 and *R* v *Manchester Crown Court, ex parte McCann* [2001] 1 WLR 1084). Therefore the procedural requirements of Article 6(2) and (3) of the Convention (**see General Police Duties, chapter 4.3**) did not apply. The court agreed that any proceedings had to be 'fair' per Article 6(1) of the Convention and also that any restriction on the defendant's liberty contained in an order against him was an 'interference' with his private life—therefore it fell to be protected under Article 8. The court, however, held that the whole point of such proceedings is to try and predict how far past behaviour gave reasonable cause to believe that an order was necessary to protect the public from serious harm. Expert evidence, particularly in proceedings concerned with sex offenders, was relevant and there was no justification for excluding it. Admitting evidence of propensity did not breach Articles 6 or 8 of the Convention and did not render the proceedings unfair. Any interference with a defendant's private life by such an order was carried out in accordance with the law and for appropriate purposes.

1.9.9.20 Interim Orders

The police can apply for an interim SOPO where an application has been made for a full order. Here the test that will be applied by the court is whether it is 'just' to do so—a wider consideration than 'necessary'. The purpose of interim orders is to allow restrictions to be placed on a defendant's conduct and movements before the full order is determined. An interim order will be for a fixed specified period (without a minimum length) during which time the defendant will be subject to the notification requirements (see above) and the relevant date will be the date of service of the interim order. The interim order will cease to have effect once a decision has been made about the full order (see generally s. 109).

There is a system by which the defendant can appeal against the making of a SOPO (including an interim order)—this is set out in s. 110. There is no equivalent section allowing the police to appeal against a decision though, in appropriate cases, a fresh application might be made, or an application for the decision to be judicially reviewed by the Administrative Court (**see Evidence and Procedure**).

For the availability of foreign travel orders **see para. 1.9.9.22.**

1.9.9.21 **Breach of an Order**

OFFENCE: **Breach of Sexual Offences Prevention Order—*Sexual Offences Act 2003, s. 113***

• Triable either way • Five years' imprisonment on indictment • Six months' imprisonment and/or fine summarily

The Sexual Offences Act 2003, s. 113 states:

(1) A person commits an offence if, without reasonable excuse, he does anything which he is prohibited from doing by—
   (a) a sexual offences prevention order;
   (b) an interim sexual offences prevention order;
   (c) an order under section 5A of the Sex Offenders Act 1997 (restraining orders);
   (d) an order under section 2, 2A or 20 of the Crime and Disorder Act 1998 (sex offender orders and interim orders made in England and Wales and in Scotland);
   (e) an order under Article 6 or 6A of the Criminal Justice (Northern Ireland) Order 1998 (S.I. 1998/2839 (N.I. 20)) (sex offender orders and interim orders made in Northern Ireland).

KEYNOTE

This offence applies to a breach, without reasonable excuse, of a SOPO—including an interim order—and also of an order under the former legislation as set out above.

Where a person is convicted of an offence under this section, it is not open to the court to make, in respect of the offence, an order for conditional discharge (s. 113(3)).

Whether or not the defendant had a reasonable excuse will be a matter of fact for the court to decide in light of all the circumstances. Examples might include where the defendant accidentally encountered a person named in the order as being someone he should not approach or have contact with, or where he is a passenger in a vehicle that is driven, without his knowledge, into a particular area where the order states he should not go.

1.9.9.22 **Foreign Travel Orders**

The Sexual Offences Act 2003, s. 114 states:

(1) A chief officer of police may by complaint to a magistrates' court apply for an order under this section (a 'foreign travel order') in respect of a person ('the defendant') who resides in his police area or who the chief officer believes is in or is intending to come to his police area if it appears to the chief officer that—
   (a) the defendant is a qualifying offender, and
   (b) the defendant has since the appropriate date acted in such a way as to give reasonable cause to believe that it is necessary for such an order to be made.
(2) An application under subsection (1) may be made to any magistrates' court whose commission area includes any part of the applicant's police area.
(3) On the application, the court may make a foreign travel order if it is satisfied that—
   (a) the defendant is a qualifying offender, and
   (b) the defendant's behaviour since the appropriate date makes it necessary to make such an order, for the purpose of protecting children generally or any child from serious sexual harm from the defendant outside the United Kingdom.

KEYNOTE

The foreign travel order is a measure provided under civil law to prevent qualifying offenders from travelling abroad.

'Qualifying offenders' are generally people who have been convicted of or cautioned for (or found not guilty by reason of insanity or to have been under disability when doing an act amounting to) an offence specified by s. 116(2). These offences are—in England and Wales—listed at paras 13 to 15 of sch. 3 (involving indecent photographs etc. of children under 16), para. 31 (trespass with intent to commit a sexual offence if the intended victim was a person under 16) and any offence within any other paragraph of the schedule, if the victim of the offence was under 16 at the time of the offence. A person will also be a qualifying offender for the purposes of s. 114 if s/he has been convicted etc. of an equivalent offence under the law in force in a country outside the United Kingdom (see s. 116(3)).

Before making the order the court must be satisfied that it is *necessary* (rather than simply desirable or appropriate) in order to protect children generally, or any child, from serious sexual harm from the defendant outside the United Kingdom. This means protecting people under 16 generally (or any particular person under 16) from serious physical or psychological harm caused by the defendant doing, outside the United Kingdom, anything which would constitute an offence listed in sch. 3 if done in any part of the United Kingdom (s. 115(2)). In other words the orders are designed to tackle so-called sex tourism and to protect children under 16 from qualifying offenders travelling from the United Kingdom.

The police can apply for a foreign travel order at the same time as applying for a SOPO (see para. 1.9.9.15) or on its own.

A foreign travel order has effect for a fixed period of not more than six months, specified in the order (s. 117(1)). The order prohibits the defendant from doing whichever of the following is specified in the order:

(a) travelling to any country outside the United Kingdom *named or described in the order*,
(b) travelling to any country outside the United Kingdom *other than* a country named or described in the order, or
(c) travelling to *any* country outside the United Kingdom. (s. 117(2)).

However, the *only* prohibitions that may be included in the order are those necessary for the purpose of protecting children generally (or any child) from serious sexual harm from the defendant outside the United Kingdom (s. 117(3)).

Most qualifying offenders who are made subject to these orders will also be subject to the relevant notification requirements (see paras 1.9.9.4 to 1.9.9.7). If for some reason the defendant is not a 'relevant offender' (see para. 1.9.9.2) at the time the order is in force, s/he will have to comply with the notification requirements of regulations made under s. 86(1).

The defendant or the chief officer who made the application (or a chief officer for the area in which the defendant resides or who reasonably believes that the defendant is in, or is intending to come to, his/her police area) may apply for the order to be varied, renewed or discharged (see s. 118). The relevant court *must* hear the person making the application and, after doing so, can impose additional prohibitions on the defendant (but only if it is necessary to do so for the purpose of protecting children generally or any child from serious sexual harm from the defendant outside the United Kingdom)—s. 118(4)). A defendant can appeal to the Crown Court against a foreign travel order or a decision made in connection with its renewal, variation or discharge (s. 119).

1.9.9.23 Breach of Foreign Travel Order

OFFENCE: **Breach of Foreign Travel Order—*Sexual Offences Act 2003, s. 122***

• Triable either way • Five years' imprisonment on indictment • Six months' imprisonment and/or fine summarily

The Sexual Offences Act 2003, s. 122 states:

(1) A person commits an offence if, without reasonable excuse, he does anything which he is prohibited from doing by a foreign travel order.

KEYNOTE

Where a person is convicted of an offence under this section, it is not open to the court to make, in respect of the offence, an order for conditional discharge (s. 122(3)).

1.9.9.24 Risk of Sexual Harm Order

The Sexual Offences Act 2003, s. 123 states:

(1) A chief officer of police may by complaint to a magistrates' court apply for an order under this section (a 'risk of sexual harm order') in respect of a person aged 18 or over ('the defendant') who resides in his police area or who the chief officer believes is in, or is intending to come to, his police area if it appears to the chief officer that—
  (a) the defendant has on at least two occasions, whether before or after the commencement of this Part, done an act within subsection (3), and
  (b) as a result of those acts, there is reasonable cause to believe that it is necessary for such an order to be made.

KEYNOTE

The Risk of Sexual Harm Order (RSHO) is a controversial measure available to the police. Before a chief officer can apply to the magistrates' court for an RSHO, it must appear to him or her that the defendant has on at least two occasions done an act within s. 123(3) and that, as a result of those acts, there is reasonable cause to believe that it is *necessary* for such an order to be made.

The acts under s. 123(3) are:

- engaging in sexual activity involving a child or in the presence of a child
- causing or inciting a child to watch a person engaging in sexual activity or to look at a moving or still image that is sexual (which will include cartoons and virtual images—s. 124(4))
- giving a child anything that relates to sexual activity or contains a reference to such activity
- communicating with a child, where any part of the communication is sexual.

A child for these purposes is a person under 16 and 'sexual activity' means an activity that a reasonable person would, in all the circumstances but regardless of any person's purpose, consider to be sexual (see s. 124). A communication or image is sexual if any *part of it* relates to sexual activity, or a reasonable person would, in all the circumstances but regardless of any person's purpose, consider that any part of the communication is sexual (see s. 124).

The court can only make an RSHO if it is satisfied that the defendant committed such an act on at least two occasions and that the order is *necessary* to protect children generally or any specific child from harm *from the defendant* (s. 123(4)). 'Protecting children generally or any child from harm from the defendant' means protecting them from physical or psychological harm, caused by the defendant doing acts within s. 123(3) to s. 124(2).

Therefore an RSHO can be made in respect of a person who has no previous convictions or whose reported activity was not sufficiently evidenced to bring a prosecution. Clearly this would be appropriate in a case such as that of Ian Huntley where an individual came to the notice of the police on several unconnected occasions but where the relevant parties were unwilling to provide statements of complaint or the evidence was doubtful.

An RSHO has effect for a fixed period (not less than two years) specified in the order or until further order and prevents the defendant from doing anything described in the order (s. 123(5)).

The court may, if it considers it just to do so, make an interim RSHO for a fixed period before the determination of the main application but any interim order will cease once that main application has been determined (s. 126).

Sections 125 and 126 create a system for variation, renewal and discharge of, and appeals against RSHOs in a similar way to that applying to other orders discussed earlier in this chapter.

1.9.9.25 Breach of RSHO

OFFENCE: **Breach of RSHO or Interim RSHO**—*Sexual Offences Act 2003, s. 128*

> • Triable either way • Five years' imprisonment on indictment • Six months' imprisonment and/or fine summarily

The Sexual Offences Act 2003, s. 128 states:

(1) A person commits an offence if, without reasonable excuse, he does anything which he is prohibited from doing by—
   (a) a risk of sexual harm order; or
   (b) an interim risk of sexual harm order.

KEYNOTE

Where a person is convicted of an offence under this section, it is not open to the court to make, in respect of the offence, an order for conditional discharge (s. 128(3)).

If a person is convicted of or cautioned for an offence under s. 128 (or found not guilty by reason of insanity or to have been under a disability), then s/he becomes subject to the relevant notification requirements until the relevant order ceases to have effect (s. 129). If the defendant is already subject to the notification requirements, s/he will remain subject to them at least until the RSHO ceases and, if his/her original notification period was longer than the RSHO, until the end of that longer period.

The 'relevant date' here will be the date on which the defendant was convicted of the above offence (s. 129(4)).

1.9.10 Offences Relating to Prostitution

There are many offences connected with the 'profession' of prostitution. Some of these offences specifically involve children and these are addressed elsewhere in this chapter (**see para. 1.9.5.11**).

While some European Union Member States have 'zones of toleration' where some forms of prostitution are permitted within controlled limits, the laws regulating prostitution and soliciting in England and Wales are quite clear and do not allow for such zones as presently drafted.

1.9.10.1 Definition of a Prostitute

Along with many other aspects of sexual offences, the Sexual Offences Act 2003 redefines prostitution and provides that a prostitute is a person (A) who:

• on at least one occasion and

- whether or not compelled to do so,
- offers or provides sexual services to another person
- in return for payment or a promise of payment to A or a third person

(s. 51(2)).

This definition applies to both men and women.

1.9.10.2   **Offence of Causing, Inciting or Controlling Prostitution**

OFFENCE: **Causing, Inciting or Controlling Prostitution for Gain—*Sexual Offences Act* 2003, ss. 52 *and* 53**
- Triable either way • Seven years' imprisonment on indictment • Six months' imprisonment and/or fine summarily

The Sexual Offences Act 2003, s. 52 states:

(1) A person commits an offence if—
  (a) he intentionally causes or incites another person to become a prostitute in any part of the world, and
  (b) he does so for or in the expectation of gain for himself or a third person.

The Sexual Offences Act 2003, s. 53 states:

(1) A person commits an offence if—
  (a) he intentionally controls any of the activities of another person relating to that person's prostitution in any part of the world, and
  (b) he does so for or in the expectation of gain for himself or a third person.

KEYNOTE

Where the victim of these offences is under 18, the specific offence under s. 48 should be considered (see para. 1.9.5.11).

The first offence above is concerned with intentional causing or inciting—in the case of the latter, this is an incomplete offence (see chapter 1.3).

The second offence above addresses those who intentionally control the activities of prostitutes (pimps).

In each case, unlike the offence involving persons under 18, you must show that the defendant acted for, or in the expectation of, gain—either for him/herself or another. Gain means any financial advantage, including the discharge of an obligation to pay or the provision of goods or services (including sexual services) gratuitously or at a discount or the goodwill of any person which is or appears likely, in time, to bring financial advantage (s. 54). This is a wide definition covering the actions of someone who hopes to build up a relationship with, say, a drug dealer who will eventually give the defendant cheaper drugs as a result of his/her activities. Although you do not need to show that money, goods or financial advantage actually passed to the defendant, you must show that he/she wanted or at least expected that someone would benefit from the conduct.

1.9.10.3   **Brothels**

There are several summary offences aimed at landlords, tenants and occupiers of premises used as brothels (see ss. 34–36 of the Sexual Offences Act 1956). The Sexual Offences Act 2003, while leaving the main offences in place, made two significant changes in this area. The first change was to extend the relevant offences so that they covered brothels used by male prostitutes (see Sexual Offences Act 2003, sch. 1); the second was to create the offence below.

OFFENCE: **Keeping a Brothel Used for Prostitution—***Sexual Offences Act 1956, s. 33A*

- Triable either way. • Seven years' imprisonment on indictment • Six months' imprisonment and/or a fine summarily

The Sexual Offences Act 1956, s. 33A states:

(1) It is an offence for a person to keep, or to manage, or act or assist in the management of, a brothel to which people resort for practices involving prostitution (whether or not also for other practices).

KEYNOTE

The above offence clearly applies to premises that have another purpose—such as massage parlours or tanning shops. While the old summary offence of keeping, managing or assisting with the management of a brothel (under s. 33) still remains, it is unlikely to be used very often in light of the above offence.

Prostitution means offering or providing sexual services, whether under compulsion or not, to another in return for payment or a promise of payment to the prostitute or a third person (see s. 51(2)).

OFFENCE: **Keeping Disorderly House—***Common Law*

- Triable on indictment • Unlimited sentence

It is an offence at common law to keep a disorderly house.

KEYNOTE

A brothel is a place to which people resort for the purposes of unlawful sexual intercourse with more than one prostitute. However, it is not necessary that full sexual intercourse takes place or is even offered. A massage parlour where other acts of lewdness or indecency for sexual gratification are offered may be a brothel.

Under s. 36, the offence is complete if the relevant premises are used by a single prostitute for the purposes of his/her habitual prostitution.

To prove the offence of keeping a disorderly house you must show that the house is 'open' (i.e. to customers); that it is unregulated by the restraints of morality; and that it is run in a way that violates law and good order (*R* v *Tan* [1983] QB 1053).

There must be 'knowledge' on the part of the defendant that a house is being so used (*Moores* v *DPP* [1992] QB 125).

The offence also requires some persistence and will not cover a single instance, e.g. of an indecent performance (*Moores* above).

The licensing of sex shops and sex cinemas is provided for by sch. 3 to the Local Government (Miscellaneous Provisions) Act 1982.

1.9.10.4 Soliciting

OFFENCE: **Soliciting by Common Prostitutes—***Street Offences Act 1959, s. 1*

- Triable summarily • Fine

The Street Offences Act 1959, s. 1 states:

(1) It shall be an offence for a common prostitute whether male or female to loiter or solicit in a street or public place for the purpose of prostitution.

(2) ...

(4) For the purposes of this section 'street' includes any bridge, road, lane, footway, subway, square, court, alley or passage, whether a thoroughfare or not, which is for the time being open to the public; and the doorways and entrances of premises abutting on a street (as hereinbefore defined), and any ground adjoining and open to a street, shall be treated as forming part of the street.

OFFENCE: **Soliciting by 'Kerb-crawling'—*Sexual Offences Act* 1985, ss. 1, 2 and 4**

- Triable summarily • Fine

The Sexual Offences Act 1985, ss. 1, 2 and 4 states:

1.—(1) A person commits an offence if he solicits another person (or different persons) for the purpose of prostitution—

(a) from a motor vehicle while it is in a street or public place; or

(b) in a street or public place while in the immediate vicinity of a motor vehicle that he has just got out of or off,

persistently or ... in such manner or in such circumstances as to be likely to cause annoyance to the other person (or any of the other persons) solicited, or nuisance to other persons in the neighbourhood.

2.—(1) A person commits an offence if in a street or public place he persistently solicits another person (or different persons) for the purpose of prostitution.

4.—(1) References in this Act to a person soliciting another person for the purpose of prostitution are references to his soliciting that person for the purpose of obtaining that person's services as a prostitute.

KEYNOTE

The Sexual Offences Act 2003 made the law applicable to both sexes.

Before a prosecution is brought under s. 1 of the Street Offences Act 1959, it is usual for the prostitute to have been cautioned for that offence at least twice in the last 12 months. This procedure is different from that of cautioning of offenders generally; it only relates to offences of soliciting under s. 1 and the details of the person concerned are recorded in a register kept for that purpose at a police station. The reasoning behind this procedure appears to be to give the person in question an opportunity to reform. It also addresses the cyclical effect of arrest–fine–re-offend to earn money to pay fines.

Note that, with the introduction of the 'final warning scheme' under the Crime and Disorder Act 1998 (as to which, **see Evidence and Procedure, chapter 2.6**) a 'prostitute's caution' can no longer be given to offenders under 18.

It is the repeat nature of the above cautioning process that marks someone out as being a 'common' prostitute (as you can become a prostitute by a single instance—see the Sexual Offences Act 2003, s. 51).

Clearly having your name recorded in a register of 'common prostitutes' is not without some stigma. Anyone who wishes to dispute the interpretation of their actions as 'soliciting' can apply to a court within 14 days of a caution being given for that caution to be expunged. A common prostitute need not actually be in the street or public place when committing the above offence. They could be in the windows of a house or on a balcony provided their solicitations can reach a person who is in a street or public place.

In the case of a prosecution for kerb-crawling you must show that there was a *likelihood* of nuisance or annoyance being caused. You do not have to show that it actually *was* caused by the defendant's conduct. Whether or not such nuisance was likely to be caused to people within the neighbourhood is a question of fact, to be determined by having regard to the type of neighbourhood involved (*Paul* v *DPP* (1989) 90 Cr App R 173).

In order to prove the 'persistent' element, you will need to show that the defendant's behaviour took place on more than one occasion. This might involve recording two or more approaches by him or her towards the same person or separate approaches made towards more than one person.

'Street' for the purposes of kerb-crawling is the same as the definition given in the Street Offences Act 1959, s. 1(4) above. Neither statute defines 'public place'. Generally the guidance developed by the courts under other statutes (e.g. the Road Traffic Act 1988; see Road Policing, chapter 3.1) may be used in determining whether or not a particular place meets the criteria.

If a person persistently follows another person in a way which causes the victim anxiety, the offence of harassment may apply, see General Police Duties, chapter 4.5.

1.9.10.5   **Placing Adverts for Prostitutes Near Public Phones**

OFFENCE: **Placing an Advertisement—*Criminal Justice and Police Act 2001, s. 46***

- Triable summarily • Six months' imprisonment and/or fine

The Criminal Justice and Police Act 2001, s. 46 states:

(1) A person commits an offence if—
   (a) he places on, or in the immediate vicinity of a public telephone, an advertisement relating to prostitution, and
   (b) he does so with the intention that the advertisement should come to the attention of any other person or persons.

KEYNOTE

Advertising the services of a prostitute by leaving stickers or cards in telephone kiosks has been held not to amount to 'soliciting' (*Weisz* v *Monahan* [1962] 1 WLR 262). Although the publisher of the stickers could be charged with the wider offence of controlling prostitutes, if appropriate (as to which, see para. 1.9.10.2), this has not been particularly helpful in relation to the people who are found placing the advert themselves. The above offence now addresses this conduct.

In proving this offence you must show that, in placing the advertisement, the defendant intended that it should come to the attention of someone else. This does not seem to be a particularly onerous requirement and will be helped by evidence of the degree of care that was taken in placing the card, sticker etc., together with its actual position. The advertisement must be for the services of a prostitute—male or female—or for premises at which such services are offered (s. 46(2)). Whether or not an advertisement 'relates to prostitution' is a question of fact. Where a reasonable person would consider that the particular advertisement was 'related to prostitution' there is a presumption that it meets the requirements of this section (s. 46(3)). This presumption is, however, rebuttable (as to which, see Evidence and Procedure, chapter 2.7).

'Public telephone' here means any telephone which is

- located in a public place *and*
- made available for use by the public or a section of the public

and includes any kiosk, booth, acoustic hood, shelter or other structure housing or attached to the telephone (s. 46(5)).

Given this wide definition, the offence will cover the placing of advertisements on or within the immediate vicinity of, not just the telephone itself, but also the kiosk, booth, etc. Therefore, although the magistrate(s) will decide whether an act fell within the immediate vicinity as a question of fact, the offence is capable of being committed by placing advertisements on pavements or shop windows immediately adjacent to a public telephone kiosk.

Section 46(5) gives a very specific definition of 'public place' for the purposes of this offence, namely:

- any place to which the public have or are permitted to have access (on payment or otherwise), *other than*
- a place to which children under 16 years of age are not permitted to have access (by law or otherwise), or
- premises used wholly or mainly as residential premises.

This means that public areas where children under 16 are not allowed, either because they are prevented by law (e.g. licensing laws) or for some other reason (e.g. where a landowner is holding a public event and has barred children from attending), will not be caught by this legislation.

Although limited to public telephones and their coverings (as defined above), this offence can be extended by regulations to cover other public structures. At the time of writing no such regulations had been made.

1.9.10.6   Trafficking for Sexual Offences

OFFENCE: **Trafficking into, within or out of the UK for Sexual Exploitation—**
Sexual Offences Act 2003, ss. 57–59

- Triable either way • 14 years' imprisonment on indictment • Six months' imprisonment and/or a fine summarily

The Sexual Offences Act 2003, s. 57 states:

(1) A person commits an offence if he intentionally arranges or facilitates the arrival in the United Kingdom of another person (B) and either—
  (a) he intends to do anything to or in respect of B, after B's arrival but in any part of the world, which if done will involve the commission of a relevant offence, or
  (b) he believes that another person is likely to do something to or in respect of B, after B's arrival but in any part of the world, which if done will involve the commission of a relevant offence.

The Sexual Offences Act 2003, s. 58 states:

(1) A person commits an offence if he intentionally arranges or facilitates travel within the United Kingdom by another person (B) and either—
  (a) he intends to do anything to or in respect of B, during or after the journey and in any part of the world, which if done will involve the commission of a relevant offence, or
  (b) he believes that another person is likely to do something to or in respect of B, during or after the journey and in any part of the world, which if done will involve the commission of a relevant offence.

The Sexual Offences Act 2003, s. 59 states:

(1) A person commits an offence if he intentionally arranges or facilitates the departure from the United Kingdom of another person (B) and either—
  (a) he intends to do anything to or in respect of B, after B's departure but in any part of the world, which if done will involve the commission of a relevant offence, or
  (b) he believes that another person is likely to do something to or in respect of B, after B's departure but in any part of the world, which if done will involve the commission of a relevant offence.

KEYNOTE

These three offences address the trafficking of people for sexual exploitation. Worded almost identically, the three sections deal with the intentional arranging or facilitation of the person's arrival in, travel within, or departure from the United Kingdom. In each case you must show the defendant's intention to do something to or in respect of the victim which would involve the commission of a relevant offence *or* the defendant's belief that someone else is likely to do so. The relevant offence, intended or believed likely by the defendant, can take place in any part of the world provided it is after the victim's arrival, during or after their journey or after their departure respectively.

A relevant offence is any offence under part I of the Sexual Offences Act 2003 (virtually all regularly occurring sexual offences) and an offence under s. 1(1)(a) of the Protection of Children Act 1978 (taking, permitting to be taken or making indecent photographs of a child—**see para. 1.9.5.8**); it also includes anything done outside England and Wales which is not an offence in that country but would be if done in England and Wales where the offender is a British citizen, a British overseas territories citizen, a British National (Overseas), a British Overseas citizen, a person who is a British subject under the British Nationality Act 1981 or a British protected person within the meaning given by s. 50(1) of that Act (s. 60).

The wording of the offences means that bringing victims into the United Kingdom temporarily on their way to another destination will be caught.

Note that it is the intention or belief of the defendant that is the central feature—the fact that the relevant sexual offence never actually took place will not prevent this offence being committed. Similarly, if the intention or belief is not present, there is no offence under these provisions. This protects transport companies and their staff who are often unwittingly used in these offences. Nevertheless, the wording of the offences is wide enough to deal with any intentional involvement in planning, organising or carrying out arrangements in furtherance of trafficking where the relevant state of mind or knowledge (**see chapter 1.1**) is present.

For the further offences of people trafficking for non-sexual exploitation **see chapter 1.15**.

1.10 Child Protection

1.10.1 Introduction

The application of the law and the use of measures to protect children and other vulnerable groups are amongst some of the most contentious issues that any police officer may be involved in. This is echoed in the amount of media interest in such matters, often as a result of tragic circumstances surrounding the death of a child or the publication of a report or inquiry related to the subject. One such report, the Bichard Inquiry Report (June 2004), provides the background for the Safeguarding Vulnerable Groups Act 2006, implementation of which is expected to be phased in during Autumn 2008. At present, the Criminal Justice and Court Services Act 2000 deals with individuals disqualified from working with children. This chapter also deals with other child related offences and corresponding legislation such as child abduction (Child Abduction Act 1984) and 'Police Protection' (Children Act 1989).

1.10.2 Protection of Children

Although many of the general provisions restricting the behaviour of sex offenders have been targeted at paedophiles, there are several significant areas of legislation which are aimed specifically at the protection of children, in both a sexual context and in other areas where their well-being is jeopardised.

1.10.2.1 Disqualification Orders

The Criminal Justice and Court Services Act 2000 introduced a number of measures aimed at preventing unsuitable people from working with children. What follows is a summary of some of the relevant provisions of the Act; for further detail see Home Office Circular 45/2000.

Part II of the 2000 Act introduces the concept of disqualification orders. These orders are aimed at disqualifying people who present a threat to children from working in certain jobs and positions. A key feature of disqualification orders is the fact that a court *must* impose them when defendants are convicted of certain offences unless, having regard to all the circumstances, the court is satisfied that it is unlikely that the defendant will commit any further offences against *any* child (ss. 28 and 29). Broadly, the requirement to pass a disqualification order arises when:

- the defendant, being 18 or over, is convicted of an 'offence against a child'. 'Offences against a child' are set out in sch. 4 to the Act and generally include most offences involving sexual activity, the use of violence and some drug-related offences (the list specifically includes the military or service law equivalent of these offences);

- a senior court passes a 'qualifying sentence' on the defendant for that offence. A qualifying sentence is generally a sentence of 12 months' imprisonment or more, a hospital or guardianship order (s. 30). 'Senior court' here means the Crown Court and the Court of Appeal. Again, these concepts are specifically extended to cover sentences imposed under service law by courts-martial and the Courts-Martial Appeal Court.

For most purposes under this part of the Act, 'child' means a person under 18. Although the disqualification order scheme was introduced in 2000, there have been some practical difficulties in their recording and implementation. As a result the Home Office has issued further guidance to chief police officers and criminal justice agencies to ensure that the importance of disqualification orders and their effect is understood (see Home Office Circular 67/2004). The Home Office advises that disqualification orders must be recorded on the Police National Computer and that it is the responsibility of the police to enforce any breaches of them.

A person convicted of an 'offence against a child' will also be automatically prevented from a number of activities involving children including carrying on or being involved in the management of a children's home or from privately adopting children unless special authority is sought first (see the Disqualification from Caring for Children (England) Regulations 2002 (SI 2002/635)).

Once an order is imposed, the person becomes a 'disqualified person' for the purposes of the Act. In addition, anyone who is included (other than provisionally) on the list kept under s. 1 of the Protection of Children Act 1999 (**see para. 1.10.2.3**) or is banned by the Secretary of State for Education and Skills under s. 142 of the Education Act 2002 (**see para. 1.10.2.4**) on the grounds that they are unsuitable to work with children is also disqualified from working with children in a regulated position (s. 35(4)). These provisions differ from those under the disqualification order regime above in that there is no requirement for a person to have been convicted of any offence in order to be placed on one of these lists.

OFFENCE: **Applying for Position while Disqualified—*Criminal Justice and Court Services Act 2000, s. 35***

> - Triable either way • Five years' imprisonment on indictment • Six months' and/or fine summarily

Section 35 states:

(1) An individual who is disqualified from working with children is guilty of an offence if he knowingly applies for, offers to do, accepts or does any work in a regulated position.

(2) An individual is guilty of an offence if he knowingly—

    (a) offers work in a regulated position to, or procures work in a regulated position for, an individual who is disqualified from working with children, or

    (b) fails to remove such an individual from such work.

(3) It is a defence for an individual charged with an offence under subsection (1) to prove that he did not know, and could not reasonably be expected to know, that he was disqualified from working with children.

KEYNOTE

There are two offences associated with being a disqualified person. The first offence arises where a disqualified person knowingly applies for, offers to do, accepts or does any work in a regulated position (s. 35(1)). Given the specific defence available (see below), it would seem that the requirement of 'knowingly' here relates to the act of applying, offering or accepting work in a regulated position. The offence would therefore not be made out if the application, offer, etc. were made without the disqualified person's knowledge or agreement. Regulated positions are generally those where the person's normal duties include working with children, whether in the public, private or voluntary sectors and also in certain senior management roles such as social services and children's charities. Examples given by the Home Office include babysitting; working as a school teacher; working in a local authority education or social services department; voluntary work at a boys' football club; and positions where the normal duties include the supervision or management of another individual who works directly with children (e.g. a member of a school governing body).

Note that a person can become disqualified either through the imposition of a disqualification order or by virtue of appearing on one of the statutory lists referred to earlier in this chapter.

The statutory defence to s. 35(1) applies if the defendant can show that he/she neither knew, nor could reasonably have been expected to know that he/she was disqualified (a difficult scenario to envisage let alone prove).

The second offence arises where a person offers or procures work in a regulated position for a person who is disqualified from working with children or fails to remove such an individual from that work (s. 35(2)). This offence is clearly aimed at employers, though it would clearly extend beyond those circumstances and it does not have the statutory defence available. This seems slightly odd given that, of the two, a prospective employer is far less likely to know of a person's disqualification than the person disqualified.

1.10.2.2 Reviews and Appeals of Disqualification Orders

The Criminal Justice and Court Services Act 2000 makes provision for a person to appeal against the imposition of a disqualification order and also to have such orders reviewed after a minimum period. More significantly for the police, s. 34 makes provision for a chief officer of police (or director of social services) to apply to the High Court to restore a disqualification order if it can be shown that:

- the person who was once subject to the order has acted (either before the order ceased or after) in such a way
- as to give reasonable cause to believe that an order is necessary
- to protect children in general or any children in particular
- from serious harm from that person.

If these conditions are made out, the High Court *must* reinstate the disqualification order.

In addition to the provisions under the Criminal Justice and Court Services Act 2000, there are several pieces of legislation that exist for the protection of children generally. Three key statutes relating to the protection of children are:

- the Protection of Children Act 1999
- the Education Act 2002
- the Children Act 1989.

1.10.2.3 Protection of Children Act 1999

The Protection of Children Act 1999 was passed to provide greater safeguards for children and to increase the restrictions on those who would seek to gain access to children in order to exploit them. One of the main pillars of the 1999 Act is the creation of a comprehensive and accessible information network. Such a network will:

- provide a consolidated list of people who are deemed to represent a particular risk to children; and

- make that list more accessible to employers and other agencies whose responsibilities include the protection of children.

The 1999 Act brings together two existing lists currently maintained by the Department of Health (the 'Consultancy List') and the Department for Education and Employment ('List 99') for the purposes of identifying those people who are unsuitable to work with children. It also makes provision for relevant organisations to apply to the Criminal Record Bureau for criminal record certificates and criminal conviction certificates utilising the relevant provisions of the Police Act 1997.

The Consultancy List maintained by the Secretary of State for the Department of Health providing access to employers' records on people considered to be unsuitable for work with children has been held not to infringe the human rights of those included on it (*R v Worcester County Council and Secretary of State for the Department of Health, ex parte W* [2000] HRLR 702). The same should therefore apply to any such list maintained by authority of the National Assembly for Wales.

The 1999 Act also creates a number of statutory duties upon child care organisations (which now includes the Welsh Assembly in performing its general child welfare functions under ss. 35 and 36 of the Children Act 2004) and those involved in the employment of people in child care positions, as well as establishing a tribunal to hear appeals from individuals whose names appear on the relevant list.

Further provisions for the protection of children in foster care are made by the Children Act 2004.

1.10.2.4 Education Act 2002

The Education Act 2002 provides the Secretary of State for Education and Skills with many powers to regulate the provisions of teaching and full-time education of children in England. In particular, s. 142 empowers the Secretary of State for Education and Skills to direct that a person may not carry out work that involves 'providing education' (not simply *teaching*) at a school, further education institution or under a contract of employment with a local education authority. The section also covers taking part in the management of an independent school and other work which brings a person regularly into contact with children. Section 142 provides the same powers to the National Assembly for Wales.

1.10.2.5 Children Act 1989

When first enacted the Children Act 1989 was the most comprehensive piece of legislation affecting children ever seen in England and Wales. The Act has been supplemented by a further substantial and far-reaching statute, the Children Act 2004. Throughout the 1989 Act, which makes provision for the care and treatment of children in virtually every aspect of their development, there is a common theme of the child's rights.

Among those rights are the right to protection from harm and the Act imposes many duties on local authorities. It also provides powers for the protection of children and, in particular, for situations where emergency protection is needed.

1.10.3 Child Abduction

There is a Convention between the United Kingdom and many other countries which is designed to help with the civil law practicalities of recovering children from other jurisdictions. The full list of such countries can be found in the Child Abduction and Custody (Parties to Conventions) Order 1986 (SI 1986/1159), as amended.

There are two offences of abducting children, one which applies to people 'connected with the child' and the second by others.

1.10.3.1 Person Connected with Child

OFFENCE: **Child Abduction—Person Connected with Child—*Child Abduction Act 1984, s. 1***
  - Triable either way • Seven years' imprisonment on indictment • Six months' imprisonment and/or a fine summarily

The Child Abduction Act 1984, s. 1 states:

(1) Subject to subsections (5) and (8) below, a person connected with a child under the age of 16 commits an offence if he takes or sends the child out of the United Kingdom without the appropriate consent.

'Connected with a Child'

The Child Abduction Act 1984, s. 1 states:

(2) A person is connected with the child for the purposes of this section if—
   (a) he is a parent of a the child; or
   (b) in the case of a child whose parents were not married to each other at the time of his birth, there are reasonable grounds for believing that he is the father of the child; or
   (c) he is a guardian of the child; or
   (d) he is a person in whose favour a residence order is in force with respect to the child; or
   (e) he has custody of the child.

'Appropriate Consent'

The Child Abduction Act 1984, s. 1 states:

(3) In this section 'the appropriate consent' in relation to a child, means—
   (a) the consent of each of the following—
      (i) the child's mother;
      (ii) the child's father, if he has parental responsibility for him;
      (iii) any guardian of the child;
      (iv) any person in whose favour a residence order is in force with respect to the child;
      (v) any person who has custody of the child; or
   (b) the leave of the court granted under or by virtue of any provision of Part II of the Children Act 1989; or
   (c) if any person has custody of the child, the leave of the court which awarded custody to him.

KEYNOTE

This offence can only be committed by those people listed in s. 1(2). To be guilty they must take or send the child out of the United Kingdom. The taking or sending must be shown to have been done without the consent of *each* of those persons listed in s. 1(3)(a) above.

The consent of the Director of Public Prosecutions is needed before a charge of child abduction is brought under this section (s. 4(2)): there are also restrictions on charging kidnapping (as to which, **see chapter 1.8**) where the offence involves an offence under s. 1 above by a person connected with the child (s. 5).

1.10.3.2   Defence for Person Connected with a Child

The Child Abduction Act 1984, s. 1 states:

   (4) A person does not commit an offence under this section by taking or sending a child out of
       the United Kingdom without obtaining the appropriate consent if—
       (a) he is a person in whose favour there is a residence order in force with respect to the child,
           and
       (b) he takes or sends him out of the United Kingdom for a period of less than one month.
  (4A) Subsection (4) above does not apply if the person taking or sending the child out of the
       United Kingdom does so in breach of an order under Part II of the Children Act 1989.
   (5) A person does not commit an offence under this section by doing anything without the con-
       sent of another person whose consent is required under the foregoing provisions if—
       (a) he does it in the belief that the other person—
            (i) has consented; or
           (ii) would consent if he was aware of all the relevant circumstances; or
       (b) he has taken all reasonable steps to communicate with the other person but has been
           unable to communicate with him; or
       (c) the other person has unreasonably refused to consent.

KEYNOTE

Note the specific defence (at s. 1(5))—if the defendant believes that the appropriate person has consented
or would have consented had they known of the circumstances.

   A further provision (s. 1(5A)) states that s. 1(5)(c) will not apply if the person who refused to consent is
a person:

- in whose favour there is a residence order in force with respect to the child; or
- who has custody of the child; or
- is, by taking or sending the child out of the United Kingdom, acting in breach of a court order in the
  United Kingdom.

1.10.3.3   Person Not Connected with Child

OFFENCE: **Child Abduction—Person Not Connected with Child—*Child
          Abduction Act 1984, s. 2***

            • Triable either way • Seven years' imprisonment on indictment • Six months'
            imprisonment and/or a fine summarily

The Child Abduction Act 1984, s. 2 states:

   (1) Subject to subsection (3) below, a person other than one mentioned in subsection (2) below,
       commits an offence if, without lawful authority or reasonable excuse, he takes or detains a
       child under the age of 16—
       (a) so as to remove him from the lawful control of any person having lawful control of the
           child: or
       (b) so as to keep him out of the lawful control of any person entitled to lawful control of the
           child.
   (2) The persons are—
       (a) where the father and mother of the child in question were married to each other at the
           time of his birth, the child's father and mother;
       (b) where the father and mother of the child in question were not married to each other at the
           time of his birth, the child's mother; and
       (c) any other person mentioned in section 1(2)(c) to (e) above.

KEYNOTE

This offence requires the taking or detaining of a child under 16 years. This will include keeping a child in the place where he/she is found and inducing the child to remain with the defendant or another person. The distinction between subss. (a) and (b) is important. You must show that the defendant acted without lawful authority or reasonable excuse. Unlike kidnapping, the consent of the victim is irrelevant. The word 'remove' for the purpose of s. 2(1)(a) means effectively a substitution of authority by a defendant for that of the person lawfully having it and physical removal from a particular place is not required (see *Foster* v *DPP* [2004] EWHC 2955).

Section 2(1)(a) requires the child *there and then* to be in the lawful control of someone entitled to it when they are taken or detained, whereas s. 2(1)(b) requires only that the child be kept out of the lawful control of someone entitled to it when taken or detained. Whether or not a person is under the lawful control of another is a question of fact (*R* v *Leather* (1993) *The Times,* 21 January). Proving the absence of reasonable excuse could be difficult. Clearly a defendant could argue, particularly in the case of a very young child, that he/she was acting in the child's best interests, a claim which might be difficult to refute. Note that s. 3 makes further practical provisions in relation to 'taking, sending and detaining'.

1.10.3.4 Defence for Person Not Connected with a Child

The Child Abduction Act 1984, s. 2 states:

(3) ... it shall be a defence for [the defendant] to prove—
  (a) where the father and mother of the child in question were not married to each other at the time of his birth—
    (i) that he is the child's father; or
    (ii) that, at the time of the alleged offence, he believed, on reasonable grounds, that he was the child's father; or
  (b) that, at the time of the alleged offence, he believed that the child had attained the age of 16.

KEYNOTE

Section 2(3)(b) provides a defence if the accused can show that he/she believed the child to be 16 or over. Given the appearance, dress and behaviour of children in their early teens, this defence may not be too difficult to establish in many cases. This should be contrasted with some sexual offences involving children (see chapter 1.9).

1.10.4 Child Cruelty

OFFENCE: **Child Cruelty—*Children and Young Persons Act 1933, s. 1***
  • Triable either way • Ten years' imprisonment on indictment • Six months' imprisonment and/or a fine summarily

The Children and Young Persons Act 1933, s. 1 states:

(1) If any person who has attained the age of 16 years and has responsibility for any child or young person under that age, wilfully assaults, ill-treats, neglects, abandons, or exposes him, or causes or procures him to be assaulted, ill-treated, neglected, abandoned, or exposed, in a manner likely to cause him unnecessary suffering or injury to health (including injury to or

loss of sight, or hearing, or limb or organ of the body, and any mental derangement), that person shall be guilty of a misdemeanour ...

KEYNOTE

The defendant must be shown both to have attained the age of 16 years *and* to have had responsibility for the child or young person. For the practical issues of proving a child's age, **see Evidence and Procedure, chapter 2.5.**

Responsibility for a child or young person can be shared and whether a person had such responsibility in each case will be a matter of both fact and law (see *Liverpool Society for the Prevention of Cruelty to Children* v *Jones* [1914] 3 KB 813). Any one having parental responsibility or any other legal liability to maintain a child or young person will be presumed to have responsibility for him/her and that responsibility does not cease simply because the person ceases to have care of him/her. Others such as babysitters and child minders may also have 'responsibility' for the child while in their care (see generally s. 17).

The Act goes on to make other specific provisions and presumptions, particularly in relation to the issues of causation. So, for example, if a parent or other person legally liable to maintain the child or young person, or a guardian, has failed to provide adequate food, clothing, medical aid or lodging for the child or young person, he/she will be deemed to have neglected the child or young person for the above purposes (see s. 1(2)).

Similarly, a person will be presumed to have neglected the child where it is proved that the child was an infant under three years old and that he/she died as a result of suffocation (other than by disease or blockage of the airways by an object) while in bed with someone of 16 years or over who was under the influence of drink when they went to bed (see s. 1(2)(b)).

A defendant may be charged with the above offence even where the child has died (see s. 1(3)(b)) but homicide should also be considered (as to which, **see chapter 1.5**).

The above section creates only one single offence, albeit one that can be committed in many different ways, by both positive acts and omission (see *R* v *Hayles* [1969] 1 QB 364). Although any aspect of neglect must be shown to have occurred in a manner likely to cause unnecessary suffering or injury to health, there is no need to show that any such suffering or injury actually came about. The usual technical arguments over recklessness and intent (**see chapter 1.1**) have been raised in connection with the wording of the offence and the advice of the Crown Prosecution Service should be sought at an early stage when bringing a charge under this section.

For over 70 years the above legislation specifically allowed for parents and others with responsibility for a child to administer 'lawful chastisement'. However, this 'defence' has been removed and battery (as to which **see para. 1.7.2**) of a child cannot be justified on the ground that it constituted reasonable punishment (see the Children Act 2004, s. 58).

For the police powers to take a child into police protection, **see para. 1.10.5.**

1.10.5 **Police Protection**

As has been discussed in the earlier paragraphs of this chapter, there may be many and various ways in which children can be threatened with or come to harm. Whatever the source, the police have specific statutory powers to deal with the threat of significant harm posed to children and these are set out below.

Section 46 of the Children Act 1989 states:

(1) Where a constable has reasonable cause to believe that a child would otherwise be likely to suffer significant harm, he may—
    (a) remove the child to suitable accommodation and keep him there; or

(b) take such steps as are reasonable to ensure the the child's removal from any hospital, or other place, in which he is then being accommodated is prevented.

(2) For the purposes of this Act, a child with respect to whom a constable has exercised his powers under this section is referred to as having been taken into police protection.

KEYNOTE

For most purposes of the 1989 Act, someone who is under 18 years old is a 'child' (s. 105).

The wording of s. 46(1) means that an officer may use the powers at s. 46(1)(a) and (b) if he/she has reasonable cause to believe that, if he/she does not use them, a child is likely to suffer significant harm. The issues arising from similar wording in relation to powers of arrest have been considered by the courts on a number of occasions. Generally, tests of reasonableness impose an element of objectivity and the courts will consider whether, in the circumstances, a reasonable and sober person might have formed a similar view to that of the officer.

'Harm' is a very broad term and is defined under s. 31(9). It covers all forms of ill treatment including sexual abuse and forms of ill treatment that are not physical. It also covers the impairment of health (physical or mental) and also physical, intellectual, emotional, social or behavioural development. The definition also extends to impairment suffered from seeing or hearing the ill-treatment *of any other person*.

When determining whether harm to a child's health or development is '*significant*', the child's development will be compared with that which could reasonably be expected of a similar child (s. 31(10)).

The power under s. 46 is split into two parts:

- a power to *remove* a child to suitable accommodation and keep him/her there, and
- a power to take reasonable steps to *prevent* the child's removal from a hospital or other place.

The longest a child can spend in police protection is 72 hours (s. 46(6)). It should be remembered that this is the *maximum* time that a child can be kept in police protection, not the norm.

As soon as is reasonably practicable after taking a child into police protection, the police officer must do a number of things as set out above. These things generally include:

- telling the local authority within whose area the child was found what steps that have been, and are proposed to be, taken and why this aspect of communicating with the local authority is a critical part of the protective powers;
- giving details to the local authority within whose area the child is ordinarily resident of the place at which the child is being kept;
- telling the child (if he/she appears capable of understanding) of what steps have been taken and why, and what further steps may be taken;
- taking such steps as are reasonably practicable to discover the wishes and feelings of the child;
- making sure that the case is inquired into by a 'designated officer' (see below);
- taking such steps as are reasonably practicable to inform:
  - ✦ the child's parents
  - ✦ every person who is not his/her parent but who has parental responsibility for the child and
  - ✦ any other person with whom the child was living immediately before being taken into police protection,

of the steps that the officer has taken under this section, the reasons for taking them and the further steps that may be taken with respect to the child. This element, of informing the child, parent and /or relevant carers of what is happening and why is also a vital part of the protective process.

Where the child was taken into police protection by being removed to accommodation which is not provided by or on behalf of a local authority or as a refuge (under s. 51), the officer must, as soon as is reasonably practicable after taking a child into police protection, make sure that the child is moved to accommodation provided by the local authority. Every local authority must receive and provide accommodation for children in police protection where such a request is made (s. 21).

The requirement under s. 46(3)(c) to give the child information, reflects the 1989 Act's theme that children should have some influence over their own destiny.

Note that, when considering action under s. 46, it is possible that the child may already be the subject of an Emergency Protection Order (EPO) applied for by a local authority or authorised body under s. 44.

In considering the proper approach under these circumstances the Court of Appeal has held that:

- There is no express provision in the Act prohibiting the police from invoking s. 46 where an EPO is in place and it is not desirable to imply a restriction which prohibits a constable from removing a child under s. 46 he/she has reasonable cause to believe that the child would otherwise be likely to suffer significant harm.
- The s. 46 power to remove a child can therefore be exercised even where an EPO is in force in respect of the child.
- Where a police officer knows that an EPO is in force, he/she should not exercise the power of removing a child under s. 46, unless there are compelling reasons to do so.
- The statutory scheme accords primacy to the EPO procedure under s. 44 because removal under that section is sanctioned by the court and involves a more elaborate, sophisticated and complete process of removal than under s. 46.
- Consequently, the removal of children should usually be effected pursuant to an EPO, and s. 46 should only be invoked where it is not reasonably practicable to execute an EPO.
- In deciding whether it is practicable to execute an EPO, the police should always have regard to the paramount need to protect children from significant harm.
- Failure to follow the statutory procedure may amount to the police officer's removal of the child under s. 46 being declared unlawful.

Langley v *Liverpool City Council and Chief Constable of Merseyside* [2006] 1 WLR 375.

1.10.5.1 Designated Officer

The reference at s. 46(3)(e) of the Act to a 'designated officer' is a reference to the appropriate officer designated for that police station for the purposes of this legislation by the relevant chief officer of police. This is a key role in ensuring the effective use of the statutory framework set up for the protection of children in these circumstances. The responsibility for ensuring that the case is inquired into by the designated officer, together with the other responsibilities under s. 46(3) and the responsibility for taking steps to inform people under s. 46(4), clearly rest with the police officer exercising the power under s. 46.

Practically, the designated officer must inquire fully and thoroughly into the case; he/she must also do what is reasonable in all the circumstances for the purpose of safeguarding or promoting the child's welfare (having regard in particular to the length of the period during which the child will be so protected) (s. 46(9)(b)).

Where a child has been taken into police protection, the designated officer must allow:

- the child's parents
- any person who is not a parent of the child but who has parental responsibility for him
- any person with whom the child was living immediately before he/she was taken into police protection
- any person in whose favour a contact order is in force with respect to the child
- any person who is allowed to have contact with the child by virtue of an order under s. 34; and
- any person acting on behalf of any of those persons,

to have such contact (if any) with the child as, in the opinion of the designated officer, is both reasonable and in the child's best interests (s. 46(10)).

The designated officer may apply for an 'emergency protection order' under s. 44 (s. 46(7)). Such an order allows the court to order the removal of the child to certain types of accommodation and to prevent the child's removal from any other place (including a hospital) where he/she was being accommodated immediately before the making of the order (s. 44(4)). An emergency protection order gives the applicant 'parental responsibility' for the child while it is in force. It also allows the court to make certain directions in relation to contact with the child and a medical or psychiatric assessment of them. Section 44A allows the court to make an order excluding certain people from a dwellinghouse where the child lives and to attach a power of arrest accordingly.

While the designated officer can apply for an emergency protection order without the local authority's knowledge or agreement (see s. 46(8)), there should be no reason why, given proper multi-agency co-operation and a well-planned child protection strategy, that this situation would come about. For further guidance on multi-agency working in the area of child protection, see *Working Together to Safeguard Children* (HMSO 1999).

On completing his/her inquiry into the case, the designated officer must release the child from police protection *unless he/she considers that there is still reasonable cause for believing that the child would be likely to suffer significant harm if released* (s. 46(5)).

While a child is in police protection, neither the officer concerned nor the designated officer will have parental responsibility for him/her (s. 46(9)(a)).

When a local authority is informed that a child is in police protection, they have a duty to make 'such enquiries as they consider necessary to enable them to decide whether they should take any action to safeguard' the child (s. 47(1)(b)). A court may issue a warrant for a constable to assist a relevant person to enter premises in order to enforce an emergency protection order.

1.10.5.2 Contravention of Protection Order or Police Protection

OFFENCE: **Acting in Contravention of Protection Order or Power Exercised under s. 46—*Children Act 1989, s. 49***

- Triable summarily • Six months' imprisonment

The Children Act 1989, s. 49 states:

(1) A person shall be guilty of an offence if, knowingly and without lawful authority or reasonable excuse, he—
   (a) takes a child to whom this section applies away from the responsible person;
   (b) keeps such a child away from the responsible person; or
   (c) induces, assists or incites such a child to run away or stay away from the responsible person.
(2) This section applies in relation to a child who is—
   (a) in care;

(b) the subject of an emergency protection order; or

(c) in police protection,

and in this section 'the responsible person' means any person who for the time being has care of him by virtue of the care order, the emergency protection order, or section 46, as the case may be.

KEYNOTE

It is arguable that, in the case of a child who is under 16, the person would also commit an offence under the Child Abduction Act 1984.

There is also a power of entry under s. 17(1)(e) of the 1984 PACE Act for 'saving life and limb'.

Where a child is taken in contravention of s. 49 above, the court may issue a 'recovery order' under s. 50. Such an order, which is also available where a child is missing or has run away, requires certain people to produce the child to an authorised person (which includes a constable (s. 50(7)(b)) or to give certain information about the child's whereabouts to a constable or officer of the court (s. 50(3)). It can also authorise a constable to enter any premises and search for the child.

Under s. 102 of the 1989 Act a court may issue a warrant to enter premises in connection with certain provisions of the Act which regulate children's homes, foster homes, child-minding premises and nursing homes for children. Section 102 allows for constables to assist any person in the exercise of their powers under those provisions. It also makes allowances for a constable to be accompanied by a medical practitioner, nurse or health visitor (s. 102(3)).

1.10.5.3 Disclosure of Information Regarding Child

Where a child is reported missing problems can arise once he/she is discovered to be safe and well but one of the parents wants the police to disclose the whereabouts of the child. This situation arose in *S v S (Chief Constable of West Yorkshire Police Intervening)* [1999] 1 All ER 281 and the Court of Appeal provided some clarification of the issues. In that case the mother left home with her three-year-old child after a marriage breakdown. The father reported the child's absence to the police who found the child and her mother in a refuge. At the request of the mother, the police advised the father that both she and the child were safe but refused to disclose their whereabouts. The father applied 'without notice' (i.e. without telling the police) to the County Court which then made an order under s. 33 of the Family Law Act 1986, requiring the police to disclose the information. The chief constable was granted leave to intervene and, following another order from the court to disclose the child's whereabouts, the chief constable appealed. Butler-Sloss LJ (one of the key figures behind the drafting of the Children Act 1989), gave the finding of the Court of Appeal. The Court held that it was only in exceptional circumstances that the police should be asked to divulge the whereabouts of a child under a s. 33 order. Their primary role in such cases should continue to be finding missing children and ensuring their safety.

However, Butler-Sloss LJ went on to say that, in such cases:

- The police are *not* in a position to give 'categoric assurances' of confidentiality to those who provide information as to the whereabouts of a child. The most they could say is that, other than by removing the child, it would be *most unlikely* that they would have to disclose the information concerning the child's whereabouts.
- An order under s. 33 provides for the information to be disclosed to the court, not to the other party or his/her solicitor.

- An order under s. 33 should not normally be made in respect of the police without their being present (*ex parte*).

Note that the provision of information by police officers in relation to civil proceedings involving children is governed by regulations; specific advice should therefore be sought before disclosing any such information.

1.10.5.4 Other Protective Legislation

In addition to the offences, powers and procedures discussed elsewhere in this Manual affecting children, there are several other statutes that have the protection of children at their heart. For instance, the framework for licensing under the Licensing Act 2003 has, as one of its key objectives, the protection of children in relation to the sale and supply of alcohol by means of specific licensing provisions regarding children (**see General Police Duties, chapter 4.11**). There are restrictions on selling tobacco or cigarette papers to a person under 16 (Children and Young Persons Act 1933, s. 7(1)). More importantly, police officers have a *duty* to seize any tobacco or cigarette papers in the possession of any person apparently under the age 16 years whom he/she *finds smoking in any street or public place* (s. 7(3)). This duty—which also applies to a park keeper in uniform—is converted into a *power* that can be conferred on a designated person under sch. 4 to the Police Reform Act 2002 (**see General Police Duties, chapter 4.2**). A designated person given this power has discretion whether or not to use it; a police officer (and park keeper), however, is under an obligation to seize the tobacco or papers and to dispose of them in accordance with local arrangements made by their employer. These provisions are reinforced by the requirement for retailers and vending machine owners to display warning signs regarding cigarettes (Children and Young Persons (Protection from Tobacco) Act 1991). The Children and Young Persons Act 1933 makes a number of provisions with regard to the protection of children such as the offence of exposing a child under 12 to the risk of burning (s. 11) and the requirement to provide safety attendants in buildings where entertainment is provided for children (Children and Young Persons Act 1993, s. 12). Finally, there are specific provisions relating to children and safety in relation to roads policing (**see Road Policing, chapter 3.7**).

1.11 | Theft and Related Offences

1.11.1 Introduction

Many of the offences contained in this chapter will be all too familiar to policing personnel. Their real life experiences will provide them with first-hand knowledge of the physical, emotional and financial cost to victims of offences such as theft, burglary and robbery. The prevalence, and consequent significant impact, that these offences have on society as a whole can leave no doubt as to their importance in terms of policing.

1.11.2 Theft

OFFENCE: **Theft—*Theft Act 1968, s. 1***

> • Triable either way • Seven years' imprisonment on indictment • Six months' imprisonment and/or a fine summarily

The Theft Act 1968, s. 1 states:

> (1) A person is guilty of theft if he dishonestly appropriates property belonging to another with the intention of permanently depriving the other of it; and 'thief' and 'steal' shall be construed accordingly.

KEYNOTE

It is important to understand each element of this offence. The Theft Act 1968 provides some detailed guidance as to parts of the above definition, while our common law has clarified some of the others.

In order for an offence of theft to exist, each element of the definition must be proved and those elements are considered in detail below.

While some thefts or acts of shoplifting can cause harassment, alarm or distress and so fall within the provisions of theCrime and Disorder Act 1998, not all thefts and acts of shoplifting fall within those criteria. Therefore it is necessary to consider the individual facts of each case, and Anti-Social Behaviour Orders (see General Police Duties, chapter 4.5) cannot be made automatically simply on the basis that the theft could potentially have caused harassment, alarm or distress—*R (On the Application of Mills)* v *Birmingham Magistrates' Court* [2005] EWHC 2732.

The component parts of theft are considered more closely below.

Note that offences of theft from businesses involving values not exceeding £200 can be dealt with by way of fixed penalty notice (see General Police Duties, para. 4.4.3).

As described above, there are five key elements to the offence of theft. These are:

- dishonesty
- appropriation

- property
- belonging to another
- intention of permanently depriving.

Dishonestly

If a person cannot be shown to have acted 'dishonestly', he/she is not guilty of theft. The decision as to whether or not a defendant was in fact dishonest is one for the jury or magistrate(s). Perhaps surprisingly given its central importance in the offence, there is no statutory definition of this term. Instead the 1968 Act sets out a number of specific circumstances where the relevant person will *not* be treated as dishonest and one circumstance where a person *may* be dishonest.

The Theft Act 1968, s. 2 states:

(1) A person's appropriation of property belonging to another is not to be regarded as dishonest—
  (a) if he appropriates the property in the belief that he has in law the right to deprive the other of it, on behalf of himself or of a third person; or
  (b) if he appropriates the property in the belief that he would have the other's consent if the other knew of the appropriation and the circumstances of it; or
  (c) (except where the property came to him as trustee or personal representative) if he appropriates the property in the belief that the person to whom the property belongs cannot be discovered by taking reasonable steps.
(2) A person's appropriation of property belonging to another may be dishonest notwithstanding that he is willing to pay for the property.

KEYNOTE

In all three instances it is the person's *belief* that is important.

Right

- Under s. 2(1)(a) if a person in dispute with a bookmaker believes he/she has a legal contractual *right* to take something of a value equal to his/her unpaid winnings from the bookmaker's stand, that person will not be regarded as dishonest—even though gambling debts are not legally enforceable. His/her belief need not even be reasonable, only honestly held, and could be based on a 'mistake' (contrast the general defence of mistake, see chapter 1.4).

Consent

- Under s. 2(1)(b) the person appropriating the property must believe both elements, i.e. that the other person would have *consented* had he/she known of the appropriation *and the circumstances of it*. If a member of a police station tea club is desperate for a cigarette and takes cash from the tea club kitty which colleagues occasionally use for such 'emergencies', the taker might well argue that s. 2(1)(b) applies. If, however, the money is taken to boost the Christmas kitty of another shift, the second condition may defeat them! Although the person need not have given his/her consent to the appropriation, the presence of such consent may be very relevant in establishing the honest existence of the defendant's belief.

Lost

- Under s. 2(1)(c), the belief has to be in relation to the likelihood of *discovering* the 'owner' by taking reasonable steps. Both the nature and value of the property, together with the attendant circumstances, will be relevant. The chances of finding the owner of a valuable, monogrammed engagement ring found after a theatre performance would be considerably greater than those of discovering the owner of a can of beer found outside Twickenham stadium following a Six Nations match between Wales and England.

Again, it is the defendant's *belief* at the time of the appropriation that is important here, not that the defendant went on to *take* reasonable steps to discover the person to whom the property belongs.

Under s. 2(2), if a person appropriates another's property, leaving money or details of where he/she can be contacted to make restitution will not *of itself* negate dishonesty (see *Boggeln* v *Williams* [1978] 1 WLR 873). The wording of s. 2(2) gives latitude to a court where the defendant was willing to pay for the property. The subsection says that such an appropriation *may* be dishonest, not that it *will always* be dishonest.

1.11.2.2 Dishonesty: The Ruling in *Ghosh*

Section 2 will not cater for every circumstance and indeed ss. 2 to 6 only affect the interpretation of the basic elements of theft as set out in s. 1 unless the Act says otherwise (s. 1(3)). Since the case of *R* v *Ghosh* [1982] QB 1053 there has been a requirement for juries to be given some form of direction where the issue of dishonesty is raised and s. 2 is of no assistance. As well as clarifying that the defendant's dishonesty is a matter for a jury to decide, the Court of Appeal in *Ghosh* also identified two aspects which the jury should consider when so deciding. If s. 2 is not applicable or helpful then a jury must decide:

* whether, according to the ordinary standards of reasonable and honest people, what was done was 'dishonest'; *and*, if it was
* whether 'the defendant himself must have realised that what was done was dishonest' *by those standards*.

This test against the standards of reasonable and honest people means that a defendant who has a purely *subjective* belief that he/she is doing what is morally right (e.g. an anti-vivisectionist taking animals from a laboratory) can still be 'dishonest'. The *Ghosh* test is probably the source of the questions so loved by some interviewing officers: 'But what would an *honest* person have done?' or 'What would have been the *honest* thing to do?'

1.11.2.3 Appropriates

The Theft Act 1968, s. 3 states:

(1) Any assumption by a person of the rights of an owner amounts to an appropriation, and this includes, where he has come by the property (innocently or not) without stealing it, any later assumption of a right to it by keeping or dealing with it as owner.

KEYNOTE

It is important to note that there can be an 'appropriation' without any criminal liability and appropriation itself does not amount to an offence; it describes one of the elements of the criminal conduct that must exist before a charge of theft can be made out. An appropriation requires no mental state on the part of the appropriator. It is an objective act.

Where an appropriation takes place and is accompanied by the required dishonesty and intention to deprive permanently, there will be a theft.

Appropriation under s. 3(1) envisages a *physical* act—*Biggs* v *R* (2003) 12 December, unreported.

When and where the particular act amounting to an appropriation took place is therefore of critical importance when bringing a charge of theft; it is also vital when establishing other offences such as robbery (see para. 1.11.3), aggravated burglary (see para. 1.11.5) and handling stolen goods (see para. 1.11.10).

Appropriation and Consent: *R* v *Gomez*

The decision of the House of Lords in *R* v *Gomez* [1993] AC 442 is significant in the development of the meaning of 'appropriation'. Gomez worked in a shop in London. He was approached by a friend who asked him to accept two building society cheques in exchange for some expensive electrical goods from the shop. Knowing the cheques to be stolen, Gomez took them to his store manager asking him to authorise the supply of goods. Gomez assured the manager that the cheques had been confirmed and that they were 'as good as cash'. With this reassurance the manager authorised the supply of the goods. Gomez paid the cheques into the store's account and the large quantity of electrical goods was dispatched to Gomez's friend. Some time later, the cheques were returned with a 'not to pay' order on them as they had been reported stolen.

Gomez was arrested for theft of the electrical goods, together with his friend, and sent for trial. There, counsel for Gomez submitted that there was no case to answer in respect of the theft because the store manager had authorised their supply and therefore there had been no 'appropriation' under s. 3(1) of the Theft Act 1968. The submission was rejected by the trial judge but was upheld on appeal on the grounds that, when Gomez's friend took possession of the electrical goods, he was entitled to do so under the terms of the contract of sale entered into by the store manager. The Court went on to say that, although the contract of sale may have been 'voidable' (that is, the other parties to it could have it set aside because they had been duped into it), nevertheless the goods were transferred to Gomez's friend with the express authority of the 'owner' (the store manager) who had consented to the transaction.

On the appeal by the Director of Public Prosecutions to the House of Lords, Lord Keith followed an earlier case (*Lawrence* v *Metropolitan Police Commissioner* [1972] AC 626). His Lordship disagreed with the argument that an act expressly or impliedly authorised by the owner can never amount to an 'appropriation' and pointed out that the decision in *Lawrence* was a direct contradiction of that proposition. The House of Lords upheld the men's convictions for theft and accepted that there are occasions where property can be 'appropriated' for the purposes of the Theft Act 1968, *even though the owner has given his/her consent or authority.*

A number of issues come from this decision:

- *Taking or depriving.* First, it is not necessary that the property be 'taken' in order for there to be an appropriation (contrast this with the offence under s. 12 of taking a conveyance, **see para. 1.11.6**), neither need the owner be 'deprived' of the property. Similarly, there is no need for the defendant to 'gain' anything by an appropriation which can also be caused by damaging or destroying property (*R* v *Graham* [1997] 1 Cr App R 395). (For offences involving criminal damage, **see chapter 1.13**.)
- *Consent.* Secondly, it is irrelevant to the issue of appropriation whether or not the owner consented to that appropriation (again, contrast the offence under s. 12, **see para. 1.11.6**). This is well illustrated in *Lawrence*, the decision followed by the House of Lords in *Gomez*. In *Lawrence* a tourist gave his wallet full of unfamiliar English currency to a taxi driver for the latter to remove the correct fare. The driver in fact helped himself to ('appropriated') far more than the amount owed. It has held that the fact that the wallet and its contents were handed over freely (with consent) by the owner did not prevent the taxi driver's actions from amounting to an 'appropriation' of it. The Court of Appeal appears—at least on one occasion—to have interpreted *Gomez* as deciding that consent *obtained by fraud* is irrelevant to the issue of appropriation (see *R* v *Mazo* [1997] 2 Cr App R 518). However, there is no such restriction placed on the decision in *Gomez* and it seems safe to assume that consent given by the owner will not prevent an 'appropriation' of property for the purposes of the Theft Act 1968.
- *Interfering with goods.* Our higher courts were greatly concerned for a number of years by the swapping of price labels on goods displayed for sale in shops and whether or not such behaviour amounted to an appropriation. A third point that is now clear from the decision in *Gomez* is that simply swapping the price labels on items displayed for sale in a shop *would* amount to an 'appropriation'. This is because to

do so, irrespective of any further intention, involves an assumption of one of the owner's rights in relation to the property. If that appropriation were accompanied by the required circumstances of dishonesty and intention to deprive, then there would be a *prima facie* case of theft.

- *More than one appropriation.* A fourth point apparent from *Gomez* is that there may be an appropriation of the same property on more than one occasion. However, once property has been *stolen* (as opposed to merely appropriated), that same property cannot be stolen again by the same thief (*R v Atakpu* [1994] QB 69). Appropriation can also be a continuing act, that is, it can include the whole episode of entering and ransacking a house and the subsequent removal of property (*R v Hale* (1978) 68 Cr App R 415). Therefore identifying the exact point at which property was appropriated with the requisite intention and accompanying dishonesty can cause practical difficulties.

Summary

The House of Lords was recently asked to rule on whether a person could 'appropriate' property belonging to another where the other person made her an absolute gift of property, retaining no proprietary interest in the property or any right to resume or recover it (*R v Hinks* [2000] 3 WLR 1590). In that case the defendant had befriended a middle aged man of limited intelligence who had given her some £60,000 over a period of time. The defendant was charged with five counts of theft and, after conviction, eventually appealed to the House of Lords. Their Lordships held that:

- in a prosecution for theft it was unnecessary to prove that the taking was without the owner's consent (as in *Lawrence* above);
- it was immaterial whether the act of appropriation was done with the owner's consent or authority (as in *Gomez*); and
- *Gomez* therefore gave effect to s. 3(1) by treating 'appropriation' as a neutral word covering 'any assumption by a person of the rights of an owner'.

Although consistent with earlier cases, this approach creates a few problems. If acceptance of the gift were treated as an 'appropriation', the defendant would seem to have had a belief that she had a right to deprive the donor of the property (see para. **1.11.2.1**) and therefore she was not 'dishonest'. Further, under s. 5 of the 1968 Act (see para. **1.11.2.6**) the prosecution has to prove that, at the time of the alleged appropriation, the relevant property belonged to another. In *Hinks* the defendant had been validly given the property, therefore it is difficult to see how the money still belonged to the donor at the time of appropriation.

These and other concerns were raised by Lord Hobhouse who pointed out that ss. 1 to 6 should be read as a whole and that attempts to 'compartmentalise' each element only lead to contradictions. However, he was in a minority and the case decision stands, compartments and all.

If a person, having come by property—innocently or not—without stealing it, later assumes any rights to it by keeping it or treating it as his/her own, then he/she 'appropriates' that property (s. 3(1)).

An exception to these circumstances is provided by s. 3 which states:

(2) Where property or a right or interest in property is or purports to be transferred for value to a person acting in good faith, no later assumption by him of rights which he believed himself to be acquiring shall, by reason of any defect in the transferor's title, amount to theft of the property.

KEYNOTE

If a person buys a car in good faith and gives value for it (i.e. a reasonable price) but then discovers it has been stolen, his/her refusal to return it to the vendor will not, without more, *attract liability for theft*. Without s. 3(2) the retention of the vehicle would be caught by s. 3(1). This narrow exemption does not mean however that the innocent purchaser gets good title to the car (see *National Employers' Mutual Insurance Association Ltd* v *Jones* [1990] 1 AC 24), nor would it provide a defence if the stolen goods are a gift and the 'donee' (recipient) subsequently discovers that they had been stolen.

1.11.2.4 Property

The Theft Act 1968, s. 4 states:

(1) 'Property' includes money and all other property, real or personal, including things in action and other intangible property.
(2) A person cannot steal land, or things forming part of land and severed from it by him or by his directions, except in the following cases, that is to say—
    (a) when he is a trustee or personal representative, or is authorised by power of attorney, or as liquidator of a company, or otherwise, to sell or dispose of land belonging to another, and he appropriates the land or anything forming part of it by dealing with it in breach of the confidence reposed in him; or
    (b) when he is not in possession of the land and appropriates anything forming part of the land by severing it or causing it to be severed, or after it has been severed; or
    (c) when, being in possession of the land under a tenancy, he appropriates the whole or part of any fixture or structure let to be used with the land.
    For purposes of this subsection 'land' does not include incorporeal hereditaments; 'tenancy' means a tenancy for years or any less period and includes an agreement for such a tenancy, but a person who after the end of a tenancy remains in possession as statutory tenant or otherwise is to be treated as having possession under the tenancy, and 'let' shall be construed accordingly.
(3) A person who picks mushrooms growing wild on any land, or who picks flowers, fruit or foliage from a plant growing wild on any land, does not (although not in possession of the land) steal what he picks unless he does it for reward or for sale or other commercial purpose. For purposes of this subsection 'mushroom' includes any fungus, and 'plant' includes any shrub or tree.
(4) Wild creatures, tamed or untamed, shall be regarded as property; but a person cannot steal a wild creature not tamed nor ordinarily kept in captivity, or the carcase of any such creature, unless either it has been reduced into possession by or on behalf of another person and possession of it has not since been lost or abandoned, or another person is in course of reducing it into possession.

KEYNOTE

Specific Types of Property

Under s. 4(1) 'things in action' would include patents and trademarks and other things which can only be enforced by legal action as opposed to physical possession. (See also the Copyright etc. and Trade Marks (Offences and Enforcement) Act 2002.) Other intangible property would include software programs and perhaps credits accumulated on 'smart cards'. Confidential information—such as the contents of an examination paper (!)—is not intangible property *per se* (see *Oxford* v *Moss* (1978) 68 Cr App R 183). However, the document itself would be property. It has been accepted by the Court of Appeal that contractual rights obtained by buying a ticket for the London Underground may amount to a 'thing in action' (see *R* v *Marshall* [1998] 2 Cr App R 282), though this view is extremely contentious.

Although an area of criminal activity causing increasing concern (and cost) is that of so-called 'identity theft', this is something of a misnomer. Adopting another person's characteristics and using their administrative data (such as national insurance number) is not theft as this information is not 'property' for these purposes, however confidential it might be.

Cheques

Cheques will be property as they are pieces of paper (albeit of very little intrinsic value). The contents of a bank or building society account, however, are also a 'thing in action' that can be stolen *provided the account is in credit or within the limits of an agreed overdraft facility* (*R* v *Kohn* (1979) 69 Cr App R 395). Therefore reducing the credit balance in one account, and transferring a like sum into your own account amounts to an 'appropriation' of property within the meaning of s. 1. This principle (set out in *Kohn*) was reaffirmed in *R* v *Williams (Roy)* [2001] 1 Cr App R 362 by the Court of Appeal.

Land

Under s. 4(2) you cannot generally steal land even though it is 'property' for the purposes of criminal damage (**see chapter 1.13**). An exception to this general rule is if you are a trustee or personal representative or someone in a position of trust to dispose of land belonging to another, you can be guilty of stealing it if, in such circumstances, you dishonestly dispose of it.

If you are in possession of land under a tenancy then things forming part of that land to be used with it are 'property' capable of being stolen. Such fittings and fixtures (including fireplaces, fitted kitchens, etc.) would be particularly relevant to agricultural tenants or those occupying council property.

Section 4(3) obliquely includes mushrooms, flowers, fruit and foliage in the ambit of 'property' unless they are growing wild on any land. If they are so growing, then the person picking them must be shown to have done so for reward, sale or other commercial purpose in order to be guilty of theft. It is arguable that, if the person does not have such a *purpose at the time of the picking*, any later intention to sell the fruit, etc. may not bring it within the provisions of s. 4(3).

Animals

Section 4(4) acknowledges that all wild creatures are 'property' but goes on to qualify the occasions when they will be capable of being the subject matter of a charge of theft. Once a person has reduced it into possession (say, by trapping, capturing or shooting it), a wild animal can be 'stolen', by another, but not the person reducing it into possession. This is why poaching is not generally theft. If the animal is lost or abandoned after it has been reduced into possession or killed then it cannot be 'stolen'.

These provisos appear to relate more to the concept of 'belonging to another' (see below) than 'property'.

Pets and animals that are tamed or ordinarily kept in captivity are always property for the purposes of theft.

1.11.2.5 What is not Property?

Human bodies are not property (*Doodeward* v *Spence* (1908) 6 CLR 406) although a driver has been convicted of stealing a specimen of his own urine (*R* v *Welsh* [1974] RTR 478). This principle was upheld by the Court of Appeal in *R* v *Kelly* [1999] QB 621, after the conviction of two people involved in the theft of body parts from the Royal College of Surgeons. The court upheld the convictions for theft on the grounds that the process of *alteration* (amputation, dissection and preservation) which the body parts had undergone did make them 'property' for the purposes of the 1968 Act. The common law rule was that there is no property in a corpse and any change to that rule would have to be made by Parliament.

Electricity is the subject of a specific offence (**see para. 1.11.9**).

1.11.2.6 Belonging to Another

The Theft Act 1968, s. 5 states:

(1) Property shall be regarded as belonging to any person having possession or control of it, or having in it any proprietary right or interest (not being an equitable interest arising only from an agreement to transfer or grant an interest).

(2) Where property is subject to a trust, the persons to whom it belongs shall be regarded as including any person having a right to enforce the trust, and an intention to defeat the trust shall be regarded accordingly as an intention to deprive of the property any person having that right.

KEYNOTE

Property can be 'stolen' from any person who has possession or control or a right or interest in that property. In one case where the defendant sneaked into a garage to recover his own recently-repaired car, he was convicted of stealing the car which at the time 'belonged to' the garage proprietor who had possession and control of it (*R* v *Turner (No. 2)* [1971] 1 WLR 901). In determining whether or not a person had 'possession' of property for the purposes of s. 5(1), the period of possession can be finite (i.e. for a given number of hours, days, etc.) or infinite (*R* v *Kelly* [1998] 3 All ER 741).

It is not necessary to show who does own the property—only that it 'belongs to' someone other than the defendant. (For rights of the Crown under the Treasure Act 1996 and other statutes, see *Blackstone's Criminal Practice*, 2008, section B4.18.)

A good example of how this principle operates can be seen in a case before the Court of Appeal where the two defendants went diving in a lake on a golf course, recovering sacks of 'lost' balls which it was believed they were going to sell. Although the defendants argued that the balls had been abandoned by their owners, the Crown had shown that they were 'property belonging to another' and therefore the convictions were safe (*R* v *Rostron*; *R* v *Collinson* [2003] EWCA Crim 2206).

Where money is given by members of the public to charity collectors it becomes the property of the relevant charitable trustees at the moment it goes into the collecting tin (*R* v *Dyke* [2002] Crim LR 153). This will be important when framing the relevant charge or indictment. If in doubt as to the 'ownership' of property that is the subject of a theft, the advice of the Crown Prosecution Service should be sought.

When a cheque is written, that will create a 'thing in action'. That thing in action belongs only to the payee. Therefore a payee of a cheque cannot 'steal' the thing in action which it creates (*R* v *Davis* (1988) 88 Cr App R 347). The piece of paper on which a cheque is printed will also be property—however low in value (**see para. 1.11.2.4**).

In proving theft, you must show that the property belonged to another *at the time of the appropriation*. This requirement has caused some difficulty where a defendant's decision not to pay for goods has been made *after* property passed to him/her. In such cases (e.g. people refusing to pay for meals after they have eaten or deciding to drive off having filled their car with petrol), the proper charge (historically) was deception but would now be covered by the Fraud Act 2006 (**see chapter 1.12**) or making off without payment (**see para. 1.11.14**). But it should be remembered that the appropriation can be an extended and continuing act (*R* v *Atakpu* [1994] QB 69). The House of Lords' ruling in *Gomez* raises some questions over such cases (**see para. 1.11.2.3**). As the consent of the owner is irrelevant to the issue of 'appropriation', the key element in such cases is whether the property 'belonged to another' at the time of the act of appropriation. If ownership of the property had passed to the defendant *before* he/she appropriated it (e.g. by virtue of the Sale of Goods Act 1979; see *Edwards* v *Ddin* [1976] 1 WLR 942) then this element of theft would not be made out and an alternative charge should be considered.

1.11.2.7 Obligations Regarding Another's Property

The Theft Act 1968, s. 5 states:

(3) Where a person receives property from or on account of another, and is under an obligation to the other to retain and deal with that property or its proceeds in a particular way, the property or proceeds shall be regarded (as against him) as belonging to the other.

KEYNOTE

'Obligation' means a legal obligation, not simply a moral one (*R* v *Hall* [1973] QB 126). Whether or not such an obligation exists is a matter of law for a trial judge to decide (*R* v *Dubar* [1994] 1 WLR 1484).

Instances under s. 5(3) most commonly involve receiving money from others to retain and use in a certain way (e.g. travel agents taking deposits; solicitors holding funds for mortgagees; or pension fund managers collecting contributions (*R* v *Clowes (No. 2)* [1994] 2 All ER 316)). The Court of Appeal has held that one effect of s. 5(3), is that property can be regarded as belonging to another even where it does not 'belong' to them on a strict interpretation of civil law (*R* v *Klineberg* [1999] 1 Cr App R 427). In that case the defendants collected money from customers in their timeshare business.

Although the customers were told that their deposits would be placed with an independent trustee, the defendants paid the sums into their company account, thereby breaching the 'obligation' under s. 5(3) to deal with the money in a particular way. Section 5(3) would also include, say, the owners of shopping malls where coins thrown into a fountain are to be donated to charity; if the owners did not deal with those coins in the way intended, the provisions of s. 5(3) may well apply.

1.11.2.8 Obligation to Restore Another's Property

The Theft Act 1968, s. 5 states:

(4) Where a person gets property by another's mistake, and is under an obligation to make restoration (in whole or in part) of the property or its proceeds or of the value thereof, then to the extent of that obligation the property or proceeds shall be regarded (as against him) as belonging to the person entitled to restoration, and an intention not to make restoration shall be regarded accordingly as an intention to deprive that person of the property or proceeds.

KEYNOTE

Before s. 5(4) was enacted, an employee who was mistakenly credited with extra money in his/her bank account could not be prosecuted for larceny (the predecessor of theft) (*Moynes* v *Cooper* [1956] 1 QB 439). In such circumstances under s. 5(4) the employee will be liable for stealing the extra money if he/she keeps it (see *Attorney-General's Reference (No. 1 of 1983)* [1985] QB 182 where a police officer's account was credited with money representing overtime which she had not actually worked).

Section 5(4) only applies where someone *other than the defendant* has made a mistake. It is clear that such a mistake can be a mistake as to a material fact; whether or not a mistake as to *law* would be covered is unclear.

Again, the obligation to make restoration is a *legal* one and, as with s. 5(3), an unenforceable or moral obligation will not be covered by s. 5(4). (See *R* v *Gilks* [1972] 1 WLR 1341 where a betting shop mistakenly paid out winnings against the wrong horse. As gambling debts are not legally enforceable the defendant was not under 'an obligation' to restore the money and therefore s. 5(4) did not apply.)

1.11.2.9   Intention of Permanently Depriving

If you cannot prove an intention permanently to deprive you cannot prove theft (see *R v Warner* (1970) 55 Cr App R 93).

If there is such an intention at the time of the appropriation, giving the property back later will not alter the fact and the charge will be made out (*R v McHugh* (1993) 97 Cr App R 335).

In certain circumstances s. 6 may help in determining the presence or absence of such an intention.

The Theft Act 1968, s. 6 states:

(1) A person appropriating property belonging to another without meaning the other permanently to lose the thing itself is nevertheless to be regarded as having the intention of permanently depriving the other of it if his intention is to treat the thing as his own to dispose of regardless of the other's rights; and a borrowing or lending of it may amount to so treating it if, but only if, the borrowing or lending is for a period and in circumstances making it equivalent to an outright taking or disposal.

KEYNOTE

The key feature of s. 6(1) is the intention to treat 'the thing' as one's own to dispose of regardless of the other's rights. An example of such a case would be where property is 'held to ransom' (*R v Coffey* [1987] Crim LR 498). The borrowing or lending of another's property is specifically caught within s. 6(1). If a person takes property from his/her employer (e.g. carpet tiles) and uses it in a way which makes restoration unlikely or impossible (e.g. by laying them in his/her living room), then s. 6(1) will apply (see *R v Velumyl* [1989] Crim LR 299).

Similarly, if a person borrowed a season ticket causing the owner to miss a match, s. 6(1) would help prove the required intention because the circumstances of the borrowing make it equivalent to an outright taking.

In a case involving robbery (see below), the defendants took the victim's personal stereo headphones from him and broke them in two, rendering them useless before returning them to him. The Administrative Court held that a person who took something and dealt with it for the purpose of rendering it useless in this way demonstrated the intention of treating that article as his/her own to dispose of. The Court did not accept the argument that the property had to be totally exhausted before s. 6 applied (see also *R v Fernandes* [1996] 1 Cr App R 175) and held that the magistrates had been wrong to accept the submission of no case to answer on this point (*DPP v J* (2002) LTL 20 February).

The Theft Act 1968, s. 6 states:

(2) Without prejudice to the generality of subsection (1) above, where a person, having possession or control (lawfully or not) of property belonging to another, parts with the property under a condition as to its return which he may not be able to perform, this (if done for purposes of his own and without the other's authority) amounts to treating the property as his own to dispose of regardless of the other's rights.

KEYNOTE

Section 6(2) deals with occasions such as pawning another's property. If there is a likelihood that the defendant will be unable to meet the conditions under which he/she parted with another person's property, s. 6(2) would help in proving an intention permanently to deprive.

1.11.3   **Robbery**

OFFENCE: **Robbery—*Theft Act 1968, s. 8***

> • Triable on indictment   • Life imprisonment

The Theft Act 1968, s. 8 states:

> (1) A person is guilty of robbery if he steals, and immediately before or at the time of doing so, and in order to do so, he uses force on any person or puts or seeks to put any person in fear of being then and there subjected to force.

KEYNOTE

The Theft Element of the Offence

For there to be a robbery, there must be a theft; so if there is no theft, then there can be no robbery. The word 'steal' in the offence relates to the offence under s. 1 of the Theft Act 1968 and, therefore, if any element of theft cannot be proved the offence of robbery will not be made out. For example, in *R* v *Robinson* [1977] Crim LR 173, D, who was owed £7 by P's wife, approached P, brandishing a knife. A fight followed, during which P dropped a £5 note. D picked it up and demanded the remaining £2 owed to him. Allowing D's appeal against a conviction for robbery, the Court of Appeal held that the prosecution had to prove that D was guilty of theft, and that he would not be (under the Theft Act 1968, s. 2(1)(a)) if he believed that he had a right in law to deprive P of the money, even though he knew that he was not entitled to use the knife to get it.

The Robbery Time Frame

Section 8(1) requires that the force must be used or the threat made 'immediately before or at the time' of the theft. There is no guidance as to what 'immediately before' means. Clearly, if the force used or threatened is *after* the offence of theft has taken place, there will be no robbery; however theft can be a continuing offence. This was decided in *R* v *Hale* (1978) 68 Cr App Rep 415, where the Court of Appeal stated that appropriation is a continuing act and whether it has finished or not is a matter for the jury to decide. From the robbery perspective, *Hale* decides that where D had assumed ownership of goods in a house, the 'time' of stealing is a continuing process. It does not end as soon as the property is picked up by the defendant and can be a continuing act so long as he is in the course of removing it from the premises. So, if D uses or threatens force to get away with the property (whilst still in the house for example), a robbery is committed. This would probably not be the case if the defendant used force outside the house as there must come a time when the appropriation ends. The issue may be resolved by asking the question, 'Was D still on the job?' (*R* v *Atakpu* [1994] QB 69).

In Order to Do So

The use or threat of force must be 'in order' to carry out the theft. Force used in any other context means the offence is not committed, for example:

- Two men have an argument outside a pub and begin fighting each other. One man punches the other in the face and the force of the blow knocks the man out. As the injured man falls the floor, his wallet drops out of his jacket pocket and onto the pavement. His opponent decides that he will steal the wallet. *No robbery is committed in these circumstances because the force is used for a purpose other than to steal.*

The question to ask in such circumstances is 'Why has the force been used and/or threatened?' If the answer is anything other than 'To enable the defendant to commit theft' then there is no offence of robbery.

Force

The slightest use of force to accomplish a theft changes that theft into a robbery. An illustration can be found in the case of *R* v *Dawson* (1976) 64 Cr App R 170, where the defendant and two others surrounded their victim. One of the attackers 'nudged' the victim and while he was unbalanced another stole his wallet. In *Dawson*, the court declined to define 'force' any further than to say that juries would understand it readily enough. In line with general principles of *actus reus* (criminal conduct), the force used by the defendant must be used voluntarily. Therefore, the accidental use of force such as when a pickpocket, in the process of stealing a wallet from his victim on a train, is pushed into his victim by the train jolting on the railway line would not be a robbery.

On Any Person

The force used to accomplish a robbery need not be used against the owner or possessor of the property. For example, a gang of armed criminals use force against a security guard in order to overpower him and steal cash from the safe he standing outside and guarding.

Force does not actually have to be used 'on' the *person* i.e. on the actual body of the victim. It may be used on something that the victim is carrying as in the case of *R* v *Clouden* [1987] Crim LR 65, where the Court of Appeal dismissed an appeal against a conviction for robbery when the defendant had wrenched the victim's shopping basket from her hand and ran off with it.

The Fear of Force

Where only the *threat* of force is involved the intention must be to put a person in fear for *himself*; an intention to put someone in fear for another is not enough (*R* v *Taylor* [1996] 10 Archbold News 2, CA). This may seem at odds with the approach to the actual *use* of force in the offence of robbery (in that force *can* be used against a third party who is unconnected with the property subject to the theft). For example:

- A man enters a betting shop and approaches the cashier. Without saying a word he passes a note to the cashier that simply says, 'Look to your left'. The cashier looks to her left and sees the man's accomplice standing several feet away and pointing a knife at the back of one of the betting shop customers. The customer is oblivious to the actions of the man's accomplice. The man passes a second note to the cashier that says, 'Give me the money in the till or else he gets it!' *At this stage there is no robbery committed as the cashier cannot fear force for the betting shop customer. However, whilst there is no robbery there would be an offence of blackmail (Theft Act 1968, s. 21).* The cashier shakes her head and refuses to hand over any money. At this point, the man signals to his accomplice who pulls the customer's head backwards and drags the knife across the side of the customer's throat causing a small cut. The customer screams in terror and at this point the cashier concedes to the man's demand and hands over the till contents. *At this point in time a robbery is committed as force is actually being used (albeit on a third party).*

State of Mind

Showing that a victim was frightened is not enough to prove the offence (*R* v *Khan* (2001) LTL 9 April); you must show that the offender intends the victim to fear the immediate use of force. As long as the offender possess such intent, it is immaterial if the victim is unconcerned by the threats of the offender.

General Points

Any threats to use force at some time in the future (even by a matter of minutes) would constitute an offence of blackmail. Threats to use force at some place other than location of the offence fall into the same category. This effectively excludes threats made via the telephone in all but the most improbable of situations.

1.11.4 Burglary

The main offence of burglary is split into two—s. 9(1)(a) and s. 9(1)(b). These are discussed below.

1.11.4.1 Section 9(1)(a)

OFFENCE: **Burglary—*Theft Act 1968, s. 9***

> • Triable on indictment if 'ulterior offence' is so triable, or if committed in dwelling and violence used; otherwise triable either way • Fourteen years' imprisonment if building/part of building is dwelling • Otherwise ten years' imprisonment on indictment • Six months' imprisonment and/or a fine summarily

The Theft Act 1968, s. 9 states:

> (1) A person is guilty of burglary if—
>   (a) he enters any building or part of a building as a trespasser and with intent to commit any such offence as is mentioned in subsection (2) below; or ...
> (2) The offences referred to in subsection (1)(a) above are offences of stealing anything in the building or part of a building in question, of inflicting on any person therein any grievous bodily harm and of doing unlawful damage to the building or anything therein.

KEYNOTE

Enters

What action on the part of the defendant constitutes 'entry' into a building or part of a building? The Theft Act 1968 does not define the term 'entry' and so we are left to resolve the meaning of this term by reference to case law and the decisions of the courts. The common law rule was that the insertion of any part of the body, *however small*, was sufficient to be considered an 'entry'. So where D pushed in a window pane and the forepart of his finger was observed in the building that was enough (*R v Davis* (1823) Russ & Ry 499). This approach was narrowed considerably in *R v Collins* [1973] QB 100, where it was said that entry needed to be 'effective and substantial'. The ruling in *Collins* was rejected by the Court of Appeal in *R v Brown* [1985] Crim LR 212, CA, where it was stated that the 'substantial' element was surplus to requirements and that entry need only be 'effective'. Whether an entry was 'effective' or not was for the jury to decide. So the decision of the Court in *Brown* appears to be the current accepted approach to defining the term; entry must therefore be 'effective'.

An 'effective' entry does not mean that the defendant has to enter a building or part of a building to such a degree that the ulterior offence, which he is entering with the intention to commit (the theft, GBH or criminal damage), can be committed (*R v Ryan* [1996] Crim LR 320, CA). Nor does it mean that the defendant must get his whole body into the building. In *Brown*, the defendant had his feet on the ground outside the building with the upper half inside the building as he searched for goods to steal; this was held to be an entry. In *Ryan*, the defendant, who had become trapped by his neck with only his head and right arm inside the window, was held to have 'entered' the building. In *Brown*, the Court of Appeal stated that it would be astounding if a smash-and-grab raider, who inserted his hand through a shop window to grab goods, was not considered to have 'entered' the building.

At common law, the insertion of an instrument would constitute entry as long as the instrument was inserted to enable the ulterior offence to take place, e.g. a hook inserted into premises to steal property or the muzzle of a gun pushed through a letterbox with a view to cause GBH. Insertion of an instrument merely to facilitate entry, e.g. using a coat hanger to open a window lock, *would not* be entry. Although there is no recent authority on the issue, it is likely that this line of reasoning in relation to the use of instruments in burglary is still acceptable.

Entry must be deliberate and not accidental.

Ultimately, whether the defendant has entered a building or not will be a question of fact for the jury or magistrate(s).

Trespasser

For a person to be guilty of the offence of burglary he must know that he is entering as a trespasser (i.e. he must know he is entering without a right by law or permission to do so) or be reckless as to that fact. Sometimes a defendant may have a general permission to enter premises from which he then steals. In such circumstances the exceeding of the granted permission places the defendant in a position of being a trespasser from the outset. In *R* v *Jones and Smith* [1976] 1 WLR 672, the defendant was convicted of burglary when he took two televisions from his father's home. He had a key to the premises and was free to come and go as he liked but when he entered his father's house (using the key) accompanied by a friend at 3am and stole the television sets, he committed burglary as it was his intention to steal—such an intent voids the general permission to enter.

1.11.4.2   Building

The Theft Act 1968 s. 9 states:

(4) References in subsections (1) and (2) above to a building,. . .and the reference in subsection (3), above,to a building which is a dwelling, shall apply also to an inhabited vehicle or vessel, and shall apply to any such vehicle or vessel at times when the person having a habitation in it is not there as well as at times when he is.

KEYNOTE

Building

A building is generally considered to be a structure of a permanent nature (*Norfolk Constabulary* v *Seekings and Gould* [1986] Crim LR 167), although a substantial portable structure with most of the attributes of a building can be a 'building' for the purposes of burglary. For example, in *B & S* v *Leathley* [1979] Crim LR 314, Crown Ct, a portable container measuring 25ft by 7ft by 7ft and weighing three tons, which had occupied the same position for three years, was connected to mains electricity and which was due to remain in the same position for the foreseeable future, was considered to be a building for the purposes of burglary. An unfinished house can be a building for the purposes of burglary (*R* v *Manning* (1871) LR 1 CCR 338). Tents and marquees are considered to fall outside the term, even if the tent is someone's home (the Criminal Law Revision Committee intended tents to be outside the protection of burglary).

The effect of s. 9(4) is to include house boats and vehicles used as potential dwellings within the term. This does depend on whether the vehicle or vessel is 'inhabited'; a canal boat used as a permanent home is capable of being burgled.

Part of a Building

A person may commit burglary when, although he is in one part of a building with legitimate access, he enters another part of it as a trespasser.

- A tenant of a block of flats has a pass-key that provides access to a communal foyer of the block of flats. He uses the pass-key to enter the foyer (*entering a building and plainly not a trespasser at this stage*) Instead of entering his own flat he forces entry to a neighbour's flat by breaking down the neighbour's door that can be accessed via the communal foyer (*moving from one part of a building to another in the process and certainly a trespasser at this stage*).

Part of a building does not mean that there has to be a physical separation of one room from another. In *R* v *Walkington* [1979] 2 All ER 716, the defendant walked behind a moveable counter in a shop with the intention to steal and was found guilty of burglary as this was held to be 'part of a building'. A 'no entry' or a rope could mark off one part of a building from another.

1.11.4.3 Intentions at the Time of Entry

The intentions must be as follows:

- Stealing—this means an intention to commit theft under s. 1 (**see para. 1.11.2**). It will not include abstracting electricity because abstracting under s. 13 is not stealing (*Low* v *Blease* [1975] Crim LR 513) (**see para. 1.11.9**), neither will it include taking a conveyance (**see para. 1.11.6**). The property which the defendant intends to steal must be in a building or part of a building.
- Inflicting grievous bodily harm—if grievous bodily harm is inflicted (**see chapter 1.7**), then the second offence under s. 9(1)(b) below would apply. In proving an intention to commit grievous bodily harm under s. 9(1)(a), it is not necessary to prove that an assault was actually committed (*Metropolitan Police Commissioner* v *Wilson* [1984] AC 242). The offence in question in respect of a burglary under s. 9(1)(a) is of grievous bodily harm contrary to s. 18 of the Offences Against the Person Act 1861.
- Causing unlawful damage—this includes damage, not only to the building but to anything in it (**see chapter 1.13**).

1.11.4.4 Conditional Intent

Provided the required intention can be proved, it is immaterial whether or not there is anything 'worth stealing' within the building (*R* v *Walkington* [1979] 1 WLR 1169). The same will be true if the person whom the defendant intends to cause serious harm is not in the building or part of the building at the time (see also criminal attempts, **chapter 1.3**).

1.11.4.5 Section 9(1)(b)

OFFENCE: **Burglary—*Theft Act 1968, s. 9***

(see para. 1.12.4.1)

The Theft Act 1968, s. 9 states:

(1) A person is guilty of burglary if—

. . .

(b) having entered any building or part of a building as a trespasser he steals or attempts to steal anything in the building or that part of it or inflicts or attempts to inflict on any person therein any grievous bodily harm.

KEYNOTE

The second type of burglary involves a defendant's behaviour *after* entering a building or part of a building.

The defendant must have entered the building or part of a building as a trespasser; it is not enough that he/she subsequently became a trespasser by exceeding a condition of entry (e.g. hiding in the public area of a shop during open hours until the shop closes). However, where a person has entered a particular building (such as a shop or a pub) lawfully and without trespassing, if he/she later moves to *another part* of the building as a trespasser, this element of the offence will be made out.

....

EXAMPLE

D enters a public house near closing time with a friend who buys him a drink from the bar. D's entry onto that part of the premises has been authorised by the implied licence extended to members of the adult public by the publican and therefore D is not a trespasser. D then goes into the lavatories to use them as such. At this point he has entered another part of a building but again his entry is made under the implied licence to customers wishing to use the lavatories. While inside the lavatory area, D decides to hide until closing time in order to avoid buying his friend a drink. He hides inside one of the cubicles. At this point, although D's intention in hiding may be considered a little mean-spirited, he has none of the required intentions for the purposes of s. 9(1)(a) (see para. 1.11.4.1).

Once the publican has shut the pub for the night, D leaves the lavatory and walks into the bar area. Now D has entered *a part of a building as a trespasser* because the licence extended to members of the public by the publican certainly does not cover wandering around in the bar after it has been closed. Having no particular intention at this point, however, D has still not committed an offence of burglary.

On seeing the gaming machines in the public bar, D decides to break into them and steal the money inside. At this point, although he has *two* of the required intentions for s. 9(1)(a) (an intention to steal and an intention to cause unlawful damage), those intentions were formed *after* his entry. Therefore, D has not committed burglary under s. 9(1)(a). Because he has not stolen/attempted to steal or inflicted/attempted to inflict grievous bodily harm on any person therein, D has not committed burglary under s. 9(1)(b) either.

D then breaks open a gaming machine. At this point he commits burglary under s. 9(1)(b). This is because, having entered a part of a building (the public bar area) as a trespasser (because the pub is closed and D knows that to be the case), he *attempts to steal*. If he simply damaged the machine without an intention of stealing the contents, D would not commit this offence because causing unlawful damage is only relevant to the offence under s. 9(1)(a).

....

Unlike s. 9(1)(a), there are only two further elements to the offence under s. 9(1)(b)—the subsequent theft/attempted theft of anything in the building or part of it, and the subsequent inflicting/attempted inflicting of grievous bodily harm to any person therein. The offence in question in respect of a burglary under s. 9(1)(b) is of grievous bodily harm contrary to s. 18 or s. 20 of the Offences Against the Person Act 1861.

1.11.5 Aggravated Burglary

OFFENCE: **Aggravated Burglary—*Theft Act 1968, s. 10***
* • Triable on indictment • Life imprisonment

The Theft Act 1968, s. 10 states:

(1) A person is guilty of aggravated burglary if he commits any burglary and at the time has with him any firearm or imitation firearm, any weapon of offence, or any explosive;...

KEYNOTE

The 'time' at which the defendant must have the weapon etc. with him/her is critical and will depend on the type of burglary with which he/she is charged. If the defendant is charged with an offence under s. 9(1)(a), he/she must be shown to have had the weapon *at the time of entry*. Therefore if several people are charged with the offence of aggravated burglary, it must be shown that one of the defendants who actually entered the building had the weapon with them (*R* v *Klass* [1998] 1 Cr App R 453). If the charge is brought under s. 9(1)(b), he/she must be shown to have had the weapon *at the time of stealing or inflicting grievous bodily harm (or attempting either)*.

....

EXAMPLE

A person (X) enters a house as a trespasser intending to steal the contents. While inside, X is disturbed by the occupier. X grabs a kitchen knife from the kitchen and threatens the occupier.

If charged with burglary under s. 9(1)(a), X does not, on these facts alone, commit the offence of aggravated burglary because he did not have the weapon (kitchen knife) *at the time* of the burglary. If, however, X grabs the knife from the kitchen and stabs the occupier, *inflicting grievous bodily harm*, he commits the offence of burglary under s. 9(1)(b) *and at the time* has with him a weapon of offence. (See *R* v *O'Leary* (1986) 82 Cr App R 341.) Therefore X would be guilty of aggravated burglary. Similarly, if X followed the occupier into another part of the house intending to stab him, he would commit aggravated burglary.

'Has with him' will require a degree of immediate control (*R* v *Pawlicki* [1992] 1 WLR 827) and will normally be the same as 'carrying' (*Klass* above).

....

In cases where a defendant has been found entering a building with a weapon *per se*, it will not be necessary to prove any intention to use that weapon during the burglary (*R* v *Stones* [1989] 1 WLR 156).

For other offences involving weapons, **see General Police Duties, chapter 4.8**.

1.11.5.1 Firearm/Weapon of Offence/Explosive

The Theft Act 1968, s. 10 goes on to state:

(1) ... and for this purpose—
   (a) 'firearm' includes an airgun or pistol, and 'imitation firearm' means anything which has the appearance of being a firearm, whether capable of being discharged or not, and
   (b) 'weapon of offence' means any article made or adapted for use for causing injury to or incapacitating a person, or intended by the person having it with him for such use; and
   (c) 'explosive' means any article manufactured for the purpose of producing a practical effect by explosion, or intended by the person having it with him for that purpose.

KEYNOTE

The 'person' whom the article is intended to injure or incapacitate under s. 9(1)(b) above need not be a person in the building/part of a building. If a burglar has a weapon that he/she intends to use to injure or incapacitate someone unconnected with the building/part of a building, he/she may be tempted to use that weapon during the course of the burglary; the very consequence behind the creation of this offence (see *Stones* above).

It would appear that the defendant must at least know they have an article with them *and* that the article is in fact a weapon of offence (see *Blackstone's Criminal Practice*, 2008, section B4.80).

Note the additional element of articles made, adapted or intended for 'incapacitating' a person. This is broader than the other legislation defining weapons and would include rope, binding tape, chloroform, handcuffs and CS spray.

1.11.6 Taking a Conveyance without Consent

OFFENCE: **Taking a Conveyance without the Owner's Consent—*Theft Act 1968, s. 12***

- Triable summarily • Six months' imprisonment and/or a fine

The Theft Act 1968, s. 12 states:

(1) Subject to subsections (5) and (6) below, a person shall be guilty of an offence if, without having the consent of the owner or other lawful authority, he takes any conveyance for his own or another's use or, knowing that any conveyance has been taken without such authority, drives it or allows himself to be carried in or on it.

KEYNOTE

As a summary offence, s. 12(1) proceedings are ordinarily subject to the time limit of six months from the day when the offence was committed (see s. 127 of the Magistrates' Courts Act 1980). However, this restriction has caused significant problems in cases where the analysis of forensic evidence has been needed. As a result, the Vehicles (Crime) Act 2001 has extended the time limit for s. 12(1) offences. Proceedings for any such offences may be brought at any time within six months from the time when sufficient evidence to bring a prosecution came to the notice of the prosecutor (s. 37). In a similarly-worded provision, it has been held that anyone actively involved in the making or prosecuting of a charge (e.g. the officer in charge of the investigation) can be 'the prosecutor' for this purpose and that the expression is not restricted to the Crown Prosecution Service (*Morgans* v *DPP* [1999] 1 WLR 968). *Morgans* v *DPP* involved a prosecution under s. 11(2) of the Computer Misuse Act 1990 (see **General Police Duties, chapter 4.12**) but the same arguments would presumably apply.

Consent

As with other offences requiring the absence of consent, any 'consent' given must be true consent if the defendant is to avoid liability. The identity of the person taking the conveyance may be of particular importance to the owner (i.e. he/she would not lend his/her car to just anybody). If that can be shown to be the case, consent would be negated by the taker pretending to be someone to whom the owner would not ordinarily lend the vehicle. However, if it cannot be shown that the person's identity was of importance to the owner (e.g. where the owner is a car hire company), simply pretending to be someone else and producing a driving licence in another's name would not, of itself, be enough to negate any 'consent' (see *Whittaker* v *Campbell* [1984] QB 318).

Misrepresentation

Where the consent is obtained by a misrepresentation as to the purpose or destination of the journey, that misrepresentation has been held not to negate the consent (see *R* v *Peart* [1970] 2 QB 672).

Going beyond the express or implied permission of the owner may also negate consent (*R* v *Phipps* (1970) 54 Cr App R 300). This is often encountered where employees deviate substantially from an agreed route in their employer's vehicle or take the vehicle for a purpose entirely different from that permitted.

Lawful authority

Lawful authority may come from many different sources. A police officer removing a vehicle which is obstructing traffic after an accident or an agent of a finance company re-possessing a vehicle would be examples of such authority. Another example would be a member of a fire and rescue services authority moving a vehicle under his/her statutory powers (**see** Road Policing, para. **3.8.10.1**).

Defence

In addition, s. 12(6) provides:

> A person does not commit an offence under this section by anything done in the belief that he has lawful authority to do it or that he would have the owner's consent if the owner knew of his doing it and the circumstances of it.

There are similarities here with the element of dishonesty under the Theft Act 1968, s. 2(1)(b) (**see para. 1.11.2.1**). In order to attract the exemption under this subsection the person taking the conveyance must show:

- a belief that he/she had lawful authority at the time of the taking, or
- a belief that he/she would have the owner's consent had the owner known *of the taking and the circumstances of it.*

....

EXAMPLE

If a police officer at a Police Training Centre usually allows her colleague to use her motor cycle to go to a local gym on Tuesdays and Thursdays, the colleague might be able to claim that s. 12(6) applies if he took the motor cycle for that purpose one Tuesday without prior permission. However, if he were to take her Nissan Micra to use in a time trials competition one Sunday afternoon without her consent, subsection (6) is unlikely to apply.

It is worth noting that any requirement for the defendant to demonstrate the relevant belief in order to make out his/her defence is purely an *evidential* burden (as to which, **see** chapter **1.4**).

....

1.11.6.1 Conveyance

The Theft Act 1968, s. 12(7) states:

> (a) 'conveyance' means any conveyance constructed or adapted for the carriage of a person or persons whether by land, water, or air, except that it does not include a conveyance constructed or adapted for use only under the control of a person not carried in or on it, and 'drive' shall be construed accordingly ...

KEYNOTE

It can be seen that this definition includes cars, motor cycles, boats or aircraft. It would also extend to pedal cycles but for the provisions of s. 12(5) which creates a parallel offence for such conveyances (**see para. 1.11.8**). The definition does not extend to hand carts or to animals used as conveyances, such as horses.

1.11.6.2 **Taking for Own or Another's Use**

To prove this offence you must show that the vehicle or conveyance was moved. It does not matter by how little the vehicle is moved but simply starting the engine is not enough (*R v Bogacki* [1973] QB 832) nor is hiding in a car or doing anything else in it while it is stationary. It is also worth noting that, as the offence is triable summarily only, there can be no 'attempt' (Criminal Attempts Act 1981, s. 1(1) and (4)).

The vehicle/conveyance must be 'taken', even if it is put onto another vehicle to do so (*R v Pearce* [1973] Crim LR 321, where a rubber dinghy was put on the roof rack of a car and taken away). The taking must be for the taker's or someone else's ultimate use as a conveyance. Pushing someone's car around the corner as a practical joke satisfies the first part ('taking') but not the second 'for one's own or another's use as a conveyance' (*R v Stokes* [1983] RTR 59). This is because, although the defendant may have 'taken' the conveyance, he/she did not do so for someone ultimately to use it as such. If the practical joker pushed the car round the corner in order for a friend to then start it out of earshot and drive it to a further location the offence *would* be committed at the time of pushing the car.

Where a person got into a Land Rover that was blocking his path and released the handbrake, allowing the vehicle to coast for several hundred metres, it was held that his actions satisfied both elements (*R v Bow* (1976) 64 Cr App R 54). This is because getting into (or onto) a conveyance and moving it is necessarily amounts to *taking it for use as a conveyance*, therefore the motives of a defendant in so doing are irrelevant. These decisions fit with the older notions of an offence of 'stealing a ride' rather than the vehicle itself.

Once a conveyance has been 'taken' it cannot be 'taken' again by the same person before it has been recovered (*DPP v Spriggs* [1994] RTR 1). This accords with the position in relation to the repeated theft of the same property by the same thief (**see para. 1.11.2.3**). However, where the original taker abandons the conveyance, it may be 'taken' by a further defendant and the original taker may be responsible for further offences arising out of its use before it is recovered (**see para. 1.11.7**).

The person taking a vehicle or conveyance must do so intentionally, i.e. not simply by moving it accidentally (*Blayney v Knight* (1974) 60 Cr App R 269).

1.11.6.3 **Allowing Self to be Carried**

If you cannot prove who took a vehicle/conveyance, you may be able to show that a defendant allowed himself/herself to be carried in or on it. You must also show that the defendant *knew* that the conveyance had been taken without the required consent or authority. Merely suspecting the conveyance to have been so taken will not suffice (though wilfully closing your eyes to the question probably will). It must also be shown that there was some movement of the vehicle while the defendant was in it (*R v Diggin* (1980) 72 Cr App R 204).

If, as often happens, all the occupants of a car so taken deny having been the driver, they can all be charged under this element of the offence provided there is sufficient evidence of *mens rea*.

1.11.7 **Aggravated Vehicle-taking**

Given the frequency of offences under s. 12, together with the anti-social and dangerous consequences, the offence of aggravated vehicle-taking was introduced.

OFFENCE: **Aggravated Vehicle-taking—*Theft Act 1968, s. 12A***
• Triable either way • If the accident under s. 12A(2)(b) caused death 14 years' imprisonment, otherwise two years' imprisonment and/or a fine on indictment • Six months' imprisonment and/or a fine summarily.

The Theft Act 1968, s. 12A states:

(1) Subject to subsection (3) below, a person is guilty of aggravated taking of a vehicle if—
  (a) he commits an offence under section 12(1) above (in this section referred to as a 'basic offence') in relation to a mechanically propelled vehicle; and
  (b) it is proved that, at any time after the vehicle was unlawfully taken (whether by him or another) and before it was recovered, the vehicle was driven, or injury or damage was caused, in one or more of the circumstances set out in paragraphs (a) to (d) of subsection (2) below.
(2) The circumstances referred to in subsection (1)(b) above are—
  (a) that the vehicle was driven dangerously on a road or other public place;
  (b) that, owing to the driving of the vehicle, an accident occurred by which injury was caused to any person;
  (c) that, owing to the driving of the vehicle, an accident occurred by which damage was caused to any property, other than the vehicle;
  (d) that damage was caused to the vehicle.

KEYNOTE

Before this offence is made out there must first of all be an offence under s. 12(1)—including an offence of 'being carried'—and the conveyance involved must be a 'mechanically propelled vehicle' (**see Road Policing, chapter 3.1**).

You need only prove that *one* of the consequential factors occurred before the vehicle was recovered (*Dawes* v *DPP* [1995] 1 Cr App R 65) namely that, between the vehicle being taken and its being recovered:

• it was driven dangerously on a road/public place;
• owing to the driving of it, an accident occurred by which injury was caused to anyone or damage was caused to any other property; or
• damage was caused to it.

If the person taking the car disposes of it in a way that amounts to an intention permanently to deprive the owner of it, he/she may commit an offence of theft.

'Dangerous driving' will require the same proof as the substantive offence (**see Road Policing, chapter 3.2**). There is no need to show any lack of care in the driving of the vehicle to prove s. 12A(2)(b), (c) or (d) (see *R* v *Marsh* [1997] 1 Cr App R 67). A vehicle will be 'recovered' once it has been restored to its owner or other lawful possession or custody (s. 12A(8)). This would include occasions where a vehicle has come into the possession of the police.

The word 'accident' for the purposes of the offence of aggravated vehicle taking gets its meaning from the context of that legislation. As such, s. 12A is intended to have regard to *the consequences of what occurred* and is not particularly concerned about the way in which those consequences came about. Therefore where a vehicle had been in motion and thereby caused the victim's death, the word 'accident' applied (*R* v *Branchflower* [2004] EWCA 2042).

1.11.7.1 Defence to Aggravated Vehicle Taking

The Theft Act 1968, s. 12A(3) states:

A person is not guilty of an offence under this section if he proves that, as regards any such proven driving, injury or damage as is referred to in subsection (1)(b) above, either—
(a) the driving, accident or damage referred to in subsection (2) above occurred before he committed the basic offence; or
(b) he was neither in nor on nor in the immediate vicinity of the vehicle when that driving, accident or damage occurred.

> **KEYNOTE**
>
> Once the prosecution has proved the occurrence of one of the aggravating factors above, it is for the defendant to prove one of the specific defences set out under s. 12A(3). Such proof will have to meet the lower standard of 'balance of probabilities' rather than the standard imposed upon the prosecution, namely 'beyond a reasonable doubt' (see Evidence and Procedure, chapter 2.7).
>
> 'Immediate vicinity' is not defined but will be a question of fact for the jury/magistrate(s) to determine in each case.

1.11.8 Pedal Cycles

It is a separate summary offence (punishable with a fine) for a person, without having the consent of the owner or other lawful authority, to take a pedal cycle for his/her own or another's use, or to ride a pedal cycle knowing it to have been taken without such authority (Theft Act 1968, s. 12(5)). The defence under s. 12(6) (see para. 1.11.6) also applies to pedal cycles.

1.11.9 Abstracting Electricity

OFFENCE: **Abstracting Electricity—*Theft Act 1968, s. 13***
- Triable either way • Five years' imprisonment on indictment • Six months' imprisonment and/or a fine summarily

The Theft Act 1968, s. 13 states:

A person who dishonestly uses without due authority, or dishonestly causes to be wasted or diverted, any electricity shall [be guilty of an offence].

> **KEYNOTE**
>
> As electricity is not 'property' (see para. 1.11.2.4), a specific offence was created to deal with its dishonest use or waste. For this reason electricity cannot be 'stolen' and therefore its dishonest use or wastage cannot form an element of burglary (see para. 1.11.4). Diverting a domestic electrical supply so as to bypass the meter or using another's telephone without authority (*Low* v *Blease* [1975] Crim LR 513) would be examples of this offence, as would unauthorised surfing on the Internet by an employee at work, provided in each case that dishonesty was present.

1.11.10 **Handling Stolen Goods**

OFFENCE: **Handling Stolen Goods—*Theft Act 1968, s. 22***
> • Triable either way • Fourteen years' imprisonment on indictment • Six months' imprisonment and/or a fine summarily

The Theft Act 1968, s. 22 states:

(1) A person handles stolen goods if (otherwise than in the course of the stealing) knowing or believing them to be stolen goods he dishonestly receives the goods, or dishonestly undertakes or assists in their retention, removal, disposal or realisation by or for the benefit of another person, or if he arranges to do so.

KEYNOTE

Handling can only be committed *otherwise than in the course of stealing*. Given the extent of theft and the fact that it can be a continuing act (see para. 1.11.2), it is critical to identify at what point the theft of the relevant property ended. It is also useful, in cases of doubt, to include alternative charges.

You must show that the defendant *knew* or *believed* the goods to be stolen. Mere suspicion, however strong, will not be enough (*R* v *Griffiths* (1974) 60 Cr App R 14). Deliberate 'blindness' to the true identity of the goods would suffice but the distinction is a fine one in practice. It can be very difficult to prove knowledge or belief on the part of, say, a second-hand dealer who 'asks no questions'. Because there are practical difficulties in proving the required *mens rea*, s. 27(3) of the 1968 Act makes special provision to allow evidence of the defendant's previous convictions, or previous recent involvement with stolen goods, to be admitted (see Evidence and Procedure).

Dishonestly retaining goods may amount to theft (see para. 1.11.2), in which case that is the relevant charge.

'Goods' will include money and every other description of property except land, and includes things severed from the land by stealing (s. 34(2)(b) of the Act).

1.11.10.1 **Stolen Goods**

The Theft Act 1968, s. 24 states:

(1) The provisions of this Act relating to goods which have been stolen shall apply whether the stealing occurred in England or Wales or elsewhere, and whether it occurred before or after the commencement of this Act, provided that the stealing (if not an offence under this Act) amounted to an offence where and at the time when the goods were stolen; and references to stolen goods shall be construed accordingly.

(2) For purposes of those provisions references to stolen goods shall include, in addition to the goods originally stolen and parts of them (whether in their original state or not),—
   (a) any other goods which directly or indirectly represent or have at any time represented the stolen goods in the hands of the thief as being the proceeds of any disposal or realisation of the whole or part of the goods stolen or of goods representing the stolen goods; and
   (b) any other goods which directly or indirectly represent or have at any time represented the stolen goods in the hands of a handler of the stolen goods or any part of them as being the proceeds of any disposal or realisation of the whole or part of the stolen goods handled by him or of goods so representing them.

(3) But no goods shall be regarded as having continued to be stolen goods after they have been restored to the person from whom they were stolen or to other lawful possession or custody, or after that person and any other person claiming through him have otherwise ceased as regards those goods to have any right to restitution in respect of the theft.

(4) For purposes of the provisions of this Act relating to goods which have been stolen (including subsections (1) to (3) above) goods obtained in England or Wales or elsewhere either by blackmail or subject to subsection (5) below, by fraud (within the meaning of the Fraud Act 2006) shall be regarded as stolen; and 'steal', 'theft' and 'thief' shall be construed accordingly.
(5) Subsection (1) above applies in relation to goods obtained by fraud as if—
  (a) the reference to the commencement of this Act were a reference to the commencement of the Fraud Act 2006, and
  (b) the reference to an offence under this Act were a reference to an offence under section 1 of that Act.

The Theft Act 1968, s. 24A states:

(7) Subsection (8) below applies for purposes of provisions of this Act relating to stolen goods (including subsection (4) above).
(8) References to stolen goods include money which is dishonestly withdrawn from an account to which a wrongful credit has been made, but only to the extent that the money derives from the credit.

KEYNOTE

If goods are not stolen there is no handling. Whether they are so stolen is a question of fact for a jury or magistrate(s). There is no need to prove that the thief, blackmailer, etc. has been convicted of the primary offence before prosecuting the alleged handler, neither is it always necessary to *identify* who that person was.

However, care needs to be taken if a defendant is to be accused of handling goods stolen *from a specific person or place*. If that is the case then ownership of the goods will become an integral part of the prosecution case and it will be necessary to provide evidence proving that aspect of the offence (*Iqbal* v *DPP* [2004] EWHC 2567 (Admin).

Goods obtained by fraud and blackmail are included in the definition of 'stolen goods' under s. 24(4) and s. 24(5). The references to fraud are to the general offence of fraud under s. 1 of the Fraud Act 2006. Clearly goods gained through robbery or burglary will, by definition, be 'stolen' as theft is an intrinsic element of both offences.

'Wrongful credits' are included within the meaning of stolen goods under certain circumstances and are dealt with later in this chapter (see para. 1.11.16).

1.11.10.2   **Section 24 Explained**

Under s. 24(1) a person can still be convicted of handling if the goods were stolen outside England and Wales but only if the goods were taken under circumstances which amounted to an offence in the other country.

Under s. 24(2), goods will be classed as stolen only if they are the property which was originally stolen or if they have at some time represented the *proceeds* of that property in the hands of the thief or a 'handler'.

Therefore if a video cassette recorder (VCR) is stolen, sold to an unsuspecting party who then part exchanges it for a new one at a high street retailer, the first VCR will be 'stolen' goods, the new one will not. If the person buying the original VCR *knew* or *believed* that it was stolen, the new VCR would be treated as stolen goods.

Tracing the proceeds of theft, fraud, blackmail, etc. can be complex; proving them to be stolen even more so. There is an overlap between this legislation—which deals with goods that have been stolen—and other legislation such as the Criminal Justice Act 1988 which relates to criminally-obtained property generally or the Drug Trafficking Act 1994. For further guidance, see *Blackstone's Criminal Practice*, 2008, section B22.

Under s. 24(3), once goods have been restored to lawful possession they cease to be stolen. This situation formerly caused practical problems when police officers recovered stolen property but waited for it to be collected by a handler (see *Houghton* v *Smith* [1975] AC 476). Since the Criminal Attempts Act 1981 and the common-law rulings on 'impossibility' (**see chapter 1.3**), this has been less problematic. In such cases you may consider:

- Theft—collecting the property will be an 'appropriation'.
- Handling—an *arrangement* to come and collect stolen goods will probably have been made while they were still 'stolen'.
- Criminal attempt—the person collecting the goods has gone beyond merely preparing to handle them.

Section 24(4) widens the occasions on which goods will be deemed to be stolen goods beyond strictly theft-based offences such as burglary and robbery.

1.11.10.3 Proof that Goods were Stolen

The Theft Act 1968, s. 27 states:

(1) In any proceedings for the theft of anything in the course of transmission (whether by post or otherwise), or for handling stolen goods from such a theft, a statutory declaration made by any person that he dispatched or received or failed to receive any goods or postal packet, or that any goods or postal packet when dispatched or received by him were in a particular state or condition, shall be admissible as evidence of the facts stated in the declaration, subject to the following conditions:—

(a) a statutory declaration shall only be admissible where and to the extent to which oral evidence to the like effect would have been admissible in the proceedings; and

(b) a statutory declaration shall only be admissible if at least seven days before the hearing or trial a copy of it has been given to the person charged, and he has not, at least three days before the hearing or trial or within such further time as the court may in special circumstances allow, given the prosecutor written notice requiring the attendance at the hearing or trial of the person making the declaration.

KEYNOTE

The above provisions allow for specific evidence to be admitted in proving that goods 'in the course of transmission' have been stolen. These provisions allow for a statutory declaration by the person dispatching or receiving goods or postal packets as to when and where they were dispatched and when or if they arrived and, in each case, their state or condition (e.g. if they had been opened or interfered with). Such a statutory declaration will only be admissible in circumstances where an oral statement would have been admissible *and* if a copy has been served on the defendant at least seven days before the hearing and he/she has not—within three days of the hearing—served written notice on the prosecutor requiring the attendance of the person making the declaration.

This section is to be construed in accordance with s. 24 generally (s. 27(5)).

1.11.10.4 Handling

Despite some views to the contrary, there is only one offence of handling stolen goods (albeit made up of many facets). Therefore to charge a defendant without specifying a particular form of handling is not bad for duplicity (*R* v *Nicklin* [1977] 1 WLR 403). However, the offence can be divided for practical purposes into two parts:

- *receiving/arranging to receive* stolen goods, in which case the defendant acts for his/her own benefit, and
- *assisting/acting for the benefit of another* person, in which case that assistance to another or benefit of another must be proved.

1.11.10.5 Receiving

Often used as shorthand for handling stolen goods generally, this is a specific part of the overall offence. Receiving does not require the physical reception of goods and can extend to exercising control over them. Things in action—such as bank credits from a stolen cheque—can be 'received'.

'Arranging to receive' would cover circumstances which do not go far enough to constitute an attempt—that is, actions which *are* merely preparatory to the receiving of stolen goods may satisfy the elements under s. 22 even though they would not meet the criteria under the Criminal Attempts Act 1981 (**see chapter 1.3**).

If the goods have yet to be stolen, then s. 22 would not apply and the offence of conspiracy (**see chapter 1.3**) should be considered (see *R* v *Park* (1987) 87 Cr App R 164).

1.11.10.6 Assisting/Acting for Another's Benefit

Assisting or acting for the benefit of another can be committed by misleading police officers during a search (see *R* v *Kanwar* [1982] 1 WLR 845).

Disposing of the stolen goods or assisting in their disposal or realisation usually involves physically moving them or converting them into a different form (see *R* v *Forsyth* [1997] 2 Cr App R 299).

If the only person 'benefiting' from the defendant's actions is the defendant himself/herself, this element of the offence will not be made out (*R* v *Bloxham* [1983] 1 AC 109).

Similarly, if the only 'other' person to benefit is a co-accused on the same charge, the offence will not be made out (*R* v *Gingell* [2000] 1 Cr App R 88).

1.11.10.7 Re-programming Mobile Phones

OFFENCE: **Re-programming Mobile Phones—*Mobile Telephones (Re-programming) Act 2002, s. 1***

> • Triable either way • Five years' imprisonment on indictment • Six months imprisonment and/or a fine summarily

The Mobile Telephones (Re-programming) Act 2002, s. 1 states:

(1) A person commits an offence if—
  (a) he changes a unique device identifier, or
  (b) he interferes with the operation of a unique device identifier.
(2) A unique device identifier is an electronic equipment identifier which is unique to a mobile wireless communications device.
(3) But a person does not commit an offence under this section if—
  (a) he is the manufacturer of the device, or
  (b) he does the act mentioned in subsection (1) with the written consent of the manufacturer of the device.

KEYNOTE

The above offence was created in direct response to the burgeoning problem of mobile phone thefts and robberies. By making several offences arising out of re-programming mobile phones (to compliment the system of handset barring that all major network providers have signed up to), the legislation attempts to reduce the attractiveness of such phones as targets for thieves and robbers. The unique device identifier is currently the International Mobile Equipment Identity (IMEI) number which identifies the handset of a mobile phone. It can be found on most mobile phones either behind the battery or by keying in the number *#06#. The wording of the section however allows for future development of mobile phones which may use different equipment identifiers. Changing the unique identifier is an offence, so too is adding a chip or otherwise interfering with that identifier.

It is the view of the Home Office that the international Global System for Mobiles (GSM) standards make it unnecessary for anyone other than a manufacturer or its agent to alter an IMEI number. For that reason, s. 1(3) creates a statutory defence for manufacturers or people with the *written* consent of the manufacturer.

1.11.10.8 Having or Supplying Anything to Facilitate Re-programming

OFFENCE: **Having or Supplying Anything for Re-programming Mobile Phones—*Mobile Telephones (Re-programming) Act 2002, s. 2*.**
- Triable either way • Five years' imprisonment on indictment • Six months imprisonment and/or a fine summarily

The Mobile Telephones (Re-programming) Act 2002, s. 2 states:

(1) A person commits an offence if—
   (a) he has in his custody or under his control anything which may be used for the purpose of changing or interfering with the operation of a unique device identifier, and
   (b) he intends to use the thing unlawfully for that purpose or to allow it to be used unlawfully for that purpose.
(2) A person commits an offence if—
   (a) he supplies anything which may be used for the purpose of changing or interfering with the operation of a unique device identifier, and
   (b) he knows or believes that the person to whom the thing is supplied intends to use it unlawfully for that purpose or to allow it to be used unlawfully for that purpose.
(3) A person commits an offence if—
   (a) he offers to supply anything which may be used for the purpose of changing or interfering with the operation of a unique device identifier, and
   (b) he knows or believes that the person to whom the thing is offered intends if it is supplied to him to use it unlawfully for that purpose or to allow it to be used unlawfully for that purpose.

KEYNOTE

Having something in your custody or under your control is wider than having it in your 'possession' (**see** General Police Duties, chapters 4.7 and 4.8).

The above offences apply to *anything* that may be used for the restricted purposes. It must be shown that, in each case, the defendant had the article, object, etc. or supplied/offered to supply it *and* that he/she had the requisite intent or knowledge at the time. For 'knowing or believing', **see para. 1.11.10**; for a discussion of 'supply', **see chapter 1.6**.

The definition of 'unique device identifier' is the same as for the s. 1 offence and a thing is used by a person unlawfully for a purpose if, in using it for that purpose, he/she commits an offence under s. 1.

1.11.11 Power to Search for Stolen Goods

The Theft Act 1968, s. 26 states:

(1) If it is made to appear by information on oath before a justice of the peace that there is reasonable cause to believe that any person has in his custody or possession or on his premises any stolen goods, the justice may grant a warrant to search for and seize the same; but no warrant to search for stolen goods shall be addressed to a person other than a constable except under the authority of an enactment expressly so providing.

(2) ...

(3) Where under this section a person is authorised to search premises for stolen goods, he may enter and search the premises accordingly, and may seize any goods he believes to be stolen goods.

(4) ...

(5) This section is to be construed in accordance with section 24 of this Act; and in subsection (2) above the references to handling stolen goods shall include any corresponding offence committed before the commencement of this Act.

KEYNOTE

Section 26 provides a general power to search for and seize stolen goods, whether identified in the search warrant or not and magistrates are entitled to act on material provided by the police that gives rise to a reasonable belief that stolen goods will be found (*R Cruikshank Ltd* v *Chief Constable of Kent County Constabulary* (2002) *The Times*, 27 December.

For the provisions governing the application for, and the execution of warrants, **see General Police Duties, chapter 4.4 and Evidence and Procedure, chapter 2.3.**

1.11.12 Advertising Rewards

OFFENCE: **Advertising a Reward—*Theft Act 1968, s. 23***
  • Triable summarily • Fine

The Theft Act 1968, s. 23 states:

Where any public advertisement of a reward for the return of any goods which have been stolen or lost uses any words to the effect that no questions will be asked, or that the person producing the goods will be safe from apprehension or inquiry, or that any money paid for the purchase of the goods or advanced by way of loan on them will be repaid, the person advertising the reward and any person who prints or publishes the advertisement shall [commit an offence].

KEYNOTE

This offence applies to both the person advertising such a reward and the person/company who prints or publishes that advertisement. This second aspect of the offence attracts 'strict liability', in that there is no need to demonstrate any particular *mens rea* on the part of the printer/publisher (*Denham* v *Scott* (1983)

77 Cr App R 210). The important features are the fact that no questions will be asked or that the person will be given some form of 'immunity' from arrest or investigation. There is no mention of any promise of immunity from prosecution or civil claim.

1.11.13 Going Equipped

OFFENCE: **Going Equipped for Stealing etc.—*Theft Act 1968, s. 25***

- Triable either way • Three years' imprisonment on indictment • Six months' imprisonment and/or a fine summarily

The Theft Act 1968, s. 25 states:

(1) A person shall be guilty of an offence if, when not at his place of abode, he has with him any article for use in the course of or in connection with any burglary or theft.

KEYNOTE

The power of search under s. 1 of the Police and Criminal Evidence Act 1984 applies to this offence (see General Police Duties, chapter 4.4).

A person's place of abode means where he/she resides; it does not include his/her place of business (unless, presumably, they are one and the same place) (*R* v *Bundy* [1977] 2 All ER 382). If a person lives in a vehicle then that vehicle will be regarded only as their 'place of abode' if it is parked at the place where the person 'abides' or intends to 'abide' (*Bundy*). Therefore it would seem that, if a person is found in his/her vehicle away from such a site and at the time has with them articles as described under s. 25, they would commit this offence.

'Has with him' is a narrower requirement than 'possession' and, as with aggravated burglary (see para. 1.11.5) generally means that the article must be readily accessible (see General Police Duties, chapters 4.7 and 4.8).

You do not need to prove that the person having the article with them intended to use it themselves and it will be enough to show that the person intended it to be used *by someone* for one of the purposes in s. 25(1) (*R* v *Ellames* [1974] 3 All ER 130). Simply being a passenger in a car where such an article is found is not enough to prove the offence (*R* v *Lester* (1955) 39 Cr App R 157). The articles must be for some future use; it is not enough to show that the defendant had articles that *had been used* in the course of, or in connection with, one of the proscribed offences.

If the articles are found at the defendant's place of abode then an alternative offence under the Criminal Damage Act 1971 (see chapter 1.13) may be appropriate.

If you can prove that the article was made, adapted or intended (see General Police Duties, chapter 4.8) for burglary or theft, that fact will be evidence that the person had it with him/her for that purpose (s. 25(3))—a provision that probably seems more helpful than it really is, given that, in many cases, it is simply stating the obvious.

Article can mean almost any object but does not include *animate* objects, e.g. a trained monkey (see *Daly* v *Cannon* [1954] 1 All ER 315).

Theft for these purposes will include the offence of taking a conveyance (as to which, see para. 1.11.6).

1.11.14 **Making Off without Payment**

OFFENCE: **Making Off without Payment—*Theft Act 1978, s. 3***
- Triable either way • Two years' imprisonment on indictment • Six months' imprisonment and/or a fine summarily

The Theft Act 1978, s. 3 states:

(1) Subject to subsection (3) below, a person who, knowing that payment on the spot for any goods supplied or service done is required or expected from him, dishonestly makes off without having paid as required or expected and with intent to avoid payment of the amount due shall be guilty of an offence.

(2) For purposes of this section 'payment on the spot' includes payment at the time of collecting goods on which work has been done or in respect of which service has been provided.

(3) Subsection (1) above shall not apply where the supply of the goods or the doing of the service is contrary to law, or where the service done is such that payment is not legally enforceable.

KEYNOTE

This offence is most frequently committed by motorists who drive off without paying for petrol, diners who run off after a meal and 'punters' who jump out of taxi cabs (see *DPP* v *Ray* [1974] AC 370; *Edwards* v *Ddin* [1976] 1 WLR 942; *R* v *Brooks* (1982) 76 Cr App R 66). Some problems can arise in cases of alleged theft where the ownership in the property has passed to the defendant before the act of appropriation (**see para. 1.11.2.6**); this offence offers a solution to some such cases.

This offence excludes occasions where the supply of goods or services is contrary to law or is not legally enforceable (s. 3(3)). Making off without payment after the provision of an unlawful service, or one for which payment is not legally enforceable (e.g. betting), would not then be caught by s. 3 though it might be an offence under s. 1. If there is some doubt as to whether the defendant has actually 'made off' from the spot then he/she can be charged with attempting the offence.

You must also prove an intention to *avoid* payment; simply delaying payment due or making someone wait for payment is not enough. In *R* v *Vincent* [2001] 1 WLR 1172, the Court of Appeal has recently acknowledged a 'loophole' in s. 3. Circumstances in which this loophole might operate can be illustrated as follows:

- A person checks into an hotel and runs up a substantial bill.
- The person deceives the proprietor into agreeing that the bill will be settled at some later date (as opposed to on departure).
- Having gained that agreement, the person checks out of th hotel and never makes any payment.

The Court pointed out that, in such a situation, there was no longer an expectation of payment at the time when the person checked out of the hotel. This expectation had been removed by the agreement; the fact that the agreement had been obtained dishonestly did not reinstate the expectation of payment on departure. The Court identified that the offence under s. 3 is a simple and straightforward one which applies to a limited set of circumstances only (and which, fortunately for the defendant, were not covered by the above facts). The limited scope of this offence would suggest that alternative charges of theft and/or fraud should be considered. If the person driving or running away from the garage, restaurant, taxi cab, etc. does so because he/she feels aggrieved at the service received or is in dispute with the supplier, then the question of fraud should be considered against the standards of ordinary, honest people (per *R* v *Ghosh* [1982] QB 1053 (**see para. 1.11.2.2**)).

1.11.15   **Blackmail**

OFFENCE: **Blackmail—*Theft Act 1968, s. 21***

  • Triable on indictment • 14 years' imprisonment

The Theft Act 1968, s. 21 states:

(1) A person is guilty of blackmail if, with a view to gain for himself or another or with intent to cause loss to another, he makes any unwarranted demand with menaces; and for this purpose a demand with menaces is unwarranted unless the person making it does so in the belief—
   (a) that he has reasonable grounds for making the demand; and
   (b) that the use of the menaces is a proper means of reinforcing the demand.
(2) The nature of the act or omission demanded is immaterial, and it is also immaterial whether the menaces relate to action to be taken by the person making the demand.

KEYNOTE

It might be better—for several reasons—if this offence were to be called 'demands with menaces'. Whatever its name, in proving this offence you must show that a defendant acted either with a view to gain for himself/herself or another or with intent to cause loss to another. The distinction here is important. The phrase 'with a view to' has been held (albeit under a different criminal statute) by the Court of Appeal to be less than 'with intent to' (*R* v *Zaman* [2003] FSR 13). In *Zaman*, the Court accepted that a lesser degree of *mens rea* (see chapter 1.1) was required to prove that a defendant acted 'with a view to' something and that this phrase meant simply that the defendant had something in his/her contemplation as *something that realistically might occur*, not that he/she necessarily intended or even wanted it to happen. Clearly this is a very different test from 'intent'. In the above offence then, it appears that the state of mind needed to prove the first element is that the defendant contemplated some gain for himself/herself or for another as being a realistically likely to flow from his/her actions. The alternative is an 'intent' to cause loss—a harder element to prove.

There is no requirement for dishonesty, deception or theft and the offence is aimed at the making of the demands rather than the consequences of them.

1.11.15.1   **Meaning of Gain and Loss**

Section 34 of the 1968 Act states:

(2) For the purposes of this Act—
   (a) 'gain' and 'loss' are to be construed as extending only to gain or loss in money or other property, but as extending to any such gain or loss whether temporary or permanent; and—
      (i) 'gain' includes a gain by keeping what one has, as well as a gain by getting what one has not; and
      (ii) 'loss' includes a loss by not getting what one might get, as well as a loss by parting with what one has;

KEYNOTE

Keeping what you already have can amount to a 'gain'. Similarly, not getting something that you might expect to get can be a 'loss'.

....

EXAMPLE

A person makes unwarranted demands with menaces with a view to getting a sports fixture cancelled and thereby to avoid losing money that he has bet on the outcome of that fixture. Here it could be argued that the intention of keeping what the defendant already had (the money at risk on the bet) amounts to 'gain' as defined under s. 34(2). Similarly, the intention of preventing others getting what they might have got (their winnings or the club's earnings) could amount to a 'loss'.

....

1.11.15.2   Criminal Conduct

The offence of blackmail is complete when the demand with menaces is made. It does not matter whether the demands bring about the desired consequences or not. If a demand is made by letter, the act of making it is complete when the letter is posted. The letter does not have to be received (*Treacy* v *DPP* [1971] AC 537).

The Court of Appeal has held that words or conduct which would not intimidate or influence anyone to respond to the demand would not be 'menaces'. As such, the term requires threats and conduct of such a nature and extent that a person of normal stability and courage might be influenced or made apprehensive so as to give in to the demands (see *R* v *Clear* [1968] 1 QB 670).

Menaces will therefore include threats but these must be significant *to the victim*. If a threat bears a particular significance for a victim (such as being locked in the boot of a car to someone who is claustrophobic) that will be enough, provided the defendant was aware of that fact. If a victim is particularly timid and the defendant knows it, that timidity may be taken into account when assessing whether or not the defendant's conduct was 'menacing' (*R* v *Garwood* [1987] 1 WLR 319).

For offences involving malicious and threatening communications, **see General Police Duties, chapter 4.5.**

1.11.15.3   Unwarranted?

If a defendant raises the issue that his/her demand was reasonable and proper, you will have to prove that he/she did not believe:

- that he/she had reasonable grounds for making the demand; and
- that the use of the particular menaces employed was not a proper means of reinforcing it.

The defendant's *belief* will be a subjective one and therefore could be entirely unreasonable. However, if the threatened action would itself be unlawful (such as a threat to rape the victim) then it is unlikely that the courts would accept any claim by a defendant that he/she believed such a demand to be 'proper' (see *R* v *Harvey* (1980) 72 Cr App R 139).

1.11.16   Retaining a Wrongful Credit

OFFENCE: **Dishonestly Retaining a Wrongful Credit—*Theft Act 1968, s. 24A***
- Triable either way • Ten years' imprisonment on indictment • Six months' imprisonment and/or a fine summarily

The Theft Act 1968, s. 24A states:

(1) A person is guilty of an offence if—
    (a) a wrongful credit has been made to an account kept by him or in respect of which he has any right or interest;
    (b) he knows or believes that the credit is wrongful; and
    (c) he dishonestly fails to take such steps as are reasonable in the circumstances to secure that the credit is cancelled.
(2) References to a credit are to a credit of an amount of money.
(2A) A credit to an account is wrongful to the extent that it derives from—
    (a) theft;
    (b) blackmail;
    (c) fraud (contrary to section 1 of the Fraud Act 2006); or
    (d) stolen goods.
    (subsections (3) and (4) repealed by the Fraud Act 2006)
    ...
(5) In determining whether a credit to an account is wrongful, it is immaterial (in particular) whether the account is overdrawn before or after the credit is made.
(6) ...
(7) Subsection (8) below applies for purposes of provisions of this Act relating to stolen goods (including subsection (2A) above).
(8) References to stolen goods include money which is dishonestly withdrawn from an account to which a wrongful credit has been made, but only to the extent that the money derives from the credit.
(9) 'Account' means an account kept with—
    (a) a bank;
    (b) a person carrying on a business which falls within subsection (10) below; or
    (c) an issuer of electronic money (as defined for the purposes of Part 2 of the Financial Services and Markets Act 2000).
(10) A business falls within this subsection if—
    (a) in the course of the business money received by way of deposit is lent to others; or
    (b) any other activity of the business is financed, wholly or to any material extent, out of the capital of or the interest on any money received by way of deposit.
(11) References in subsection (10) above to a deposit must be read with—
    (a) section 22 of the Financial Services and Markets Act 2000;
    (b) any relevant order under that section; and
    (c) Schedule 2 of that Act;
    but any restriction on the meaning of deposit which arises from the identity of the person making it, is to be disregarded.
(12) For the purposes of subsection (10) above—
    (a) all the activities which a person carries on by way of business shall be regarded as a single business carried on by him; and
    (b) 'money' includes money expressed in a currency other than sterling.

KEYNOTE

The introduction of this offence was prompted by the decision in *R* v *Preddy* [1996] AC 815. The Law Commission were anxious to ensure that the transferee of funds obtained dishonestly could be charged with 'handling' those funds. As there were considerable problems created by applying the existing legislation under s. 22 (**see para. 1.11.10**), these further offences were introduced.

The wrongful credit to an account can occur in two ways: it may come from the circumstances outlined under s. 1 of the Fraud Act 2006 or it may come from one of the dishonest sources set out in s. 2A above.

These offences will generally be restricted to transactions involving the crediting of accounts held with financial institutions.

There is a requirement for dishonesty (as to which, **see para. 1.11.2.2**). However, there is no requirement for any *deception*.

The effects of s. 24A(8) are that *money* derived from credit received under s. 24A of the Theft Act 1968 may amount to stolen goods. The provisions governing the status of the credit itself (i.e. not as cash but as a 'thing in action') are more complicated. If the proceeds of a theft by A are paid into his/her bank account they are stolen goods because they represent the stolen goods in the hands of the thief (s. 24(4)).

If they are then transferred into B's bank account, they cease to be stolen goods. This is because the 'thing in action' (the credit balance) created by the transfer in B's name is a different 'thing in action' from the one originally created by A (see *R* v *Preddy* [1996] AC 815). As such, the credit balance in B's name has never represented the proceeds of the theft *in the hands of the thief*. If B withdraws money from the credited account, that money then, by virtue of s. 24A(8), becomes stolen goods once more.

To quote from *Blackstone's Criminal Practice*, 2008, section B4.148:

> It may seem strange that the proceeds of A's original theft can be classed as stolen goods when paid into A's own bank account, cease to be so classified when effectively 'transferred' to B's account, and yet revert to being stolen goods when dishonestly withdrawn as cash by B; but such is now the law.

This offence is also unusual in that the *actus reus* not only *can be* satisfied by an 'omission', but necessarily *involves* an omission or a failure to act (**see chapter 1.2**).

1.12 Fraud

1.12.1 Introduction

On 15th January 2007 the Fraud Act 2006 came into force. Until this time there was no single, general fraud law in English law; instead there were a number of statutory crimes (under the Theft Acts 1968 and 1978) such as 'obtaining property by deception' and 'obtaining services by deception' that catered for such criminal behaviour. The inadequacy of existing law to deal with activities carried out utilising computer technology, and several loopholes in preceding anti-fraud legislation, provided the impetus for the new Act which has replaced previous legislation with more contemporary offences that the Government say are far more suited to modern fraud. The Act provides for a general offence of fraud with three ways of committing it (by false representation, by failing to disclose information, and by abuse of position) as well as creating new offences of obtaining services dishonestly, and possessing, making, and supplying articles for use in fraud. It also creates offences in relation to fraudulent business activities by sole traders and companies but these are beyond the scope of this manual.

1.12.2 Fraud

OFFENCE: **Fraud—*Fraud Act 2006, s. 1***
- Triable either way • Ten years imprisonment and/or fine on indictment
- Twelve months' imprisonment and/or fine summarily

The Fraud Act 2006 states:

(1) A person is guilty of fraud if he is in breach of any of the sections listed in subsection (2) (which provide for different ways of committing the offence).
(2) The sections are—
   (a) section 2 (fraud by false representation),
   (b) section 3 (fraud by failing to disclose information), and
   (c) section 4 (fraud by abuse of position)

KEYNOTE

The heart of all three methods of committing the offence of fraud is in the *conduct and ulterior intent* of the defendant. This differs from previous deception related offences where the *consequences* of the defendant's actions were important. The effect of this approach is that a defendant's unsuccessful 'attempt' to commit the offence of fraud may amount to the commission of the substantive offence, effectively excluding the possibility of an offence under the Criminal Attempts Act 1981.

1.12.3 Fraud by False Representation

Fraud Act 2006, s. 2 states:

(1) A person is in breach of this section if he—
    (a) dishonestly makes a false representation, and
    (b) intends, by making the representation—
        (i) to make a gain for himself or another, or
        (ii) to cause loss to another or to expose another to the risk of loss.
(2) A representation is false if—
    (a) it is untrue or misleading, and
    (b) the person making it knows that it is, or might be, untrue or misleading.
(3) 'Representation' means any representation as to fact or law, including a representation as to the state of mind of—
    (a) the person making the representation, or
    (b) any other person.
(4) A representation may be express or implied.
(5) For the purposes of this section a representation may be regarded as made if it (or anything implying it) is submitted in any form to any system or device designed to receive, convey or respond to communications (with or without human intervention).

KEYNOTE

Dishonestly

The 'dishonestly' referred to in s. 2(1)(a) is a reference to the test of dishonesty established in *R* v *Ghosh* [1982] QB 1053 (**see chapter 1.11**). The same test applies to ss. 3 and 4 of the Act.

Gain and Loss

Section 2(1)(b) refers to 'gain' and 'loss' and that the person making the representation must do so with the intention of making a gain or causing a loss or risk of loss to another. *The gain or loss does not actually have to take place* (the terms 'gain' and 'loss' are discussed at **para. 1.12.6**.

Representation

A representation is false if it is untrue or misleading *and* the person making it knows this is or knows this might be the case. Therefore, an untrue statement made in the honest belief that it is in fact true, would not suffice. The words 'or might be' must involve a subjective belief (**see chapter 1.1**) on the part of the person making the representation.

The representation may be express or implied and can be communicated in words or conduct. There is no limitation on the way in which the representation must be expressed, so it could be written, spoken or posted on a website. A representation may also be implied by conduct. For example, a person dishonestly misusing a credit card to pay for items hands the card to a cashier without saying a word. By handing the card to the cashier he is falsely representing that he has authority to use it for that transaction. It is immaterial that the cashier accepting the card for payment is deceived by the representation. The fact that the cashier's state of mind plays no part in the commission of the offence marks a significant departure from the previous law governing this type of activity. Deception offences under the Theft Acts 1968 and 1978 required the 'target' of the deception to be deceived by the words or conduct of the defendant; if this element were not present there would only be an attempted deception. The Fraud Act 2006 removes this requirement so that where a defendant makes a false representation knowing that it is false or might be, the offence of fraud is complete. Any representation made must be one as to fact or law, so a broken promise is not in itself a false representation. However, a statement may be false if it misrepresents the current intentions or state of mind of the person making it or anyone else. For example, D visits V's house and tells V that he needs emergency work carried out on his roof. D states that he is in a position to do the work immediately but only if V pays him £1000 there and then. V gives D the money and D then leaves without carrying out the work; the truth of the matter was that D had never intended to carry out the work. Such a 'promise' by D would amount to an offence as it involved a false representation i.e. he never intended to keep the promise.

The offence is complete the moment the false representation is made (a similar position can be found with the offence of blackmail (**see para. 1.11.15**)). The representation need never be heard nor communicated to the recipient and if carried out by post, would be complete when the letter is posted (*Treacy* v *DPP* [1971] AC 537).

Phishing

The offence would also be committed by someone who engages in 'phishing'. This is the practice of sending out e-mails in bulk, purporting to represent a well-known brand in the hope of sending victims to a bogus website that tricks them into disclosing bank account details. 'Phishing kits' have long been available on the Internet but it was difficult to prosecute sellers. The offence under s. 2 now covers such activity.

Machines

Under the old law, a machine could not be deceived and any activity carried out that fooled a machine or computer would not amount to deception. Section 2(5) of the Fraud Act enables the offence of fraud to apply in such cases, as necessity for human involvement in any response from the person making the false representation has been dispensed with (for example where a person enters a number into a 'Chip and PIN' machine).

1.12.4 Fraud by Failing to Disclose

The Fraud Act 2006, s. 3 states:

A person is in breach of this section if he—
    (a) dishonestly fails to disclose to another person information which he is under a legal duty to disclose, and
    (b) intends, by failing to disclose the information—
      (i) to make a gain for himself or another, or
      (ii) to cause loss to another or to expose another to a risk of loss.

KEYNOTE

Section 3 creates an offence of dishonestly failing to disclose information where there is a legal duty to do so. The term 'legal duty' has not been defined but will include duties under oral contracts as well as written contracts. The Law Commission's *Report on Fraud* dealt with the concept of legal duty and stated that duties might arise:

- from statute
- where the transaction is one of the utmost good faith
- from the express or implied terms of a contract
- from the custom of a particular trade or market, or
- from the existence of a fiduciary relationship between parties.

The legal duty to disclose information will exist if:

- the defendant's actions give the victim a cause in action for damages or
- if the law gives the victim the right to set aside any change in his or her legal position to which he or she may have consented as a result of the non-disclosure.

A fiduciary relationship is one relating to the responsibility of looking after someone else's money in a correct way. Examples of such behaviour would include a solicitor failing to share vital information with a client in the context of their work relationship, in order to carry out a fraud upon that client, or if a person intentionally failed to disclose information relating to a heart condition when making an application for life insurance.

1.12.5 Fraud by Abuse of Position

The Fraud Act 2006, s. 4 states:

(1) A person is in breach of this section if he—
  (a) occupies a position in which he is expected to safeguard, or not to act against, the financial interests of another person,
  (b) dishonestly abuses that position, and
  (c) intends, by means of the abuse of that position—
    (i) to make a gain for himself or another, or
    (ii) to cause loss to another or to expose another to a risk of loss.
(2) A person may be regarded as having abused his position even though his conduct consisted of an omission rather than an act.

KEYNOTE

The crux of this offence is the financial and dishonest abuse of a privileged position of trust. An offence under s. 4 may be committed in a variety of ways as the 'position' that the defendant occupies may be the result of an assortment of relationships. The Law Commission explained the meaning of 'position' at paragraph 7.38:

> The necessary relationship will be present between trustee and beneficiary, director and company, professional person and client, agent and principle, employee and employer, or between partners. It may arise otherwise, for example within a family, or in the context of voluntary work, or in any context where the parties are not at arm's length.

The term 'abuse' is not defined by the Act.

Liability for the offence could develop from a wide range of conduct, for example:

- An employee of a software company uses his position to clone software products with the intention of selling the products on.
- An estate agent values a house belonging to an elderly person at an artificially low price and then arranges for his brother to purchase the house.
- A person who is employed to care for a disabled person and has access to that person's bank account, abuses his position by transferring funds to invest in a high-risk business venture of his own.

The offence can also be committed by omission, for example:

- An employee fails to take up the chance of a crucial contract in order that an associate or rival company can take it up instead of and at the expense of the employer.

1.12.6   **Gain and Loss**

The Fraud Act 2006, s. 5 states:

(1) The references to gain and loss in sections 2 to 4 are to be read in accordance with this section.

(2) 'Gain' and 'loss'—

    (a) extend only to gain and loss in money or other property;

    (b) include any such gain or loss whether temporary or permanent;

    and 'property' means any property whether real or personal (including things in action and other intangible property).

(3) 'Gain' includes a gain by keeping what one has, as well as getting what one does not have.

(4) 'Loss' includes a loss by not getting what one might get, as well as a loss by parting with what one has.

KEYNOTE

The definition of 'gain' and 'loss' is very similar to that of the 'gain' and 'loss' in blackmail (see para. 1.11.15.1). It is important to note that the 'gain' and 'loss' relates only to *money and other property*. The definition of property covers all forms of property including intellectual property and is based on the definition of 'property' contained in s. 4(1) of the Theft Act 1968 (see para. 1.11.2.4).

1.12.7   **Possession or Control of Articles for Use in Frauds**

OFFENCE: **Possession or Control of Articles for Use in Frauds—**
              Fraud Act 2006, s. 6

              • Triable either way • Five years' imprisonment and/or fine on indictment • Twelve months' imprisonment and/or fine summarily

The Fraud Act 2006, s. 6 states:

(1) A person is guilty of an offence if he has in his possession or under his control any article for use in the course of or in connection with any fraud.

KEYNOTE

This offence replaces the 'cheat' element of the offence of 'going equipped' (see para. 1.11.13) under s. 25 of the Theft Act 1968. It has far more scope than its predecessor, as the limitation of the 'going equipped' offence to circumstances when the defendant was 'not at his place of abode' has been excluded. This means that the offence under s. 6 can be committed *anywhere at all*. It also widens times that the defendant may commit the offence as not only is it committed when the defendant has articles in his possession but also when he has them in his control—a term that indicates that the defendant may be some distance away from the articles and yet still commit the offence. Further, the 'cheat' element of 'going equipped' only applied to the offence of 'obtaining property by deception'; the offence under s. 6 applies to *all fraud offences* under the 2006 Act. However, much like the offence of 'going equipped' the offence is only committed in respect of *future* offences and not offences that have already taken place. The offence can be committed if possession or control is to enable *another* to commit an offence of fraud. The definition of the term 'article' is discussed at para. 1.12.9.

1.12.8 Making or Supplying Articles for Use in Frauds

OFFENCE: **Making or Supplying Articles for Use in Frauds**—*Fraud Act 2006, s.7*
> • Triable either way • Ten years' imprisonment on indictment and/or fine • Twelve months' imprisonment and/or fine summarily

The Fraud Act 2006, s. 7 states:

> (1) A person is guilty of an offence if he makes, adapts, supplies or offers to supply any article—
> > (a) knowing that it is designed or adapted for use in the course of or in connection with fraud, or
> > (b) intending it to be used to commit, or assist in the commission of, fraud.

KEYNOTE

The broad terms of the offence ensure that any activity in respect of the making, supplying etc. of any 'article' for use if fraud offences is an offence. Making an 'offer to supply' would not require the defendant to be in possession of the 'article' (a similar situation to offering to supply a controlled drug, **see para. 1.6.5.3**). Examples of such behaviour include:

- A person makes a viewing card for a satellite TV system, enabling him to view all satellite channels for free.
- The same person then offers to sell similar cards to work colleagues although he has only made the one prototype card and does not actually have further cards to sell.
- A number of the person's work colleagues express an interest in buying the cards, so the person makes a dozen more cards and then actually supplies them to his work colleagues.

1.12.9 'Article'

The Fraud Act 2006, s. 8 states:

> (1) For the purposes of—
> > (a) sections 6 and 7, and
> > (b) the provisions listed in subsection (2), so far as they relate to articles for use in the course of or in connection with fraud,
> >
> > 'article' includes any program or data held in electronic form.
> (2) The provisions are—
> > (a) section 1(7)(b) of the Police and Criminal Evidence Act 1984 (c 60),
> > (b) ...
> > (c) ...

Section 8 extends the meaning of 'article' for the purposes of ss. 6 and 7 of the Act to include any program or data held in electronic form. Examples of cases where electronic programs or data could be used in fraud are:

- A computer program that generates credit card numbers
- A computer template that can be used for producing blank utility bills
- A computer file that contains lists of other people's credit card details.

1.12.10   **Obtaining Services Dishonestly**

OFFENCE: **Obtaining Services Dishonestly**—*Fraud Act 2006, s. 11*

> • Triable either way • Five years' imprisonment and/or fine on indictment • Twelve months' imprisonment and/or fine summarily

The Fraud Act 2006, s. 11 states:

> (1) A person is guilty of an offence under this section if he obtains services for himself or another—
> (a) by a dishonest act, and
> (b) in breach of subsection (2)
> (2) A person obtains services in breach of this subsection if—
> (a) they are made available on the basis that payment has been, is being or will be made for or in respect of them,
> (b) he obtains them without any payment having been made for in respect of them or without payment having been made in full, and
> (c) when he obtains them, he knows—
> (i) that they are being made available on the basis described in paragraph (a), or
> (ii) that they might be,
> but intends that payment will not be made, or will not be made in full.

KEYNOTE

The offence under s. 11 of the Fraud Act 2006 replaces the offence of 'obtaining services by deception' under s. 1 of the Theft Act 1978. It is important to note that unlike the other offences created as a consequence of the Fraud Act 2006, the offence under s. 11 is not a conduct crime; it is a *result crime* and requires the *actual obtaining* of the service. However, the offence does not require a fraudulent representation or deception. A person would commit this offence if, intending to avoid payment, he slipped into a concert hall to watch a concert without paying for the privilege. The offence can be committed where the defendant intends to avoid payment or payment in full but the defendant must know that the services are made available on the basis that they are chargeable, i.e. services provided for free are not covered by the offence. The terms 'service' and 'obtaining' are not defined by the Act.

1.12.11   **Falsification of Documents and Other Instruments**

In addition to the offence of fraud, there are a series of closely-related offences which deal with falsification of documents or other 'instruments'.

1.12.11.1   **False Accounting**

OFFENCE: **False Accounting**—*Theft Act 1968, s. 17*

> • Triable either way • Seven years' imprisonment on indictment • Six months' imprisonment and/or a fine summarily

The Theft Act 1968, s. 17 states:

> (1) Where a person dishonestly, with a view to gain for himself or another or with intent to cause loss to another,—
> (a) destroys, defaces, conceals or falsifies any account or any record or document made or required for any accounting purpose; or

(b) in furnishing information for any purpose produces or makes use of any account, or any such record or document as aforesaid, which to his knowledge is or may be misleading, false or deceptive in a material particular;

he shall [commit an offence].

(2) For purposes of this section a person who makes or concurs in making in an account or other document an entry which is or may be misleading, false or deceptive in a material particular, or who omits or concurs in omitting a material particular from an account or other document, is to be treated as falsifying the account or document.

KEYNOTE

This section creates two offences: destroying, defacing, etc. accounts and documents; and using false or misleading accounts or documents in furnishing information.

An offence under s. 17 can be committed by omission as well as by an act. Failing to make an entry in an accounts book, altering a till receipt or supplying an auditor with records that are incomplete may, if accompanied by the other ingredients, amount to an offence.

Unlike theft there is no requirement to prove an intention permanently to deprive but there is a need to show dishonesty (as to both points, see chapter 1.11). The requirement as to gain and loss is the same as for blackmail (see chapter 1.11).

The misleading, false or deceptive nature of the information furnished under s. 17(1)(b) must be 'material' to the defendant's overall purpose, i.e. the ultimate gaining or causing of loss. Such an interpretation means that the defendant's furnishing of information need not relate directly to an accounting process and could be satisfied by lying about the status of a potential finance customer (see *R* v *Mallett* [1978] 1 WLR 820).

Where the documents falsified are not intrinsically 'accounting' forms, such as insurance claim forms filled out by policyholders, you must show that those forms are treated for accounting purposes by the victim (*R* v *Sundhers* [1998] Crim LR 497).

There is also a further offence (triable and punishable as the above offences), of company officers making false statements with intent to deceive members or creditors (Theft Act 1968, s. 19).

1.12.11.2 Forgery

The traditional image of forgery conjures up images of skilled printers with inky fingers using sophisticated plates to create high quality bank notes. In reality the offences classed as forgery include virtually every kind of document *except* bank notes. Coins and currency are the subject of a separate group of offences classed as counterfeiting and are dealt with later in this chapter.

For the specific offences of making, possessing, etc. registration cards under the Immigration Act 1971, **see chapter 1.15**.

Many of the offences dealt with below are divided into two categories:

• Offences where there is an *intention* by the defendant to pass the document, note or coin off as being genuine. These, more serious offences, attract higher penalties.

• Offences where there is no requirement to prove any *ulterior* intent.

1.12.11.3 Police Powers Regarding False Instruments

A warrant to search for and seize false instruments and materials may be issued under s. 7 of the 1981 Act.

1.12.11.4 False Instruments

OFFENCE: **Making a False Instrument with Intent**—*Forgery and Counterfeiting Act 1981, s. 1*

> • Triable either way • Ten years' imprisonment on indictment • Six months' imprisonment and/or a fine summarily

The Forgery and Counterfeiting Act 1981, s. 1 states:

> A person is guilty of forgery if he makes a false instrument, with the intention that he or another shall use it to induce somebody to accept it as genuine, and by reason of so accepting it to do or not to do some act to his own or any other person's prejudice.

OFFENCE: **Using a False Instrument with Intent**—*Forgery and Counterfeiting Act 1981, s. 3*

> • Triable either way • Ten years' imprisonment on indictment • Six months' imprisonment and/or a fine summarily

The Forgery and Counterfeiting Act 1981, s. 3 states:

> It is an offence for a person to use an instrument which is, and which he knows or believes to be, false, with the intention of inducing somebody to accept it as genuine, and by reason of so accepting it to do or not to do some act to his own or any other person's prejudice.

OFFENCE: **Copying a False Instrument with Intent**—*Forgery and Counterfeiting Act 1981, s. 2*

> • Triable either way • Ten years' imprisonment on indictment • Six months' imprisonment and/or a fine summarily

The Forgery and Counterfeiting Act 1981, s. 2 states:

> It is an offence for a person to make a copy of an instrument which is, and which he knows or believes to be, a false instrument, with the intention that he or another shall use it to induce somebody to accept it as a copy of a genuine instrument, and by reason of so accepting it to do or not to do some act to his own or any other person's prejudice.

OFFENCE: **Using a Copy of a False Instrument with Intent**—*Forgery and Counterfeiting Act 1981, s. 4*

> • Triable either way • Ten years' imprisonment on indictment • Six months' imprisonment and/or a fine summarily

The Forgery and Counterfeiting Act 1981, s. 4 states:

> It is an offence for a person to use a copy of an instrument which is, and which he knows or believes to be, a false instrument, with the intention of inducing somebody to accept it as a copy of a genuine instrument, and by reason of so accepting it to do or not to do some act to his own or any other person's prejudice.

KEYNOTE

The essence of these offences is that they concern documents or instruments which purport to be something which they are not; that is, they 'tell a lie about themselves'.

In the defining terms used by s. 9 of the 1981 Act they are:

(1) An instrument is false for the purposes of this Part of this Act—
  (a) if it purports to have been made in the form in which it is made by a person who did not in fact make it in that form; or

(b) if it purports to have been made in the form in which it is made on the authority of a person who did not in fact authorise its making in that form; or

(c) if it purports to have been made in the terms in which it is made by a person who did not in fact make it in those terms; or

(d) if it purports to have been made in the terms in which it is made on the authority of a person who did not in fact authorise its making in those terms; or

(e) if it purports to have been altered in any respect by a person who did not in fact alter it in that respect; or

(f) if it purports to have been altered in any respect on the authority of a person who did not in fact authorise the alteration in that respect; or

(g) if it purports to have been made or altered on a date on which, or at a place at which, or otherwise in circumstances in which, it was not in fact made or altered; or

(h) if it purports to have been made or altered by an existing person but he did not in fact exist.

KEYNOTE

The list of ways in which instruments can be false might be remembered by the following mnemonic. An instrument may be false if:

F it falsely claims to have been made in a **F**orm or in terms by, or on the authority of, another

A it falsely claims to have been **A**ltered by, or on the authority of, another

L it **L**ies about the date, place or any other circumstances in which it claims to have been made or altered

S it falsely claims to have been made or altered by **S**omeone who did not in fact

E **E**xist.

This list is exhaustive; if an instrument cannot be brought under one of these heads it will not be regarded as 'false'. However, you do not have to specify which of the heads an action comes under in a charge or indictment.

Section 9 goes on to say that:

(2) A person is to be treated for the purposes of this part of this Act as making a false instrument if he alters an instrument so as to make it false in any respect (whether or not it is false in some other respect apart from that alteration).

An 'instrument' is defined in s. 8 of the 1981 Act which states:

(1) Subject to subsection (2) below, in this Part of this Act 'instrument' means—
  (a) any document, whether of a formal or informal character;
  (b) any stamp issued or sold by a postal operator;
  (c) any Inland Revenue stamp; and
  (d) any disc, tape, sound track or other device on or in which information is recorded or stored by mechanical, electronic or other means.

(2) A currency note within the meaning of Part II of this Act is not an instrument for the purposes of this Part of this Act.

(3) A mark denoting payment of postage which a postal operator authorises to be used instead of an adhesive stamp is to be treated for the purposes of this Part of this Act as if it were a stamp issued by the postal operator concerned.

(3A) In this section, 'postal operator' has the same meaning as in the Postal Services Act 2000.

(4) In this Part of this Act 'Inland Revenue stamp' means a stamp as defined in section 27 of the Stamp Duties Management Act 1891.

KEYNOTE

The reference at s. 8(1)(d) above does not extend to electronic impulses keyed into a computer and therefore simply 'hacking' into a computer cannot amount to forgery (*R* v *Gold* [1988] AC 1063). For the offences under the Computer Misuse Act 1990, **see General Police Duties, chapter 4.12**).

Note that 'document' is not defined. As discussed above, this definition does not include currency notes which are the subject of a specific offence (see counterfeiting below).

1.12.11.5 Specific Instruments

In addition to the above offences which apply to any instrument, there are several specific offences which apply to specific types of 'formal' instrument.

OFFENCE: **Having Custody or Control of Specific Instruments and Materials with Intent—*Forgery and Counterfeiting Act 1981, s. 5(1) and (3)***
- Triable either way • Ten years' imprisonment on indictment • Six months' imprisonment and/or a fine summarily

The Forgery and Counterfeiting Act 1981, s. 5 states:

(1) It is an offence for a person to have in his custody or under his control an instrument to which this section applies which is, and which he knows or believes to be, false, with the intention that he or another shall use it to induce somebody to accept it as genuine, and by reason of so accepting it to do or not to do some act to his own or any other person's prejudice.

(2) ...

(3) It is an offence for a person to make or to have in his custody or under his control a machine or implement, or paper or any other material, which to his knowledge is or has been specially designed or adapted for the making of an instrument to which this section applies, with the intention that he or another shall make an instrument to which this section applies which is false and that he or another shall use the instrument to induce somebody to accept it as genuine, and by reason of so accepting it to do or not to do some act to his own or any other person's prejudice.

OFFENCE: **Having Custody or Control of Specific Instruments and Materials— *Forgery and Counterfeiting Act 1981, s. 5(2) and (4)***
- Triable either way • Two years' imprisonment on indictment • Six months' imprisonment and/or a fine summarily

The Forgery and Counterfeiting Act 1981, s. 5 states:

(2) It is an offence for a person to have in his custody or under his control, without lawful authority or excuse, an instrument to which this section applies which is, and which he knows or believes to be, false.

(3) ...

(4) It is an offence for a person to make or to have in his custody or under his control any such machine, implement, paper or material, without lawful authority or excuse.

The instruments to which the above offences under s. 5 apply are:

(5) ...
- (a) money orders;
- (b) postal orders;
- (c) United Kingdom postage stamps;
- (d) Inland Revenue stamps;
- (e) share certificates;

(f)   passports and documents which can be used instead of passports;

(fa) immigration documents;

(g)   cheques and other bills of exchange;

(h)   travellers' cheques;

(ha) bankers' drafts;

(hb) promissory notes;

(j)   cheque cards;

(ja) debit cards;

(k)   credit cards;

(l)   certified copies relating to an entry in a register of births, adoptions, marriages or deaths and issued by the Registrar General, the Registrar General for Northern Ireland, a registration officer or a person lawfully authorised to register marriages; and

(m)   certificates relating to entries in such registers.

(6) In subsection (5)(e) above 'share certificate' means an instrument entitling or evidencing the title of a person to a share or interest—

(a) in any public stock, annuity, fund or debt of any government or state, including a state which forms part of another state; or

(b) in any stock, fund or debt of a body (whether corporate or unincorporated) established in the United Kingdom or elsewhere.

(7) An instrument is also an instrument to which this section applies if it is a monetary instrument specified for the purposes of this section by an order made by the Secretary of State.

...

KEYNOTE

Many of these 'instruments' are self explanatory. Note that passports and immigration documents are covered by the above offence. 'Immigration document' essentially means a card, adhesive label or other instrument given under the Immigration Acts to someone to confirm their right of entry to or residence in the United Kingdom. The expression extends to cards, labels and other instruments which carry information (including information wholly or partly stored electronically) about the leave granted to that person. For a further discussion of the relevant immigration offences and the implications of having false documents see chapter 1.15.

1.12.11.6   Prejudice and Induce

The *ulterior intent* (**see chapter 1.1**) of *inducing* somebody to accept an instrument with the result that he/she does something to his/her own *prejudice* must be read in the light of s. 10 of the 1981 Act which states:

(1) Subject to subsections (2) and (4) below, for the purposes of this Part of this Act an act or omission intended to be induced is to a person's prejudice if, and only if, it is one which, if it occurs—

(a) will result—

(i) in his temporary or permanent loss of property; or

(ii) in his being deprived of an opportunity to earn remuneration or greater remuneration; or

(iii) in his being deprived of an opportunity to gain a financial advantage otherwise than by way of remuneration; or

(b) will result in somebody being given an opportunity—

(i) to earn remuneration or greater remuneration from him; or

(ii) to gain a financial advantage from him otherwise than by way of remuneration; or

(c) will be the result of his having accepted a false instrument as genuine, or a copy of a false instrument as a copy of a genuine one, in connection with his performance of any duty.

(2) An act which a person has an enforceable duty to do and an omission to do an act which a person is not entitled to do shall be disregarded for the purposes of this Part of this Act.

(3) In this Part of this Act references to inducing somebody to accept a false instrument as genuine, or a copy of a false instrument as a copy of a genuine one, include references to inducing a machine to respond to the instrument or copy as if it were a genuine instrument or, as the case may be, a copy of a genuine one.

KEYNOTE

This section extends the meaning of inducing someone to accept something as genuine to *machines*. The extension is limited to offences under part I of the 1981 Act and therefore does not apply to offences contained elsewhere such as counterfeiting (as to which, see below).

1.12.11.7 Acknowledging Bail

OFFENCE: **Acknowledging Bail in the Name of Another—*Forgery Act 1861, s. 34***

- Triable on indictment • Seven years' imprisonment

The Forgery Act 1861, s. 34 states:

Whosoever, without lawful authority or excuse (the proof whereof shall lie on the party accused), shall in the name of any other person acknowledge any recognisance or bail,...or judgment or any deed or other instrument, before any court, judge, or other person lawfully authorized in that behalf, shall be guilty of felony ...

KEYNOTE

Provided the bail or recognisance is valid, this offence would appear to apply equally to bail granted by a court or the police.

1.12.11.8 Counterfeiting

The offences of counterfeiting apply to currency notes and coins. These terms are defined within the Forgery and Counterfeiting Act 1981, s. 27, which states:

(1) In this Part of this Act—
    'currency note' means—
      (a) any note which—
          (i) has been lawfully issued in England and Wales, Scotland, Northern Ireland, any of the Channel Islands, the Isle of Man or the Republic of Ireland; and
          (ii) is or has been customarily used as money in the country where it was issued; and
          (iii) is payable on demand; or
      (b) any note which—
          (i) has been lawfully issued in some country other than those mentioned in paragraph (a)(i) above; and
          (ii) is customarily used as money in that country; and
    'protected coin' means any coin which—
          (i) is customarily used as money in any country: or
          (ii) is specified in an order made by the Treasury for the purposes of this Part of this Act.

Section 28 defines counterfeit as:

(1) For the purposes of this Part of this Act a thing is a counterfeit of a currency note or of a protected coin—

    (a) if it is not a currency note or a protected coin but resembles a currency note or protected coin (whether on one side only or on both) to such an extent that it is reasonably capable of passing for a currency note or protected coin of that description; or

    (b) if it is a currency note or protected coin which has been so altered that it is reasonably capable of passing for a currency note or protected coin of some other description.

(2) For the purposes of this Part of this Act—

    (a) a thing consisting of one side only of a currency note, with or without the addition of other material, is a counterfeit of such a note;

    (b) a thing consisting—

        (i) of parts of two or more currency notes; or

        (ii) of parts of a currency note, or of parts of two or more currency notes, with the addition of other material,

    is capable of being a counterfeit of a currency note.

(3) References in this part of this Act to passing or tendering a counterfeit of a currency note or a protected coin are not to be construed as confined to passing or tendering it as legal tender.

KEYNOTE

Currency notes and protected coins can therefore originate from another country (see, however, the offences under ss. 18 and 19 below).

Now that the Euro has arrived in most EC countries, and it is accepted by a growing number of outlets in the United Kingdom, this area of criminal law is expected to become of more relevance to everyday policing. As a result of these Europe-wide concerns, the government passed the Protection of the Euro against Counterfeiting Regulations 2001 (SI 2001/3948). These Regulations impose a duty on certain institutions to notify—among other people—the Serious Organised Crime Agency.

Counterfeit currency or coins can be either:

- things which are not in fact currency notes or coins but which resemble them sufficiently enough to be passed as such;

- things which *are* in fact currency notes or coins but which have been altered to resemble different ones.

1.12.11.9   Counterfeiting with Intent to Pass or Tender as Genuine

OFFENCE: **Making Counterfeit Note or Coin with Intent—*Forgery and Counterfeiting Act 1981, s. 14(1)***

        • Triable either way • Ten years' imprisonment on indictment • Six months' imprisonment and/or a fine summarily

The Forgery and Counterfeiting Act 1981, s. 14 states:

(1) It is an offence for a person to make a counterfeit of a currency note or of a protected coin, intending that he or another shall pass or tender it as genuine.

KEYNOTE

Although there is a requirement to prove an ulterior intent, there is no need to show that the defendant intended to induce someone to do something to his/her own prejudice.

OFFENCE: **Having Custody or Control of Counterfeit Note or Coin with Intent—** *Forgery and Counterfeiting Act 1981, s. 16(1)*

- Triable either way • Ten years' imprisonment on indictment • Six months' imprisonment and/or a fine summarily

The Forgery and Counterfeiting Act 1981, s. 16 states:

(1) It is an offence for a person to have in his custody or under his control any thing which is, and which he knows or believes to be, a counterfeit of a currency note or of a protected coin, intending either to pass or tender it as genuine or to deliver it to another with the intention that he or another shall pass or tender it as genuine.

OFFENCE: **Passing Counterfeit Notes or Coins with Intent—***Forgery and Counterfeiting Act 1981, s. 15(1)(a) and (b)*

- Triable either way • Ten years' imprisonment and/or a fine on indictment • Six months' imprisonment and/or a fine summarily

The Forgery and Counterfeiting Act 1981, s. 15 states:

(1) It is an offence for a person—
    (a) to pass or tender as genuine any thing which is, and which he knows or believes to be, a counterfeit of a currency note or of a protected coin; or
    (b) to deliver to another any thing which is, and which he knows or believes to be, such a counterfeit, intending that the person to whom it is delivered or another shall pass or tender it as genuine.

1.12.11.10 Making and Delivering Counterfeit Note or Coin

OFFENCE: **Making Counterfeit Note or Coin—***Forgery and Counterfeiting Act 1981, s. 14(2)*

- Triable either way • Two years' imprisonment on indictment • Six months' imprisonment and/or a fine summarily

The Forgery and Counterfeiting Act 1981, s. 14 states:

(2) It is an offence for a person to make a counterfeit of a currency note or of a protected coin without lawful authority or excuse.

OFFENCE: **Having Custody or Control of Counterfeit Note or Coin—***Forgery and Counterfeiting Act 1981, s. 16(2)*

- Triable either way • Two years' imprisonment and/or a fine on indictment • Six months' imprisonment and/or a fine summarily

The Forgery and Counterfeiting Act 1981, s. 16 states:

(2) It is an offence for a person to have in his custody or under his control, without lawful authority or excuse, any thing which is, and which he knows or believes to be, a counterfeit of a currency note or of a protected coin.
(3) It is immaterial for the purposes of subsections (1) and (2) above that a coin or note is not in a fit state to be passed or tendered or that the making or counterfeiting of a coin or note has not been finished or perfected.

OFFENCE: **Delivering Counterfeit Notes or Coins—***Forgery and Counterfeiting Act 1981, s. 15(2)*

- Triable either way • Two years' imprisonment and/or a fine on indictment • Six months' imprisonment and/or a fine summarily

The Forgery and Counterfeiting Act 1981, s. 15 states:

(2) It is an offence for a person to deliver to another, without lawful authority or excuse, any thing which is, and which he knows or believes to be, a counterfeit of a currency note or of a protected coin.

1.12.11.11 Materials for Counterfeiting

OFFENCE: **Having Custody or Control of Materials for Counterfeiting with Intent—*Forgery and Counterfeiting Act 1981, s. 17(1)***
- Triable either way • Ten years' imprisonment and/or a fine on indictment • Six months' imprisonment and/or a fine summarily

The Forgery and Counterfeiting Act 1981, s. 17 states:

(1) It is an offence for a person to make, or to have in his custody or under his control any thing which he intends to use, or to permit any other person to use, for the purpose of making a counterfeit of a currency note or of a protected coin, with the intention that it be passed or tendered as genuine.

OFFENCE: **Having Custody or Control of Materials for Counterfeiting—*Forgery and Counterfeiting Act 1981, s. 17(2) and (3)***
- Triable either way • Two years' imprisonment and/or a fine on indictment • Six months' imprisonment and/or a fine summarily

The Forgery and Counterfeiting Act 1981, s. 17 states:

(2) It is an offence for a person without lawful authority or excuse—
   (a) to make; or
   (b) to have in his custody or under his control,
   any thing which, to his knowledge, is or has been specially designed or adapted for the making of a counterfeit of a currency note.
(3) Subject to subsection (4) below, it is an offence for a person to make, or to have in his custody or under his control, any implement which, to his knowledge, is capable of imparting to any thing, a resemblance—
   (a) to the whole or part of either side of a protected coin; or
   (b) to the whole or part of the reverse of the image on either side of a protected coin.

Defence

Section 17 of the 1981 Act states:

(4) It shall be defence for a person charged with an offence under subsection (3) above to show—
   (a) that he made the implement or, as the case may be, had it in his custody or under his control, with the written consent of the Treasury; or
   (b) that he had lawful authority otherwise than by virtue of paragraph (a) above, or a lawful excuse, for making it or having it in his custody or under his control.

KEYNOTE

This defence only applies to s. 17(3) above. In all other cases the legal burden (**see Evidence and Procedure, chapter 2.7**) to disprove lawful authority lies with the prosecution.

Police Powers

A warrant to search for and seize counterfeit currency and materials may be issued under s. 24 of the 1981 Act.

1.12.11.12   **British Currency and Coins**

OFFENCE: **Reproducing British Currency Note—*Forgery and Counterfeiting Act 1981, s. 18***

> • Triable either way • Fine

The Forgery and Counterfeiting Act 1981, s. 18 states:

(1) It is an offence for any person, unless the relevant authority has previously consented in writing, to reproduce on any substance whatsoever, and whether or not on the correct scale, any British currency note or any part of a British currency note.

(2) In this section—

'British currency note' means any note which—

  (a) has been lawfully issued in England and Wales, Scotland or Northern Ireland; and

  (b) is or has been customarily used as money in the country where it was issued; and

  (c) is payable on demand; and

'the relevant authority', in relation to a British currency note of any particular description, means the authority empowered by law to issue notes of that description.

OFFENCE: **Making Imitation British Coins—*Forgery and Counterfeiting Act 1981, s. 19***

> • Triable either way • Fine

The Forgery and Counterfeiting Act 1981, s. 19 states:

(1) It is an offence for a person—

  (a) to make an imitation British coin in connection with a scheme intended to promote the sale of any product or the making of contracts for the supply of any service; or

  (b) to sell or distribute imitation British coins in connection with any such scheme, or to have imitation British coins in his custody or under his control with a view to such sale or distribution, unless the Treasury have previously consented in writing to the sale or distribution of such imitation British coins in connection with that scheme.

(2) In this section—

'British coin' means any coin which is legal tender in any part of the United Kingdom; and

'imitation British coin' means any thing which resembles a British coin in shape, size and the substance of which it is made.

KEYNOTE

These offences require no *ulterior* intent that anyone be fooled into thinking that the notes or coins are genuine. They are offences of *basic* intent (see chapter 1.1), and are designed to prevent any duplication under the proscribed circumstances. If any fraudulent use was made or intended then one of the earlier offences discussed above would be committed.

1.13 | Criminal Damage

1.13.1 Introduction

The chances of any police officer going through their career without dealing in some way with an offence of criminal damage are minuscule. The prevalence of offences of criminal damage is well documented and damage in all forms has harmful effect on the environment, the community and the economy.

1.13.1.1 Types of Offence

There are extensive civil remedies available for people whose property is damaged by others. In cases involving a course of conduct or behaviour that causes widespread public nuisance, other offences and remedies may apply (**see General Police Duties, chapter 4.5**). The law regulating *criminal* damage, however, is largely contained within one statute, the Criminal Damage Act 1971. This Act deals with occasions where a person:

- actually damages or destroys the property of another (simple damage);
- damages or destroys his/her own property or that of another where there are 'aggravating' factors or circumstances (aggravated damage);
- threatens to damage or destroy property;
- has articles to be used for damaging or destroying property.

In addition, the Crime and Disorder Act 1998 created an offence of racially or religiously aggravated criminal damage.

1.13.2 Simple Damage

OFFENCE: **Simple damage—*Criminal Damage Act 1971, s. 1(1)***
- Triable either way • Ten years' imprisonment on indictment • Six months' imprisonment and/or a fine summarily

OFFENCE: **Racially or Religiously Aggravated—*Crime and Disorder Act 1998, s. 30(1)***
- Triable either way • Fourteen years' imprisonment and/or a fine on indictment
- Six months' imprisonment and/or a fine summarily

The Criminal Damage Act 1971, s. 1 states:

(1) A person who without lawful excuse destroys or damages any property belonging to another intending to destroy or damage any such property or being reckless as to whether any such property would be destroyed or damaged shall be guilty of an offence.

KEYNOTE

Although triable either way, if the value of the property destroyed or the damage done is less than £5,000, the offence is to be tried summarily (Magistrates' Courts Act 1980, s. 22). If the damage in such a case was caused by fire (arson) (**see para. 1.13.4**) then this rule will not apply.

The fact that the substantive offence is, by virtue of the value of the damage caused, triable only summarily does not make simple damage a 'summary offence' for all other purposes. If it did, you could only be found guilty of *attempting* to commit criminal damage if the value of the intended damage was more than £5,000 (because the Criminal Attempts Act 1981 does not extend to summary offences) (**see chapter 1.3**). Therefore, where a defendant tried to damage a bus shelter in a way that would have cost far less than £5,000 to repair, his argument that he had only attempted what was in fact a 'summary offence' was dismissed by the Divisional Court (*R v Bristol Magistrates' Court, ex parte E* [1998] 3 All ER 798). Note that offences of damage involving values not exceeding £200 can be dealt with by way of fixed penalty notice (**see General Police Duties, chapter 4.4.3**).

If the offence involves only the painting or writing on, or the soiling, marking or other defacing of, any property by whatever means, the power to issue a graffiti notice may apply (as to which **see para. 1.13.7**).

The racially or religiously aggravated form of this offence (see below) is triable either way irrespective of the cost of the damage.

For the special evidential provisions in relation to criminal damage offences (under s. 9), **see Evidence and Procedure**.

1.13.2.1 Racially or Religiously Aggravated Damage

The racially or religiously aggravated circumstances set out at s. 28(1)(a) of the Crime and Disorder Act 1998 (**see General Police Duties, chapter 4.5**) deal with situations where the defendant demonstrates hostility:

- at the time of
- or immediately before or after

committing the offence, towards the *victim* and that hostility is *based on the victim's membership or presumed membership of a racial or religious group*. The courts have shown that they are prepared to adopt a wide approach when interpreting this important legislation. This can be seen in two particular cases. In the first, the Divisional Court confirmed that the relevant hostility can be demonstrated even if the victim is no longer present—*DPP* v *Parry* [2004] EWHC 3112. However, the need for any such hostility to be demonstrated *immediately* means that it must be shown to have taken place in the immediate context of the criminal damage offence. In *Parry* the only evidence of the racial hostility towards the victim came in the form of comments made to the officers attending the scene *some 20 minutes after* the defendant had caused the damage (by throwing nail polish at a neighbour's door). The court held that the wording of the statute meant that any hostility had to be demonstrated *immediately* before or *immediately* after the substantive offence and that the courts below had not been entitled to consider the retrospective effect of the comments made later by the defendant.

In another case where a juvenile used the words 'bloody foreigners' immediately before smashing the window of a kebab shop, the Divisional Court held that this was capable of amounting to an expression of hostility based on a person's membership or presumed membership of a racial group for the purposes of the Crime and Disorder Act 1998, s. 28(1)(a)—*DPP* v *M* [2004] 1 WLR 2758. Although the statutory wording used the expression 'a racial group', the court held that a specific and inclusive definition of such a group had to be used by the defendant (e.g. the defendant did not have to single out a specific nationality) and the size of group referred to by a defendant (such as all 'foreigners') was irrelevant. However, in the case of *M* the youth court had inadvertently mixed the two tests of hostility and motivation under s. 28(1)(b) and his appeal was allowed. Therefore, when considering whether an offence was racially motivated under s. 28 of the Crime and Disorder Act 1998, hostility demonstrated to foreign nationals simply because they are 'foreign' can be just as objectionable as hostility based on some more limited racial characteristic. This was clarified by the Court of Appeal in *R* v *Rogers* [2005] EWCA Crim 2863 where the defendant had called three Spanish women 'bloody foreigners' and told them to 'go back to your own country'. The prosecution case was that the defendant had demonstrated hostility based on the women's membership of a racial group. The court's decision clarifies the position that, for an offence to be aggravated under s. 28 the defendant has first to form a view that the victim is a member of a racial group (within the definition in s. 28(4)—**see General Police Duties, para. 4.5.2.4**) and then has to say (or do) something that demonstrates hostility towards the victim based on membership of that group. However, the Court of Appeal noted that the very wide meaning of racial group under s. 28(4) gives rise to a danger of aggravated offences being charged where mere 'vulgar abuse' had included racial epithets that did not truly indicate hostility to the race in question. Consequently, s. 28 should not be used unless the prosecuting authority is satisfied that the facts truly suggest that the offence was aggravated (rather than simply accompanied) by racism.

To clarify such situations in relation to racially or religiously aggravated damage, s. 30(3) provides that the person to whom the property belongs or is treated as belonging, will be treated as the 'victim'.

This provision is helpful where the aggravated offence is one under s. 28(1)(a)—the 'demonstration' type of aggravation—and the property is privately owned.

Where the property is owned by a corporate body (e.g. a bus shelter or tube station) however, there will clearly be problems in proving that the defendant's hostility was based on the *victim's* membership/presumed membership of a racial or religious group. Even though property for these purposes may be treated as belonging to more than one person (**see para. 1.13.2.4**) this means that, where the damage is caused by racist graffiti in publicly-owned places or on property owned by large corporations, the most suitable charge will probably be under s. 28(1)(b) of the Act—by far the harder to prove. Harder still would be the situation where any such graffiti is of a *religious* nature and the hostility was based on the victim's membership of a religious group. The revised wording of s. 28 of the Crime and Disorder Act 1998 (amended after the events of 11 September 2001) now includes 'religious groups'—and these will include groups of people defined, not only by their religious belief, but also their *lack* of any such belief.

The provisions of s. 30 of the Crime and Disorder Act 1998 only apply to the offence of 'simple' damage under s. 1(1) of the 1971 Act; they do not apply to any of the other offences in this chapter.

1.13.2.2 Destroy or Damage

Although a key feature of the 1971 Act, the terms 'destroy' or 'damage' are not defined. The courts have taken a wide view when interpreting these terms. 'Destroying' property would suggest that it has been rendered useless but there is no need to prove that 'damage' to property is in any way permanent or irreparable.

....

EXAMPLE

A group of youths in a shopping precinct walk up to a grocery display and begin juggling with some apples. They drop several apples, some of which smash on the pavement while others are soiled and bruised.

....

In the example above, the apples which were smashed were clearly 'destroyed'; those which were soiled, even though they could be washed, would probably be unfit for sale and therefore 'damaged' for the purposes of s. 1(1).

Whether an article has been damaged will be a question of fact for each court to determine on the evidence before it. Situations where courts have accepted that property has been damaged include the defacing of a pavement by an artist using only water-soluble paint (*Hardman* v *Chief Constable of Avon and Somerset* [1986] Crim LR 330). It has also been held by the Divisional Court that graffiti smeared in mud can amount to damage, even though it is easily washed off (*Roe* v *Kingerlee* [1986] Crim LR 735).

A good operational example of the courts' approach can be seen in *R* v *Fiak* [2005] EWCA Crim 2381. In that case the defendant had been arrested and placed in a police cell which he flooded by stuffing a blanket down the cell lavatory and repeatedly flushing. The defendant argued that there was no evidence that the blanket or the cell had been 'damaged'; the water had been clean and both the blanket and the cell could be used again when dry. The Court of Appeal disagreed and held that, while the effect of the defendant's actions in relation to the blanket and the cell was remediable, the reality was that the blanket could not be used until it had been dried and the flooded cell was out of action until the water had been cleared. Therefore both had sustained damage for the purposes of the Act.

It can be seen therefore that putting property temporarily out of use—even for a short time and in circumstances where it will revert to its former state of its own accord—may fall within the definition of 'damage'.

1.13.2.3 Property

Property is defined in the 1971 Act by s. 10 which states:

(1) In this Act 'property' means property of a tangible nature, whether real or personal, including money and—
   (a) including wild creatures which have been tamed or are ordinarily kept in captivity and any other wild creatures or their carcasses if, but only if, they have been reduced into possession...or are in the course of being reduced into possession; but
   (b) not including mushrooms growing wild on any land or flowers, fruit or foliage of a plant growing wild on any land.
   ...

KEYNOTE

This definition has similarities with the definition of 'property' for the purposes of theft (see chapter 1.11) but 'real' property (i.e. land and things attached to it) can be damaged even though it cannot be stolen. Trampling flower beds, digging up cricket pitches, chopping down trees in a private garden and even pulling up genetically-modified crops may all amount to criminal damage if accompanied by the required circumstances.

It is important to remember when dealing with disputes involving pets or farm animals that they are property for the purposes of this Act. Cases of horses being mutilated would, in addition to the offence of 'cruelty' itself, amount to criminal damage. There may also be occasions—such as domestic or neighbour disputes—involving harm or cruelty to such animals where it will be more appropriate and effective to consider offences under the 1971 Act.

Note that the destroying or damaging of another's property can amount to treating that property as your own, or otherwise falling within the parameters of s. 6 of the Theft Act (**see chapter 1.11**).

1.13.2.4 Belonging to Another

Section 10 states:

(2) Property shall be treated for the purposes of this Act as belonging to any person—
  (a) having the custody or control of it;
  (b) having in it any proprietary right or interest (not being an equitable interest arising only from an agreement to transfer or grant an interest); or
  (c) having a charge on it.

KEYNOTE

This extended meaning of 'belonging to another' is similar to that used in the Theft Act 1968 (**see chapter 1.11**). One result is that if a person damages his/her own property, he/she may still commit the offence of simple criminal damage if that property also 'belongs to' someone else.

1.13.2.5 Lawful excuse

Section 5 of the Criminal Damage Act 1971 provides for two occasions where a defendant may have a 'lawful excuse'. These can be remembered as 'permission' (s. 5(2)(a)) and 'protection' (s. 5(2)(b)). Both involve the belief of the defendant. The wording of s. 5 indicates that these particular defences are not the only ones available to a charge of criminal damage and other general defences (**see chapter 1.4**) may apply.

1.13.2.6 Permission

A person shall be treated as having lawful excuse under s. 5(2):

(a) if at the time of the act or acts alleged to constitute the offence he believed that the person or persons whom he believed to be entitled to consent to the destruction of or damage to the property in question had so consented, or would have so consented to it if he or they had known of the destruction or damage and its circumstances . . .

KEYNOTE

An example of 'lawful excuse' under s. 5(2)(a) would be if you, as a police officer, were asked by a motorist to help them get into their partner's car after locking the keys inside. If, during that attempt you damaged the rubber window surround, s. 5(2)(a) would provide you with a statutory defence to any later charge of criminal damage by the owner. The key elements here would be:

• the consent of someone whom you believed to be entitled to consent to that damage, and
• the circumstances under which it was caused.

If the driver was not available and your reason for opening the door was to get a better look at some personal documents for intelligence purposes, it is unlikely that the driver or the owner would have consented,

---

either to the damage or the circumstances in which it was caused. Therefore you could not use this particular defence.

1.13.2.7 Protection

A person shall be treated as having lawful excuse under s. 5(2):

(b) if he destroyed or damaged or threatened to destroy or damage the property in question or, in the case of a charge of an offence under section 3 above, intended to use or cause or permit the use of something to destroy or damage it, in order to protect property belonging to himself or another or a right or interest in property which was or which he believed to be vested in himself or another, and at the time of the act or acts alleged to constitute the offence he believed—

(i) that the property, right or interest was in immediate need of protection; and

(ii) that the means of protection adopted or proposed to be adopted were or would be reasonable having regard to all the circumstances.

KEYNOTE

Situations where such a defence can be used involve causing damage to property in order to protect other property. This defence also applies to the offence of having articles for causing damage (**see para. 1.13.6**). Key features of this defence are the immediacy of the need to protect the property and the reasonableness of the means of protection adopted. This defence has attracted the most attention of the courts in cases involving demonstrators claiming to be acting in furtherance of their political beliefs. For instance, in a case involving 'peace campaigners' it was held that the threat presented by a possible nuclear attack in the future did not excuse the carrying of a hacksaw for cutting through the perimeter fence of an airbase (*R* v *Hill* (1989) 89 Cr App R 74).

The 1971 Act goes on to say that it is immaterial whether a 'belief' above was justified as long as it was honestly held (s. 5(3)). This test is problematic because, although it is supposed to be an *objective* one, the evidence will be based largely on what was going through a defendant's mind at the time—or sometimes what was *not* going through their mind! In *Jaggard* v *Dickinson* [1981] QB 527 the defendant had broken a window to get into a house. Being drunk at the time, she had got the wrong house but the court accepted that her belief (that it was the right house and that the owner would have consented) had been honestly held, and that it did not matter whether that belief was brought about by intoxication, stupidity, forgetfulness or inattention. (For further discussion of drunkenness as a defence generally, **see chapter 1.4.**) That is not to say, however, that *any* honestly held belief will suffice. An example of someone claiming—though unsuccessfully—a defence under both s. 5(2)(a) and (b) can be seen in *Blake* v *DPP* [1993] Crim LR 586. There the defendant was a vicar who wished to protest against Great Britain's involvement in the Gulf War. In order to mark his disapproval, the defendant wrote a quotation from the Bible in ink on a pillar in front of the Houses of Parliament. He claimed:

- that he was carrying out God's instructions and therefore had a lawful excuse based on his belief that God was the person entitled to consent to such damage and that he had in fact consented or would have done so (s. 5(2)(a)); and

- that he had damaged the property as a reasonable means of protecting other property located in the Gulf from being damaged by warfare (s. 5(2)(b)).

Perhaps unsurprisingly the Divisional Court did not accept either proposition holding that, in the first case a belief in The Almighty's consent was not a 'lawful excuse' and, in the second, that the defendant's conduct was too remote from any immediate need to protect property in the Gulf States. The test in relation to the defendant's belief appears then to be largely subjective (i.e. what was/was not going on in his/her head at the time) but with an objective element in that the judge/magistrate(s) must decide whether, on the facts as believed by the defendant, his/her acts were capable of protecting property.

A similar approach was tried more recently in a case where the defendant was arrested after making 22 cuts in a perimeter fence of a base where nuclear warheads were produced. The defendant claimed that the activity at the base was unlawful in international law and therefore acts to prevent that activity amounted to a lawful excuse under the 1971 Act. The Divisional Court did not accept this argument, nor the argument that the defendant's acts were merely an expression of her opinion under Article 10 of the European Convention on Human Rights (as to which, **see General Police Duties, chapter 4.3**) (*Hutchinson* v *DPP* (2000) *Independent*, 20 November). Taking a different tack, peace campaigners in *R* v *Jones (Margaret)* [2004] EWCA Crim 1981 argued that their fear of the consequences of war in Iraq—which they claimed to be illegal—prompted them to conspire to cause damage at an airbase and that such fear amounted both to duress (as to which **see para. 1.4.7**) and lawful excuse under s. 5(2)(b) above. The Court of Appeal held that a jury would be entitled to consider some of the subjective beliefs of the defendants in determining the reasonableness of their actions.

Finally, a demonstrator at the Guildhall Gallery knocked the head off a statue of Baroness Thatcher and claimed that he acted in fear for his son's future which had been placed in jeopardy by the joint actions of the US and UK governments, and for which Baroness Thatcher was partly responsible. His appeal against conviction brought under s. 5(2)(b)—with a few technicalities added on—failed (*R* v *Kelleher* [2003] EWCA Crim 2846).

The Act also states, at s. 5(4), that a right or interest in property includes any right or privilege in or over land, whether created by grant, licence or otherwise.

Section 5(5) allows for other general defences (**see chapter 1.4**) at criminal law to apply in addition to those listed under s. 5.

It is not an offence to damage your own property unless there are aggravating circumstances (**see para. 1.13.3**). Even if the intention in doing so is to carry out some further offence—such as a fraudulent insurance claim—this fact still does not make it an offence under s. 1(1) of the Criminal Damage Act 1971 (*R* v *Denton* [1981] 1 WLR 1446). (It may, however, give rise to other offences of dishonesty (**see chapter 1.11**).)

1.13.2.8 Recklessness

An offence of criminal damage under s. 1(1) can be proved by showing that the defendant was 'reckless' (**see chapter 1.1**). The former concept of *objective* or 'Caldwell' recklessness (as set out in *Metropolitan Police Commissioner* v *Caldwell* [1982] AC 341) has now gone and the law has been restored to its former position by *R* v *G & R* [2003] 3 WLR 1060. In that case, the House of Lords decided that 'recklessness' in the context of criminal damage did not mean something different from the previous requirement of 'malicious damage'—namely that the defendant had foreseen the risk yet gone on to take it. Their Lordships held that a person acts recklessly for the purposes of s. 1(1) of the Act:

- with respect to a circumstance when he/she is aware of a risk that existed or would exist;
- with respect to a result or consequence when s/he is aware of a risk that it would occur and it is, in the circumstances known to him/her, unreasonable to take the risk.

In the *R* v *G & R* case, two children (aged 11 and 12), set fire to some newspapers in the rear yard of a shop premises while camping out. The children put the burning papers under a wheelie bin and left them, expecting the small fire to burn itself out on the concrete floor of the yard. In fact the fire spread causing around £1,000,000 of damage. Under the former law (*Caldwell*), the children were convicted on the basis that the risk of the fire would have been obvious to any reasonable bystander. However, their convictions were quashed by the House of Lords who reinstated the general subjective element described above.

1.13.3 Aggravated Damage

OFFENCE: **Aggravated damage—*Criminal Damage Act 1971, s. 1(2)***
- Triable on indictment • Life imprisonment

The Criminal Damage Act 1971, s. 1 states:

(2) A person who without lawful excuse destroys or damages any property, whether belonging to himself or another—
  (a) intending to destroy or damage any property or being reckless as to whether any property would be destroyed or damaged; and
  (b) intending by the destruction or damage to endanger the life of another or being reckless as to whether the life of another would be thereby endangered;
  shall be guilty of an offence.

KEYNOTE

The aggravating factor in this offence, and the reason why it attracts such a heavy maximum sentence, is the ulterior intention of endangering life or recklessness as to whether life is endangered. As such, evidence of self-induced intoxication may provide a defence to a charge under this section (**see chapter 1.4**). This form of 'aggravation' should not be confused with the 'racially or religiously aggravated' form of criminal damage.

The reference to 'without lawful excuse' does not refer to the statutory excuses under s. 5 (**see para. 1.13.2.5**) which are not applicable here, but to general excuses such as self-defence or the prevention of crime (**see chapter 1.4**).

For the relevant test of recklessness **see para. 1.13.2.8**.

You must also show that the defendant either intended or was reckless as to each of the following consequences:

- the damage being caused, and
- the *resultant* danger to life.

It does not matter that the *actual* damage caused by the defendant turned out to be minor. What matters is the *potential* for damage and danger created by the defendant's conduct.

Where a defendant set fire to furniture in a house which was unoccupied at the time, the court nevertheless found him guilty of this offence. The court's reasoning for doing so turned on the fact that, had a reasonable bystander been present, he/she would have seen the possible risk that the fire might cause to the lives of others in the area, even though with hindsight it was shown that there had been no likelihood of the fire spreading to neighbouring properties (*R* v *Sangha* [1988] 1 WLR 519). This decision was taken while the concept of 'objective' or *Caldwell* recklessness (as to which, **see chapter 1.1**) was still in place for criminal damage offences. As a result, it will need to be reconsidered and it will probably be necessary to show that there *was* some likelihood of life being endangered. In this case there was clearly recklessness as to the damage caused *and* recklessness as to the danger to life *presented by the damage*. In contrast, where a defendant fired a gun through a window pane he was clearly reckless as to the damage his actions would cause. However, the court felt that, even though two people were standing behind the window and that they were obviously put in some danger, it was the *missile* which endangered their lives and not the result of the damage. Therefore the court held that the defendant was not guilty of this particular offence

(*R* v *Steer* [1988] AC 111). This distinction seems to be a fine one, particularly if you are the person behind the window.

If someone were to smash the windscreen of a moving car or to cause a large display window to collapse into a busy street, this would probably be enough to support a charge under s. 1(2) (see *R* v *Webster* [1995] 2 All ER 168).

1.13.4 Arson

OFFENCE: **Arson—*Criminal Damage Act 1971, s. 1(3)***
- Triable either way • Life imprisonment on indictment • Where life is not endangered six months' imprisonment and/or a fine summarily

The Criminal Damage Act 1971, s. 1 states:

(3) An offence committed under this section by destroying or damaging property by fire shall be charged as arson.

KEYNOTE

In any of the above cases of criminal damage, if the destruction or damage is caused by fire, the offence will be charged as 'arson'. Given the potential for extensive damage and danger to life that fire-raising has, the restrictions on the mode of trial for simple damage under s. 1(1) (see para. 1.13.2) do not apply to cases of arson.

Again, in light of the potential for serious injury and death, the link between this offence and the various homicide offences (see chapter 1.5) often arises. An example of where criminal liability for either gross negligence or unlawful act manslaughter arose from an offence of arson can be seen in *R* v *Willoughby* (2004) *The Times*, 21 December. In that case the defendant enlisted the help of another man in burning down a public house on which the defendant owed money. Having poured petrol around the inside of the building, the defendant set fire to it, killing the other person and injuring himself in the process. The defendant was convicted of both arson and manslaughter. The Court of Appeal held that by convicting the defendant of arson, the jury had showed that they were sure that he (on his own or jointly) had deliberately spread petrol by being reckless or with the intention that the premises would be destroyed. Provided that such conduct had been the cause of the death, the jury were therefore also bound to convict the defendant of manslaughter.

Aggravated damage caused by arson is triable only on indictment and carries a maximum penalty of life imprisonment.

1.13.5 Threats to Destroy or Damage Property

OFFENCE: **Threats to destroy or damage property—**
Criminal Damage Act 1971, s. 2
- Triable either way • Ten years' imprisonment on indictment • Six months' imprisonment and/or a fine summarily

The Criminal Damage Act 1971, s. 2 states:

A person who without lawful excuse makes to another a threat, intending that that other would fear it would be carried out,—

(a) to destroy or damage any property belonging to that other or a third person; or

(b) to destroy or damage his own property in a way which he knows is likely to endanger the life of that other or a third person;

shall be guilty of an offence.

KEYNOTE

This is an offence of *intention*, that is, the key element is the defendant's intention that the person receiving the threat fears it would be carried out.

The s. 2 offence, which originates from the need to tackle protection racketeers, is very straightforward: there is no need to show that the other person actually feared or even believed that the threat would be carried out. There is no need to show that the defendant intended to carry it out; nor does it matter whether the threat was even capable of being carried out.

....

EXAMPLES

If a person, enraged by a neighbour's inconsiderate parking, shouts over the garden wall, '*When you've gone to bed I'm going to T-cut that heap with paint stripper!*', the offence will be complete, provided you can show that the person making the threat intended the neighbour to fear it would be carried out.

Where a group of protestors staged a protest in the pods of the London Eye and threatened to set fire to themselves, their conduct was held by the Court of Appeal to be capable of amounting to a threat to damage the property of another contrary to s. 2(a) (*R v Cakmak* [2002] 2 Cr App R 10).

In *Cakmak* the court held that the gist of the offence under s. 2(a) was the making of a threat and that any such threat had to be considered objectively.

Whether:

• there has been such a threat to another

• the threat amounted to 'a threat to damage or destroy property'

• the defendant had the necessary state of mind (*mens rea*, **see** chapter 1.1) at the time

are all questions of fact for the jury to decide (per *Cakmak*).

....

While not usually enough to amount to the substantive offence under s. 2 above, a person's *conduct* which represents a threat to damage property may be relevant in triggering police action. This can be seen in yet another case involving a political protest against war. In *Clements v DPP* [2005] EWHC 1279 several protestors left a public highway, crossed a ditch and approached the perimeter fence of an RAF base. The defendant ignored a police warning to return to the road and the police attempted to restrain the protestors in order to prevent criminal damage to the fence. After a scuffle the defendant was subsequently convicted of assaulting a police constable in the execution of his duty (as to which **see para. 1.7.3.3**). The key issues at trial were whether the police officer had acted in the course of his duty and the extent to which the officer had reasonable grounds to believe that the defendant would cause criminal damage. The Divisional Court held that the officer had to consider the whole event in context and at the relevant time a political protest was ensuing; the defendant had deliberately left the public highway and refused to return to it; he had no legitimate reason to approach the fence; and it was plainly reasonable for the police officer to believe that he could cause criminal damage to the fence.

For other offences involving threats, harassment or nuisance, **see General Police Duties, chapter 4.5**.

1.13.6 Having Articles with Intent to Destroy or Damage Property

OFFENCE: **Having articles with intent to destroy or damage property—**
Criminal Damage Act 1971, s. 3

> • Triable either way • Ten years' imprisonment on indictment • Six months' imprisonment and/or a fine summarily

The Criminal Damage Act 1971, s. 3 states:

> A person who has anything in his custody or under his control intending without lawful excuse to use it or cause or permit another to use it—
> (a) to destroy or damage any property belonging to some other person; or
> (b) to destroy or damage his own or the user's property in a way which he knows is likely to endanger the life of some other person;
> shall be guilty of an offence.

KEYNOTE

Often referred to as 'possessing articles' for causing damage, this offence is, in reality, far wider than that. Although it also originates from the need to control organised crime, this offence covers *anything* which a defendant has *'in his custody or under his control'*, a deliberately broader term than 'possession'. (Compare this with the narrower expression—'has with him'—used in the law preventing the carrying of weapons, **see General Police Duties, chapter 4.8** and the Theft Act 1968, **chapter 1.11.**)

As a result, this offence applies to graffiti 'artists' carrying aerosols, advertisers with adhesives for sticking illicit posters and neighbours with paint stripper. The key element, once again, is an *intention*. This time the required intention is that the 'thing' be used to cause criminal damage to another's property or to the defendant's own property in a way which he/she knows is likely to endanger the life of another. Such articles are now 'prohibited' articles for the purposes of the power of stop and search under s. 1 of the Police and Criminal Evidence Act 1984 (**see General Police Duties, chapter 4.4**). For the specific offence of selling aerosol paint to children **see para. 1.13.7**.

If the person's intention is to use the articles for contaminating goods or making it appear that goods have been contaminated, a separate offence exists under the Public Order Act 1986, s. 38(3) (**see para. 1.13.8**).

A conditional intent—that is, an intent to use something to cause criminal damage if the need arises—will be enough (*R v Buckingham* (1976) 63 Cr App R 159).

Just as it is not an offence to damage your own property in a way which endangers no-one else, neither is it an offence to have something which you intend to use to cause damage under those circumstances.

. . . .

EXAMPLE

If the owner of a 10 metre high conifer decides to trim the top with a chainsaw and a ladder, putting himself—but no-one else—at considerable risk, he commits no offence, either by causing the damage or by having the chainsaw. If he intends to fell the tree in a way which a reasonable bystander would say presents a danger to his neighbours or passers by, then he may commit offences on both counts.

. . . .

Police Powers

There is a statutory power to apply to a magistrate for a search warrant under s. 6.

1.13.7   **Penalty and Removal Notices for Graffiti**

Where an authorised officer of a local authority has reason to believe that a person has committed a relevant offence in the area of that authority, s/he may give that person a penalty notice under s. 43 of the Anti-social Behaviour Act 2003 (unless the offence amounts to a racially or religiously aggravated damage offence).

Examples of a 'relevant offence' include:

- s. 1(1) of the Criminal Damage Act 1971 (**see para. 1.13.2**) which involves only the painting or writing on, or the soiling, marking or other defacing of, any property by whatever means
- s. 132(1) of the Highways Act 1980 (painting or affixing things on structures on the highway etc.)
- para. 10 of s. 54 of the Metropolitan Police Act 1839 (affixing posters etc.)
- s. 20(1) of the London County Council (General Powers) Act 1954 (defacement of streets with slogans etc.)
- s. 131(2) of the Highways Act 1980 (including that provision as applied by s. 27(6) of the Countryside Act 1968) which involves only an act of obliteration
- s. 224(3) of the Town and Country Planning Act 1990 (displaying advertisement in contravention of regulations). (s. 44).

These provisions, along with those regulating the sale of aerosol paint to children (see below), will be extended by the Clean Neighbourhoods and Environment Act 2005 when its relevant provisions come into force.

Police community support officers and accredited employees under schs 4 and 5 to the Police Reform Act 2002 (**see General Police Duties**) can be given the power to issue these penalty notices.

In addition, where a local authority is satisfied that a relevant surface in an area has been defaced by graffiti and the defacement is detrimental to the amenity of the area or is offensive, the authority may serve a defacement removal notice upon any person who is responsible (s. 48). A 'relevant surface' means broadly the surface of any street or of any building, structure or other object in or on any street, or the surface of any land owned, occupied or controlled by an educational institution or any building, structure etc. on any such land (see s. 48(9)). For further practical advice in relation to these powers see the guidance provided by the Secretary of State under s. 50.

OFFENCE: **Sale of Aerosol Paint to Children**—*Anti-social Behaviour Act 2003, s. 54*
- Triable summarily • Fine

The Anti-social Behaviour Act 2003, s. 54 states:

(1) A person commits an offence if he sells an aerosol paint container to a person under the age of sixteen.

(2) ...

(3) ...

(4) It is a defence for a person charged with an offence under this section in respect of a sale to prove that—

(a) he took all reasonable steps to determine the purchaser's age, and

(b) he reasonably believed that the purchaser was not under the age of sixteen.

(5) It is a defence for a person charged with an offence under this section in respect of a sale effected by another person to prove that he (the defendant) took all reasonable steps to avoid the commission of an offence under this section.

KEYNOTE

An 'aerosol paint container' means a device which contains paint stored under pressure, and is designed to permit the release of the paint as a spray (s. 54(2)).

Once the elements in relation to the selling and the age of the buyer are proved, the offence is complete. There is no need to show that the person buying the aerosol intended to use it for causing damage (though if this can be shown, the offence under s. 3 of the Criminal Damage Act 1971 should be considered—see para. 1.13.6).

Note the two different elements of the defence that will be available in the relevant circumstances under subss. (4) and (5) above.

1.13.8 Contamination or Interference with Goods

OFFENCE: **Contamination or interference with goods—*Public Order Act 1986, s. 38(1)***

- Triable either way • Ten years' imprisonment and/or a fine on indictment • Six months' imprisonment and/or a fine summarily

The Public Order Act 1986, s. 38 states:

(1) It is an offence for a person, with the intention—

  (a) of causing public alarm or anxiety, or

  (b) of causing injury to members of the public consuming or using the goods, or

  (c) of causing economic loss to any person by reason of the goods being shunned by members of the public, or

  (d) of causing economic loss to any person by reason of steps taken to avoid any such alarm or anxiety, injury or loss,

  to contaminate or interfere with goods, or make it appear that goods have been contaminated or interfered with, or to place goods which have been contaminated or interfered with, or which appear to have been contaminated or interfered with in a place where goods of that description are consumed, used, sold or otherwise supplied.

(2) It is also an offence for a person, with any such intention as is mentioned in paragraph (a), (c) or (d) of subsection (1), to threaten that he or another will do, or to claim that he or another has done, any of the acts mentioned in that subsection.

(3) It is an offence for a person to be in possession of any of the following articles with a view to the commission of an offence under subsection (1)—

  (a) materials to be used for contaminating or interfering with goods or making it appear that goods have been contaminated or interfered with, or

  (b) goods which have been contaminated or interfered with, or which appear to have been contaminated or interfered with.

(4) ...

(5) In this section 'goods' includes substances whether natural or manufactured and whether or not incorporated in or mixed with other goods.

(6) The reference in subsection (2) to a person claiming that certain acts have been committed does not include a person who in good faith reports or warns that such acts have been, or appear to have been, committed.

KEYNOTE

Section 38 creates two offences. The first involves the contamination of, interference with or placing of goods with the intentions set out at s. 38(1)(a)–(d). This is a crime of 'specific' intent (**see chapter 1.1**) and the particular intention of the defendant must be proved.

Section 38(2) involves the making of threats to do, *or* the claiming *to have done* any of the acts in s. 38(1), with any of the intentions set out at s. 38(1)(a), (c) or (d). It is difficult to see how a threat or claim made with the intention of causing injury to the public (s. 38(1)(b)) would not also amount to an intention to cause them alarm or anxiety.

Given the sensitivity of food preparation and production to some sections of the community, there may be occasions where deliberate interference with foodstuffs amounts to an offence of racially or religiously aggravated criminal damage (as to which **see para. 1.13.2.1**).

Section 38(6) allows for people to communicate warnings in good faith where such acts appear to have been committed.

Where threats to contaminate goods are made there may also be grounds for charging blackmail (**see chapter 1.11**). This type of 'product' sabotage is increasing, evidenced by the increasingly elaborate sealing devices used by manufacturers. Perhaps the most notorious example of this offence—and the overlap with blackmail—is the case of *R* v *Witchelo* (1991) 13 Cr App R (S) 371 where the defendant, a police officer, was sentenced to 13 years' imprisonment after obtaining £32,000 from food producers to whom he had sent threatening letters.

Additionally, where the defendant's behaviour is designed to influence the government, to intimidate the public or where it creates a serious risk to health and safety, the offences may fall within the definition of 'terrorism' under the Terrorism Act 2000. For a full discussion of this area, **see General Police Duties, chapter 4.6**.

1.14 Offences Against the Administration of Justice and Public Interest

1.14.1 Introduction

This chapter deals with a wide range of offences against the administration of justice and also the public interest. The first group of offences involve some form of interference with the machinery of justice. Some such offences, such as perjury and tendering false statements in evidence, affect the administration of justice directly while others, like corruption, have an indirect effect on the process. The offences grouped in the next chapter deal with issues of immigration, nationality and asylum-seekers.

1.14.2 Perjury

OFFENCE: **Perjury in Judicial Proceeding—*Perjury Act 1911, s. 1***
  - Triable on indictment • Seven years' imprisonment

The Perjury Act 1911, s. 1 states:

(1) If any person lawfully sworn as a witness or as an interpreter in a judicial proceeding wilfully makes a statement material in that proceeding, which he knows to be false or does not believe to be true, he shall be guilty of perjury...
(2) The expression 'judicial proceeding' includes a proceeding before any court, tribunal, or person having by law power to hear, receive, and examine evidence on oath.
(3) Where a statement made for the purposes of a judicial proceeding is not made before the tribunal itself, but is made on oath before a person authorised by law to administer an oath to the person who makes the statement, and to record or authenticate the statement, it shall, for the purposes of this section, be treated as having been made in a judicial proceeding.

KEYNOTE

To commit this offence a defendant must have been *lawfully sworn* (see the Evidence Act 1851, s. 16). The statement made in 'judicial proceeding' can be one given orally before the court or tribunal, or it can be given in the form of an affidavit (sworn statement). If a witness tenders a false statement (MG 11) used under the Criminal Justice Act 1967, s. 89 he/she commits a separate, lesser offence (see para. 1.14.3).

'Wilful' in this case means deliberate as opposed to accidental.

A 'statement material in that proceeding' means that the content of the evidence tendered in that case must have some importance to it and not just be of passing relevance. Whether something is material to a case is a question of law for a judge to decide. Whether a motorist had taken a drink between the time of his/her having a road traffic accident and being breathalysed would be such a material issue, and to get a witness to provide false evidence about that matter would be a 'statement material in that proceeding' (*R v Lewins* (1979) 1 Cr App R (S) 246).

To prove perjury you must also show that the defendant *knew* the statement to be false or *did not believe it to be true.*

Evidence of an opinion provided by a witness who does not genuinely hold such an opinion may also be perjury.

Perjury may be proved by using a court transcript or the evidence of others who were present at the proceeding in question (see Perjury Act 1911, s. 14).

Corroboration is required in cases of perjury (see Perjury Act 1911, s. 13 and Evidence and Procedure, chapter 2.10). The requirement for corroboration is solely in relation to the *falsity* of the defendant's statement. There is no requirement under s. 13 for corroboration of the fact that the defendant *actually made* the alleged statement, nor that he/she knew or believed it to be untrue. However, as that corroboration can be documentary and may even come from the defendant's earlier conduct (*R v Threlfall* (1914) 10 Cr App R 112) this requirement does not appear to present much of a hurdle to the prosecution.

Evidence given by live TV link under the provisions of the Criminal Justice Act 1988, s. 32 is also subject to the offence of perjury.

1.14.2.1 Aiding and Abetting

OFFENCE: **Aiding and Abetting Perjury—*Perjury Act 1911, s. 7***
- If principal offence is contrary to s.1 triable on indictment • Seven years imprisonment • Otherwise either way • Two years' imprisonment on indictment
- Six months' imprisonment and/or a fine summarily

The Perjury Act 1911, s. 7 states:

(1) Every person who aids, abets, counsels, procures, or suborns another person to commit an offence against this Act shall be liable to be proceeded against, indicted, tried and punished as if he were a principal offender.
(2) Every person who incites...another person to commit an offence against this Act shall be guilty of a misdemeanour.

KEYNOTE

'Subornation' is the same as procuring. This specific section does not appear to add anything to the general offences of aiding and abetting principal offenders (**see chapter 1.2**).

1.14.3 Offences Similar to Perjury

The offence of False Testimony of Unsworn Child Witness—Children and Young Persons Act 1933, s. 38(2), has been repealed by the Youth Justice and Criminal Evidence Act 1999, s. 67(3), Schedule 6. This has had effect since 1st April 2000 following SI 3427/1999.

OFFENCE: **False Statements in Criminal Proceedings—*Criminal Justice Act 1967, s. 89***

  • Triable either way • Two years' imprisonment and/or a fine on indictment • Six months' imprisonment and/or a fine summarily

The Criminal Justice Act 1967, s. 89 states:

(1) If any person in a written statement tendered in evidence in criminal proceedings by virtue of section 9 of this Act, or in proceedings before a court-martial...wilfully makes a statement material in those proceedings which he knows to be false or does not believe to be true, he shall be liable...
(2) The Perjury Act 1911 shall have effect as if this section were contained in that Act.

OFFENCE: **False Statements on Oath—*Perjury Act 1911, s. 2***

  • Triable either way • Seven years' imprisonment and/or a fine on indictment • Six months' imprisonment and/or a fine summarily

The Perjury Act 1911, s. 2 states:

If any person—
(1) being required or authorised by law to make any statement on oath for any purpose, and being lawfully sworn (otherwise than in a judicial proceeding) wilfully makes a statement which is material for that purpose and which he knows to be false or does not believe to be true;...
he shall be [guilty of an offence].

KEYNOTE

The first offence covers witnesses who tender false statements in criminal proceedings. The second offence covers the making of false statements under an oath which is not sworn in connection with a judicial proceeding.

The Perjury Act 1911 makes further provision for the making of false statements in relation to marriage licences (s. 3) and the making of false statements in relation to the registration of births and deaths (s. 4).

The 1911 Act also creates offences of making false declarations and of suppressing documents. For a full discussion of these offences, see *Blackstone's Criminal Practice*, 2008, section B14.

1.14.4 Perverting the Course of Justice

OFFENCE: **Perverting the Course of Justice—*Common Law***

  • Triable on indictment • Life imprisonment and/or a fine

It is an offence at common law to do an act tending and intended to pervert the course of public justice.

KEYNOTE

'The course of public justice' includes the process of criminal investigation (see *R* v *Rowell* (1977) 65 Cr App R 174).

Although traditionally referred to—and charged—as 'attempting' to pervert the course of justice, it is recognised that behaviour which is *aimed* at perverting the course of public justice does just that and the substantive offence should be charged (see *R* v *Williams* (1991) 92 Cr App R 158).

One way in which this offence is commonly committed is where a prisoner uses a false identity when he/she is arrested. Although the offence of perverting the course of justice may be made out in these—or similar—circumstances in connection with a number of other substantive offences, the Court of Appeal has held that, in many cases, the addition of such a charge is unnecessary and only serves to complicate the sentencing process (*R v Sookoo* (2002) *The Times*, 10 April). Where, as in *Sookoo*, a defendant makes an unsophisticated attempted to hide their identity and fails, the Court felt that a specific separate count of perverting the course of justice should not be laid. If it was shown that there were serious aggravating features, for instance where a lot of police time and resources had been involved or innocent members of the public had been arrested as a result, a specific charge may be appropriate and could be justified (for the specific offence of wasting police time, see para. 1.14.10).

Perverting the course of justice requires positive acts by the defendant, not merely standing by and allowing an injustice to take place. The offence will include cases where evidence is deliberately destroyed, concealed or falsified as well as cases where witnesses and jurors are intimidated (see para. 1.14.5).

Admitting to a crime to enable the true offender to avoid prosecution would fall under this offence (*R v Devito* [1975] Crim LR 175), as would abusing your authority as a police officer to excuse someone of a criminal charge (*R v Coxhead* [1986] RTR 411). Other examples include:

- making a false allegation of an offence (*R v Goodwin* (1989) 11 Cr App R (S) 194 (rape));
- giving another person's personal details when being reported for an offence (*R v Hurst* (1990) 12 Cr App R (S) 373);
- destroying and concealing evidence of a crime (*R v Kiffin* [1994] Crim LR 449).

It is important that the requisite intention is proved in every case as that intention cannot be implied, even from admitted facts (*R v Lalani* [1999] 1 Cr App R 481).

Where a person makes a false allegation to the police justifying a criminal investigation with the possible consequences of detention, arrest, charge or prosecution and that person intends that the allegation be taken seriously, the offence of perverting the course of justice is prima facie made out—whether or not the allegation is capable of identifying specific individuals. This is clear from *R v Cotter* [2002] 2 Cr App R 29, a case involving the boyfriend of a well-known black Olympic athlete who claimed to have been attacked as part of a racist campaign.

1.14.5 Considerations Affecting Witnesses, Jurors and Others

Great care is needed by police officers in handling witnesses. Any behaviour that is seen as interfering with witnesses (or potential witnesses) by promises of favours and rewards or by threats will be a contempt of court (see *R v Kellett* [1975] 3 All ER 468). However, there is no 'property' in a witness. Protecting witnesses is one thing but trying to restrict the way in which defendants and/or their legal advisers obtain evidence for their defence—e.g. by properly approaching witnesses—can also amount to a contempt of court (see *Connolly v Dale* [1996] 1 All ER 224).

So far as the police are concerned there are several significant areas of common and statute law to consider when considering witnesses. First there is the situation where the witness is also a victim of crime. The detail of relevant schemes in place to protect victims of crime and give effect to their wishes is beyond the scope of this Manual, but the code of practice (issued under s. 33(7) of the Domestic Violence, Crime and Victims Act 2004) for victims should be consulted when dealing with victims of criminal conduct. Then there is the legislative framework involved where it is felt that the witness (who may be a police officer or other person engaged in policing) requires some specific form of protection. Again, the full detail of witness protection arrangements are beyond the scope of this Manual. However the main legislative provisions are set out below.

The Serious Organised Crime and Police Act 2005 sets out specific provisions relating to witness protection arrangements. In fact these arrangements stretch beyond witnesses and extend to a series of people involved in the criminal justice process, including people who are *or have been*:

- constables
- employees accredited under the Police Reform Act 2002
- jurors
- magistrates (or their equivalent outside the United Kingdom)
- holders of judicial office (whether in the United Kingdom or elsewhere)
- the DPP, criminal prosecutors and staff of the Crown Prosecution Service

(see the Serious Organised Crime and Police Act 2005, sch. 5).

Chapter 4 of the Act allows for the making of arrangements to protect these and other relevant people ordinarily resident in the United Kingdom where the 'protection provider' (usually the Chief Officer of Police or the Director General of the Serious Organised Crime Agency) considers that the person's safety is at risk by virtue of their being a witness, constable, juror etc. (s. 82(1)). A protection provider may vary or cancel any arrangements made by him/her under subs. (1) if he/she considers it appropriate to do so. Joint arrangements (e.g. between police forces) can be made where appropriate, and public authorities (other than courts and tribunals or parliament) are under a duty to take reasonable steps to assist protection providers where requested to do so (see ss. 83 and 85).

OFFENCE: **Disclosing Information about Protection Arrangements—*Serious Organised Crime and Police Act 2005, s. 86***
- Triable either way • Two years' imprisonment and/or fine on indictment
- 12 months' imprisonment and/or fine summarily

The Serious Organised Crime and Police Act 2005, s. 86 states:

(1) A person commits an offence if—
   (a) he discloses information which relates to the making of arrangements under section 82(1) or to the implementation, variation or cancellation of such arrangements, and
   (b) he knows or suspects that the information relates to the making of such arrangements or to their implementation, variation or cancellation.

KEYNOTE

The above offence requires proof of both elements, namely that the defendant disclosed information which did in fact relate to the protection arrangements (or their implementation, variation or cancellation) *and* that he/she knew or suspected it related to those arrangements.

The Act contains a whole series of defences to the above offence. In summary, there is a defence where:

- the person disclosed the information for the purposes of safeguarding national security or for the purposes of the prevention, detection or investigation of crime;
- a protection provider (or person involved in the making of arrangements under s. 82(1) or their implementation, variation or cancellation) makes the disclosure for the purposes of making, implementing, varying or cancelling such arrangements;
- the person was or had been a 'protected person' (i.e. arrangements had been made for their protection under s. 82(1) and had not been cancelled), the information related only to arrangements made for

his/her protection or for the protection of a person associated with him/her and at the time it was not likely that the disclosure would endanger the safety of *any* person;
- as above but, although it was not the protected person who made the disclosure, the information was disclosed the information with his/her agreement. (see s. 87).

Where the person has been given a new identity as part of their protection arrangements there is a separate offence (see below).

OFFENCE: **Disclosing Information Relating to People Assuming New Identity—*Serious Organised Crime and Police Act 2005, s. 88***
- Triable either way • Two years' imprisonment and/or fine on indictment
- 12 months' imprisonment and/or fine summarily

The Serious Organised Crime and Police Act 2005, s. 88 states:

(1) A person (P) commits an offence if—
  (a) P is or has been a protected person,
  (b) P assumed a new identity in pursuance of arrangements made under section 82(1),
  (c) P discloses information which indicates that he assumed, or might have assumed, a new identity, and
  (d) P knows or suspects that the information disclosed by him indicates that he assumed, or might have assumed, a new identity.
(2) A person (D) commits an offence if—
  (a) D discloses information which relates to a person (P) who is or has been a protected person,
  (b) P assumed a new identity in pursuance of arrangements made under section 82(1),
  (c) the information disclosed by D indicates that P assumed, or might have assumed, a new identity, and
  (d) D knows or suspects—
    (i) that P is or has been a protected person, and
    (ii) that the information disclosed by D indicates that P assumed, or might have assumed, a new identity.

KEYNOTE

The first offence is committed by the protected person themselves; the second is where someone else makes the disclosure.

As with the more general offence under s. 86 you need to show that the disclosure was in fact made and that the defendant had the relevant knowledge or suspicion.

The new identity adopted by the protected person must have been in pursuance of arrangements made under s. 82(1). Therefore if a witness simply takes it on themselves to assume a new name without any involvement by the protection provider, the above offences will not apply. Similarly, this offence will not generally apply where the identity is one that has been adopted by an undercover officer in the course of his/her duties.

Again there are several defences to the above. In summary these are:

- if, at the time when the *protected person* disclosed the information, it was not likely that its disclosure would endanger the safety of *any* person;
- where another person disclosed the information for the purposes of safeguarding national security or for the purposes of the prevention, detection or investigation of crime;

- where a protection provider (or person involved in the making of arrangements under s. 82(1) or their implementation, variation or cancellation) made the disclosure for the purposes of making, implementing, varying or cancelling such arrangements;
- where another person disclosed the information with the agreement of the protected person and at the time it was not likely that its disclosure would endanger the safety of *any* person.

The Act goes on to make provisions for transitional arrangements, issues relating to liability and circumstances where the person in need of protection cannot understand the arrangements being made on their behalf.

Even without the special arrangements referred to above, witnesses are in a special category of people, separate and apart from ordinary members of the public. As a result, a witness is entitled to look to the state for a reasonable level of protection from risks that the police know about. Failure to take appropriate and proportionate measures to protect witnesses from such risks can render the police liable to civil actions for breach of their obligations under Article 2 of the European Convention on Human Rights (see **General Police Duties, chapter 4.3**)— *Van Colle (Administrator of the Estate of Giles Van Colle, Deceased)* v *Chief Constable of Hertfordshire* [2006] EWHC 360.

There are several statutory measures designed to protect witnesses, jurors and others involved in the judicial process. These can be separated into measures aimed at protecting those involved in *criminal* trials and/or investigations and offences aimed at protecting those involved in other proceedings.

1.14.5.1 Witnesses or Jurors in Investigation or Proceedings for an Offence

The first measure can be found in the Criminal Justice and Public Order Act 1994.

OFFENCE: **Intimidating Witnesses and Jurors—*Criminal Justice and Public Order Act 1994, s. 51***

- Triable either way • Five years' imprisonment and/or a fine on indictment
- Six months' imprisonment and/or a fine summarily

The Criminal Justice and Public Order Act 1994, s. 51 states:

(1) A person commits an offence if—
    (a) he does an act which intimidates, and is intended to intimidate, another person ('the victim'),
    (b) he does the act knowing or believing that the victim is assisting in the investigation of an offence or is a witness or potential witness or a juror or potential juror in proceedings for an offence, and
    (c) he does it intending thereby to cause the investigation or the course of justice to be obstructed, perverted or interfered with.
(2) A person commits an offence if—
    (a) he does an act which harms, and is intended to harm, another person or, intending to cause another person to fear harm, he threatens to do an act which would harm that other person,
    (b) he does or threatens to do the act knowing or believing that the person harmed or threatened to be harmed ('the victim'), or some other person, has assisted in an investigation into an offence or has given evidence or particular evidence in proceedings for an offence, or has acted as a juror or concurred in a particular verdict in proceedings for an offence, and
    (c) he does or threatens to do it because of that knowledge or belief.
(3) For the purposes of subsections (1) and (2) it is immaterial that the act is or would be done, or that the threat is made—

  (a) otherwise than in the presence of the victim, or
  (b) to a person other than the victim.
(4) The harm that may be done or threatened may be financial as well as physical (whether to the person or a person's property) and similarly as respects an intimidatory act which consists of threats.
(5) The intention required by subsection (1)(c) and the motive required by subsection (2)(c) above need not be the only or the predominating intention or motive with which the act is done or, in the case of subsection (2), threatened.

KEYNOTE

As discussed above, this section is aimed at protecting people involved in the investigation or trial of criminal offences.

These offences are designed to exist alongside the common-law offence of perverting the course of justice (see para. 1.14.4) and there will be circumstances which may fall under both the statutory and the common-law offences. Such behaviour may also be punishable as a contempt of court, see *Blackstone's Criminal Practice*, 2008, section B14.69 and para. 1.14.11 below.

This is an offence of 'specific intent' (see chapter 1.1) or perhaps even multiple intent as it must be shown that the act was done with the intentions set out in s. 51(1)(a) and (c). It must also be shown that the defendant knew or believed the other person to be assisting in the investigation of an offence or that he/she was going to testify/appear on the jury in proceedings for an offence.

For 'knowing or believing' in this context the prosecution must present evidence that an investigation was in fact being carried out at the time of the alleged offence (*R v Singh* [2000] 1 Cr App R 31). In a decision that appears to contradict the specific wording of the statute, the Court of Appeal has confirmed that 'an act which intimidates' does not have to result in the victim *actually* being intimidated. In *R v Patrascu* [2004] 4 All ER 1066 the Court held that a person did an act which intimidated another, within the meaning of s. 51(1) if he/she put that other person in fear, or sought by threat or violence to deter him or her from some relevant action such as giving evidence. However mere pressure which did not put the victim in fear or contained no element of threat or violence was insufficient. Therefore, if a defendant seeks to deter the victim from giving evidence, the offence could be made out even if the victim was not in fear. While slightly odd in the light of the words of the Act above, this reasoning is in line with the law relating to assault (as to which see para. 1.7.2.2).

'Harm' for the purposes of s. 51(2) means physical harm and not simply an assault or battery. Therefore spitting at a person does not amount to 'harm' for these purposes (even though it would amount to other public order or assault offences) (*R v Normanton* [1998] Crim LR 220).

Section 51(2) provides a similar offence for acts done or threatened in the knowledge or belief that the person, *or another person*, has so assisted or taken part in proceedings. Doing acts to third parties in order to intimidate or harm the relevant person is also covered by this offence (s. 51(3)). Making threats by telephone will amount to 'doing an act to another' (*DPP v Mills* [1997] QB 300).

Section 51(8) creates a statutory presumption under certain circumstances that the defendant had the required motive at the time of his/her actions or threats.

Making a *threat* via a third person knowing it will be passed on and that the ultimate recipient would be intimidated by it amounts to an offence under s. 51(1) (*Attorney-General's Reference (No. 1 of 1999)* [1999] 3 WLR 769).

The intention to obstruct, pervert or interfere with the course of justice need not be the only or even the main intention (s. 51(5)).

1.14.5.2 Intimidation of Witnesses in Other Proceedings

In addition to the measures aimed at protecting those involved in the investigation and trial of criminal offences, there are further statutory measures designed to protect witnesses and others who are (or may become) involved in other proceedings. Guidance on the practical application of these measures can be found in Home Office Circular 12/2001.

OFFENCE: **Intimidation of Witnesses—*Criminal Justice and Police Act 2001, s. 39***

- Triable either way • Five years' imprisonment on indictment • Six months' imprisonment and/or fine summarily

The Criminal Justice and Police Act 2001, s. 39 states:

(1) A person commits an offence if—
   (a) he does an act which intimidates, and is intended to intimidate, another person ('the victim');
   (b) he does the act—
      (i) knowing or believing that the victim is or may be a witness in any relevant proceedings; and
      (ii) intending, by his act, to cause the course of justice to be obstructed, perverted or interfered with;
      and
   (c) the act is done after the commencement of those proceedings.

KEYNOTE

This offence has some similarities to the Criminal Justice and Public Order Act 1994 offence in the earlier paragraph. References to doing an act include threats—against a person and/or their property—and the making of any other statement (s. 39(6)). The key difference is that this offence is concerned with protecting people who are in some way connected with 'relevant proceedings' which are '*any proceedings in or before the Court of Appeal, the High Court, the Crown Court or any county or magistrates' court which are not proceedings for an offence*' (s. 41(1)). This means that the offence will be relevant if the proceedings involved are civil proceedings in the higher courts or the county court or if they are non-offence proceedings in the Crown Court or magistrates' court. Examples of the latter would be a hearing to deal with a breach of a community order or an application for an anti-social behaviour order (as to which, **see General Police Duties, chapter 4.5**). You must show that the relevant proceedings had already commenced by the time of the offence.

Note that some proceedings, such as inquests or police conduct hearings, will not be covered by the s. 41 definition and therefore the offences above.

As with the Criminal Justice and Public Order Act offence, this requires proof of 'multiple' intent in that, as well as showing the intimidatory act, it must also be shown that the elements set out at s. 39(1)(a)–(c) are present. However, if you can prove that the defendant:

- did any act that intimidated, and was intended to intimidate, another person, and
- that he/she did that act knowing or believing that that other person was or might be a 'witness' in any relevant proceedings that had already commenced,

there will be a presumption that the defendant did the act with the intention of causing the course of justice to be obstructed, perverted or interfered with (s. 39(3)). This presumption is, however, rebuttable (as to which, **see Evidence and Procedure, chapter 2.7**). 'Witness' here is a very wide expression and extends to anyone who provides, or is able to provide, any information, document or other thing which might be used in evidence in those proceedings (see s. 39(5)).

In proving the offence it is immaterial whether the act:

- is done in the presence of the victim
- is done to the victim himself/herself or to another person

or whether or not the intention to obstruct, pervert or interfere with the course of justice is the main intention of the person doing it (s. 39(2)).

This offence is intended to exist alongside the common law offence of perverting the course of justice (as to which, **see para. 1.14.4**) and came into force on 1 August 2001.

For the specific measures involving witness protection programmes **see para. 1.14.5.**

1.14.6 **Harming Witnesses**

OFFENCE: **Harming Witnesses—*Criminal Justice and Police Act 2001, s. 40***
- Triable either way • Five years' imprisonment on indictment • Six months' imprisonment and/or fine summarily

The Criminal Justice and Police Act 2001, s. 40 states:

(1) A person commits an offence if in circumstances falling within subsection (2)—
    (a) he does an act which harms, and is intended to harm, another person; or
    (b) intending to cause another person to fear harm, he threatens to do an act which would harm that other person.
(2) The circumstances fall within this subsection if—
    (a) the person doing or threatening to do the act does so knowing or believing that some person (whether or not the person harmed or threatened or the person against whom harm is threatened) has been a witness in relevant proceedings; and
    (b) he does or threatens to do that act because of that knowledge or belief.

KEYNOTE

A distinction between this and the s. 39 offence is that the offence above refers to someone who *has been* (or is believed to have been) a witness in relevant proceedings. Again, 'witness' is very wide and extends to anyone who has provided any information, document, etc. which was (or might have been) used in evidence in those proceedings (see s. 40(7)). For 'relevant proceedings' see the s. 39 offence. This offence is aimed is the general protection of people who have been involved in relevant proceedings. Therefore there is no requirement here for any intention to pervert or interfere with the course of justice. The harm caused or threatened does not have to be directed towards the witness themselves; the key element is the motivation of the defendant. In relation to that motivation, the Act creates a presumption as follows. If you can prove that, between the start of the proceedings and one year after they are concluded, the defendant:

- did an act which harmed, and was intended to harm, another person, or
- threatened to do an act which would harm another person intending to cause that person to fear harm

with the knowledge or belief required by s. 40(2)(a) above, he/she will be presumed to have acted because of that knowledge or belief (s. 40(3)). Again, this is rebuttable (**see Evidence and Procedure, chapter 2.7**). It is immaterial whether the act or threat is made (or would be carried out) in the presence of the person who is or would be harmed, or of the person threatened or whether the motive mentioned in

s. 40(2)(b) is the main motive. The harm done or threatened can be physical or financial and can be made to a person or property (s. 40(4)). This offence came into force on 1 August 2001.

For the specific measures involving witness protection programmes see para. 1.14.5.

1.14.7 Assisting Offenders

OFFENCE: **Assisting Offenders—*Criminal Law Act 1967, s. 4***

• Triable on indictment; either way if original offence is either way • Where sentence for original offence is fixed by law (ten years' imprisonment and/or a fine on indictment; six months' imprisonment and/or a fine summarily) • Where sentence for original offence is 14 years (seven years' imprisonment and/or a fine on indictment; six months' imprisonment and/or a fine summarily) • Where sentence for original offence is ten years (five years' imprisonment and/or a fine on indictment; six months' imprisonment and/or a fine summarily) • Otherwise (three years' imprisonment and/or a fine on indictment; six months' imprisonment and/or a fine summarily)

The Criminal Law Act 1967, s. 4 states:

(1) Where a person has committed a relevant offence, any other person who, knowing or believing him to be guilty of the offence or of some other relevant offence, does without lawful authority or reasonable excuse any act with intent to impede his apprehension or prosecution shall be guilty of an offence.

(1A) In this section and section 5 below, 'relevant offence' means—

(a) an offence for which the sentence is fixed by law,

(b) an offence for which a person of 18 years or over (not previously convicted) may be sentenced to imprisonment for a term of five years (or might be so sentenced but for the restrictions imposed by section 33 of the Magistrates' Courts Act 1980).

KEYNOTE

This offence must involve some positive act by the defendant; simply doing or saying nothing will not suffice.

Although there is no duty on people to assist the police in their investigations generally (though, see chapter 1.7), this offence and the one below create a negative duty not to interfere with investigations after an offence has taken place.

For there to be an offence under s. 4 or 5 (para. 1.14.8) there must first have been a relevant offence committed by someone. That relevant offence must, in the case of the above offence, have been committed by the 'assisted' person.

The defendant can commit the offence before the person he/she has assisted is convicted of committing the relevant offence.

It must be shown that the defendant knew or believed the person to be guilty of that, *or some other* relevant offence. Therefore, if the defendant believed that the 'assisted' person had committed a robbery when in fact he/she had committed a theft, that mistaken part of the defendant's belief will not prevent a conviction for this offence.

By analogy with the requirements for handling stolen goods (see chapter 1.11) mere *suspicion*, however strong, that the 'assisted' person had committed a relevant offence will not be enough.

This offence requires the consent of the Director of Public Prosecutions before a prosecution is brought (s. 4(4)).

This offence cannot be 'attempted' (Criminal Attempts Act 1981, s. 1(4)).

1.14.8 Concealing Relevant Offences

OFFENCE: **Concealing Relevant Offences—*Criminal Law Act 1967, s. 5***
- Triable on indictment; either way if original offence is triable either way
- Two years' imprisonment on indictment • Six months' imprisonment and/or a fine summarily

The Criminal Law Act 1967, s. 5 states:

(1) Where a person has committed a relevant offence, any other person who, knowing or believing that the offence or some other relevant offence has been committed, and that he has inform- ation which might be of material assistance in securing the prosecution or conviction of an offender for it, accepts or agrees to accept for not disclosing that information any consider- ation other than the making good of loss or injury caused by the offence, or the making of reasonable compensation for that loss or injury, shall be liable. . .

KEYNOTE

This offence also requires the consent of the Director of Public Prosecutions before a prosecution can be brought (s. 5(3)).

It is also excluded from the provisions of the Criminal Attempts Act 1981 (s. 1(4)).

Again, someone must have committed a relevant offence before this particular offence can be committed. The main focus of this offence is:

- the acceptance of, or agreement to accept 'consideration' (i.e. anything of value)
- beyond reasonable compensation for loss/injury *caused by the relevant offence*
- in exchange for not disclosing material information.

'Disclosure' does not appear to be confined to information passed to the police. It would probably extend to other agencies with a duty to investigate offences but is perhaps even wider than that.

This offence requires proof, not only of the defendant's knowledge or belief that a relevant offence had been committed, but also that he/she has information that might be of material assistance in securing the *prosecution or conviction* of *an offender* for it. Given this very broad wording, the possession of information that might provide useful intelligence in an investigation into relevant offences may meet the requirements of s. 5, although *proving* that the defendant had the required knowledge or belief presents considerable practical problems.

1.14.9 Miscellaneous Offences Relating to Offenders

OFFENCE: **Escaping—*Common Law***
- Triable on indictment • Unlimited punishment

It is an offence at common law to escape from legal custody.

KEYNOTE

The 'custody' from which a person escapes must be shown to have been lawful. The offence applies to both police custody (or police detention—see the Police and Criminal Evidence Act 1984, s. 118) or custody following conviction.

Whether a person was 'in custody' is a question of fact and the word 'custody' is to be given its ordinary and natural meaning—*E* v *DPP* [2002] Crim LR 737. (See also *Richards* v *DPP* [1988] QB 701.) In proving that a person was in custody at a particular time it should be shown that their liberty was restricted in a way that meant that he/she was confined by another and that their freedom of movement was controlled; it is not necessary, however, to show that the person's actual ability to move around was physically impeded, e.g. in secure accommodation (*E* v *DPP* above).

People may be in lawful custody even if not directly in the custody of a sworn police officer, for example those people who are being dealt with by investigating officer or escort officers under sch. 4 to the Police Reform Act 2002 (as to which, **see General Police Duties, chapter 4.2**).

People detained under the Mental Health Act 1983, s. 36, are also in lawful custody (**see chapter 1.9**).

If a defendant uses force to *break out* of a prison or a police station, he/she may commit an offence of prison breach, again at common law and attracting the same punishment and mode of trial as escaping.

Under the Prisoners (Return to Custody) Act 1995, s. 1, a person who has been temporarily released under the Prison Act 1952 commits a summary offence if he/she remains unlawfully at large or fails to respond to an order of recall to prison.

Escort officers designated under sch. 4 to the Police Reform Act 2002 have a duty to prevent the escape of people in their charge who they are escorting in accordance with their statutory powers (see the Police Reform Act 2002, sch. 4, part 4, para. 35). For a general discussion of the powers and roles of escort officers and other designated staff under the Police Reform Act 2002, **see General Police Duties, chapter 4.2**.

OFFENCE: **Assisting Escape—*Prison Act 1952, s. 39***
- Triable on indictment • Ten years' imprisonment

The Prison Act 1952, s. 39 states:

Any person who aids any prisoner in escaping or attempting to escape from a prison or who, with intent to facilitate the escape of any prisoner, sends anything (by post or otherwise) into a prison or to a prisoner or places any thing anywhere outside a prison with a view to its coming into the possession of a prisoner, shall be guilty of [an offence].

OFFENCE: **Harbouring Offenders—*Criminal Justice Act 1961, s. 22(2)***
- Triable either way • Ten years' imprisonment and/or a fine on indictment
- Six months' imprisonment and/or a fine summarily

The Criminal Justice Act 1961, s. 22 states:

(2) If any person knowingly harbours a person who has escaped from a prison or other institution to which the said section thirty-nine applies, or who, having been sentenced in any part of the United Kingdom or in any of the Channel Islands or the Isle of Man to imprisonment or detention, is otherwise unlawfully at large, or gives to any such person any assistance with intent to prevent, hinder or interfere with his being taken into custody, he shall be liable...

KEYNOTE

The offences under s. 39 of the 1952 Act and s. 22 of the 1961 Act do not apply to a prisoner who escapes while in transit to or from prison (*R* v *Moss and Harte* (1986) 82 Cr App R 116).

> There is a particular offence, punishable by two years' imprisonment, of inducing or assisting a patient detained in a mental hospital to escape or to absent themselves without leave (Mental Health Act 1983, s. 128).
>
> It also appears that there is a common law offence of forcibly rescuing another from lawful custody (see *Blackstone's Criminal Practice*, 2008, section B14.67).

1.14.10 Wasting Police Time

OFFENCE: **Wasting Police Time—*Criminal Law Act 1967, s. 5(2)***
> • Triable summarily • Six months' imprisonment and/or a fine

The Criminal Law Act 1967, s. 5 states:

> (2) Where a person causes any wasteful employment of the police by knowingly making to any person a false report tending to show that an offence has been committed, or to give rise to apprehension for the safety of any persons or property, or tending to show that he has information material to any police inquiry, he shall be liable...

KEYNOTE

It is widely thought that there is a minimum number of hours which must be wasted before a prosecution can be brought for this offence. There is no reliable authority on this point. Consideration should also be given to the offence of perverting the course of justice (**see para. 1.14.4**). This offence is a 'penalty offence' for the purposes of s. 1 of the Criminal Justice and Police Act 2001 (**see General Police Duties, chapter 4.4**).

It is unclear whether this offence will extend to any wasted activities of non-sworn police personnel such as those designated under the Police Reform Act 2002 (as to which, **see General Police Duties, chapter 4.2**).

1.14.11 Contempt of Court

Acts which amount to contempt of court can be divided into criminal and civil contempt. Criminal contempt is defined at common law as 'behaviour involving interference with the due administration of justice' (*Attorney-General* v *Newspaper Publishing plc* [1988] Ch 333 and see *Blackstone's Criminal Practice*, 2008, section B14.69).

Contempt can be committed in many different ways including misbehaviour in court, publication of matters prejudicial to a trial and taking photographs inside a court building. For a full explanation of the subject together with the extensive powers of courts to deal with contempt, see *Blackstone's Criminal Practice*, 2008, section B14.69 *et seq.*

1.14.12 Corruption

Corruption offences, like conspiracies (**see chapter 1.3**), can be divided into common law and statutory offences.

1.14.12.1 Common Law Offences

OFFENCE: **Corruption—*Common Law***

- Triable on indictment • Unlimited punishment

'[A person] accepting an office of trust concerning the public is answerable criminally to [the Crown] for misbehaviour in his office' (*R* v *Bembridge* (1783) 3 Doug 327 and see *Blackstone's Criminal Practice*, 2008, section B15.1).

KEYNOTE

As well as a public official accepting a bribe (which would amount to 'misbehaviour'), it is also a similar offence at common law to *bribe* such an office-holder.

In addition to these offences, there are two overlapping statutory offences of corruption (see below).

In relation to any offence of bribery at common law, such an offence can be committed and prosecuted in England and Wales even if the person involved is a UK national (or company) but carries out any relevant act in another country. Additionally, it does not matter whether the functions of the person receiving or being offered a reward have no connection with the United Kingdom and are carried out in another country. These provisions were added by the Anti-terrorism, Crime and Security Act 2001 after the events of 11 September 2001.

1.14.12.2 Statutory Offences

OFFENCE: **Corruption—*Public Bodies Corrupt Practices Act 1889, s. 1***

- Triable either way • Seven years' imprisonment and/or a fine on indictment
- Six months' imprisonment and/or a fine summarily

The Public Bodies Corrupt Practices Act 1889, s. 1 states:

(1) Every person who shall by himself or by or in conjunction with any other person, corruptly solicit or receive, or agree to receive, for himself, or for any other person, any gift, loan, fee, reward, or advantage whatever as an inducement to, or reward for, or otherwise on account of any member, officer, or servant of a public body as in this Act defined, doing or forbearing to do anything in respect of any matter or transaction whatsoever, actual or proposed, in which the said public body is concerned, shall be guilty of [an offence]

(2) Every person who shall by himself or by or in conjunction with any other person corruptly give, promise, or offer any gift, loan, fee, reward, or advantage whatsoever to any person, whether for the benefit of that person or of another person, as an inducement to or reward for or otherwise on account of any member, officer, or servant of any public body as in this Act defined, doing or forbearing to do anything in respect of any matter or transaction whatsoever, actual or proposed, in which such public body as aforesaid is concerned, shall be guilty of [an offence].

KEYNOTE

The consent of the Attorney-General (or Solicitor-General) is required before bringing a prosecution for this offence.

The definition of a public body (to be found in s. 7) does not include a government department or the Crown (*R* v *Natji* (*Naci Vedat*) [2002] 1 WLR 2337).

The meaning of the word 'corruptly' is circular in that it has been usefully held to be 'doing an act which the law forbids as tending to corrupt'! (See *R* v *Wellburn* (1979) 69 Cr App R 254.) The offence of corruption under s. 1(1) is concerned with the 'instigation of a corrupt bargain'. This was reaffirmed by

---

the Court of Appeal in *R* v *Harrington* (2000) LTL 29 September. That case involved the defendant asking for money from someone who was being investigated for 'fixing' a horse race. The defendant claimed that he could make the case 'go away' but said that he would need money in order to bribe the police officer conducting the investigation. The defendant never met the officer in question, nor did he ever communicate with him. The person whom the defendant asked for the money was acting as an informant and there was never any intention that the police officer investigating the case was going to be 'bribed' into dropping it. The Court held that it was not necessary to prove an intention by the defendant that the corrupt transaction would actually involve a public official or an employee of a public body in order to establish the state of mind required by the offence. Consequently, the defendant's conviction was upheld. (For some general issues arising out of covert police operations, **see para. 1.3.6.**)

Giving improper gifts, payments or favours to officers or servants of a public body would usually amount to corruption.

In relation to the offence of corruption in a public office, this offence can also be committed and prosecuted in England and Wales even if the person involved is a UK national (or company) but carries out any relevant act in another country. A public body here will include any equivalent body or local authority which exists in a country outside the United Kingdom (see the Anti-terrorism, Crime and Security Act 2001, ss. 108 and 109).

As with the common law, both the giving and the receiving of the gift can amount to this offence. It will not be a defence for either the giver or the recipient to show that the latter was not in fact influenced by it (*R* v *Parker* (1986) 82 Cr App R 69). There are circumstances where there will be a rebuttable presumption (**see Evidence and Procedure, chapter 2.7**) that any gift etc. was given or received corruptly (see below).

OFFENCE: **Corruption of Agents—*Prevention of Corruption Act 1906, s. 1***
- Triable either way • Seven years' imprisonment and/or a fine on indictment
- Six months' imprisonment and/or a fine summarily

The Prevention of Corruption Act 1906, s. 1 states:

(1) If any agent corruptly accepts or obtains, or agrees to accept or attempts to obtain, from any person, for himself or for any other person, any gift or consideration as an inducement or reward for doing or forbearing to do, or having after the passing of this Act done or forborne to do, any act in relation to his principal's affairs or business, or for showing or forbearing to show favour or disfavour to any person in relation to his principal's affairs or business; or

If any person corruptly gives or agrees to give or offers any gift or consideration to any agent as an inducement or reward for doing or forbearing to do, or for having after the passing of this Act done or forborne to do, any act in relation to his principal's affairs or business, or for showing or forbearing to show favour or disfavour to any person in relation to his principal's affairs or business; or

If any person knowingly gives to any agent, or if any agent knowingly uses with intent to deceive his principal, any receipt, account, or other document in respect of which the principal is interested, and which contains any statement which is false or erroneous or defective in any material particular, and which to his knowledge is intended to mislead the principal;

he shall be guilty of [an offence]...

(2) For the purposes of this Act the expression 'consideration' includes valuable consideration of any kind; the expression 'agent' includes any person employed by or acting for another; and the expression 'principal' includes an employer.

(3) A person serving under the Crown or under any corporation or any borough, county, or district council, or any board of guardians, is an agent within the meaning of this Act.

KEYNOTE

The consent of the Attorney-General or the Solicitor-General is required before a prosecution can be brought under s. 1. There is an overlap between this offence and the offence under s. 1 of the 1889 Act. However, 'agent' does not include persons such as local counsellors who would fall under the Public Bodies Corrupt Practices Act 1889. Examples of the corruption of agents range from the securing of Ministry of Defence contracts in return for personal payments of £2 million (*R* v *Foxley* (1995) 16 Cr App R (S) 879) to the attempted bribery of police officers with free meals in a restaurant (*R* v *Ozdemir* (1985) 7 Cr App R (S) 382).

In relation to the offences of bribes being given to or obtained by agents under s. 1(1) above, those offences can still be committed and prosecuted in England and Wales if the person involved is a UK national (or company) but carries out any relevant act in another country. Additionally, it does not matter whether the principal's affairs or business, or the agent's functions have no connection with the United Kingdom and are carried out in another country. These provisions were added by the Anti-terrorism, Crime and Security Act 2001, s. 108(2) after the events of 11 September 2001.

1.15 | Offences Arising from Immigration, Asylum and People Exploitation

1.15.1 Introduction

Immigration, asylum and the criminal exploitation of people has become an increasingly significant area of criminal activity in England and Wales. As a result, the government's legislative programme has made important amendments to the law governing this area of policing, including the introduction of a number of serious criminal offences. The key aspects of the recent legislation and the longer-standing provisions are the subject of this chapter.

1.15.2 Illegal Entry to the United Kingdom

One of the most controversial and pressing policing issues at the start of the 21st century arose from the enormous increase in illegal entry to the United Kingdom. Whatever the reason behind this increase, the law regulating immigration is substantial, extending far beyond the scope of this Manual. That legislation was itself reinforced by a raft of additional measures contained in the Immigration and Asylum Act 1999 designed to address the issues arising from asylum seekers and also from those criminals who specialise in smuggling illegal entrants into the country. Then came 11 September 2001, prompting swift and significant changes to legislation in a number of jurisdictions throughout the world. As well as bringing changes in other areas of law, the Anti-terrorism, Crime and Security Act 2001 made several amendments in relation to immigration and asylum.

1.15.2.1 General Powers Regarding People Entering the United Kingdom

There are general powers to arrest, detain and ultimately deport people under the Immigration Act 1971. Of direct relevance to police officers are the provisions in sch. 2 to the 1971 Act, for the following reasons:

- Immigration officers are given very wide powers in respect of people entering the United Kingdom. This includes powers to issue directions in relation to people embarking from aircraft, ships and vessels and to detain those people while considering whether or not to issue such directions.
- Many of these powers come from sch. 2, para. 16.
- A person liable to be detained under sch. 2, para. 16, may be arrested without warrant by an immigration officer (sch. 2, para. 17).

- These general powers also apply to suspected international terrorists (Anti-terrorism, Crime and Security Act 2001, s. 23).

Note that immigration officers also have the power to require operators of aircraft and ships entering or leaving the United Kingdom to provide passenger lists, and a copy of all or part of a document relating to a passenger which contains passenger information, either in relation to a particular journey or generally over a specified time period (see sch. 2, para. 27B to the 1971 Act).

1.15.2.2 Nationality, Immigration and Asylum

The areas of nationality, immigration and asylum have become of increased importance to everyday policing. The activities of 'people smugglers' in the United Kingdom have attracted considerable international attention and the issues arising from this whole subject area are now among the most sensitive and time-consuming of modern policing topics.

While most of the relevant legislation is still contained in the Immigration Act 1971 as described above, that Act has been amended in relation to offences and powers, while the whole framework for nationality and asylum was created by the Nationality, Immigration and Asylum Act 2002.

The Act is split into seven parts, each addressing a different aspect of this vast subject. In summary, the provisions for establishing citizenship, naturalisation and nationality can be found in Part 1, while Part 2 contains the measures for establishing and maintaining 'accommodation centres'. Parts 3 and 4 deal with support for asylum seekers and the measures available to the government to control entry to the United Kingdom—including powers to detain and remove asylum seekers. Parts 5 and 6 provide for the immigration and asylum application and appeals procedures. The more important aspects of the Act for the police can be found in Part 7 which sets out a number of offences, the key aspects of which are set out in the remainder of this chapter. Note however that the offences to people trafficking for sexual purposes are now contained in the Sexual Offences Act 2003 (**see chapter 1.9**). The 2002 Act has been reinforced and extended by the Asylum and Immigration (Treatment of Claimants etc.) Act 2004 which was designed to streamline the immigration and asylum appeals system, deal with undocumented arrivals in the United Kingdom and enhance the powers of the Office of the Immigration Services Commissioner. In addition to making further provision for the practicalities of managing asylum applications and increasing the powers available to immigration officers, the Act creates a number of significant criminal offences, some of which are addressed throughout this chapter.

Specialist advice is available from the Home Office in all areas involving immigration and asylum. However, there are several key offences—and accompanying powers—that are immediately relevant to police officers who may find themselves dealing with incidents involving people suspected of having entered the United Kingdom unlawfully or of having assisted others to do so.

In addition, the Home Office has published a Circular (HOC 70/2004) reminding police officers of the availability of deportation orders which are available on the recommendation of a court (see s. 3(6) of the Immigration Act 1971). Before a court can make such a recommendation the person to be deported must have been served with a warning notice at least seven days before sentence is imposed. Responsibility for service of such notices will usually fall to the police, and the Home Office Immigration and Nationality Directorate advises that such a notice should normally be served where a person who appears to be eligible for deportation is charged with an offence punishable by imprisonment.

1.15.2.3   Illegal Entry

OFFENCE: **Illegal Entry—*Immigration Act 1971, s. 24***

> • Triable summarily • Six months' imprisonment and/or fine

The Immigration Act 1971, s. 24 states:

> (1) A person who is not a British citizen shall be guilty of an offence...in any of the following cases—
>   (a)   if contrary to this Act he knowingly enters the United Kingdom in breach of a deportation order or without leave;
>   (aa) ...
>   (b)   if, having only a limited leave to enter or remain in the United Kingdom, he knowingly either—
>   (i)   remains beyond the time limited by the leave; or
>   (ii) fails to observe a condition of the leave;
>   (c)   if, having lawfully entered the United Kingdom without leave by virtue of section 8(1) above, he remains without leave beyond the time allowed by section 8(1);
>   (d)   if, without reasonable excuse, he fails to comply with any requirement imposed on him under Schedule 2 to this Act to report to a medical officer of health or to attend, or submit to a test or examination, as required by such an officer;
>   (e)   if, without reasonable excuse, he fails to observe any restriction imposed on him under Schedule 2 or 3 to this Act as to residence, as to his employment or occupation or as to reporting to the police or to an immigration officer or to the Secretary of State;
>   (f)   if he disembarks in the United Kingdom from a ship or aircraft after being placed on board under Schedule 2 or 3 to this Act with a view to his removal from the United Kingdom;
>   (g)   if he leaves or seeks to leave the United Kingdom through the tunnel system in contravention of a restriction imposed by or under an Order in Council under section 3(7) of this Act.

1.15.2.4   Use of Deception to Enter or Remain

OFFENCE: **Use of Deception—*Immigration Act 1971, s. 24A***

> • Triable either way • Two years' imprisonment on indictment • Six months' imprisonment and/or a fine summarily

The Immigration Act 1971, s. 24A states:

> A person who is not a British citizen is guilty of an offence if, by means which include deception by him—
>   (a) he obtains or seeks to obtain leave to enter or remain in the United Kingdom; or
>   (b) he secures or seeks to secure the avoidance, postponement or revocation of enforcement action against him.

KEYNOTE

The first offence above (s. 24) is concerned generally with non-British citizens who enter the UK illegally or who 'overstay' having been granted only limited leave to be here; it also addresses occasions where such people disregard some other lawful requirements placed upon them. The reference in s. 24(1)(c) to 'section 8(1)' refers to the special provisions made for seamen, aircrew, etc. landing lawfully in the United Kingdom.

   The second offence (s. 24A) is relatively new and is broadly aimed at the more calculated actions by non-British citizens to get (or try to get) leave to enter or stay in the United Kingdom, or to evade deportation. 'Deception' here would appear to have its ordinary meaning and is not defined within the 1971 Act. It is worth noting that the relevant criminal conduct (*actus reus*: **see chapter 1.2**) by the defendant here can be *any means which include deception by him/her*. Therefore, although the entire course of conduct by the defendant need not amount to a deception, it will be necessary to show that the defendant himself/herself carried out some act of deception (e.g. giving false details, providing misleading information, etc.). It will not be enough for this offence to show that someone else practised a deception in order to bring about the consequences at s. 24A(a) and (b) for another person (but see below for further offence of assisting and harbouring).

1.15.3 People Trafficking and Exploitation

A very specific and increasingly prevalent form of offence involving unlawful immigration is that falling under the general heading of 'people trafficking'. The people seeking immigration in this way are often very vulnerable by reason of their economic, legal or political circumstances and the opportunities for exploiting such vulnerability has created the need for a number of specific offences over and above the more generic immigration offences. For the specific offences relating to the trafficking of people for *sexual* exploitation **see chapter 1.9**.

1.15.3.1 Assisting Unlawful Immigration and Asylum-seekers

OFFENCE: **Assisting Unlawful Immigration to Member State—**
Immigration Act 1971, s. 25

- Triable either way • 14 years' imprisonment on indictment • Six months' imprisonment and/or a fine summarily

The Immigration Act 1971, s. 25 states:

(1) A person commits an offence if he—
  (a) does an act which facilitates the commission of a breach of immigration law by an individual who is not a citizen of the European Union,
  (b) knows or has reasonable cause for believing that the act facilitates the commission of a breach of immigration law by the individual, and
  (c) knows or has reasonable cause for believing that the individual is not a citizen of the European Union.

KEYNOTE

This very broadly worded offence requires that the defendant facilitated the commission of any breach of immigration law by someone who is not an EU citizen. 'Immigration law' means a law in a Member State and which controls, in respect of some or all people who are not nationals of the State, entitlement to enter, travel across or be in the State (s. 25(2)). The above section has been amended to allow the Secretary of State to make an order prescribing additional States which are to be regarded as 'Member States' for the purposes of the section if he/she considers it necessary for the purpose of complying with the United Kingdom's EU obligations (see s. 25(7)). A document issued by the relevant government of a Member State will be conclusive in certifying any matter of law in this regard (s. 25(3)).

You must show that, in doing so, the defendant knew or had reasonable cause for believing that both his/her act facilitated the commission of the breach of immigration law *and* also that the person was not an EU citizen.

This offence can be committed outside the United Kingdom by British citizens and others with relevant forms of British citizenship (see s. 25(5)).

It is worth noting the Court of Appeal's observations that drivers and others involved in these type of offences are often of good previous character—in fact that is one of the criteria by which they are selected by the main organisers so as not to arouse suspicion of the authorities (*R v Salem* (2003) LTL 5 February).

The courts' powers to order forfeiture of vehicles, ships and aircraft under s. 25C apply to this offence (see below).

OFFENCE: **Helping Asylum-seeker to Enter United Kingdom—**
Immigration Act 1971, s. 25A
- Triable either way • 14 years' imprisonment on indictment • Six months' imprisonment and/or a fine summarily

The Immigration Act 1971, s. 25A states:

(1) A person commits an offence if—
  (a) he knowingly and for gain facilitates the arrival in the United Kingdom of an individual, and
  (b) he knows or has reasonable cause to believe that the individual is an asylum-seeker.

KEYNOTE

In order to prove this particular offence you must show that the defendant acted in the knowledge that he/she was facilitating the arrival in the United Kingdom of a person whom he/she knew was (or had reasonable cause to believe to be) an asylum-seeker *and* that, in so doing, that he/she acted 'for gain'.

'Asylum-seeker' means a person who intends to claim that to remove him/her from, or require him/her to leave the United Kingdom would be contrary to the United Kingdom's obligations under the Refugee Convention or the Human Rights Convention (in each case as defined under s. 167(1) of the Immigration and Asylum Act 1999) (s. 25 A(2)).

The above offence does not apply to anything done by a person acting on behalf of an organisation which aims to assist asylum-seekers and *does not charge for its services* (s. 25A(3)).

The courts' powers to order forfeiture of vehicles, ships and aircraft under s. 25C apply to this offence (see below). For the specific provisions setting out the penalties for operators of vehicles (including rail freight wagons), see the Immigration and Asylum Act 1999, s. 32.

OFFENCE: **Assisting Entry to United Kingdom in Breach of Deportation**
Order—Immigration Act 1971, s. 25B
- Triable either way • 14 years' imprisonment on indictment • Six months' imprisonment and/or a fine summarily

The Immigration Act 1971, s. 25B states:

(1) A person commits an offence if he—
  (a) does an act which facilitates a breach of a deportation order in force against an individual who is a citizen of the European Union, and
  (b) knows or has reasonable cause for believing that the act facilitates a breach of the deportation order.
(2) ...
(3) A person commits an offence if he—
  (a) does an act which assists the individual to arrive in, enter or remain in the United Kingdom,
  (b) knows or has reasonable cause for believing that the act assists the individual to arrive in, enter or remain in the United Kingdom, and

(c) knows or has reasonable cause for believing that the Secretary of State has personally directed that the individual's exclusion from the United Kingdom is conducive to the public good.

KEYNOTE

As with the earlier offences under s. 25 and 25A, the state of mind (*mens rea*—see chapter 1.1) here is important to note.

For the first offence, there must be a deportation order in force and this will need to be proved before someone can be convicted. Additionally, the defendant must have known or had reasonable cause for believing that his/her act facilitated a breach of that order (therefore he/she must have known/had reasonable cause to believe that there was such an order in existence). This offence also applies where the Secretary of State personally directs that the exclusion from the United Kingdom of an individual who is a citizen of the European Union is conducive to the public good (an exclusion order) (s. 25B(2)).

The second offence is broader in scope than the offence under s. 25A (see above) and applies to acts that assist the person to arrive in, enter or remain in the United Kingdom. Again, however, the relevant knowledge or cause for belief are crucial.

The courts' powers to order forfeiture of vehicles, ships and aircraft under s. 25C apply to this offence (see below).

1.15.3.2 Powers of Seizure and Forfeiture

Where a person has been arrested for an offence under s. 25, 25A or 25B, a police officer may detain any vehicle or certain smaller ships and aircraft where he/she has reasonable grounds for believing that:

- the vehicle, ship or aircraft has been used or was intended to be used in carrying out the arrangements in respect of the offence, and
- the person arrested is the owner, driver or, in the case of a ship or aircraft, the captain (see generally s. 25D).

Extensive powers for entry and search under warrant are made for immigration officers and the police under ss. 28A and 28B.

Following the conviction of a defendant for a relevant offence, a court may order the forfeiture of any vehicle used or intended to be used in connection with the offence if the person owned or was driving the vehicle at the time the offence was committed, or was a director, manager or secretary of a company that owned the vehicle at the time (see s. 25C).

This power will extend to ships and aircraft but there are minimum requirements in relation to the size of the vessel or aircraft and to the number of illegal entrants carried on board

1.15.3.3 Trafficking People for Exploitation

People seeking asylum or refuge in any country can be particularly vulnerable and that vulnerability can provide a lever by which they can be exploited by criminals, either individually or on a highly organised basis. This area of criminal activity has become a significant feature for policing in recent years, with people trafficking becoming increasingly prevalent. As a result, in addition to the more general immigration offences and provisions

discussed elsewhere in this chapter, there are specific statutory measures designed to increase the effectiveness of the police and other agencies in this area.

OFFENCE: **Trafficking People for Exploitation—*Asylum and Immigration
(Treatment of Claimants etc.) Act 2004, s. 4***
- Triable either way • On indictment 14 years' imprisonment and/or fine
- 12 months, and/or fine summarily (unless committed before the commencement of
  s. 154 of the Criminal Justice Act 2003, in which case the reference to 12 months is
  six months)

The Asylum and Immigration (Treatment of Claimants etc.) Act 2004, s. 4 states:

(1) A person commits an offence if he arranges or facilitates the arrival in the United Kingdom of
an individual (the 'passenger') and—
  (a) he intends to exploit the passenger in the United Kingdom or elsewhere, or
  (b) he believes that another person is likely to exploit the passenger in the United Kingdom or
  elsewhere.
(2) A person commits an offence if he arranges or facilitates travel within the United Kingdom
by an individual (the 'passenger') in respect of whom he believes that an offence under subsection (1) may have been committed and—
  (a) he intends to exploit the passenger in the United Kingdom or elsewhere, or
  (b) he believes that another person is likely to exploit the passenger in the United Kingdom or
  elsewhere.
(3) A person commits an offence if he arranges or facilitates the departure from the United Kingdom of an individual (the 'passenger') and—
  (a) he intends to exploit the passenger outside the United Kingdom, or
  (b) he believes that another person is likely to exploit the passenger outside the United Kingdom.

KEYNOTE

The above offence is very widely drafted and covers arranging or facilitating the arrival in, departure from
or travel within the United Kingdom of a whole series of different vulnerable categories of person, in each
case with the relevant intention or belief with regard to that person's exploitation. For the purposes of this
section a person is exploited if:

- they are the victim of behaviour that contravenes Article 4 of the European Convention on Human Rights
  (slavery and forced labour)—as to which see General Police Duties, para. 4.3.8;
- they are encouraged, required or expected to do anything as a result of which they (or another person)
  would commit an offence under the Human Organ Transplants Act 1989;
- they are subjected to force, threats or deception designed to induce them to provide services, to provide
  another person with benefits or to enable another person to acquire benefits of any kind;
- they are requested or induced to undertake *any activity*, having been chosen on the grounds that they
  are mentally or physically ill or disabled, young or have a family relationship with a person and a person
  without the illness, disability, youth or family relationship would be likely to refuse the request or resist
  the inducement (s. 4(4)).

Where the offence is committed within the context of employment there are further considerations and
offences and the advice of the Home Office Immigration and Nationality Directorate should be sought.

Sections 25C and 25D of the Immigration Act 1971 (forfeiture or detention of vehicle etc.) apply in
relation to an offence under s. 4 above.

1.15.3.4   The Gangmasters (Licensing) Act 2004

The deaths of 20 immigrant workers in Morecambe Bay in February 2004 drew widespread attention to a particular aspect of unlawful exploitation of vulnerable groups of people within England and Wales. As a response to the ensuing governmental report on the need to regulate the activities of those providing teams of temporary or seasonal workers within the agricultural industry, Parliament introduced the Gangmasters (Licensing) Act 2004. The Act establishes a regulatory body (the Gangmasters Licensing Authority—GLA) whose remit includes the issuing and inspection of licences and the provision of information held by it to specified persons in accordance with the Act.

The definition of a gangmaster is very wide. In summary a gangmaster is a person who supplies a worker to do work to which the Act applies for another person (s. 4). The 'work' to which the Act applies is essentially agricultural work, gathering shellfish and includes processing or packaging any produce derived from agricultural work, shellfish, fish or products derived from shellfish or fish (s. 3). It does not matter whether the worker supplied in this way is supplied directly or indirectly or whether the work done is for the purposes of a business carried on by the recipient of the worker or in connection with services provided by him/her to another person. Similarly, it does not matter whether the gangmaster supplies the worker him/herself or procures that the worker is supplied, whether the worker works under a contract or whether the work is done under the control of the gangmaster, recipient or an intermediary (see generally s. 4(3)). A person will still be a 'worker' for the purposes of the Act even if he/she has no right to be, or to work, in the United Kingdom (s. 26). The Secretary of State may make further detailed provision in the form of regulations setting out the fine detail of the regulatory framework for gangmasters and these should be consulted when considering offences under the legislation.

OFFENCE: **Acting as a Gangmaster without Licence etc.—**
Gangmasters (Licensing) Act 2004, s. 12
- Triable either way • 10 years' imprisonment and/or fine on indictment
- 12 months' imprisonment, fine or both summarily if committed before the commencement of s. 154(1) of the Criminal Justice Act 2003, six months

The Gangmasters (Licensing) Act 2004, s. 12 states:

(1) A person commits an offence if he acts as a gangmaster in contravention of section 6 (prohibition of unlicensed activities).
(2) A person commits an offence if he has in his possession or under his control—
    (a) a relevant document that is false and that he knows or believes to be false,
    (b) a relevant document that was improperly obtained and that he knows or believes to have been improperly obtained, or
    (c) a relevant document that relates to someone else,
    with the intention of inducing another person to believe that he or another person acting as a gangmaster in contravention of section 6 is acting under the authority of a licence.

KEYNOTE

Section 6 of the Act provides for the issuing of licences as monitored by the GLA. A person acting as a gangmaster does not contravene s. 6 by reason only of the fact that he/she breaches a condition of the licence (s. 12(1)).

A relevant document is a licence or any document issued by the GLA in connection with a licence (s. 12(6)).

The offence at subs. (2) requires both the possession/control of the relevant document *and* the intention set out above. (For a discussion of possession **see para. 1.6.3**).

The concept of 'false' documents is the same as that used in the wider legislation relating to forgery (**see para. 1.12.11.4**).

It is a further summary offence to enter into an arrangement with a gangmaster where, in supplying the workers or services, the gangmaster contravenes s. 6 (s. 13(1)).

The Act makes provision for the appointment of enforcement officers and extends certain powers of arrest and enforcement to those officers; it also allows for the appointment of compliance officers (s. 15). Intentional obstruction of these officers in the exercise of their functions is a summary offence, as is failure without reasonable cause to comply with their proper instructions (s. 18).

1.15.4 Registration Cards

OFFENCE: **Misuse etc. of Registration Card—*Immigration Act 1971, s. 26A***
  - Triable either way ● Ten years' imprisonment on indictment ● Six months' imprisonment, and/or a fine summarily

The Immigration Act 1971, s. 26A states:

(3) A person commits an offence if he—
  (a) makes a false registration card,
  (b) alters a registration card with intent to deceive or to enable another to deceive,
  (c) ...
  (d) uses or attempts to use a false registration card for a purpose for which a registration card is issued,
  (e) uses or attempts to use an altered registration card with intent to deceive,
  (f) makes an article designed to be used in making a false registration card,
  (g) makes an article designed to be used in altering a registration card with intent to deceive or to enable another to deceive ...
  (h) ...

KEYNOTE

A registration card here is a document which:

- carries information about a person (whether or not wholly or partly electronically), and
- is issued by the Secretary of State to the person wholly or partly in connection with a claim for asylum (whether or not made by that person) (s. 26A(1)).

These offences require different degrees of intent and the wording of each needs to be considered carefully. They are similar to the more general offences of forgery (as to which, **see chapter 1.12**).

'False registration card' means a document which is designed to appear to be a registration card (s. 26A(4)).

OFFENCE: **Possession of Registration Card or Immigration Stamp—*Immigration Act 1971, s. 26A(3)(c) and (h) and s. 26B***
  - Triable either way ● Two years' imprisonment on indictment ● Six months' imprisonment and/or a fine summarily

The Immigration Act 1971, s. 26A states:

> (3) A person commits an offence if he—
>
> ...
>
> (c) has a false or altered registration card in his possession without reasonable excuse,
>
> ...
>
> (h) has an article within paragraph (f) or (g) in his possession without reasonable excuse.

The Immigration Act 1971, s. 26B states:

> (1) A person commits an offence if he has an immigration stamp in his possession without reasonable excuse.
> (2) A person commits an offence if he has a replica immigration stamp in his possession without reasonable excuse.

KEYNOTE

These lesser offences should be read in conjunction with the other s. 26A offences (see above).

As with the other offences, 'false registration card' here means a document which is designed to appear to be a registration card (s. 26A(4)).

'Immigration stamp' means a device which is designed for the purpose of stamping documents in the exercise of an immigration function; 'replica immigration stamp' means a device which is designed for the purpose of stamping a document so that it appears to have been stamped in the exercise of an immigration function; and 'immigration function' means a function of an immigration officer or the Secretary of State under the Immigration Acts (s. 26B(3)).

An immigration officer may arrest without warrant a person who has committed, or whom he/she has reasonable grounds for suspecting has committed an offence under s. 26A or 26B (s. 28A(9A)).

1.15.5 Passport Offences

OFFENCE: **Making Untrue Statement to Procure Passport—*Criminal Justice Act 1925, s. 36***

> • Triable either way • Two years' imprisonment on indictment • Six months and/or fine summarily

The Criminal Justice Act 1925, s. 36 states:

> (1) The making by any person of a statement which is to his knowledge untrue for the purpose of procuring a passport, whether for himself or any other person, shall be [an offence].

KEYNOTE

This offence, which has been around for many years, has attracted increased police attention lately as a result of the growing concerns with controlling and monitoring the movement of individuals in and out of the United Kingdom.

OFFENCE: **Entering United Kingdom without Passport etc.—**
Asylum and Immigration (Treatment of Claimants etc.) Act 2004, s. 2
• Triable either way • two years' imprisonment on indictment • 12 months' imprisonment, fine or both summarily if after the commencement of s. 154 of the Criminal Justice Act 2003, otherwise six months.

The Asylum and Immigration (Treatment of Claimants etc.) Act 2004, s. 2 states:

(1) A person commits an offence if at a leave or asylum interview he does not have with him an immigration document which—
  (a) is in force, and
  (b) satisfactorily establishes his identity and nationality or citizenship.
(2) A person commits an offence if at a leave or asylum interview he does not have with him, in respect of any dependent child with whom he claims to be travelling or living, an immigration document which—
  (a) is in force, and
  (b) satisfactorily establishes the child's identity and nationality or citizenship.

KEYNOTE

'Immigration document' means a passport or a document which relates to a national of a state other than the United Kingdom and which is designed to serve the same purpose as a passport (s. 2(12)).

The above section creates two offences. Subsection (8) provides that a person shall be presumed for the purposes of this section not to have a document with them if they fail to produce it to an immigration officer or official of the Secretary of State on request. Therefore the first offence is effectively committed where a person is unable to produce a current passport or similar document at a 'leave' or 'asylum' interview. The second offence applies where the person at such an interview is unable to produce a current passport or similar document in respect of a dependent child with whom he/she claims to be living or travelling.

The person does not commit the offences if the interview takes place *after* the person has entered the United Kingdom and within the period of three days (beginning with the date of that interview) the person provides a passport or similar immigration document to an immigration officer or to the Secretary of State (s. 2(3)).

A document which purports to be, or is designed to look like, a passport or relevant immigration document, is a false immigration document. In addition, if a passport (or document) is used outside the period for which it is expressed to be valid, if it is used by or in respect of a person other than the person to or for whom it was issued or it is used contrary to any formal provisions for its use it will be regarded as a false immigration document (see s. 2(13)). There are several specific defences to these offences. In addition to the more obvious ones (e.g. having a reasonable excuse for not being in possession of the passport being a European Economic Area national exercising a right in respect of entry/residence in the United Kingdom) it is also a defence to some of the above offences for a person to produce a *false passport or immigration document* and to prove that he/she used it as an immigration document for all purposes in connection with his/her journey to the United Kingdom (see s. 2(4)). This is both important and unusual in that the defence to the offence above is itself an offence (see para. 1.12.11.5).

The section makes other detailed provisos as to when this specific defence will apply and what will amount to a 'reasonable excuse' in relation to the more general defence.

1.15.6 Suspected International Terrorists

Under the Anti-terrorism, Crime and Security Act 2001, the Secretary of State may issue a certificate in respect of a person suspected of being a terrorist where the Secretary of State believes that the person's presence in the United Kingdom is a risk to national security (s. 21). Broadly, a terrorist for this purpose is a person who:

- is or has been concerned in the commission, preparation or instigation of international terrorism; or
- is a member of, supports or assists an international terrorist group.

Terrorism is defined in s. 1 of the Terrorism Act 2000 (**see General Police Duties**). Generally, this means the use or threat of action which:

- involves serious violence against a person
- involves serious damage to property
- endangers another person's life
- creates a serious risk to the health or safety of the public
- is designed seriously to interfere with or seriously to disrupt an electronic system and
- the use or threat is designed to influence the government or to intimidate the public or a section of the public, and
- the use or threat is made for the purpose of advancing a political, religious or ideological cause.

The Court of Appeal has held that the power to detain foreign nationals on the ground that they pose a risk to national security under these provisions does not breach Article 14 of the European Convention on Human Rights (see *A* v *Secretary of State for the Home Department* [2003] 2 WLR 564).

There are, however, several legal restrictions on the powers under the 2001 Act in relation to suspected international terrorists.

Index